Elusive stability

Studies in Monetary and Financial History

EDITORS: Michael Bordo and Forrest Capie

Barry Eichengreen, *Elusive Stability: Essays in the History of International Finance, 1919–1939*

Elusive stability

Essays in the history of international finance, 1919–1939

Barry Eichengreen

CAMBRIDGE UNIVERSITY PRESS

Published by the Press Syndicate of the University of Cambridge
The Pitt Building, Trumpington Street, Cambridge CB2 1RP
40 West 20th Street, New York, NY 10011-4211, USA
10 Stamford Road, Oakleigh, Victoria 3166, Australia

First published 1990
First paperback edition 1993

Library of Congress Cataloging-in-Publication Data

Eichengreen, Barry J.
Elusive stability: essays in the history of international
finance, 1919–1939 / Barry Eichengreen.
p. cm. – (Studies in monetary and financial history)
Bibliography: p.
Includes index.
ISBN 0-521-36538-4
1. International finance – History – 20th century. I. Title.
II. Series.
HG3881.E346 1989
332'.042'0904 – dc20   89–7189
                                                                            CIP

British Library Cataloguing in Publication Data

Eichengreen, Barry J.
Elusive stability: essays in the history of
international finance, 1919–1939. – (Studies in
monetary and financial history)
1. International finance, history
I. Title   II. Series
332'.042'09

ISBN 0-521-36538-4 hardback
ISBN 0-521-44847-6 paperback

Transferred to digital printing 2004

Contents

Tables

Figures

Acknowledgments

I am grateful to the following publishers for permission to reprint articles that appeared originally as cited below. I have made a few minor changes in text and documentation, and in two cases I have dropped subtitles.

Many thanks also go to the *European Economic Review* and North-Holland Publishers for permission to reprint "Real Exchange Rate Behavior Under Alternative International Monetary Regimes: Interwar Evidence," from vol. 32, 1988; to the *Rivista di Storia Economica* to reprint "Understanding 1921–1927: Exchange Rates and Economic Recovery in the 1920s," from second ser., vol. 3, International Issue, 1986; to the *Economic Journal* and the Royal Economic Society to reprint "Bank Rate Policy Under the Interwar Gold Standard: A Dynamic Probit Model," from vol. 95, no. 379, 1985; to *Explorations in Economic History* and Academic Press to reprint "The Bank of France and the Sterilization of Gold, 1926–1932," from vol. 23, no. 1, 1986; to Cambridge University Press to reprint "International Policy Coordination in Historical Perspective: A View from the Interwar Years," from Willem Buiter and Richard Marston (eds.), *International Economic Policy Coordination* (Cambridge and New York, 1985); to MIT Press for permission to reprint "The Economic Consequences of the Franc Poincaré," from Elhanan Helpman et al., *Economic Effects of Government Expenditure* (Cambridge, MA, 1988); to the International Finance Section and Princeton University Press to reprint "Sterling and the Tariff, 1929–32," from *Princeton Studies in International Finance* no. 48, 1981; to the *Journal of Economic History* and the Economic History Association to reprint "Exchange Rates and Economic Recovery in the 1930s," from vol. LXV, no. 4, 1985; and to the Brookings Institution to reprint "Hegemonic Stability Theories of the International Monetary System," from Richard Cooper, Barry Eichengreen, Randall Henning, Gerald Holtham, and Robert Putnam, *Can Nations Agree?* (Washington, DC, 1989).

1. Introduction

Two themes run through this collection of essays. The first concerns the role of the international monetary system in the functioning of the global economy. The intricacies of international finance tend to be dismissed by analysts of economic growth, who focus on the accumulation of capital and labor inputs and on technical change in the production function that transforms them into outputs of final goods. In fact, as recent events have underscored, this dichotomy can lead to an incomplete and misleading picture of the aggregate economy. Economic growth is predicated on a stable macroeconomy, which in turn requires a stable financial environment. As new technologies link national financial markets ever more tightly together, the international monetary system through which cross-border transactions are settled comes to play an increasingly central role in the operation of the macroeconomy and its financial sector.

By highlighting the connection between the international monetary system and the macroeconomy, turbulence in financial markets has led to renewed calls for international monetary reform. This raises a host of questions about the optimal design of international monetary institutions. Theory can shed light on the operating characteristics of different institutional arrangements. But it delivers useful results only by stripping away complications that yield ambiguous conclusions in the abstract. For those concerned with the operation of different international monetary arrangements not in theory but in practice, there is no substitute for concrete evidence from historical experience.

But why focus on the decades between World Wars I and II? A first reason is that the interwar period provides an exceptionally rich menu of international monetary experience. Following the collapse of the international gold standard during World War I, the early 1920s witnessed a period of floating exchange rates the like of which the industrial economies have experienced neither before nor since. Between 1921 and 1925 the major currencies fluctuated against one another in the virtual absence of central bank intervention, providing the closest approximation yet witnessed to the

1

textbook model of freely floating exchange rates. Modern opinions about
the advantages and drawbacks of floating rates – including the fear that they
might prove excessively volatile and be destabilized by speculation – were
formed largely on the basis of this historical experience.[1]

There followed an equally short-lived experience with fixed exchange
rates in the context of the reconstructed gold standard. Just as the preceding
period did much to form modern opinion about floating rates, the interwar gold-exchange standard of 1925–31 was the crucible on which modern
views of pegged exchange rates were forged. The notion that the stability
of fixed-rate regimes is readily undermined by destabilizing flows of short-
term capital ("hot money") was encouraged by the abrupt collapse of this
laboriously reconstructed system. Memory of the experience played a role
in the retention of capital controls for more than a decade after the establishment of the Bretton Woods System following World War II. The notion
that fixed-rate regimes which bind policymakers' hands can be counterproductive from a macroeconomic point of view was similarly shaped by the
exceptional severity of the Great Depression in those countries which clung
to their gold standard parities.

Interpretation of this episode has been complicated by disagreement over
the proper characterization of the fixed-rate system that prevailed between
1925 and 1931. Some have questioned whether the interwar gold (or gold-
exchange) standard was a true gold standard, others whether it differed
significantly from Bretton Woods. I suggest below that although the interwar system had elements in common with both its predecessor and its
successor, in certain crucial respects it more closely resembled the former.
Admittedly, the gold-exchange standard of 1925–31 differed from the textbook model of the gold standard by virtue of central bank intervention,
the use of foreign deposits as international reserves, and the fact of exchange rate changes. So had the classical gold standard, however. Rather
than differences in kind, the differences between the prewar and interwar

---

[1] The single most influential account of the operation of floating rates and single most powerful statement of the dangers of destabilizing speculation remains Ragnar Nurkse, *International Currency Experience* (Geneva, 1944). His interpretations have not gone undisputed,
viz. Milton Friedman, "The Case for Flexible Exchange Rates," in *Essays in Positive Economics* (Chicago, 1953), 157–203. Other influential accounts of exchange rate behavior in
this period include William Adams Brown, *The International Gold Standard Reinterpreted,
1914–1934* (New York, 1940); E.L. Dulles, *The French Franc 1914–1928* (New York,
1929); M. Wolfe, *The French Franc Between the Wars, 1919–1939* (New York, 1951); S.C.
Tsiang, "Fluctuating Exchange Rates in Countries with Relatively Stable Economies," *Staff
Papers* 7 (1959), 244–73; and Robert Z. Aliber, "Speculation in the Foreign Exchanges:
The European Experience," *Yale Economic Essays* 2 (1962), 171–245.

gold standards were differences in extent (more active management, more reliance on nongold reserves, more frequent exchange rate changes between the wars). Although the interwar gold standard bore a strong resemblance to the system constituted at Bretton Woods, it differed by the absence of a dominant reserve currency to which other participants pegged their exchange rates and of a single center country in response to whose initiatives they adjusted their policies.

The collapse of the gold-exchange standard in 1931 cleared the way for a period of managed floating. Between 1932 and 1936, most of the major exchange rates fluctuated, as in the first half of the 1920s, but were actively managed, as in the second half of that decade. Intervention tended to occur unilaterally with a minimum of international consultation or policy coordination. The experience of the thirties did much to mold modern opinions about the hazards of international monetary systems which permit unilateral exchange-rate changes. According to the standard interpretation of the period, countries initiated beggar-thy-neighbor devaluations which imposed costs on their trading partners, and engaged in an expensive and ultimately futile tug of war over the exchange rates linking their currencies.

That the interwar system of fixed rates was at the same time more actively managed than its predecessor and more decentralized than its successor provides a further rationale for focusing on the period. Any international monetary reform in our lifetime is certain to share these features. Though faith in the merits of activist stabilization policy will continue to wax and wane, future policymakers are unlikely to adopt binding rules or attach priority to external balance to the same extent as their 19th century predecessors. The interwar period, when policymakers intervened actively in response to conflicts between internal and external balance, more closely resembles the situation that is likely to prevail. Similarly, the trend toward an increasingly multipolar international monetary system is certain to persist into the 21st century. Hence, any new set of institutions will be required to accommodate the objectives of a number of nations possessing roughly comparable financial and monetary resources. The precedent for this situation is neither the classical gold standard nor the Bretton Woods System but interwar experience.

The second recurring theme of this collection of essays is the connection between the international monetary system and the Great Depression, the unparalleled macroeconomic catastrophe of modern times. The most influential work on the Depression concentrates on the United States, which is treated essentially as a closed economy. Both Milton Friedman and Anna

Schwartz, on the one hand, and Peter Temin, on the other, portray the Great Depression basically as a domestic affair.[2] While the international dimension is not totally absent from either book, neither is it central. Friedman and Schwartz share with Temin the view that the events which converted a garden-variety recession into a Great Depression originated primarily in the United States. They attribute to feedbacks from overseas at most a subsidiary role in the Depression's depth and duration.

A central message of these essays is that the Great Depression was at root an international phenomenon. The international monetary system served as one of the channels through which deflationary impulses were propagated and constrained the economic policies adopted in response. Although I concur with Friedman and Schwartz and with Temin in the importance they attach to economic policy, I differ in my emphasis on its international dimension. Policy had important cross-border effects through its impact on foreign economies and foreign policymakers. The failure of officials to take these effects into account played a significant role in the international slump. The analogy is with a couple competing in a three-legged race. Progress hinges on their ability to coordinate their efforts. Steps taken without coordination will lead to their downfall. So it was in the Depression, when unilateral initiatives of national policymakers often worked at cross-purposes, leaving everyone worse off.

The first of the essays sets the stage for the subsequent analysis, summarizing the behavior of real and nominal exchange rates under the three interwar monetary regimes. (Nominal exchange rates are those quoted in the newspaper. Real exchange rates adjust nominal rates for domestic and foreign prices.) The contrasts among periods are striking. Not just nominal exchange rates but relative prices were much more volatile under the free float of the 1920s than under the managed float of the 1930s, and much more volatile under managed floating than under the fixed parities of the gold-exchange standard. It is tempting to interpret this correlation in causal terms – to argue that volatility in foreign-exchange markets gave rise to relative price (real exchange rate) instability which distorted patterns of production and consumption, with real economic costs.

2 The references are to Milton Friedman and Anna Schwartz, *A Monetary History of the United States, 1857–1960* (Princeton, 1963) and Peter Temin, *Did Monetary Forces Cause the Great Depression?* (New York, 1976). An important exception is Charles Kindleberger, *The World in Depression, 1929–1939* (Berkeley, 1973). And as I hope to make clear, there are still others who have considered the economics of the interwar years from an international perspective.

This is the interpretation favored by authors writing in the tradition of interwar commentators such as Ragnar Nurkse. In this view, nominal exchange rates are subject to destabilizing speculation, and domestic prices respond sluggishly to exchange rate movements. Speculators buy or sell currencies in anticipation of capital gains and losses that otherwise would not occur. Since commodity prices adjust more slowly than exchange rates, destabilizing speculation distorts the structure of relative prices. In the 1920s destabilizing speculation was especially prevalent, it is argued, in countries experiencing inflation at rates ranging from the moderate (France, Belgium, Italy) to the extreme (Germany, Austria, Hungary, Poland). But whereas evidence of sluggish price adjustment is abundant, that for destabilizing speculation is not. In Eichengreen (1982) I asked whether speculation destabilized the French franc in the 1920s, finding little evidence that it did. That study, however, predated the recent literature on "rational" (self-fulfilling) bubbles in asset markets, which suggests different tests for destabilizing speculation.[3] This is an area ripe for reexamination.

But there exist alternative explanations for the correlation between real and nominal exchange rates. A second interpretation, which I personally favor, is that during floating-rate periods nominal exchange rates are perturbed by divergences among national policies (rather than by speculation), and that nominal exchange-rate volatility results in real exchange-rate volatility for the reasons just described. A commitment to fixed parities that is at least temporarily binding constrains national policymakers to harmonize their policies internationally. With policies adapted to eliminate variations in nominal rates, the volatility of real rates is minimized. A commitment to fixed nominal exchange rates is no panacea, since it solves neither the "after you, Alphonse" problem of which nation's policymakers move first nor the "too many Indians" problem of which ones determine the overall thrust of policy. This is evident in the early phases of the Great Depression, when fixed rates succeeded in limiting the volatility of real exchange rates even in an exceptionally turbulent period but did not prevent policy from being highly deflationary.

---

[3] Work on rational or self-fulfilling speculative bubbles was largely instigated by the articles of Robert Flood and Peter Garber, for example, "Market Fundamentals versus Price-Level Bubbles: First Tests," *Journal of Political Economy* 88 (1980), 745–70. Two applications to the foreign exchange market are K. West, "A Standard Monetary Model and the Variability of the Deutchemark-Dollar Exchange Rate," *Journal of International Economics* 23 (1987), 57–76, and Wing T. Woo, "The Monetary Approach to Exchange Rate Determination under Rational Expectations, *Journal of International Economics* 18 (1985), 1–16.

A third interpretation emphasizes the tendency of disturbances to wreak havoc with both real and nominal exchange rates. Causality may run in the other direction, according to this view, from real disturbances through relative prices to the financial system and the nominal exchange rate. Although there is no reason to question the existence of real disturbances in the interwar period, it need not follow that they were greatest in the years of floating rates. Many observers would argue that the real shocks of the early years of the Great Depression, when nominal exchange rates remained fixed, dwarfed those of either the early twenties or the mid-thirties.

None of this justifies a blanket indictment of flexible exchange rates. Even if exchange-rate flexibility had costs, in the form of the relative price volatility to which it gave rise, it may have also had benefits. This, in fact, is what standard theory suggests. When countries suffer an external shock such as World War I or the Great Depression, restoration of macroeconomic equilibrium can be expedited by a depreciation which raises prices and profitability and redeploys resources faster than is possible through adjustments in the entire spectrum of domestic prices and costs. This is the "daylight-savings-time" argument for flexible rates. Chapter 3 demonstrates its applicability to the 1920s (as does Chapter 9 for the 1930s). The benefits of exchange-rate adjustments are apparent in the wake of World War I, when countries which depreciated their currencies recovered more rapidly than those which restored their prewar gold standard parities, and in the wake of the Depression, when countries which devalued recovered more quickly than those which clung to the gold standard.

The next several chapters consider the second of the three interwar monetary regimes: the reconstructed gold standard. Its unsatisfactory operation is evident in its early collapse and in the onset of the Great Depression with which its short existence coincided. The question is why the system performed so poorly. Was it riddled by structural flaws which undermined its operation, or did central banks simply fail to manage it effectively? Most of those who blame inadequate management concentrate on the three leading central banks, those of Britain, France, and the United States. Chapter 4 takes a close look at the actions of the Bank of England. Throughout the gold standard period Britain experienced external difficulties, due to a conjuncture of developments, prominent among which was the restoration of the prewar parity in 1925. Contemporaries criticized the Bank of England for failing to stem Britain's gold losses and thereby for undermining the stability of sterling, which was, along with the dollar, one of the two key currencies of the interwar system. Chapter 4 demonstrates that the Bank of England felt compelled to respond not only to disturbances to the external accounts but to domestic economic conditions, and suggests that these played a role in the sterling crisis and in the gold standard's collapse.

The Bank of France also has been allotted a significant share of the blame for the instability of the interwar gold standard. It is indicted for sterilizing inward gold flows (for eliminating their impact on domestic financial markets), much as the Bank of England sterilized outflows. Not only did France's absorption of gold intensify the difficulties experienced by the Bank of England, but it placed downward pressure on gold supplies and prices worldwide, the last thing needed on the eve of the Great Depression. The popular explanation for this behavior is that Paris was indulging a characteristic French appetite for gold. Chapter 5 emphasizes instead the limited capacity of the French central bank to stem gold inflows. The new statutes under which the Bank of France operated following stabilization in 1926 precluded expansionary open market operations, whereas the other instruments of policy available to the Bank were not up to the task. These new statutes were themselves a response to the perception that further restrictions were needed to insulate the Bank of France from pressure to monetize government budget deficits, pressure it had proven unable to resist in the first half of the decade.

Indirectly, then, the gold flows and consequent instabilities of the period following 1925 were a legacy of the experience of the preceding years.[4] The incapacity of the Bank of France to slow its absorption of gold arose out of structural features of the French gold standard bequeathed by the inflationary experience of the first half of the 1920s. The difficulties experienced by the Bank of England, in part a result of the decision to restore the prewar parity, similarly reflected interwar perceptions of Britain's experience in prewar years. In both cases, historical experience influenced the structure and conditioned perceptions of the international monetary system.

These analyses of the French and British central banks have two implications for how the interwar gold standard should be viewed. First, that gold standard was neither a purely rules-based nor a purely discretionary system. Rules and discretion combined in its operation, and either might dominate at the worst possible moment. Second, the structure and operation of the interwar system – both the nature of its rules and the ways in which discretion was utilized – hinged on political as much as economic

---

[4] Harold James, *The German Slump* (Oxford, 1986) makes a similar argument for interwar Germany.

considerations. This is not to suggest that politics were isolated from economics. In both Britain and France political pressures responded to recent economic events: in the case of Britain, the foreign challenge to sterling's status as a key currency, which fueled the mandate to restore the prewar parity; in the case of France, the postwar experience with inflation, which created the demand for new constraints on monetary management.

Neither British nor French policy was formulated in isolation from the other or from the policy of the Federal Reserve. Chapter 6 focuses on the interaction of central banks and on the implications for the operation of the international monetary system. It assesses the argument, advanced by Clarke (1967), that the failure of central bank cooperation, by undermining the stability of the gold-exchange standard, exacerbated the Great Depression. That argument is important, since it suggests a role for the international monetary system in the post-1929 slump. It is at the same time perplexing, since its emphasis on policy coordination is at odds with the conventional view of the gold standard as a decentralized system. I argue that the interwar gold-exchange standard was in reality anything but a decentralized system comprised of autonomous members; rather, economies were highly interdependent and systemic stability required collective management. The immediate problem for policy coordination was that the demand for reserves by central banks exceeded the available supply. Possessing incompatibly large desires for scarce global gold stocks, central banks engaged in a self-defeating struggle to acquire gold from one another through the adoption of higher and higher interest rates. As Keynes described the situation on the eve of the Depression, "What helps each central bank is not a high Bank rate but a higher rate than the others. So that a raising of rates all round helps no one until, after an interregnum during which the economic activity of the whole world has been retarded, prices and wages have been forced to a lower level." [5] Herein lay the scope for policy coordination. Had they acknowledged the dilemma and negotiated a cooperative solution to this game, central banks could have achieved the same international distribution of gold without putting the world economy through a deflationary wringer.

Since not all national economies suffered equally from the deflation of the 1920s, the expansion which served as prelude to the Great Depression took on different shapes in different countries. Britain suffered dispropor-

---

[5] John Maynard Keynes, "Is There Enough Gold? The League of Nations Inquiry," *The Nation and Athenaeum* (19 January 1929). Reprinted in D. Moggridge (ed.), *The Collected Writings of John Maynard Keynes, Activities 1922-1929: The Return to Gold and Industrial Policy* (Cambridge, 1981), Part II, pp. 775-80.

tionately throughout the second half of the 1920s and did not have far to fall when the Depression struck. France, after enjoying a modest boom and remaining immune from the worst effects of the Depression until the end of 1930, suffered an exceptionally severe depression when its prosperous economy collapsed. The traditional explanation for their contrasting experiences in the 1920s emphasizes the exchange rate – that the pound sterling was overvalued, by some ten percent according to Keynes, whereas the French franc was undervalued by approximately the same amount. The mystery is how decisions about nominal exchange rates taken in 1925 or 1926 could continue to exercise such powerful effects five years later. An increasing number of authors agree that insofar as these effects persisted, they did so through their interaction with other structural and policy problems.[6] In the case of Britain, the exchange rate mattered in conjunction with wage and price rigidities which prevented costs from quickly coming into line and in conjunction with the restrictive monetary policies mandated by the exchange-rate constraint. In the case of France, as Chapter 7 shows, its effects are comprehensible only when considered alongside those of other policy instruments, notably taxation and government expenditure. International monetary policy provides an important part of the explanation for the shape of the run-up to the Depression, but only a part.

Among the side-effects of exchange-rate instability was mounting protectionist pressure. Protectionist sentiment had been on the rise throughout the 1920s, culminating in the worldwide round of tariff increases sandwiched between the U.S. Smoot-Hawley tariff of 1930 and the British General Tariff of 1932. Whether or not one subscribes to the argument that trade warfare contributed significantly to the Great Depression, a view which I have questioned elsewhere (Eichengreen, 1989), it remains true that whatever macroeconomic objectives nations achieved through the imposition of tariffs, they could have obtained more efficiently through a combination of exchange-rate adjustments and other changes in domestic policy. While decisions to raise tariff barriers have been a favorite topic for study by economists and historians alike, the connection between exchange rates and protection has gone almost unnoticed.[7] As Chapter 8 documents, the

---

6 The cases of France and Britain are both considered by J. Bradford DeLong, "Returning to the Gold Standard: A Macroeconomic History of Britain and France in the 1920s," Ph.D. dissertation, Harvard University (1987). Another perspective on the British case is provided by Kent Matthews, "Was Sterling Overvalued in 1925?" *Economic History Review* (sec. ser., 1987), 572–98, and by the authors whose work he cites.

7 Representative of recent studies of the political economy of protection in this period are Forrest Capie, "The British Tariff and Industrial Protection in the 1930s," *Economic History Review* 31 (sec. ser., 1978), 399–409; Barry Eichengreen, "The Political Economy

exchange rate contributed to protectionist pressure through two channels. First, misaligned exchange rates created problems of internal and external balance and exacerbated the difficulties of particular sectors, generating pressure for a tariff to offset exchange-rate effects and as a final line of defense for the gold standard. Second, distrust of floating rates inherited from the 1920s sustained the pressure for a tariff even after the gold standard had collapsed and adjustment through exchange-rate changes was again feasible. Protection was attractive as a defense against the specter of excessive depreciation which might ignite an inflationary spiral.

Although the devaluation of sterling in 1931 did not prevent Britain from imposing a tariff, it transformed the policy environment in other ways. More than two dozen countries followed Britain off the gold standard, the remaining members of the Gold Bloc successively falling by the wayside between 1932 and 1936.[8] These competitive devaluations have been widely blamed for the severity of the Great Depression. But as Jeffrey Sachs and I suggest in Chapter 9, they may have received more than their fair share of criticism. Rather than ineffectual or counterproductive policy initiatives, currency depreciation in the 1930s had a powerful stimulative effect on the devaluing countries. Besides switching demand toward them – the beggar-thy-neighbor effect criticized by successive generations of historians – devaluation increased the scope for expansionary monetary policy by relaxing the gold standard constraint. Admittedly, devaluation was contractionary abroad in the sense that the stimulative effects of domestic monetary expansion were dominated by the beggar-thy-neighbor expenditure-switching effects.[9] But as we point out in that chapter, this is not to say that had the policy been adopted even more widely it would not have hastened recovery from the Great Depression.

A possible caveat is that competitive depreciation could have worsened

of the Smoot-Hawley Tariff," *Research in Economic History* 11 (1989), 1–44, and J. Goldstein, "Ideas, Institutions and American Trade Policy," *International Organization* 42 (1987), 179–218.

8 Studies of the 1931 devaluation of sterling have proliferated in recent years. The most recent generation of analyses includes Alec Cairncross and Barry Eichengreen, *Sterling in Decline* (Oxford, 1983), Stephen Broadberry, *The British Economy Between the Wars: A Macroeconomic Survey* (Oxford, 1986), and Diane Kunz, *Britain's Battle for the Gold Standard in 1931* (Kent, 1987).

9 The theoretical point, that devaluation under a gold standard need not be beggar-thy-neighbor, because the expenditure-increasing effect of monetary expansion may dominate the expenditure-switching effect, is developed in Barry Eichengreen and Jeffrey Sachs, "Competitive Devaluation and the Great Depression: A Theoretical Reassessment," *Economics Letters* 22 (1986), 67–71.

the Depression by leading to the destruction of international reserves. The ensuing reserve shortage would have put downward pressure on national money supplies whose levels were still linked to reserve availability. The mechanism worked as follows. Because currency depreciation was not coordinated internationally, it gave rise to exchange-rate uncertainty. The risk of exchange-rate changes, and specifically the danger of devaluation, threatened arbitrary capital losses on foreign deposits. Given the heightened riskiness of holding foreign-exchange reserves, central banks liquidated a substantial fraction of their foreign deposits in the years following 1930. Whether this had deflationary consequences hinges upon whether it was simply a liquidation of excess reserves or simultaneously an attempt to shift into gold. Seeking to acquire gold would have entailed the same kind of noncooperative scramble and increasingly restrictive monetary policies as in the 1920s. In contrast, simply liquidating excess foreign-exchange reserves would not have had the same deflationary effects. Chapter 10 finds that, although the liquidation of foreign exchange reserves is indisputable, evidence for a shift into gold with deflationary monetary consequences is not. Thus, it does not appear that the uncertainties created by competitive devaluation – at least those which operated through this channel – were serious enough to render the policy counterproductive overall. It remains true, however, that if devaluation had been coordinated internationally it would have been more effective.

To what, then, should the problems of international monetary relations in the period 1919–39 be ascribed? Were the problems structural, due to excessive restrictions on central banks attempting to implement reflationary initiatives but constrained by the gold standard rules, and to the inherent instabilities of a system relying on both gold and foreign-exchange reserves? Or were they the result of misguided policies? Though these essays acknowledge a role for both sets of factors, they suggest that the central problem was one of policies rather than institutions – policies that were not adapted to circumstances and, just as critically, that were not coordinated internationally.

But why was policy so inept? One popular explanation, associated with the work of Charles Kindleberger, is that policy tends to be successfully adapted to circumstances and coordinated internationally when it is organized under the leadership of a dominant power. Britain played this role before World War I, the United States after World War II. Between the wars, to echo Kindleberger, Britain was no longer capable of managing the system, while the United States was unwilling to accept its new responsibilities. Chapter 11 assesses this "hegemonic stability" theory of the international monetary system, not only for the interwar years but also for the periods before World War I and after World War II. As with any powerful theory, this one's appeal derives from its parsimony: from its seeming ability to explain events in terms of a select few facets of a complex history. Broadening the focus somewhat, I suggest in this final essay that the contrast between periods has been overdrawn. The extent of British dominance before World War I and of American dominance after World War II has been exaggerated. International monetary stability has always required international cooperation and collaboration. Interwar experience only provides a particularly dramatic illustration of the general point. Neither clever institutional design nor the hope for a renewal of hegemonic dominance vitiates the need for collaboration in international monetary affairs.

Both the questions addressed and the methodology utilized in this volume straddle the disciplines of economics and history. It has been my purpose neither to employ the tools of economic theory to correct misapprehensions of historians, nor to invoke the historian's approach to correct misinterpretations of economists. My intent has been to draw on the methods of the two disciplines as needed to provide straightforward answers to concrete questions. Reflecting their hybrid nature, these essays first appeared in a variety of economics journals, history journals, and conference volumes, all of which neither historians nor economists were likely to encounter.[10] This, I hope, provides some justification for collecting them here.

The many debts I incurred in the course of writing these essays are noted at the beginning of each. In addition, I should like to acknowledge some obligations that are both more general and more specific. Specifically in connection with this book, I thank Michael Bordo for his encouragement. I am delighted by its appearance as the first volume in the series on monetary and financial history edited by Michael together with Forrest Capie. I thank the Institute of International Studies of the University of California at Berkeley for supporting the preparation of the manuscript, and UC Berkeley's Institute of Business and Economic Research for wordprocessing and research assistance.

[10] One of the essays, Chapter 10, has not previously appeared in complete form. Some of the evidence it contains was reported in Barry Eichengreen, "Did International Economic Forces Cause the Great Depression?" *Contemporary Policy Issues* 6 (1988), 90–114, however. I have made minor changes to the published versions, indicating for example the place of publication of citations still unpublished at the time of writing.

More generally, I owe three additional debts of thanks. First, to my collaborators, Jeffrey Sachs, Mark Watson, Charles Wyplosz, and Richard Grossman, whose influence extends beyond the essays of which they are coauthors. Second, to my steadfast correspondents, Michael Bordo, Peter Kenen, Charles Kindleberger, and Peter Temin, who have commented on more than their fair share of chapters. Third, to my teachers, William N. Parker and Carlos F. Diaz-Alejandro, for guidance and inspiration. It is to Bill and to the memory of Carlos that this volume is dedicated.

2. Real exchange rate behavior under alternative international monetary regimes

1. Introduction

One of the most disturbing features of the system of floating but managed exchange rates which has prevailed since 1973 is the surprising degree of real exchange rate volatility. This observation, common even among journalists and politicians, has served as a focal point for the attention of economists. For example, Mussa (1986) contrasted the behavior of real exchange rates in the period of predominantly fixed nominal exchange rates prior to 1973 and in the subsequent period of managed floating. He confirmed that the variability of real rates was significantly greater during the period of floating nominal rates, and that the increased variability of nominal rates was the proximate source of the increased variability of real rates. The reason for interest in such findings is apparent: if the increased variability of real rates reflects an increased incidence of deviations from equilibrium relative prices, then systems of floating exchange rates may have welfare costs not anticipated by their early advocates.

Unfortunately, the generality of the findings of Mussa and others derived from the experience of recent decades is not entirely clear. Rather than yielding general conclusions about the operating properties of fixed and flexible exchange rate regimes, recent experience may tell us more about the particular shocks to which the international monetary system was subjected and about the special features of Bretton Woods and of the post-Bretton-Woods nonsystem. It is conceivable, for instance, that the relative stability of real exchange rates under Bretton Woods reflects a peculiar absence of supply-side shocks in the two decades immediately following World War II. The instability of real exchange rates following the dissolution of Bretton Woods may likewise reflect a peculiar sequence of macroeconomic shocks: OPEC I, OPEC II, and Reagan budget deficits. Alternatively, it is conceivable that the relative stability of real exchange rates under Bretton Woods reflects the beneficent effects of a system of pegged

I thank Jeffrey Frankel, Francesco Giavazzi, and Lars Jonung for helpful comments.

but adjustable rates, in contrast to systems of immutably fixed rates like the textbook gold standard. The instability of real exchange rates following the dissolution of Bretton Woods may likewise reflect the detrimental effects of a system of managed floating, in contrast to systems of freely floating exchange rates.

One way to probe the generality of these findings is to analyze the relationship of real exchange rate behavior to nominal exchange rate regimes in different historical periods. In this chapter I analyze real exchange rate behavior under the three international monetary regimes that prevailed during the interwar years: free floating in the early 1920s, pegged and essentially unadjustable exchange rates in the late 1920s, and managed floating in the early 1930s. I consider the experiences of ten European countries and the United States. Not only does the methodology differ from Mussa's but so do the questions asked. Here I am concerned with three questions. First, what was the variability of real exchange rates under these three international monetary regimes? Second, what was the association between the variability of real and nominal rates? Third, when real exchange rates were disturbed, what was the speed of convergence to equilibrium under the alternative international monetary regimes?

2. International monetary regimes, 1922–1936

Anyone who attempts to analyze the properties of alternative international monetary regimes is immediately confronted by the gap between textbook models of international monetary systems and historical experience. Rather than being demarcated by distinct beginning and end points, the transition between regimes is often gradual. Rather than neatly incapsulating the features of a theoretical model of fixed or floating rates, actual international monetary systems often combine features of different models. While these problems prevail in the interwar period as in any other, it is relatively straightforward to break the two decades between the wars into three distinct international monetary regimes.

The period through 1926 can be fairly characterized as one of freely floating nominal rates. In the spring of 1919, the support operations that had stabilized the British pound and French franc against the U.S. dollar during the latter part of World War I were terminated, and these and other currencies were permitted to float against one another. Of the major currencies, only the dollar remained pegged to gold. A distinguishing characteristic of this period was the virtual absence of exchange-market intervention by the monetary authorities. Those few cases of intervention which occurred – notably by the Bank of France in 1924 and 1926 – were exceptions to the rule (Eichengreen, 1982). Toward the end of the period, the European currencies were pegged to gold and the dollar at intervals, starting with Sweden and followed by Germany, Britain, and finally France in December 1926.

The years from 1927 through 1931 comprise the gold-exchange standard era. The major European currencies remained pegged against one another from France's de facto stabilization at the end of 1926 until Britain's forced departure from gold in September 1931 (for details, see Eichengreen, 1985). While pegging operations did not preclude small variations in bilateral rates (mostly within the gold points), these were of negligible proportions. Transactions in foreign currency were freely permitted at official rates. The major exception occurred in the summer of 1931, when Germany experienced a balance-of-payments crisis and responded with the imposition exchange control. Still, this period is fairly characterized as one of unified, fixed exchange rates.

Following Britain's departure from the gold standard in 1931, some two dozen other countries devalued their currencies. By early 1932, Britain, the Commonwealth and Dominions, Japan, and the Scandinavian and Latin American nations all had reverted to floating rates. But in contrast with the early 1920s, floating was managed, usually through the active intervention of specially constituted Exchange Equalization Funds. In 1933, the U.S. joined the list of countries whose currencies were floating if managed; in 1935 Belgium joined. The German and Italian currencies were regulated by exchange control. Only the members of the gold bloc (France, the Netherlands, Poland, and Switzerland) continued to peg their currencies against gold and one another until France's devaluation in September 1936.

While all such periodizations are approximate, the interwar years can fairly be said to offer three international monetary regimes whose operating properties may be compared: free floating through 1926, fixed rates through August 1931, and managed floating through August 1936.

3. Real exchange rate variability and the speed of convergence

Tables 2.1, 2.2, and 2.3 analyze the behavior of bilateral exchange rates against the British pound. As in any analysis of bilateral rates, a benchmark currency is required; for the interwar period sterling and the dollar

Table 2.1: *Real exchange rate behavior under floating, 1922–1926*

Country	Standard deviation	Time trend	Convergence regression			
			Constant	Lagged real rate	Time trend	R^2
Belgium	8.74	0.42	36.11	0.66	0.13	0.80
		(0.04)	(10.40)	(0.10)	(0.05)	
Denmark	4.74	−0.17	18.03	0.82	−0.04	0.78
		(0.03)	(8.26)	(0.08)	(0.02)	
Finland	4.12	0.03	14.88	0.83	0.02	0.76
		(0.73)	(5.69)	(0.06)	(0.02)	
France	8.01	0.38	34.95	0.64	0.14	0.80
		(0.03)	(10.11)	(0.11)	(0.05)	
Italy	9.49	0.29	8.91	0.92	−0.01	0.85
		(0.06)	(6.36)	(0.06)	(0.03)	
Netherlands	4.26	0.14	10.58	0.90	0.01	0.85
		(0.03)	(6.55)	(0.07)	(0.02)	
Norway	9.23	−0.14	8.69	0.93	−0.05	0.88
		(0.07)	(5.56)	(0.05)	(0.03)	
Sweden	6.02	0.32	26.22	0.75	0.07	0.92
		(0.02)	(9.78)	(0.10)	(0.03)	
U.S.A.	3.33	0.01	8.79	0.91	0.01	0.84
		(0.03)	(5.18)	(0.05)	(0.01)	

Note: Standard errors in parentheses. Monthly data are used. All real exchange rate indices are normalized to 100 in January 1922. The standard deviation and time trend are calculated for the period January 1922–December 1926. The sample period for the convergence regression is February 1922–December 1926 to allow for the lagged variable.

are the logical candidates. Here I consider rates against sterling. While the choice of sterling as the benchmark currency has minimal implications for comparisons of exchange rate stability across periods, it has significant implications for rankings of exchange rate stability across countries within periods. Specifically, countries which made a practice of pegging to sterling will appear to have had more stable exchange rates than would be the case were the dollar rate or an effective exchange rate used in place of sterling. Hence cross-country comparisons within periods must be interpreted with caution.

I consider the behavior of nine European currencies and the U.S. dollar. In the early 1920s Germany is omitted, however, due to the exceptional difficulty of measuring real exchange rates in a period of hyperinflation

Table 2.2: *Real exchange rate behavior under the gold-exchange standard, 1927–1931*

| Country | Standard deviation | Time trend | Convergence regression | | | |
			Constant	Lagged real rate	Time trend	R^2
Belgium	2.08	−0.09	22.98	0.77	−0.02	0.78
		(0.01)	(9.16)	(0.09)	(0.01)	
Denmark	1.09	−0.01	63.72	0.36	−0.01	0.14
		(0.01)	(12.94)	(0.13)	(0.01)	
Finland	4.04	−0.18	6.67	0.93	−0.02	0.92
		(0.02)	(5.59)	(0.06)	(0.01)	
France	2.21	−0.05	22.52	0.77	−0.01	0.65
		(0.02)	(8.84)	(0.09)	(0.01)	
Germany	3.56	−0.20	18.58	0.81	−0.04	0.96
		(0.01)	(8.02)	(0.08)	(0.02)	
Italy	3.06	0.07	16.14	0.83	0.02	0.76
		(0.02)	(7.04)	(0.07)	(0.01)	
Netherlands	3.94	0.19	13.29	0.85	0.05	0.94
		(0.02)	(5.02)	(0.05)	(0.01)	
Norway	3.13	−0.11	11.77	0.89	−0.02	0.87
		(0.02)	(6.60)	(0.06)	(0.01)	
Sweden	2.05	−0.02	6.99	0.93	−0.01	0.81
		(0.02)	(6.00)	(0.06)	(0.01)	
U.S.A.	2.72	−0.14	22.76	0.77	−0.03	0.88
		(0.01)	(8.91)	(0.09)	(0.01)	

Note: Standard errors in parentheses. Monthly data are used. All real exchange rate indices are normalized to 100 in January 1927. The standard deviation and time trend are calculated for the period January 1927–August 1931. The sample period for the convergence regression is February 1927–August 1931 to allow for the lagged variable.

and currency reform. The countries included experienced at most moderate rates of inflation or deflation; it is to such countries that the generalizations in this chapter should be thought to apply. Real exchange rates are measured as the ratio of foreign wholesale prices, converted to sterling by the bilateral rate, relative to British wholesale prices. Monthly data (monthly averages wherever possible) are drawn from the League of Nations' *Monthly Bulletin of Statistics*, supplemented by Tinbergen (1934) and Methorst (1938).

I consider first the behavior of nominal exchange rates. Since the regimes are defined according to the behavior of nominal rates, it follows that their

Table 2.3: *Real exchange rate behavior under managed floating, 1932–1936*

Country	Standard deviation	Time trend	Convergence regression			
			Constant	Lagged real rate	Time trend	R^2
Belgium	8.12	0.35	18.29	0.81	0.08	0.82
		(0.05)	(8.18)	(0.08)	(0.04)	
Denmark	4.66	0.03	17.97	0.83	−0.01	0.71
		(0.04)	(7.78)	(0.07)	(0.02)	
Finland	3.04	0.16	33.01	0.65	0.07	0.85
		(0.01)	(9.70)	(0.10)	(0.02)	
France	2.15	0.01	33.49	0.66	0.01	0.43
		(0.02)	(10.41)	(0.10)	(0.01)	
Germany	8.28	−0.45	9.87	0.90	−0.04	0.95
		(0.03)	(7.57)	(0.07)	(0.04)	
Italy	4.76	−0.23	21.81	0.79	−0.05	0.85
		(0.03)	(8.66)	(0.08)	(0.03)	
Netherlands	5.17	−0.12	10.36	0.90	−0.01	0.82
		(0.04)	(6.84)	(0.07)	(0.02)	
Norway	2.42	0.05	24.68	0.76	0.01	0.64
		(0.02)	(8.78)	(0.08)	(0.01)	
Sweden	1.15	0.01	24.74	0.76	−0.01	0.59
		(0.02)	(9.09)	(0.09)	(0.01)	
U.S.A.	12.09	0.46	7.62	0.94	0.01	0.93
		(0.08)	(4.99)	(0.05)	(0.04)	

Note: Standard errors in parentheses. Monthly data are used. All real exchange rate indices are normalized to 100 in January 1932. The standard deviation and time trend are calculated for the period January 1932–August 1936. The sample period for the convergence regression is February 1932–August 1936 to allow for the lagged variable.

variability should differ across periods. But the extent of the difference is striking. Nominal rates were almost four times as volatile (measured by their standard deviation) during the free float of the early 1920s as during the managed float of the early 1930s. Similarly, under the 1930s managed float, nominal rates were four times as volatile as under the pegged rate system of the late 1920s. Clearly, there was a significant difference in the extent of nominal-exchange-rate variability under these alternative exchange rate regimes.

I consider next the standard deviation of real exchange rates in the three periods. That standard deviation averages 6.46 under floating in the early 1920s, 2.79 under fixed rates in the late 1920s, and 5.18 under managed floating in the early 1930s. (These and other cross-country averages cited in the text are simple arithmetic means.) This is striking confirmation that the variability of real exchange rates was positively associated with the free- dom of the float. Moreover, when nominal rates were floating, there was a positive correlation between the variability of nominal rates and the vari- ability of real rates. Looking across countries, in both the early 1920s and early 1930s, the correlation between the standard deviation of nominal rates and the standard deviation of real rates is positive and significantly greater than zero at the 99 percent confidence level. In both periods of floating, nominal exchange rate variability was a significant source of real exchange rate variability. This was not the case, however, during the gold-exchange standard era. For this period there is no strong association between the variability of nominal and real exchange rates. Looking across countries, the correlation between the standard deviations of the two variables, while positive, is significant only at levels below 70 percent.

Differences in the stability of nominal exchange rates do not provide the entire explanation for differences in the stability of real exchange rates across periods, however. There are also striking differences in the speed with which real exchange rates converged to their equilibrium levels when perturbed by nominal exchange rate movements or price level shocks. To analyze the speed of convergence I estimate variants of the following model (see also Frankel, 1986). The change in the real rate is hypothesized to depend on the deviation of the current rate R_t from its equilibrium level R_t^*

$$(R_t - R_{t-1}) = \theta(R_{t-1}^* - R_{t-1}),\tag{1}$$

where θ is the speed of convergence. I consider the case where R^* is a linear function of time $(R_t^* = \alpha + \beta TIME)$, which nests the case where R^* is constant $(\beta = 0)$. Then

$$R_t = \alpha\theta + (1 - \theta)R_{t-1} + \beta\theta TIME.\tag{2}$$

If convergence is completed within the period, the coefficient on R_{t-1} should be zero. If convergence requires additional time, that coefficient should significantly exceed zero. If the real exchange rate has a unit root, that coefficient should equal one.

Regressions are run using ordinary least squares. Standard t-statistics are constructed to test for coefficients greater than zero and Dickey–Fuller tests for lagged dependent variables less than one. In every case, whatever the exchange-rate regime, the coefficients on R_{t-1} significantly exceed zero at the 99 percent confidence level. Equally, in every case but one (Denmark under the gold-exchange standard), it is impossible to reject the hypothesis that this coefficient equals one. Yet the coefficient estimates display patterns, both across countries and over time, that have plausible interpretations within the convergence-to-equilibrium paradigm but would seem impossible to interpret within the unit-root framework. Hence I discuss the results in terms of convergence to equilibrium. Under the free float of the early 1920s, on average 18 percent of any deviation from the equilibrium real exchange rate was eliminated within a month. Under the gold-exchange standard, the comparable figure was 28 percent; under the managed float of the early 1930s, it was 20 percent. Just as there is a positive association between the stability of nominal rates and the stability of real rates across regimes, there is, more surprisingly, a positive association between the stability of nominal rates and the speed with which real exchange rates converged to their equilibrium levels. Thus, real rates were relatively stable under the gold-exchange standard both because nominal rates were stable and because the speed of convergence was high. By contrast, real rates were relatively unstable during the period of freely floating exchange rates that preceded the return to gold both because nominal rates were volatile and because the speed of adjustment was low. One might speculate that faster convergence under more stable nominal exchange rates reflected less uncertainty about the equilibrium level of real exchange rates.

If the negative association between the variability of real and nominal exchange rates on the one hand and the speed of convergence on the other is robust, one would expect to observe it within each period when looking across countries as well as in comparisons across periods. This is generally the case. Regressing the speed of convergence (one minus the coefficient on the lagged dependent variable) on a constant and the standard deviation of the real exchange rate for each cross section of countries yields a negative slope coefficient for two of three cross sections. The coefficient estimate is more than three and a half times its standard error for the early 1930s, more than two and a half times for the late 1920s. The exception is the early 1920s, when the slope coefficient is positive if small, with a coefficient estimate little more than half its standard error. Plotting the data reveals that the absence of a negative correlation between real exchange rate variability and speed of convergence for this period is due entirely to the exceptional behavior of France and Belgium. While these two countries had the most variable real exchange rates, they also exhibited the fastest rates of convergence. Of the countries in the sample, these two experienced the highest and most variable rates of inflation and nominal depreciation. It is tempting to speculate that the usually high degree of inflation and nominal exchange rate depreciation experienced by these countries altered the manner in which domestic prices were set and the frequency with which they were adjusted, and that the more frequent adjustment of domestic prices facilitated the process of real exchange rate convergence. If this is correct, then the relationship between real exchange rate variability and speed of convergence identified here holds only in periods of relatively moderate inflation.

Since the findings of this analysis are striking, it is important to note their limitations. Confirming that differences across periods in the standard deviation of real exchange rates are statistically robust will require additional tests to establish the constancy of those standard deviations within periods. Similarly, establishing that greater real exchange rate variability had real economic costs will require additional work to construct an expected real exchange rate and thereby measure unanticipated variability. Finally, observing a correlation between real and nominal exchange rates does not definitively establish causation. It could be that the real shocks to which exchange rates were subjected varied significantly across periods, and that these real shocks, rather than the degree of nominal exchange rate flexibility, account for the differing behavior of real rates. In other words, definitive conclusions will require a full structural model of the equilibrium real exchange rate toward which the current rate converges. Indeed, the entire notion of an equilibrium exchange rate toward which the current rate converges requires further substantiation, since it is rarely possible to reject the hypothesis of a unit root. Still, the close correspondence between this paper's results for the interwar period and the findings of other investigators concerned with the experience of recent years creates a presumption that more than a peculiar constellation of real shocks accounts for the divergent behavior of real exchange rates under the alternative nominal exchange rate regimes.

4. Conclusion

The evidence presented in this chapter generalizes the findings of investigators of post–World War II exchange rate systems. Comparing interwar monetary systems, regimes characterized by greater nominal exchange rate stability were also characterized by greater real exchange rate stability. This was true both because movements in nominal rates perturbed real rates to a lesser extent under pegged and managed rate systems and because, once perturbed, real rates converged to their equilibrium levels more quickly when nominal rates were relatively stable.

3. Understanding 1921–1927: inflation and economic recovery in the 1920s

The 1920s were for the industrial nations of the western world a decade of reconstruction and recovery. World War I had wrought destruction of two kinds of productive capacity: the physical capacity to produce goods and services, and the institutional capacity to mobilize productive resources and distribute the fruits of their labor. The first set of effects is more easily observed. Approximately 8.5 million soldiers, amounting to 15 percent of those mobilized, 2 percent of Europe's population, and nearly 8 percent of its adult male workers, died in active service. The number of casualties doubles when the permanently disabled are included and triples with the addition of civilian deaths. In parts of Europe, notably portions of France, Belgium, and northern Italy, where trench warfare had been waged, extensive destruction of industrial capacity had occurred. Restoring basic infrastructure, rebuilding plant and equipment, reconverting capacity from war- to peace-time uses, and training replacements for skilled workers proved to be a drawn-out process. The upward trend in industrial production over the first postwar decade is typically understood to reflect the gradual reconstruction of this type of productive capacity.

The impact of the war on economic institutions, while more difficult to quantify and measure, was equally profound. In the domestic sphere, wartime exigencies had undermined monetary stability, fiscal orthodoxy, and accepted standards of labor-management relations. In the international sphere, they had disrupted foreign trade, led to the gold standard's abandonment, and impeded the free international movement of capital. During the war, the imposition of controls had suppressed the effects of many of these changes, which then asserted themselves with a vengeance following postwar decontrol. The monetary and financial instability which resulted was seen as creating uncertainty which undermined confidence, impeding reconstruction and recovery. Almost without exception, the goal of policymakers in the 1920s was to restore prewar institutional arrange-

I am grateful for comments from Michael Bordo, Carol Heim, Charles Kindleberger, Larry Summers, Gianni Toniolo, and Herman van der Wee.

ments, notably balanced budgets, monetary stability, and an international gold standard incorporating prewar rates of exchange. In some accounts, the upward trend of industrial production reflects steady progress along these lines.

Yet the stabilization of prices interacted with economic activity not only through the reduction of uncertainty but through the macroeconomic policies by which stabilization was achieved.[1] Countries which returned to the gold standard at prewar rates of exchange were forced to endure a reduction of wages and prices sufficient to reverse much of the wartime inflation. Those such as France, Belgium, and Italy which ultimately returned to the gold standard at parities below those prevailing before the war were unable to prevent inflation from continuing into the mid-1920s. Keynes's view, as expressed in *The Tract on Monetary Reform* (published in 1923), was that these deflationary and inflationary trends powerfully conditioned the course of recovery from the war. With wages and interest rates slow to adjust, countries such as Britain which endured deflation experienced declining competitiveness which caused growth to stagnate, while countries such as France which experienced inflation benefited from the boost it provided for the recovery process.

The notion that inflation was conducive to economic recovery in the 1920s has not been given much weight in the recent literature in which the period is discussed. That view is quite inconsistent with the neutrality of money, a basic postulate of classical economics. It contradicts the literature in which the depressing effects of price-level uncertainty are emphasized.[2] It has been undermined by subsequent research on inflationary eras in which the generality of the Keynesian wage-lag hypothesis has been questioned.[3] Enthusiasm for the proposition surely has been tempered by the experience of the post–World-War-II era, in which inflation and economic growth have been anything but compatible.[4]

I argue here that price-level changes exercised a powerful influence over

---

[1] Notable comparative studies adopting this perspective include H.W. Arndt, *The Economic Lessons of the 1930s* (London, 1944), and W.A. Lewis, *Economic Survey, 1919–1939* (London, 1949).

[2] See especially Dulles, *The French Franc*, but also Eleanor Lansing Dulles, *The Dollar, the Franc and Inflation* (New York, 1933) and G. Cassel, *The Downfall of the Gold Standard* (London, 1936).

[3] See R.A. Kessel and A.A. Alchian, "The Inflation-Induced Lag of Wages," *American Economic Review* 50 (1960), 43–66, and T.F. Cargill, "An Empirical Investigation of the Wage-Lag Hypothesis," *American Economic Review* 59 (1969), 806–16.

[4] The literature on this subject is reviewed by W. Baer and I. Kerstenetzky, *Inflation and Growth in Latin America* (Homewood, 1964).

the economic recovery of the industrial nations in the 1920s. Those countries marked by moderate inflation expanded more rapidly and recovered
more quickly from the after-effects of the First World War than did those
which endured deflation. Economic policies, which worked through a combination of supply- and demand-side channels suggested by modern variants
of the Keynesian model, significantly influenced real economic fluctuations
in the early postwar years.

To argue that inflation was conducive to economic recovery in the early
1920s is not to argue the stimulus to expansion was free of costs. In several
countries rapid growth in the period of rising prices had as its counterpart
relatively slow growth once financial stability was restored. The point is
not that different inflation rates explain differences across countries in rates
of long-term economic growth, but that different inflation rates contributed to differences across countries in the pattern and character of postwar
recovery.

To argue that inflation was conducive to economic recovery in the early
1920s is not to argue that the process was without limits. The discussion
here is limited to countries experiencing moderate changes in the level of
prices, avoiding collapse of the monetary standard through hyperinflation.
Hyperinflations like those which took place in Germany, Austria, Hungary,
and Poland produce changes in economic structure, notably in the ways
wages and prices are set and quoted, which qualitatively alter the inflation
process.[5] Hyperinflations still affect economic activity through several of
the channels identified here, but because of the changes in structure they
produce, the operation of these effects is hidden – indeed dominated –
by the influence of others. Hence the Central European experience with
hyperinflation does not figure in the discussion that follows.

Finally, to argue that inflation was conducive to economic growth in the
twenties is not to argue that the same is necessarily true in other times and
places. The argument is historically specific. Inflation had pronounced real

---

[5] For example, the lag of domestic prices behind import prices is eliminated once producers
index prices to foreign exchange quotations. The lag of wages behind prices may be eliminated by similar indexing and by payment in commodities. Recent contributions which
emphasize such developments include G.D. Feldman, "Socio-Economic Structures in the
Industrial Sector and Revolutionary Potentialities, 1917–1922," in C. Bertrand, ed. *Revolutionary Situations in Europe, 1917–1922* (Montreal, 1977); G.H.B. Franco, "The Rentenmark 'Miracle'," *Rivista di Storia Economica* (sec. ser., 1987), 96–117; R. Dornbusch,
"Lessons from the German Inflation Experience of the 1920s," in R. Dornbusch, S. Fischer,
and J. Bossons (eds.), *Macroeconomics and Finance* (Cambridge, MA, 1987), 337–366;
and S.B. Webb, "Four Ends to the Big Inflation in Germany, 1920–1924," unpublished,
University of Michigan (1985).

effects in the immediate postwar years precisely because of the economic and intellectual legacy of the prewar era. The effects of that legacy operated so powerfully because of its influence over not just the public but also the policymakers whose actions brought the inflation about.

1. Sources and perceptions of inflation

Changes in prices over the period 1921–27 were associated with changes in money supplies, the major instances of which were fiscal in origin. In countries such as Belgium and France where inflation reached double-digit levels and persisted for a period of years, monetary expansion resulted from the methods used to finance government budget deficits. Typically, central banks were encouraged or compelled to extend advances to the state when government expenditures increased, although sometimes the fiscal authorities augmented the supply of credit directly by issuing liquid assets. *Bons de la défense nationale* issued in France in the early 1920s were sufficiently liquid to serve as close substitutes for money.[6] In Italy, short-dated Treasury bills served the same function and had similar effects. In Belgium, highly liquid Treasury bills were issued to finance nearly half the deficits of the period 1919–24. In countries such as Britain where deflation prevailed, the money supply was reduced or its rate of growth restricted through fiscal austerity (balanced budgets or relatively small deficits), reinforced as necessary by high central bank discount rates and open market sales.

Evidence on the association between inflation and monetary growth appears in Table 3.1. In the first equation, the change in wholesale prices over the period 1921–27 is related to the change in M1 in 12 countries (eight European, two North American, Australia, and Japan), except for Britain where reliable M1 figures are unavailable for 1921 and M3 is used instead.[7] There is a strong positive association of changes in money sup-

---

[6] French monetary trends in this period are the subject of B. Eichengreen, "Did Speculation Destabilize the French Franc in the 1920s?" *Explorations in Economic History* 19 (1982), 71–100; J.H. Rogers, *The Process of Inflation in France, 1914–1927* (New York, 1929); and G.C. Schmid, "The Politics of Currency Stabilization; The French Franc, 1926," *Journal of European Economic History* 3 (1976), 359–77.

[7] This refers to the M1 and M3 estimates of F. Capie and A. Webber, *Monetary History of the United Kingdom, 1870–1982, vol. I: Data, Sources, Methods* (London, 1985). In preparation for this study, statistics were assembled for a total of 15 countries: the United Kingdom, France, Norway, Sweden, Belgium, Italy, Spain, Denmark, Holland, Finland, Switzerland, Canada, the United States, Australia, and Japan. No experimentation was done with the sample of countries. The intention was to include all non-hyperinflationary countries for which adequate statistics were available. Some of the analysis discussed below is based on

Table 3.1: *Price levels and money supplies,*
1921–1927

Eq.	Sample period	Constant	Money supply	R^2	n
1.	1921–27	−0.55 (2.28)	1.38 (6.77)	.82	12
2.	1921–27	−0.17 (1.01)	0.64 (4.01)	.67	10

Notes: t-statistics in parentheses. In Eq. 1. Holland, Finland, and Switzerland are the omitted countries. France and Belgium are also omitted from Eq. 2.

Dependent variable is the ratio of wholesale prices at the end and the start of the period.

plies with changes in wholesale prices. However, the constant term differs significantly from zero at the 95 percent level, suggesting that factors other than M1 growth may have contributed to inflation over the period, while the coefficient on monetary growth is greater than unity, not less than unity as would be expected if monetary policy had real effects and resulted partly in higher prices and partly in increased production.[8]

Figure 3.1, where the country data are plotted, suggests that this result hinges upon inclusion of Belgium and France. Excluding them, as in the second line of Table 3.1, yields a constant term insignificantly different from zero at standard confidence levels and a point estimate on the money supply term which is less than unity. France and Belgium (and perhaps also Italy) appear to have been different due to the internal circulation of substantial quantities of highly liquid short-term government securities which were close substitutes for components of the narrowly defined money supply, and in whose absence the international relationship of M1 growth to inflation underestimates the increase in their price levels.

Policymakers in these countries shared a desire to return to the gold standard at their prewar parities. Restoring the traditional domestic-currency price of gold and the exchange rate against the U.S. dollar, thought to signal the restoration of normalcy, required prices and money supplies to be reduced toward the levels that had prevailed in prewar years. So long as

subsets of countries when one or more variables do not exist. Sources and definitions of the time series used in this chapter appear in the data appendix.

[8] Note, however, that one cannot reject at the 95 percent level the null hypothesis that this coefficient is less than unity.

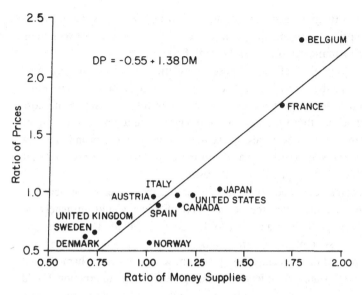

Figure 3.1. Changes in money supplies and price levels, 1921–1927.

the authorities remained committed to this objective and their commitment was credible, current movements in prices did not lead the private sector to revise its estimate of the level of prices that would prevail in the future. Hence the more inflation and monetary expansion witnessed in preceding or current periods, the less was anticipated to follow. In France, persistent central government deficits were the source of credit creation which not only ratified price increases that had occurred during the war but permitted wholesale prices nearly to double between 1921 and 1926. With the exchange rate's downward spiral and the political turmoil of 1924, faith that the French authorities would ultimately succeed in reversing years of double-digit inflation began to erode. But even after 1924 a sizeable segment of the French public retained the belief that the authorities would ultimately reverse the course of postwar inflation. That their hopes were not entirely misplaced is suggested by the extended discussions of the question among French policymakers between Poincaré's return to power in 1926 and the franc's de jure stabilization in 1928. The situation in Belgium was similar. Despite persistent inflation, the public remained confident of the franc's eventual return to par until the failure of the abortive Jansson stabilization scheme of September 1925. In Italy, the inflationary mechanism was basically the same, although the price level rose markedly only after 1924. Mussolini expressed his commitment to price stability in the same terms as the Belgians and French, and following the Italian stabilization, wholesale prices were actually permitted to fall by 23 percent between their peak in the summer of 1926 and the end of 1927.[9]

The real economic effects of postwar inflations were pronounced precisely because they were expected to be reversed. Workers were less militant in demanding higher wages to compensate for increases in the cost of living because those increases were thought to be temporary. Creditors when extending loans were less insistent on compensation for inflation because they expected current changes in the price level to be reversed and the real value of their principal to be restored.

What seems remarkable in retrospect is the resilience of the belief in inflationary countries that the prewar level of prices would ultimately be restored. The public's attachment to the idea that inflation was a temporary and reversible phenomenon must be understood as a legacy of the fact that Europe had only recently emerged from several decades characterized by a relatively stable price level and the operation of an international gold standard. These two factors – the gold standard and stable prices – were associated with one another in the minds of the public and policymakers alike, who shared the belief that postwar efforts to reconstruct the prewar gold standard would ultimately succeed. Add to this the extent to which restoration of the gold standard symbolized the official commitment to restoring normalcy and economic prosperity, and one begins to understand the faith of contemporaries that stabilization would be achieved.

2. Inflation and growth in the 1920s

Britain and France are the two countries most often juxtaposed when the real economic effects of inflation in the 1920s are discussed. Figure 3.2 displays the course of inflation and industrial production growth in the two countries. While there is broad conformance in the two time series for each country after 1922, there are exceptions to the rule. In Britain, the rate of growth of industrial production is exceptionally low relative to the rate of inflation in 1926, reflecting the effects of the General Strike. Similarly, rapid growth between 1926 and 1927 is a function of putting idle resources back to work. In France, rates of inflation and industrial production are in step after 1923 but not before. Slower growth in 1923 than would be

9 See D.T. Jack, *The Restoration of European Currencies* (London, 1927), p. 138, as well as J.S. Cohen, "The 1927 Revaluation of the Lira: A Study in Political Economy," *Economic History Review*, new ser., 25 (1972), 642–54.

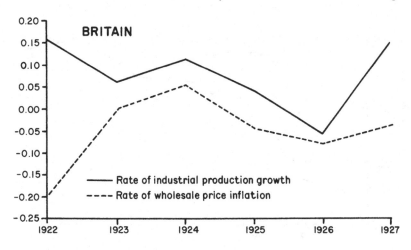

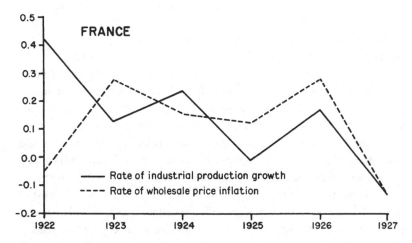

Figure 3.2. Inflation and economic growth in Britain and France, 1922–1927.

predicted from the subsequent relationship between inflation and industrial production may be understood in terms of the uncertainties associated with France's occupation of the Ruhr and with the Reparations tangle.[10]

In both countries, the rate of economic growth is high in 1922 despite the fact that the rate of price increase is low. This could be a rubber-band effect in the wake of the severe but short-lived recession of 1920–21, during which wholesale prices had fallen by fully 36 percent in Britain and

[10] See the discussion of these relations in W.F. Ogburn and W. Jaffe, *The Economic Development of Postwar France* (New York, 1929), p. 158.

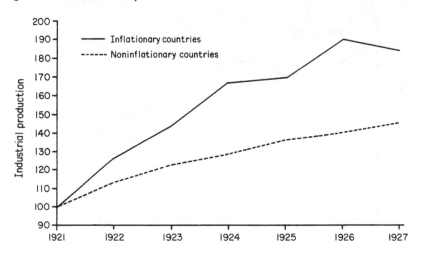

Figure 3.3. Growth of inflationary and noninflationary countries, 1921–1927.

31 percent in France. But there are reasons to suppose that the positive association between the price level and economic activity was not as prevalent before 1922 as after. In 1919 and 1920, Britain and a number of other countries experienced increases in unit labor costs, despite a rise in the price level, due to reductions in weekly hours.[11] In 1920, labor leaders acknowledged that prices and hence wages were above the levels expected to prevail in the future. Wages then fell with prices in 1920–21 at a rate not witnessed previously or duplicated subsequently. This rapid adjustment was facilitated by the operation of sliding-scale clauses in labor contracts, under whose provisions wages were indexed to product prices or the cost of living. While sliding scales had prevailed in certain industries and countries prior to the war, in response to wartime inflation their scope was considerably expanded. Following the rapid deflation of 1920–22, sliding scales fell gradually from favor, and comparable wage flexibility did not recur.[12]

For evidence of an association between inflation and economic activity to be convincing, it must extend beyond the cases of Britain and France. Figure 3.3 displays the growth of industrial production separately for three

[11] See J.A. Dowie, "1919–1920 Is in Need of Attention," *Economic History Review* 28, sec. ser. (1975), 429–50.
[12] Wartime labor unrest and the rise and fall of sliding scales in Britain are discussed by S. Pollard, *The Development of the British Economy, 1914–1967* (2nd ed., Bath, 1969). The spread of indexation in Sweden is discussed by K. Fregert and L. Jonung, "Monetary Regimes and the Length of Wage Contracts," unpublished manuscript, University of Lund (1986).

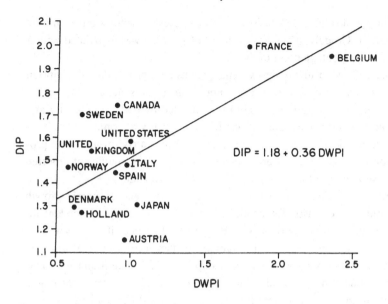

Figure 3.4. Inflation and economic growth, 1921–1927.

inflationary countries (France, Belgium, and Italy) and ten countries which did not experience sustained inflation (six European, two North American, plus Australia and Japan).[13] The inflationary countries grow more rapidly over the period 1921–27 with two interruptions: 1924–25 and 1926–27. The second hiatus is by no means inconsistent, since stabilization was achieved in 1926 and prices fell thereafter in both Italy and France. The first hiatus is more perplexing, since in 1924–25 prices were only temporarily stabilized in Belgium while continuing to rise rapidly in Italy and France.

Overall trends disguise considerable variation within both groups of countries. Figure 3.4 therefore plots the change in industrial production against the change in the price level over the period 1921–27. There is a positive relationship between these two variables. Ordinary least squares regression yields:

$$INDUSTRIAL\ PRODUCTION\ GROWTH\ =\ 1.18\ +\ 0.36\ \pi,$$
$$(9.16)\quad (3.08)$$

---

[13] These are unweighted averages. This comparison of industrial production growth rates excludes Finland and Switzerland, since authorities there constructed the series from the middle of the 1920s.

with an R^2 of 0.46 and t-statistics in parentheses. π denotes inflation over the period. Crudely, a percentage point of inflation was associated with a third of a percentage point of growth.

This regression involving two endogenous variables is data description rather than a test of a theory. The point estimate and standard error on the coefficient for inflation are likely to be affected by both simultaneity and omitted-variables bias. Corrections for simultaneity are unlikely to eliminate the relationship, since by the quantity theory a rise in industrial production should put downward pressure on prices. The coefficient reported above should therefore be interpreted as a lower bound.

Omitted variables correlated with both inflation and economic growth constitute more reason for doubt. Since the relationship is dependent for its strength on the experiences of Belgium and France, if other variables were mainly responsible for the rapidity of their economic growth, little evidence would remain of a relationship between inflation and recovery. At the same time, it is possible that such omitted variables contributed heavily to the relatively rapid growth of Sweden and Canada in the face of price stability, or the relatively slow growth of Australia and Japan. It is appropriate, therefore, to turn to other determinants of economic growth.

3. Wartime dislocation, reconstruction, and economic expansion

The other obvious determinant of rates of economic growth in the early 1920s is the extent of wartime disturbances to production. Where those disturbances took the form of damage to transport and communications systems, the repair of railway and telegraph lines offered considerable scope for rapid growth. Especially in the main theaters of the war, bridges and roadbeds were in poor repair. In the ten northern departments of France invaded by hostile forces, half the roads had been torn up, 600 bridges and 1500 miles of railway demolished, and 700 miles of canal routes damaged. More than a year after the armistice, over a large part of Europe fewer than half of all locomotives were in working order.[14] Inadequate transport impeded the supply of raw materials to industry and the supply of output to home and foreign markets.

---

14 This situation was most serious in Central and Eastern Europe: at the beginning of 1920, only 27 and 29 percent of locomotives were usable in Hungary and Rumania, respectively. League of Nations, *Europe's Overseas Needs, 1919–1920* (Geneva, 1943). On France, see Sir Robert Cahill, *Economic Conditions in France, 1928* (London, 1928).

Interruptions to the steady flow of raw materials and semi-manufactured inputs to industry were particularly disruptive given the low level of inventories. Where blockades had cut off foreign sources of supply, stocks had been run down in the course of the war. The Dutch textile industry, for example, suffered shortages of raw cotton, while iron and steel industries across Europe experienced shortages of coal. Not until 1921, and in some instances later, did inventories again approach working levels.

The destruction of plant and equipment was the most visible evidence of wartime devastation. Industries deemed nonessential had suffered the removal of parts and of equipment containing copper and other metals vital to the war effort. Machinery had been deliberately destroyed by retreating armies. In parts of Belgium and Northern France, factories had been leveled: in France's 10 northern departments alone, 9,000 factories employing 10 or more persons had been crippled or razed, and half of the looms and spindles in the region had been put out of service.[15] Nearly every coalmining shaft in the Nord and Pas-de-Calais had been destroyed.

Where damage was superficial, production could be restarted quickly. The installation of a few parts could provide a dramatic boost to industrial production. But where damage was extensive, the process of reconstruction was drawn out and continued well into the 1920s.

The very extent of destruction offered opportunities for modernization. The greatest effects were generally felt by capital- rather than consumer-goods industries; the former had been frequent targets of retreating armies and were favored recipients of government subsidies. Thus, coalmining shafts which had been damaged were not only repaired but improved. The French iron and steel industry, to take another prominent example, was almost entirely reconstructed. Missions of experts were sent to the United States to study ore mining, blast furnace, and steel mill practice.[16]

According to Lewis, physical destruction was not the war's most important consequence for industrial capacity.[17] More pervasive and persistent were continued impediments to international trade. The most heavily damaged nations found their capacity to export diminished and their gold and exchange reserves depleted. In the absence of foreign loans, they found it difficult to import intermediate inputs. The absence of foreign loans was clearly war related: the burden of reparations and allied war debts, along

---

[15] Ogburn and Jaffe, *Economic Development*, p. 28.

[16] Tom Kemp, *The French Economy, 1913–1939* (London, 1972), p. 68; Sir Robert Cahill, *Economic Conditions in France, 1934* (London, 1934), pp. 213–14.

[17] Lewis, *Economic Survey*, p. 35.

with the political upheavals that accompanied demobilization, raised questions about the ability of potential capital importers to service additional foreign debts.[18] Moreover, all of the belligerents had imposed new restrictions on imports and exports, which they were slow to relax following the conclusion of hostilities. The United States raised its rates of import taxation with the passage of the Fordney-McCumber Tariff in 1922, which shifted resources out of the production of exports and into import substitutes. In the absence of established tax systems, the new nations of Central and Eastern Europe typically imposed high tariffs as a means of raising revenues. For all these reasons, many nations found it difficult to import the capital goods and raw materials needed for production.

Changes in the composition of production induced by wartime exigencies contributed to both the postwar slump in industrial production and the subsequent recovery. Manpower, plant, and equipment had been shifted out of consumer goods industries into the production of capital equipment and war matériel. Rapid expansion occurred, for example, in the engineering industry in general and machine tool production in particular. Similarly, in all but the neutral countries, shipbuilding capacity was considerably increased over the second decade of the 20th century. Given the number of ships constructed in the course of hostilities, there was little need for new production in the 1920s.[19] Hence readjustment to a peace-time footing required a shift of resources back toward the production of consumer goods, a process often delayed by the maintenance of controls, but which in any case would have required time and disrupted activity until complete.

War and its aftermath also unsettled labor-management relations, strengthening at least temporarily the bargaining position of organized labor. In some countries, workers' representatives had been given new influence over the organization of production, prerogatives not easily withdrawn following the armistice. In others, skilled workers were radicalized by the erosion of traditional piece rates and wage differentials. In the engineering industries, they rebelled against the introduction of semi-automatic machinery which made possible the increasing subdivision of work, the employment of women and children, and the spread of scientific management.[20] The concentration of industrial workers in large enterprises, a trend common to Germany, Italy, and other belligerents, was conducive also to

---

[18] B. Eichengreen and R. Portes, "Debt and Default in the 1930s: Causes and Consequences," *European Economic Review* 30 (1986), pp. 599–640.

[19] See C.E. Fayle, *The War and the Shipping Industry* (New Haven, 1927), chaps. 21–5.

[20] J.B. Jeffreys, *The Story of the Engineers* (London, 1945).

the growth of labor militancy. Many of these enterprises drew on women, immigrants, and young workers new to the labor force, who were sympathetic to industrial action.[21] One measure of labor militancy was the number of organized workers, another the frequency of disputes. In Italy, the General Confederation of Labor more than doubled its membership over the course of the war. Following the conclusion of hostilities, workers on the land seized farms and those in industry occupied factories. In France, union membership rose by more than 50 percent between 1913 and 1919, and 1919–20 was marked by a strike wave involving miners, metalworkers, and building laborers. In Britain, the number of trade union members doubled between 1914 and 1920. The immediate postwar period was marked by agitation for workers' control of industry and for nationalization. Serious strikes took place in coal mining, iron, and the railways. During 1919 the 2.6 million British workers directly involved in labor disputes lost on average 13 days apiece. Labor militancy and the severity of disruptions to production declined gradually over subsequent years, a process symbolized in Britain by the failure of the General Strike of 1926.[22]

No single measure can encapsulate these developments. Nonetheless, an attempt can be made to capture the extent of wartime disruptions to productive capacity and organization with the ratio of industrial production at the start of the period to industrial production in 1913. Since there was exceptional scope for output growth where war-related disruptions had been most severe, the lower the ratio of production in the early twenties to production in 1913, the more rapid should have been the rate of economic growth. The results in Table 3.2 confirm this expectation when the economy's growth rate is computed from a 1921 base and are not inconsistent with it when growth is computed from 1922.[23] Plausibly enough, the positive association between reconstruction and growth is most important in the early part of the 1920s.

Introducing this measure of postwar reconstruction fails to eliminate the

[21] See Feldman, "Socio-economic Structures"; J. Hinton, *The First Shop Stewards' Movement and Workers' Control* (London, 1973); J. Saposs, *The Postwar Labor Movement in France* (New York, 1931).

[22] On Italy, see S.B. Clough, *The Economic History of Modern Italy* (New York, 1964). On France, see D. Geary, *European Labour Protest, 1848–1939* (London, 1981) and Saposs, *Labor Movement*. On Britain, see R. Currie, *Industrial Politics* (Oxford, 1979), chap. 4, and A.C. Pigou, *Aspects of British Economic History, 1918–1925* (London, 1947).

[23] Note from Eq. (7) that this remains true whether or not the inflationary cases (Belgium and France) are included in the sample. In contrast, the statistical significance of the coefficient on prices hinges upon their inclusion.

Table 3.2: *Inflation, reconstruction, and industrial production growth, 1921–1927*

Eq.	Sample period	Constant	π	Start/1913	R^2	n
1.	1921–27	1.72 (8.47)	0.26 (2.86)	−0.49 (3.03)	.72	13
2.	1921–26	1.56 (6.59)	0.38 (3.41)	−0.49 (2.74)	.75	13
3.	1922–27	1.35 (6.92)	0.14 (1.80)	−0.18 (1.30)	.42	13
4.	1922–26	1.27 (5.82)	0.21 (2.23)	−0.19 (1.33)	.51	13
5.	1921–25	1.63 (6.97)	0.30 (1.98)	−0.56 (3.96)	.73	13
6.	1922–25	1.47 (6.66)	0.05 (0.36)	−0.28 (2.67)	.50	13
7.	1921–27	1.71 (6.24)	0.23 (0.67)	−0.46 (2.17)	.63	11

Note: *t*-statistics in parentheses. Finland and Switzerland are the omitted countries. France and Belgium have also been omitted from Eq. (7).

Dependent variable is the ratio of industrial production at the end and start of the period.

positive association between inflation and economic growth. It does, however, somewhat attenuate the effect.

4. Mechanisms linking inflation with activity

Evidence on the relationship between inflation and economic activity must be buttressed by evidence on the mechanisms through which these variables were linked. According to the early Keynesian view epitomized by the *Tract on Monetary Reform*, inflation promoted economic activity by reducing real wages and real interest rates. As Keynes described the wage mechanism, "It has been a commonplace of economic text-books that wages tend to lag behind prices, with the result that the real earnings of the wage earner are diminished during a period of rising prices."[24] Similarly, in 1928 Sir Josiah Stamp noted how,

it is insufficiently realised that slowly falling prices are a deadening influence on business itself . . . they provide good times for the people who are in work because

[24] J.M. Keynes, *Tract on Monetary Reform* (London, 1923), p. 27.

they steadily increase the value of money wages, but they gradually reduce the number that are in work, for they continually restrict the area of business. Only if prices have remained stable at a lower level for some time are these effects overcome.[25]

Complementary arguments applied to the behavior of interest rates. According to Keynes,

When prices are rising, the business man who borrows money is able to repay the lender with what, in terms of real value, not only represents no interest, but is even less than the capital originally advanced; that is, the real rate of interest falls to a negative value, and the borrower reaps a corresponding benefit. It is true that, in so far as a rise in prices is foreseen, attempts to get advantage from this by increased borrowing force the money rates of interest upwards . . . . Nevertheless in a period of rapidly changing prices, the money rate of interest seldom adjusts itself adequately or fast enough to prevent the real rate from becoming abnormal.[26]

Similarly, writing in 1928 of recent French experience, Ogburn and Jaffe concluded that "It was mainly through its effects on the cost of production that inflation exerted a direct influence on industrial output. This is fairly obvious in the case of that element of cost which consists of interest paid on capital charges."[27] Many of these observers noted that, insofar as the authorities' commitment to prewar gold standard parities was credible, inflation was likely to give rise to expectations of subsequent deflation. Thus, in the early stages of an inflation, nominal interest rates might actually decline, and the demand for wage increases to compensate for a rise in the cost of living would be moderated by expectations of deflation. "The public is so much accustomed to thinking of money as the ultimate standard, that, when prices begin to rise, believing that the rise must be temporary, they tend to hoard their money and to postpone purchases, with the result that they hold in monetary form a larger aggregate value than before."[28]

Tables 3.3 and 3.4 report the relationship of inflation to real wages and real interest rates. The first two rows of Table 3.3 suggest that, between 1921–22 and 1926–27, a percentage point of wholesale price inflation reduced the rate of growth of the real wage by a quarter of a percentage point.[29] The pooled time-series cross-section regression using annual rates

[25] J. Stamp, *Papers on Gold and the Price Level* (London, 1931), p. 4.
[26] Keynes, *Tract*, pp. 21–2.
[27] Ogburn and Jaffe, *Economic Development*, p. 160.
[28] Keynes, *Tract*, p. 45.
[29] Since both the dependent and independent variables contain the wholesale price index, the dependent variable in its denominator and the independent variable in its numerator, any measurement error in the price index will give rise to a negative coefficient. However, regressing the nominal wage on the price index leads to precisely the same conclusion; the coefficient on prices is in this case consistently positive but significantly less than unity

Table 3.3: *Inflation and real wage growth,*
1921–1927

Eq.	Sample period	Constant	π	R^2	n
1.	1921–27	1.35 (12.50)	−0.23 (2.31)	.31	14
2.	1922–27	1.34 (15.82)	−0.22 (3.02)	.43	14
3.	1921–26	1.39 (12.15)	−0.31 (2.95)	.40	14
4.	1922–26	1.39 (15.22)	−0.30 (3.89)	.54	14
5.	1920–27*	1.06 (62.59)	−0.009 (7.92)	.40	97
6.	1921–27*	1.44 (21.36)	−0.42 (6.24)	.32	84

Notes: *t*-statistics in parentheses. * denotes pooled time-series cross-section estimates. In Eqs. 1–4, Spain is the omitted country. In Eq. 5, the Netherlands are omitted due to missing wage data for 1920.
Dependent variable is the ratio of real wages at the end and start of the period.

of change for the period 1921–27 confirms this result. The change in the slope coefficient which results when 1920 is added to the sample reinforces the presumption that, for reasons discussed above, labor market behavior in 1920–21 differed fundamentally from behavior in subsequent years. Although one still cannot reject the hypothesis that inflation altered real wages, the magnitude of the effect is considerably reduced.

As with the relationship of inflation to industrial production, it is important to acknowledge the possibility that war-related disruptions rather than the policies associated with inflation were responsible for the behavior of wages, especially since, of the countries in the sample, those experiencing the most rapid inflation and erosion of real wages were also those suffering

at the 99 percent confidence level. Readers may question the direction of causality, since in the presence of mark-up pricing and/or monetary accommodation, real wage increases may lead to inflation. Note, however, that this implies a *positive* relationship between inflation and real wages. To the extent that this linkage was operative, it would tend to bias upward the negative coefficient on the inflation term which should therefore be interpreted as a conservative estimate of the impact of inflation on real wages.

Table 3.4: *Discount rates and inflation,*
1921–1927

Eq.	Sample period	Constant	π	R^2	n
1.	1921–27	0.67 (7.63)	1.001 (2.06) (0.01)	.25	15
2.	1922–27	0.82 (7.76)	0.663 (1.44) (0.73)	.14	15
3.	1921–27*	0.38 (4.02)	0.60 (6.21) (4.21)	.30	90
4.	1922–27*	0.50 (4.60)	0.50 (4.66) (4.76)	.23	75

Note: Where a coefficient appears above a pair of t-statistics, the first tests whether it differs from zero and the second whether it differs from one. The asterisks by the sample period for Eqs. 3 and 4 denote estimates based upon pooled time-series cross-sectional data.

Dependent variable is the change in discount rate between the end and the start of the period.

the most extensive disruptions. Adding the ratio of production at the start of the period to production in 1913 has no impact on the results, however. Neither the coefficient estimate nor the standard error on the price variable is noticeably altered, and the added variable never has a t-statistic as large as one.

Unfortunately in light of the importance of the link between inflation and interest rates, it is all but impossible to assemble market interest rates on assets with roughly comparable maturities and risk characteristics. The only possibility is to analyze the relationship of wholesale price inflation to the change in the central bank discount rate, as in Table 3.4. Where central banks discounted freely, market interest rates on eligible paper could not diverge markedly from the rate charged by the monetary authorities. But since many central banks rationed credit and limited discount privileges, the discount rate is likely to be an imperfect indicator of the cost of credit. Still, discount rates are, as expected, positively related to inflation. Moreover, it is impossible to reject the hypothesis that, by the end of the period, countries experiencing one additional percentage point of annualized inflation had raised their discount rates, relative to 1921 or 1922 levels, by exactly a point. However, this adjustment took time. From rows 3 and 4 of Table 3.4, the hypothesis that rates adjusted fully to inflation within the year can be rejected at the 99 percent confidence level. Although interest rates responded to inflation even in the short run, the rate of price change was still negatively associated with the real interest rate.

Again it is possible that the association between inflation and interest rates reflects the common influence of omitted factors, such as the extent of wartime dislocation, especially since the discount-rate–inflation-rate relationship hinges on the experiences of Belgium and France. As with real wages, however, adding the ratio of industrial production at the start of the period to production in 1913 alters none of the results, and the reconstruction variable never enters with a t-statistic as large as unity.

This evidence suggests only that actual inflation was imperfectly incorporated into nominal interest rates, not that lenders failed to fully incorporate expected inflation into the rates charged. It suggests, therefore, that lenders failed to fully anticipate the price trends of the early 1920s, which may simply reflect the notion that in inflationary countries they expected the upward course of prices to be reversed. Thus, there is no evidence here that *ex ante* real interest rates upon which savings and investment decisions depend were much affected by price level movements. Insofar as the imperfect adjustment of interest rates had real economic effects, another mechanism was at work. Keynes in the *Tract* emphasized the windfall gains and losses accruing to businessmen with an unanticipated change in the price level. Typically, producers borrow on short term to finance production and inventory carrying costs or on long term to finance fixed investment. An unanticipated rise in the price level not reflected in interest rates reduces the value of their liabilities by inflating away a portion of their debts. With this burden lightened, the entrepreneur is willing to borrow more to expand the volume of production. Under circumstances like those described by Keynes in 1923, it is through these balance-sheet effects rather than by altering anticipated rates of return that the incomplete adjustment of interest rates to inflation makes its influence felt.

The international comparisons discussed in this and the preceding section suggest that much of the variation across industrial countries in the pace of economic expansion in the 1920s is explicable in terms of two factors: (i) the extent of wartime disruptions to the productive machinery and consequent scope for growth through reconstruction, and (ii) the inflationary and deflationary policies of governments. Even after factoring reconstruction into the picture, the macroeconomic policies responsible for inflation retain their importance. This evidence supports what might be called the early Keynesian view of the 1920s, that the real effects of inflation were transmitted through real wages and real interest rates. Yet nothing has been said about the length of time over which these effects persisted. Given the channels through which they operated, the impact of price-level changes on economic recovery should have been only transitory. Considering the length of time over which these effects operated requires an explicitly dynamic analytical framework. It is to the elaboration of such a model that I now turn.

5. The dynamic effects of price-level changes

The model of inflation and economic activity discussed in this section is designed to capture the early Keynesian view that business cycles in the 1920s were driven by the slower adjustment of wages than of asset and commodity prices. It combines a Phillips Curve relationship linking the change in money wages to deviations of output from normal levels with continuously clearing money and goods markets. This model is used to analyze the cyclical response to price-level changes. In the 1920s, the nature of this response hinged on the extent to which the public viewed as credible the authorities' commitment to return to the gold standard at prewar rates of exchange – in other words, whether they believed that an increase in the price level implied offsetting deflation in the future. These issues provide the focus of the analysis that follows.

The framework is a variant of the Mundell-Fleming model of an open economy under flexible exchange rates, extended to incorporate forward-looking behavior in asset markets and determinants of aggregate supply.[30] The assumption of forward-looking behavior on the part of asset market participants facilitates analysis of the notion that inflation in the early 1920s was expected to be reversed. The addition of a supply side and labor market adjustment allows the wage lag hypothesis to be addressed.

The supply of money m in this economy is assumed to be determined by the authorities, while money demand depends on output y and the nominal interest rate i. (Throughout, lower-case letters indicate variables measured in logs, except for interest rates, which are measured in levels.)

---

[30] The first feature is patterned after R. Dornbusch, "Expectations and Exchange Rate Dynamics," *Journal of Political Economy* 84 (1976), 1161–76, the second after B. Eichengreen, "A Dynamic Model of Tariffs, Output and Employment Under Flexible Exchange Rates," *Journal of International Economics* 11 (1981), 341–59.

$$m - p = \varphi y - \lambda i. \tag{1}$$

Here p is the price of domestic products. Aggregate supply is an increasing function of profitability (equivalently, a declining function of the real product wage):

$$y = q(p - w), \tag{2}$$

where w is the money wage and q is the elasticity of aggregate supply. Aggregate demand depends on relative prices and the interest rate:

$$y = -\delta(p - e - p^*) - \beta i, \tag{3}$$

where p^* is the exogenous foreign-currency price of competing goods produced overseas, and e is the market exchange rate (the domestic price of one unit of foreign exchange).

Two equations provide the dynamics of the system. The first is open interest parity:

$$\dot{e} = i - i^*, \tag{4}$$

where i^* is the exogenous foreign interest rate, and a dot over a variable indicates its rate of change. The domestic interest rate equals the foreign interest rate plus the expected rate of depreciation of the exchange rate under the assumptions of perfect substitutability of domestic and foreign interest-bearing assets and perfect international capital mobility. I assume that exchange-rate expectations are formed rationally, so the same notation may be used for expected and actual values. While overly simplistic, rational expectations is a tractable way of analyzing forward-looking behavior by asset-market participants, which is needed if anticipated policies are to be discussed.

The second differential equation specifies labor market adjustment. The nominal wage rises when output exceeds the level corresponding to the natural rate of unemployment $\bar{y}$ and falls when output falls short of $\bar{y}$.

$$\dot{w} = \theta(y - \bar{y}) \tag{5}$$

Substituting the other equations into (4) and (5) reduces the model to its state-space representation:

$$\begin{bmatrix} \dot{e} \\ \dot{w} \end{bmatrix} = \begin{bmatrix} \dfrac{\delta}{\lambda[q+\delta+\beta/\lambda]} & \dfrac{q}{\lambda[q+\delta+\beta/\lambda]} \\ \dfrac{\theta\varphi q\delta}{q+\delta+\beta/\lambda} & \dfrac{-\theta\varphi[\delta q+q\beta/\lambda]}{q+\delta+\beta/\lambda} \end{bmatrix} \begin{bmatrix} e - \bar{e} \\ w - \bar{w} \end{bmatrix} \tag{6}$$

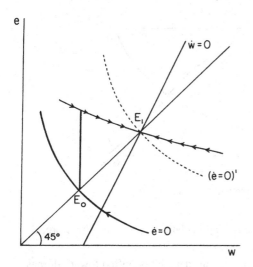

Figure 3.5. Equilibrium dynamics of the model.

which is depicted graphically in Figure 3.5. The downward-sloping $\dot{e} = 0$ locus depicts combinations of e and w along which the exchange rate does not change. If the exchange rate depreciates aggregate demand is stimulated, and the domestic interest rate must rise to clear the money market; this higher interest rate is associated with expected depreciation. For the exchange rate to remain stable, this effect must be offset by a fall in the money wage. The upward-sloping $\dot{w} = 0$ locus depicts combinations of e and w along which the money wage is stable. A rise in e, which shifts demand toward domestic goods, by increasing output puts upward pressure on wages; for wage stability it must be offset by a rise in w now. The system is saddle-point stable, and there is a unique path, marked with arrows, along which this economy approaches its resting point.

I use this model to analyze the cyclical response to two types of monetary expansion: a permanent increase in the money supply, and an increase now which the public assumes will be reversed later. The effects of the permanent increase, depicted in Figure 3.5, are straightforward. Since a larger money supply implies a correspondingly higher price level and depreciated exchange rate once adjustment is complete, the exchange rate depreciates now in anticipation of subsequent developments. But since money supply rises relative to initial demand, interest rates must fall to clear the money market. With domestic interest rates below foreign rates, speculators' ex-

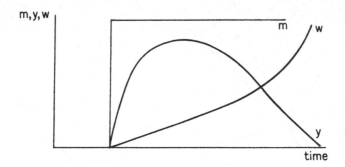

Figure 3.6. Dynamic response to monetary expansion.

pectations must be of exchange rate appreciation over time. Therefore, the exchange rate overshoots its long-run value.

With the exchange rate's depreciation, demand is shifted toward domestic goods. This puts upward pressure on the domestic price level which, in the presence of nominal wage inertia, reduces the real wage on impact. Output rises and the real wage falls with the inflationary impulse. Over time, the money wage rises to restore the real wage to its market-clearing level, and output gradually falls to normal levels.

The dynamic effects of this inflationary impulse are depicted in Figure 3.6. Output initially responds positively to the inflation. But with production temporarily above its permanent level, output must respond negatively to inflation with a lag until adjustment is complete.

The effects of an increase in the money supply which the public expects to be reversed later are more complex than those of a permanent increase. As before, when the money supply is increased, the economy's evolution is governed by the laws of motion represented by the arrows surrounding the high-money-supply equilibrium E' in Figure 3.7. Even though the price-level increase is known to be temporary, the exchange rate must depreciate, so the monetary expansion still has expansionary effects. But if the public expects the price-level increase to be reversed in the future, stability and the assumption of perfect foresight require that the economy be on the stable arm corresponding to the laws of motion represented by the arrows surrounding the low-money-supply equilibrium E at the time the monetary expansion is reversed. The initial depreciation is smaller because agents anticipate that it is to be reversed. Just as when no reversal is anticipated, the exchange rate appreciates following its initial depreciation, at which point real wages begin to rise. Because the economy is below the

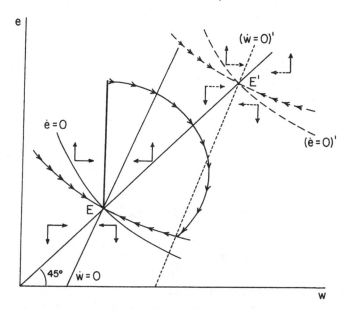

Figure 3.7. Further equilibrium dynamics.

stable arm corresponding to the higher money supply, the exchange rate now appreciates too quickly to lead the economy to its steady state at E'. In Figure 3.7, the economy moves off in a southeastward direction until the monetary expansion is reversed. At that instant, the economy reaches the stable arm corresponding to the reduced money supply, and exchange-rate appreciation gives way to depreciation. Since the money wage has been rising, it now must fall to return to the level from which it started. However, if money wages adjust rapidly and the reversal of the money supply increase is expected to occur sufficiently long in the future, the money wage may reverse course even before the contraction takes place. (This is the case depicted in Figure 3.7.) Wages will have risen so much that output is depressed below the natural rate despite the fact that the exchange rate is still undervalued relative to its steady state level.

The business cycle that accompanies this adjustment is depicted in Figure 3.8. With the initial depreciation, output rises and the real wage falls, although by less than before. Output and employment gradually decline as the exchange rate appreciates, switching demand away from domestic goods, and the real wage recovers. However, the real wage, rather than simply rising to offset any erosion caused by inflation, continues to rise relative to its long-term level, so that over a portion of the transition path

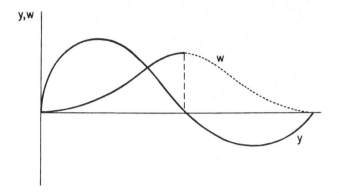

Figure 3.8. Dynamic response to reversible monetary expansion.

output is depressed. Finally, the real wage reverses, and activity recovers until the normal level of employment is restored.

As with the permanent increase in the price level, output responds positively to inflation in the short run but negatively over a subsequent span of time. When the public anticipates that the authorities intend eventually to reverse any change in the price level, the negative association between lagged inflation and current output should be especially pronounced.

6. Inflation-growth cycles in the 1920s

The model analyzed above predicts a cyclical response of real wages and industrial production to inflationary shocks. Table 3.5 shows the relationship of industrial production in the 1920s to recent and lagged price-level changes and to the reconstruction variable introduced above. As anticipated, industrial production is positively related to recent inflation and negatively related to inflation lagged, although the significance of the lagged response is sensitive to changes in the sample period. The coefficient on recent inflation consistently exceeds in absolute value the coefficient on inflation lagged, although the model analyzed above implies that the two effects should be equal once real variables are given sufficient time to adjust. This suggests that the real economic effects of early-1920s inflation were not entirely played out by 1925–27. The coefficients on recent and lagged inflation shift as the sample period is extended from 1925 to 1927, with the coefficient on recent inflation shrinking and that on lagged inflation growing, consistent with the notion that the longer the period and the

Table 3.5: *Cycles of inflation and economic growth, 1921–1927*

Eq.	Sample period		Constant	π	π_{-1}	Start/1913	R^2	n
1.	Dep:	1921–25	0.24	1.52	−0.003	−0.44	.91	12
			(0.64)	(4.92)	(1.76)	(4.46)		
	π:	1923–25						
	π_{-1}:	1920–23						
2.	Dep:	1921–25	−0.83	2.15	−0.002		.69	12
			(1.62)	(4.14)	(0.58)			
	π:	1923–25						
	π_{-1}:	1920–23						
3.	Dep:	1921–26	0.88	0.99	−0.006	−0.42	· .88	12
			(3.27)	(5.30)	(1.98)	(2.92)		
	π:	1923–26						
	π_{-1}:	1920–23						
4.	Dep:	1921–26	0.29	1.19	−0.005		.75	12
			(1.20)	(5.00)	(1.36)			
	π:	1923–26						
	π_{-1}:	1920–23						
5.	Dep:	1921–27	1.37	0.81	−0.18	−0.52	.72	12
			(4.68)	(2.48)	(0.52)	(3.29)	·	
	π:	1924–27						
	π_{-1}:	1920–24						
6.	Dep:	1921–27	0.93	1.00	−0.50		.34	12
			(2.50)	(2.17)	(1.04)			
	π:	1924–27						
	π_{-1}:	1920–24						

Note: t-statistics in parentheses. Omitted countries are Spain, Finland, and Switzerland.
Dependent variable is the ratio of industrial production at the end and the start of the period.

less credence invested in the authorities' commitment to restore prices to their previous level, the smaller the real economic effects of inflation.

Table 3.6 shows the relationship of real wages to recent and lagged price-level changes. Real wages are related negatively to recent inflation and positively to inflation lagged, although the second effect is small in magnitude and weak statistically relative to the first. Again, it appears that by 1927 the full effects of the postwar inflations and deflations had not fully worked their way through the industrial economies.

Thus, inflation and deflation in the 1920s set off a cyclical response. Countries which grew with exceptional rapidity in the early 1920s due to the adoption of inflationary policies decelerated subsequently, although the full effects of this deceleration had not been felt by 1927. Conversely,

Table 3.6: *Cycles of inflation and real wage growth, 1921–1927*

Eq.	Sample period		Constant	π	π_{-1}	R^2	n
1.	Dep:	1921–27	1.35	−0.24	0.001	.33	14
			(12.06)	(2.28)	(0.58)		
	π:	1921–27					
	π_{-1}:	1920–21					
2.	Dep:	1922–27	0.93	−0.28	0.54	.54	14
			(3.33)	(3.58)	(1.60)		
	π:	1922–27					
	π_{-1}:	1921–22					
3.	Dep:	1923–27	1.33	−0.46	0.28	.48	14
			(0.57)	(2.56)	(1.03)		
	π:	1923–27					
	π_{-1}:	1921–23					
4.	Dep:	1924–27	1.55	−0.86	0.42	.76	14
			(15.66)	(5.32)	(2.67)		
	π:	1924–27					
	π_{-1}:	1921–24					
5.	Dep:	1925–27	1.42	−0.51	0.19	.74	14
			(16.89)	(3.84)	(1.85)		
	π:	1925–27					
	π_{-1}:	1921–25					

Note: t-statistics in parentheses. Spain is the omitted country.

countries which grew more slowly in the early 1920s due to their governments' deflationary stance recovered and grew with greater-than-average speed over the second half of the decade.

7. New light on recovery in the industrial economies

The framework and evidence developed above can be used to interpret the differing character of recovery experiences across the industrial economies. This section demonstrates their applicability in the cases of Britain, France, Italy, the Netherlands, and Japan.

As is evident from Figure 3.9, where the growth of its industrial production is compared with the average for 13 countries, Britain's recovery, rather than the classic example of disappointing economic performance suggested by much of the historical literature, emerges as remarkably representative of recovery experience in the 1920s. The only marked divergence

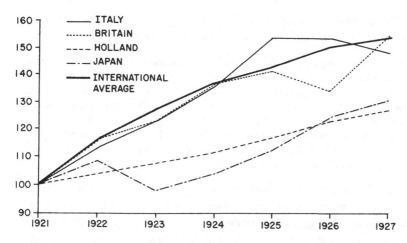

Figure 3.9. Industrial production and the international average, 1921–1927.

between recovery in Britain and the international average is associated with the 1926 General Strike. This parallelism reflects two offsetting effects. First, prices, which fall only slightly on average in the sample of 13 countries, decline in Britain by some 27 percent between 1921 and 1927. Estimates in Table 3.2 imply that this deflation reduced the growth of British industrial production over the period from 62 to 54 percent. One reason the British cycle so closely follows the international average is that the timing of its deflation, which was 3.2 times as great in 1920–24 as in 1924–27, follows quite closely the international average (for which the comparable ratio is 3.8). Second, exceptional scope for growth was provided by the relatively low level from which the British recovery started. While physical capacity had not been destroyed by the war, the reconversion of industry to peacetime uses and the loss of skilled workers contributed to depressing 1921 industrial production to 80 percent of its 1913 level, compared to 90 percent in the sample as a whole. This scope for faster-than-average growth roughly offset the effects of British deflation.

France is a second country where industrial production started from relatively low levels, and a country where the effects of inflation on industry and trade should be readily discernible. While France experienced inflation over much of the first half of the 1920s, it was not until 1925, or so it has been argued, that the persistence of inflation was widely anticipated.[31]

[31] Ogburn and Jaffe, *Economic Development*, p. 124.

Especially in the early period, when wholesale prices moved quickly, wages followed with a lag. In the words of Ogburn and Jaffe,

Since the prevailing tenor of the post-war period was one of rising prices, and since all evidence points to a sluggishness in the wage movement to keep pace with the wholesale price movement in either its upward or downward course, it is probable that in respect to labor costs industry in post-war France profitted generally by the monetary disorder . . . in spite of all the forces tending to increase wages, and in spite of the uncertain nature of the data, it is clear that wages did not rise to the same extent as wholesale prices – and industry in times of inflation thus enjoyed relatively low labor cost as well as low interest.[32]

As a subsequent observer noted to his surprise, "The sharp rise in prices provided a stimulus to general business activity. Even the depreciation of the franc was not an unqualified disaster; since it proceeded at a faster rate than the rise in the costs of production in France, it made French goods and services relatively cheap and tended to provide a favorable balance of current payments."[33]

Figures 3.2 and 3.3 are consistent with this characterization. Except for the stabilization recessions of 1924–25 and 1926–27, French growth consistently exceeds growth elsewhere. Different price-level trends account for approximately twice as much of the differential as differing reconstruction requirements.

In contrast to France and Britain, war brought more prosperity than dislocation to Japan. Contemporary observers concluded that the war had been responsible for a greater transformation of industry there than in any other country outside the war zone.[34] Capital, rather than continuing to be invested primarily in finance and transportation, was directed increasingly toward the construction of iron works, paper mills, and factories for the manufacture of drugs, dyes, paints, and textiles. As early as 1916, small goods and fancy articles previously exported by Austria and Germany to Britain were increasingly supplied by Japanese producers.[35] These developments were reflected in a level of industrial production in 1921 some two-thirds above 1913 levels. Thus, in the 1920s there was no scope in Japan for expansion through reconstruction and relatively little for growth through investment and modernization, since possibilities for the latter had

[32] Ibid., pp. 163–4.
[33] Wolfe, French Franc, p. 52.
[34] Keynes, Tract; I. Lippincott, Problems of Reconstruction (New York, 1919), p. 247.
[35] A.W. Kirkaldy, Labour, Finance and the War (London, 1916), p. 5.

been exploited in the previous decade. These factors help to account for the poorer-than-average growth performance of the Japanese economy evident in Figure 3.9.[36] In contrast, price trends contributed little to the difference, with wholesale prices in Japan rising on average by only one-half percent per annum over the period.

Italy was another country where manufacturing had been stimulated by the war. Great progress occurred in the chemical, electrical, and metallurgical industries which, following war-related disruptions to trade, moved into the production of hundreds of articles traditionally imported from abroad.[37] Industrial production in 1921 was therefore only 6 percent below 1913 levels, not far different from the average for the 13 countries. If anything, this would suggest slightly slower growth of Italian industry in the 1920s than of industry elsewhere. But this effect was offset by a rate of inflation considerably above the international average. Italian inflation accelerated most rapidly in 1925; as shown in Figure 3.9, this was also the year when Italian output rose most rapidly relative to the sample average.

Holland provides a final example of a country where industrial production was stimulated rather than depressed by the war. The exceptions were Dutch industries producing luxury goods and some, such as bottle factories and grain mills, which were adversely affected by raw material shortages. Other industries were stimulated by disruptions to the supply of competing imports, including clothing (which expanded by 50 percent) and rubber goods (which expanded five-fold).[38] As a result of this wartime stimulus, Dutch industry had less scope than, say, British for rapid growth in the early 1920s. In addition, prices in Holland declined over the period at a pace exceeding the international average. For both reasons, Dutch industry expanded less rapidly than the industries of other advanced economies. It is notable that, compared to other countries considered here, Dutch deflation is relatively rapid in the first half of the period. As predicted by the model of Section 5, there is some sign of the Netherlands beginning to close the gap in growth rates after 1924.

---

[36] The 1922–3 recession, which was not synchronized with foreign business cycles, is typically ascribed to the discount rate increase taken at the beginning of 1922 in response to a balance of trade deterioration, to a reduction of Japanese military expenditures, to Chinese boycotts of Japanese goods, and to a wave of bank failures set off by the so-called Ishii Teihichi affair.

[37] Lippincott, *Problems*, p. 245.

[38] C.J.P. Zaalberg, *The Netherlands and the World War. Vol. 2: The Manufacturing Industry* (New Haven, 1928), pp. 11–12.

8. Conclusions

Increasingly, skepticism has attended accounts of economic fluctuations in the 1920s which attach weight to government policies affecting the exchange rate and the general level of prices. There is reason for skepticism when the period considered is marked by the persistence of wartime disruptions to output, extensive reconstruction, and generalized uncertainty about economic conditions. Nonetheless, the evidence marshalled here suggests that policies affecting prices had pronounced real economic effects. Inflation, by reducing real wages and real interest rates, promoted the expansion of industrial production in the years immediately following its occurrence. As real wages and interest rates recovered subsequently, however, growth slowed both absolutely and relative to trend. Inflation and deflation therefore elicited a cyclical response.

Given the variation across countries in inflationary experience, the effects considered are likely to have been large. Macroeconomic policies thus emerge as first-order determinants of economic fluctuations in the 1920s.

To some readers, this chapter's central conclusion – that inflation in the 1920s had real economic effects – will seem far from surprising. Economic expansion is the natural consequence of demand stimulus in a wide variety of Keynesian models. Yet with their failure to provide an adequate explanation for macroeconomic fluctuations in the 1970s and 1980s, Keynesian models have tended to fall from favor. Simultaneously, economic historians of the interwar period, their outlooks presumably influenced by these same developments, have grown skeptical of the ability of such models to illuminate macroeconomic fluctuations in the interwar years.[39] This chapter can be read as a corrective to that view. It has shown that the model developed by Keynes with the 1920s in mind remains an illuminating framework for understanding the macroeconomic fluctuations of that pivotal decade.

Data Appendix

Sources and definitions of the variables used in the text are as follows.

Prices: Wholesale price indices for European countries are taken from

---

[39] See for example D. Benjamin and L. Kochin, "Searching for an Explanation for Unemployment in Interwar Britain," *Journal of Political Economy* 87 (1979), 449–78; M. Beenstock, B. Griffiths and F. Capie, "Economic Recovery in the United Kingdom in the 1930s," Bank of England Panel of Academic Consultants paper no. 23 (1984).

B. R. Mitchell, *European Historical Statistics, 1750–1970* (London, 1975). The series for Japan is from K. Ohkawa and H. Rosovsky, *Japanese Economic Growth* (Stanford, 1973), p. 308, col. 3, and for the remaining countries from the *Monthly Statistical Bulletin* of the League of Nations.

Wages: Money wages for European countries are from Mitchell, *European Historical Statistics*, except for Belgium, which are from I. Cassiers, "Une statistique des salaires horaires en Belgique, 1919–1939," *Recherches Economiques de Louvain*, 46 (1980), p. 63. The series for Japan is from Ohkawa and Rosovsky, *Japanese Economic Growth*, p. 316, col. 6, and for the remaining countries from Tinbergen, *International Abstract of Economic Statistics.*

Industrial Production: Indices for most European countries are taken from Mitchell, *European Historical Statistics*. That for France, as well as those for Canada and the U.S., are from Tinbergen, *Abstract*. Series for Denmark and the Netherlands are from A. Maddison, *Economic Growth in the West* (New York, 1964). That for Australia is from B. D. Haig, "Manufacturing Output and Productivity, 1910 to 1948/9," *Australian Economic History Review* 14 (1974), pp. 136–55, while the Japanese index is from Ohkawa and Rosovsky, *Japanese Economic Growth*, p. 284, col. 2.

Discount Rate: Most series are from the *Monthly Statistical Bulletin* of the League of Nations. That for the United States is the New York Reserve Bank rate on 60–90 day commercial paper, and that for Canada is the interest rate on Dominion Bonds (from Tinbergen, *Abstract*).

Money Supplies: Sources of M1 are as follows. U.S.: M. Friedman and A. Schwartz, *A Monetary History of the United States, 1867–1960* (Princeton, 1963); France: C. Saint-Etienne, "L'offre et la demande de monnaie dans la France de l'entre-deux-guerres (1920–1939)," *Revue Economique*, 34 (1983), pp. 344–67; Belgium: H. van der Wee and K. Tavernier, *La Banque Nationale de Belgique et l'histoire monétaire entre les deux guerres mondiales* (Brussels, 1975); Canada (currency outside banks plus chartered bank deposits less float): M. C. Urquhart and K. A. H. Buckley, *Historical Statistics of Canada* (Cambridge, 1965); Australia and New Zealand: N. G. Butlin, "Select Comparative Economic Statistics 1900–1941," Department of Economic History, Research School for Social Sciences, Australian National University, Source Paper No. 4, 1984; M3 for the U. K. is from F. Capie and A. Webber, *Monetary History of the United Kingdom, 1870–1982, vol. I: Data, Sources, Methods* (London, 1985). Japanese figures (bills in circulation plus total ordinary bank deposits) from K. Yamamura,

"Then Came the Great Depression: Japan's Interwar Years," in H. van der Wee, ed., *The Great Depression Revisited* (The Hague, 1972). Remaining series are from Tinbergen, *Abstract.* Sweden: bills in circulation plus deposits of joint stock banks; Italy: bills in circulation, postal deposits plus ordinary deposits; Denmark: bills in circulation plus commercial bank sight and time deposits; Norway: bills in circulation plus savings bank deposits.

4. Bank Rate policy under the interwar gold standard

With Mark W. Watson and Richard S. Grossman

In truth, the gold standard is already a barbarous relic. All of us, from the Governor of the Bank of England downwards, are now primarily interested in preserving the stability of business, prices, and employment, and are not likely, when the choice is forced upon us, deliberately to sacrifice these to the outworn dogma, which had value once, of £3. 17s. 10½d. per ounce.

J. M. KEYNES (1923), p. 172

The classical gold standard occupies an almost mystical position in the literature of international finance. In popular accounts the gold standard is portrayed as a remarkably durable and efficient mechanism for achieving price and exchange rate stability and for relieving balance of payments pressures. The system's resilience is attributed to the willingness of national monetary authorities to refrain from impeding the international adjustment process. When central banks intervened in financial markets, it is said, they did so mechanically, obeying 'rules of the game' which dictated that they reinforce the impact on domestic money and credit of changing balance of payments conditions.

Succeeding generations of economists and historians have sought to qualify this popular view. The recent contributions of Bordo (1981) and Cooper (1982) provide a critical assessment of extravagant claims concerning price and exchange rate stability under the classical gold standard. Other authors have extended the research of Bloomfield (1959), Ford (1962), and

An extended version of this paper (Eichengreen, Watson, and Grossman, 1983) is available from the Harvard Institute of Economic Research as Discussion Paper Number 1008. An earlier version was presented at Yale, Brown, and Stanford Universities, to the Harvard-MIT Joint Econometrics Seminar, to the Seminaire d'économie monétaire international (Paris), and to a meeting of the International Finance Section at Princeton University. We are grateful to seminar participants, to Peter Kenen, Charles Kindleberger, and Peter Temin, and to two referees of *The Economic Journal* for comments. We acknowledge the permission of Her Majesty's Stationery Office to quote materials in the Public Record Office. Mark Watson thanks the National Science Foundation for financial support.

Triffin (1964), who emphasized the special conditions that permitted the classical gold standard's smooth operation and cast doubt on the tendency of national monetary authorities to adhere faithfully to 'rules of the game.' [1]

All too often, scant mention is made of the interwar gold standard, for it is not evident how interwar experience fits into either view. Certain facts are clear. It is clear that the interwar standard was far from durable; Britain's resumption of gold payments in 1925 usually is taken to mark the gold standard's resurrection, just as her devaluation a mere 6 years later is taken as its demise. In the interim many of the major participants suffered serious balance of payments pressures that threatened to render their exchange rates indefensible. The system was anything but conducive to stability; it precluded neither price nor income fluctuations, as the Great Depression dramatically illustrated.

Numerous explanations have been advanced for the interwar gold standard's unsatisfactory performance. [2] Many critics cite governments' choices of inappropriate exchange rates, notably an overvalued British pound and an undervalued French franc, which created balance of payments difficulties and intensified problems of structural adjustment. Others argue that the worldwide maldistribution of gold stocks, which were concentrated to a great extent in the United States and France, shifted the burden of adjustment onto countries with precarious reserve positions. [3] Perhaps the most popular villains are the major central banks. Following the reestablishment of the gold standard, it is alleged, central banks failed to play by the 'rules of the game.' Where previously they had been seen as intervening through open market operations to amplify the impact on domestic asset supplies of an imbalance in the external accounts, after 1925 they sterilized gold flows instead. While the desire to maintain their gold standard parities lim-

---

[1] See C.A.E. Goodhart, *The Business of Banking* (London, 1972); J. Dutton, "The Bank of England and the "Rules of the Game" Under the International Gold Standard: New Evidence," in M. Bordo and A. Schwartz (eds.), *A Retrospective on the Classical Gold Standard* (Chicago, 1984), 173–202; and J. Pippinger, "Bank of England Operations, 1893–1913," in Bordo and Schwartz, *Retrospective,* 203–32.

[2] The principals in this debate are too many to mention by name. Although there are many valuable studies of individual national experiences, few authors have attempted to analyze the international system as a whole. Contributions along these lines include Brown, *International Gold Standard;* Nurkse, *Currency Experience;* S.V.O. Clarke, *Central Bank Cooperation 1924–1931* (New York, 1967); Kindleberger, *World in Depression;* B. Eichengreen, "Central Bank Cooperation under the Interwar Gold Standard," *Explorations in Economic History* 21 (1984), 64–87; and Chapter 6.

[3] For contemporary analysis of the problem, see League of Nations, *Selected Documents on the Distribution of Gold* (Geneva, 1931).

ited the extent of the sterilization operations that deficit countries could conduct, there were no such constraints on surplus countries such as the United States and France.[4] The resulting asymmetry in central bank behaviour is blamed for undermining the efficiency of the adjustment process. The same case is made with special force concerning the most visible of central bank instruments: the discount rate. Although central banks were compelled to raise their discount rates when confronted by a sustained loss of gold, all too often they refrained from reducing those rates when acquiring reserves.[5] Some central banks, sensitive to political pressures, hesitated to adjust their discount rates at all, while others which traditionally had used their discount rates to influence the external accounts now directed them at other targets. By hesitating to act or formulating their discount rate policies with these other targets in mind, central banks may have impeded the international adjustment process during the interwar period.

These criticisms have been levelled with particular force at the Bank of England (see Section I below). In the 19th century, the Bank had played a special role in managing the international monetary system. The single most important instrument of which it availed itself to promote external adjustment was Bank Rate, the rate charged by the Bank of England for loans to discount houses and other dealers in Treasury and commercial bills. A change in Bank Rate affected the rates on bank loans and overdrafts and on fixed interest securities, with implications for the capital account. The Bank resorted to frequent discount rate changes, which helped it to maintain the sterling parity despite remarkably slender reserves. Bank Rate was changed 202 times between 1855 and 1874, and as often as 24 times in a single year. In the interwar period, it was the immobility of Bank Rate that was notable. Between 1925 and 1931, Bank Rate was changed only half as often as it had been over the 6 year period preceding the War, or as it had been on average over the period 1890–1913. Between 1925 and 1931, Bank Rate was left unchanged for more than a year on three sepa-

---

[4] The classic indictments of gold sterilization by the Federal Reserve System and Bank of France are Nurske, *Currency Experience*, pp. 73–4; C. Hardy, *Credit Policies of the Federal Reserve System* (Washington DC, 1932); and Friedman and Schwartz, *Monetary History*.

[5] The existence of this asymmetry is noted in the British case by D.E. Moggridge, *British Monetary Policy 1924–1931* (New York, 1972), but without a critical judgment. This argument should be distinguished from the quite different point that certain banks' interwar discount rates were maintained at high average levels. For example, a high Bank of England discount rate could be explained in terms of the weakness of an overvalued pound sterling. The discussion here, however, concentrates on patterns of adjustment and not average levels.

Bank Rate

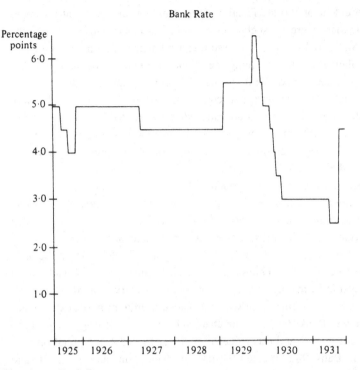

Figure 4.1. Bank Rate.

rate occasions, whereas comparable stability had been achieved only once between 1890 and 1913 (see Figure 4.1). Although it appeared that Bank Rate eventually was adjusted in the required direction, it seemed as if the Bank of England had grown reluctant to act and was waiting for conditions to deteriorate past a critical threshold before responding to events.[6]

The discount rate was only one of several instruments at the Bank of England's command. The others included open market operations, intervention in gold and foreign exchange markets, and the use of moral suasion. Bank Rate is by no means the perfect measure of the stance of monetary policy. However, Bank Rate was 'that most orthodox instrument of monetary control' and a crucial barometer for many domestic interest rates and expectations.[7] It was the most visible and controversial of the Bank's

---

6 R.S. Sayers, *The Bank of England, 1891–1944* (London, 1976), on the basis of his study of the Bank's records, finds no recorded explanations for this contrast with earlier periods. His suggested explanation is quite similar to the one given here.
7 Moggridge, *British Monetary Policy*, pp. 147, 164. As Sayers, op. cit., puts it, '. . . the accepted doctrine both inside and outside the Bank, was that its most important action was

instruments, and as such is the variable most likely, when subjected to detailed analysis, to yield information on the pressures and considerations influencing the formulation of policy.

In this chapter we take a close look at Bank Rate policy in the period 1925–31, the years of Britain's participation in the interwar gold standard. We begin with an analysis of contemporary views of discount rate management.[8] This account suggests that an appraisal of whether the Bank of England's discount rate policy contributed to the instability of the interwar gold standard must start by addressing three questions. First, was policy asymmetric in the sense that the Bank raised its discount rate upon losing reserves but failed to lower it upon gaining them? Second, was the Bank responsive not only to the balance of payments but also to internal conditions when making Bank Rate decisions? Third, did the Bank take domestic conditions into account primarily when the level of Bank Rate and numbers unemployed exceeded a certain level?

To address these questions, we employ a reaction function framework in the spirit of those applied previously to the study of discount policy under the classical gold standard by Goodhart (1972), Dutton (1984), and Pippinger (1984). Our analysis differs from previous efforts in a number of important respects. Decisions about Bank Rate typically were made weekly, at Thursday morning meetings of the Bank's Court of Directors. Recognizing this fact, we depart from previous practice and use weekly data for all our variables, thereby minimizing problems of aggregation and simultaneity. Our review of opinion on the effects of Bank Rate suggests the possibility that the Bank of England may have grown increasingly concerned about the domestic repercussions of its discount rate policy once Bank Rate exceeded a certain level. Therefore, we incorporate nonlinearities in the relationship between Bank Rate and the targets of policy into our empirical specification.

To estimate this relationship, we develop a dynamic econometric model designed to account for the discrete quality of our dependent variable. Bank Rate was changed very infrequently during our sample period, and each change that took place was in increments of fifty basis points. To model its determinants, we specify and estimate a dynamic generalization of the static ordered probit model. This model is discussed in detail in Section II. The likelihood function associated with the model involves a

---

the fixing of Bank Rate, announced each week before the Court of Directors proceeded to less important business.'

[8] We supplement this analysis with a narrative account of movements in Bank Rate between 1925 and 1931 in our unpublished working paper of the same title.

normal distribution of the same dimension as the sample size. Evaluation of this distribution poses significant computational difficulties. Fortunately, the underlying density has a special Markov form which makes the evaluation of the distribution possible. In the Appendix we present our method for evaluating the required multivariate normal distribution.

I. Bank Rate and the adjustment process

The phrase 'rules of the game' gained currency following the appearance of Sir Robert Kindersley, the influential Director of the Bank of England, before the Macmillan Committee in February 1930.[9] However, the idea that Bank Rate should be used systematically to protect the gold reserve was already commonplace. In answers to questions submitted to the Governor and Directors of the Bank of England by the U.S. National Monetary Commission (1910, pp. 26-7), a 'prompt and adequate increase' in Bank Rate was cited as the most effective measure to protect the Bank's gold reserves. The Bank described its practice as raising the discount rate to attract gold to the country or prevent it from leaving, and lowering the rate when it was completely out of touch with market interest rates or it was no longer necessary to attract gold imports.[10] The Bank admitted no limitations on a higher discount rate's ability to defend the reserve position, nor did it mention domestic economic or political considerations which might lead it to hesitate in making such an adjustment.[11]

---

[9] Committee on Finance and Industry, *Report* (London, 1931), Question 1595, 6 February 1930. A. Bloomfield, *Monetary Policy Under the International Gold Standard: 1880–1914* (New York, 1959) attributes the phrase to Keynes, but provides no citation. It does appear in Keynes's 1925 polemic, "The Economic Consequences of Mr. Churchill." The Committee on Finance and Industry was known as the Macmillan Committee after its chairman, H.P. Macmillan.

[10] The concept of a Bank Rate policy can be traced to the discussions of monetary management stimulated by the 1837–8 financial crisis and by the Bank of England's response to the 1847–8 crisis. R.S. Sayers, *Bank Rate in Keynes' Century* (London, 1979); Keynes, *Treatise*, p. 186. The Bank of England's response to the 1837–8 crisis is discussed by R. Hawtrey, *A Century of Bank Rate* (London, 1938), while its use of Bank Rate during the 1847 crisis is studied by R. Dornbusch and J.A. Frenkel, "The Gold Standard and the Bank of England in the Crisis of 1847," in Bordo and Schwartz, *Retrospective*, 233–64. Among the advocates of an active Bank Rate policy at that time were H.D. MacLeod, *The Theory and Practice of Banking* (London, 1856), and G.J. Goschen, *The Theory of Foreign Exchanges* (London, 1863).

[11] As one official put it in 1929, "In prewar days a change in bank rate was no more regarded as the business of the Treasury than the colour which the Bank painted its front door. . . ." Public Record Office (hereafter PRO) T176/13, Niemeyer to Phillips, 18 February 1929. Still, subject to the constraints posed by its overriding commitment to the gold parity,

In the Macmillan Committee evidence of Bank of England officials, the maintenance of convertibility was identified uniformly as the paramount goal of policy.[12] What emerges clearly from the evidence of Montagu Norman, Governor of the Bank of England during the period under study here, is the absence of an optimizing strategy. Bank of England policy was formulated by rules of thumb: in assessing the present and prospective stability of the sterling price of gold, the Bank focused on major bilateral exchange rates, the gold reserve, the relation of interest rates in London to those prevailing abroad, and other manner of 'foreign influence.' This evidence was evaluated in light of general financial market conditions, the state of the domestic economy, the time of year, and special circumstances, if any.

Keynes and other members of the Macmillan Committee questioned Bank of England officials on the issue of whether the possible domestic repercussions of a change in the discount rate influenced Bank Rate policy. These queries elicited guarded replies. The most revealing comment was made by Sir Ernest Harvey, Deputy Governor of the Bank, to the effect that the Bank of England sought to 'afford reasonable assurance of the convertibility of the currency into gold in all circumstances, and within the limits imposed by that objective to adjust the price and volume of credit to the requirements of industry and trade.'[13] Of course, the directors may have attached greater weight to domestic considerations than they were willing to admit to outsiders. Sayers (1976, vol. 1, p. 219) concludes, on the basis of Bank of England records to which he alone has had access, that the Bank went as far as it could to protect industry and trade from monetary difficulties, given the gold standard constraints. Moggridge (1972, Chapter 7) comes to much the same conclusion on the basis of Treasury and Cabinet papers.

Internal conditions could have influenced Bank Rate policy for a number of reasons, including Treasury pressure for lower interest rates to reduce the cost of debt service, ministerial pressure for lower rates to promote economic recovery, or genuine concern within the Bank of England for the state of British industry. There is ample evidence that the Treasury at-

the Bank's policy was "always to create as favourable conditions as it could for home trade. . . ." See R.S. Sayers, *Central Banking After Bagehot* (Oxford, 1957).

[12] See, for example, Norman's Macmillan Committee evidence, in Committee on Finance and Industry, Question 3319, 26 March 1930, reprinted in Sayers, *Bank of England, 1891–1944*, Vol. 3, p. 174. The remainder of this paragraph draws on Moggridge, *British Monetary Policy*, pp. 145–6, where an interpretation of the Bank of England's operating procedures is presented.

[13] Sayers, *Bank of England, 1891–1944*, Vol. 3, Question 7512 (2 July 1930).

tempted to influence the Bank to refrain from raising Bank Rate and to lower it whenever possible. Throughout the interwar period the foremost goal of Treasury policy was to reduce the burden of debt service charges, which had risen from 11% of central government spending in 1913 to 24% in 1920 and more than 40% by the end of the decade. Hence, between 1925 and 1929 the Treasury objected strenuously to each rise in Bank Rate and lobbied intensively for discount rate reductions. Compared to Montagu Norman, Treasury officials also may have harboured more concern for the domestic repercussions, particularly on unemployment, of changes in Bank Rate policy.[14] Their viewpoint was conveyed to the Governor and other high officials within the Bank via telephone and in person.[15] This divergence in outlook between the Treasury and the Bank of England contributed greatly to the politicization of Bank Rate, and it could not have encouraged the Bank to employ its discount rate actively in pursuit of external targets.

There was some disagreement among contemporaries concerning the channels through which Bank Rate operated to restore external balance. The discussion elicited by Keynes's private evidence before the Macmillan Committee in February 1930 illustrates the terms of this debate.[16] Keynes chose to begin his analysis of the relationship of finance to industry by describing the effects of Bank Rate.[17] A change in Bank Rate, he argued, tended to restore external balance through effects transmitted via two channels. The first effect was the one emphasized by Bank of England officials since at least the time of Bagehot (1873): by raising short-term interest rates at home relative to abroad, a Bank Rate increase attracted funds from overseas, thus strengthening the capital account.[18] The second effect was less familiar: by raising the price and restricting the quantity of bank lend-

14 For discussion, see D. Williams, "Montagu Norman and Banking Policy in the 1920's, *Yorkshire Bulletin of Economic and Social Research* 11 (1959), 38–55.

15 See, for example, PRO T176/13, Leith-Ross Memorandum, 3 December 1925.

16 PRO T200/4, T200/5, and T200/6, 20 February–5 December 1930, reprinted in J.M. Keynes, *Activities 1929–31: Rethinking Employment and Unemployment Policies*, vol. XX of *The Collected Writings of John Maynard Keynes* (London, 1981). The modus operandi of Bank Rate also is the subject of chapter 13 of Keynes, *Treatise*, the framework upon which Keynes's Macmillan Committee evidence draws. Keynes's evidence before the Macmillan Committee is also discussed in Chapter 8.

17 Here we concentrate on Keynes's views of Bank Rate per se. In much of his evidence, Keynes referred to what he called "Bank Rate policy" as distinct from Bank of England's official discount rate. This reflected a belief in the importance of discussing the discount rate in conjunction with other policies affecting the volume and cost of bank loans.

18 Note should be made of R. Hawtrey, *Currency and Credit* (London, 1950) and his dissenting view. Hawtrey argues that interest differentials were generally incapable of inducing an international flow of funds from 1871 onwards.

ing to industry and commerce, a Bank Rate increase damped down the level of economic activity, strengthening the balance on current account. 'The beauty of the Bank Rate,' according to Keynes, lay precisely in this 'double effect.'[19]

According to Keynes's account, a rise in Bank Rate depressed domestic activity in two ways. By raising the price of bank credit, it increased the cost of holding inventories, thereby inducing businessmen to liquidate their stocks, reducing final goods prices, and discouraging additional production.[20] At the same time, the higher cost of credit rendered physical investment less attractive. Together these two effects depressed the level of employment and ultimately put downward pressure on money wages. Once costs fell sufficiently to restore full employment, British goods again would be rendered competitive in international markets and external balance would be insured.[21]

If, according to Keynes, Bank Rate restored external balance by creating unemployment, the gospel according to Montagu Norman was of a very different sort. In Norman's view, the ill effects of an increase in Bank

[19] Keynes, *Activities 1929-31*, p. 41-2; see also Committee on Currency and Foreign Exchanges after the War, *First Interim Report* (London, 1918). Although Keynes attempted to put across this second effect, which had also been mentioned by the Cunliffe Committee, as part of the "traditional doctrine," his account was disputed from the outset, and these matters were to be the subject of extended exchanges over the course of subsequent weeks.

[20] This point could be attributed to R. Hawtrey, *Good and Bad Trade* (London, 1913), although it appears also in the *First Interim Report* of the Cunliffe Committee (Committee on Currency and Foreign Exchanges, 1918). See also Hawtrey, *Currency and Credit*, pp. 163-4, and R. Hawtrey, *Toward the Rescue of Sterling* (London, 1954). A similar argument is applied to 19th century experience by R. Triffin, "National Central Banking and the International Economy," in Federal Reserve System, *Postwar Economic Studies* no. 7 (Washington, DC, 1947) and R. Triffin, "The Evolution of the International Monetary System: Historical Reappraisal and Future Perspectives," *Princeton Studies in International Finance* no. 12 (Princeton, 1964), and to the 20th century by H.G. Johnson, "The Revival of Monetary Policy in Britain," *Three Banks Review* 30 (June 1956), 3-20.

[21] It is instructive to contrast this description of the adjustment process with the price specie flow mechanism associated with David Hume. The price specie flow model emphasizes the impact of relative prices on commodity trade and hence on the balance of payments and international reserve flows. A deterioration in the external accounts leads to reserve losses, monetary deflation, and falling wages and prices. This enhances the competitiveness of domestic goods, restoring external balance. In the model described by Keynes before the Macmillan Committee, the link between monetary deflation and wages was broken, at least in the short run. With wages slow to respond, the loss of reserves, reinforced by the impact of an increase in Bank Rate on the domestic credit base, checked demand and gave rise to unemployment. Given prices, monetary contraction reduced the supply of real balances, requiring higher interest rates to clear the money market. Spending would be reduced by both the wealth effect on consumption and the interest rate effect on investment. Only with time as wage rates fell would industrial employment recover.

Rate were greatly exaggerated and 'more psychological than real.' While admitting that a rise in Bank Rate would induce holders of inventories to liquidate their stocks, Norman denied that industrial activity would be noticeably affected.[22] Insofar as industrial investment responded to interest rate fluctuations, it was long-term rates that he thought relevant. And according to the conventional wisdom, a rise in Bank Rate would fall primarily on the cost of short-term bank credit. Only when a high Bank Rate was maintained for an extended period would long-term interest rates and, by inference, industrial investment respond.

Another distinction commonly drawn was between the effects of a change in a low Bank Rate and the effects of a change in a high one. According to this view, the link between Bank Rate and interest rates on bank credit was binding only when Bank Rate exceeded a certain threshold. It was argued that Bank Rate had little if any effect on the cost of bank loans and overdrafts until it exceeded 4%. Although advances regarded as 'fair banking risks' typically were extended at rates 1% above Bank Rate, these rates normally were subject to a floor of 5%. (The same convention applied to large customers, except that the margin over Bank Rate was half a point with a floor of 4½%.) Thus, Sir Ernest Harvey could tell the Macmillan Committee, 'We have always understood that there are minimum rates at which money is lent to trade, and that the minimum in most cases would not be below, if indeed as low as, 4½%.'[23] So long as Bank Rate remained at or below 4%, as it did for portions of 1925, 1930, and 1931 and as had been the case for most of the decade preceding the War, supporters of Bank of England policy could argue that the cost of bank advances was little affected by the discount rate.

Other contemporary observers were critical of this characterization of the instances in which changes in Bank Rate affected the rates on com-

22 Here Norman was echoing the opinion of Alfred Marshall, *Evidence Before the Gold and Silver Commission*, Official Papers, no. 9677–9981 (London, 1887). See Norman's Macmillan Committee evidence, Committee on Finance and Industry, Questions 3328–3517, 26 March 1930, reprinted in Sayers, *Bank of England, 1891–1944*, Vol. 3, pp. 172–253.

23 Sayers, *Bank of England, 1891–1944*, Vol. 3, Question 7597. Rates below the 5 percent floor also could be extended on loans to customers who put up gilt-edged securities as collateral. This paragraph draws on the accounts of British banking practice in W. Leaf, *Banking* (London, 1926); A.T.K. Grant, *A Study of the Capital Market in Postwar Britain* (London, 1937); Hawtrey, *Century of Bank Rate*, pp. 57–62; T. Balogh, *Studies in Financial Organization* (Cambridge, 1947); and Sayers, *Central Banking After Bagehot*, p. 17.

mercial bank advances and overdrafts. Hawtrey (1938, p. 60), who also appeared before the Macmillan Committee, later argued that exceptions to the practice of maintaining a 5% minimum loan charge were 'numerous and important.' He asserted that almost any customer with good credit might succeed in having the minimum waived. Yet it is not clear that the Bank of England shared this view.

Another possibility is that we observe fewer changes in Bank Rate under the interwar gold standard not because of a new sensitivity to either internal economic conditions or political pressures but because of new operating procedures. Prior to 1917, the Bank had raised or lowered Bank Rate by increments of half a point, one point, or more as the occasion demanded. From 1917 the Bank adhered to a new rule of raising Bank Rate in one-point steps and lowering it in half point steps.[24] Fewer upward movements of Bank Rate may have occurred simply because the new operating procedures dictated that the Bank wait until conditions warranted a full point adjustment.

Thus, the extent to which the Bank of England formulated its discount rate policy with domestic repercussions in mind remains an open question. It is conceivable that internal considerations exerted a powerful influence over policy. Alternatively, the Bank may have treated domestic considerations as largely outside its realm of responsibility, so that what appears as a new hesitancy to raise Bank Rate in the face of deteriorating internal conditions may have simply reflected the Bank's new operating procedures. Another possibility is that the Bank concentrated on Bank Rate's implications for the short-term interest rates to which it was known to be related. Indeed, such considerations may have only come into play once the discount rate exceeded a certain level and was thought to affect the cost of bank advances. These hypotheses can only be evaluated by considering the Bank of England's actual behaviour, to which we now turn.

---

[24] The new convention has a curious history. It seems to have originated in a footnote added to a new edition of Walter Bagehot's *Lombard Street* (London, 1873) in 1901 by the editor E. Johnstone. Bagehot had quoted Goschen to the effect that changes in discount rates exert a weak influence over international gold flows and then attributed to him (apparently erroneously) the suggestion that Bank Rate increases for the purpose of attracting gold be taken in one-point steps. The new footnote in the 1901 edition reads: "Occasionally the Bank now moves by steps of 1/2 per cent; but the rule that may be said to be broadly observed is that, while in lowering the rate it may be expedient to move by steps of 1/2 per cent, in raising it the advance should be by steps of 1 per cent" (PRO T176/13, Hawtrey to Niemeyer; undated but apparently November 1923).

2. Specification and estimation

This section describes the model and the methods used in our econometric analysis of Bank Rate policy during the period 1925–31. The type of reaction function we consider is familiar from the targets-instruments literature. We model Bank Rate as a dependent variable which depends on a vector of predetermined variables. Since the discount rate is one of several instruments available to the central bank, this reaction function should be interpreted as a reduced form. In some applications, such reaction functions have been derived as a first-order condition of a central bank's maximization problem, where the authorities are assumed to possess an objective function with a set of policy targets as arguments, and where the discount rate is taken as a control variable. However, the preceding discussion casts doubt on whether it is appropriate to model Bank Rate policy during the interwar period as optimizing behaviour. Instead, we hypothesize that Bank Rate policy was formulated by rules of thumb and postulate a reaction function of the form:

$$\Delta BR = f(\Delta G, E, i - i^*, BR - i, \Delta TB, Q, BR_{high}). \tag{1}$$

The first variable upon which the change in Bank Rate (ΔBR) depends is the change in the Bank of England's reserve position (ΔG). To allow for the possibility that the Bank responded asymmetrically to increases and decreases in reserves, we enter reserve gains and losses separately. The level of the exchange rate (E) and the differential between domestic and foreign interest rates ($i - i^*$) are entered as additional indicators of external conditions. Since the Bank of England apparently was concerned with the relationship of Bank Rate to market interest rates, we enter $BR - i$ as a separate variable. The Bank may have been concerned with the attractiveness of new debt issue by the Treasury. This suggests a negative relationship between new Treasury Bills issued, TB, and the level of Bank Rate. We therefore include ΔTB as a possible determinant of ΔBR. Finally, we include two proxies designed to capture any concern the Bank of England may have had for the impact of Bank Rate policy on the state of trade and industry. Q is a measure of the level of economic activity. BR_{high} is designed to capture the possibility that the authorities believed that Bank Rate only affected the cost of bank credit and influenced the state of industry once it was at or above 4%; BR_{high} is defined as the level of Bank Rate except when Bank Rate was below 4%, in which case the variable takes on a value of zero.

The variables which are entered in levels in the reaction function and the feedback effects from Bank Rate to its determinants stabilize the dynamic properties of the dependent variable. Inclusion of the term $BR - i$ prevents Bank Rate from straying too far from the market rate. A negative response of ΔBR to BR_{high} prevents Bank Rate from indefinitely diverging above 4.5%. These lagged values and feedback effects are particularly important because of the allowance in our empirical specification for asymmetries in the response of ΔBR to ΔG. When equation (1) is integrated it might appear that the level of Bank Rate will depend separately on the accumulated gains and losses of reserves and not just on their level. Nothing would appear to rule out the possibility that an asymmetric response to gains and losses will lead to ever increasing or decreasing levels of Bank Rate; but in fact the feedback effects from Bank Rate to the other variables and the presence in the reaction function of lagged values of the level of BR preclude this type of behaviour.

It is obvious from our data that the Bank of England did not adjust Bank Rate continuously in response to economic conditions. The discount rate was altered only 16 times during our 328 week sample. Of these 16 changes in the rate, 12 were decreases and the remaining 4 were increases. Each of the decreases was exactly 50 basis points and each of the increases was exactly 100 basis points.

This discrete quality of our data indicates that standard time series regression techniques are inappropriate. We require an econometric model which explicitly accounts for the discrete nature of the dependent variable. Unfortunately, most econometric methods which account for the discrete nature of the data fail to account for its serial correlation.[25] Here we develop a model which is a dynamic generalization of the static ordered probit model in order to capture both the discreteness and the serial correlation in the data.

We will denote the level of Bank Rate at time t by BR_t and collect the independent variables at time t into a $k \times 1$ vector $\mathbf{X}_t$. In our sample ΔBR_t can take on only three values, -50, 0, or 100 basis points. Our dynamic econometric model will determine the probability of these events as func-

[25] Notable exceptions are J. Heckman, "Statistical Models for Discrete Panel Data," in C. Manski and D. McFadden (eds.), *Structural Analysis of Discrete Data with Econometric Applications* (Cambridge, 1981); R.A. Avery, L.P. Hansen, and V.J. Klotz, "Multiperiod Probit Model and Orthogonality Condition Estimation," *International Economic Review* 24 (1983) 21–35; and P. Ruud, "Conditional Minimum Distance Estimation and Autocorrelation in Limited Dependent Variable Models," Ph.D. dissertation, MIT (1981).

tions of current X_t and past values of both X_t and BR_t. We denote this information set by J_t, so that the econometric model will determine

$$\text{Prob}\,[\Delta BR = -50|J_t] = P_{1t}(J_t), \tag{2}$$

$$\text{Prob}\,[\Delta BR_t = 0|J_t] = P_{2t}(J_t), \tag{3}$$

and

$$\text{Prob}\,[\Delta BR_t = 100|J_t] = P_{3t}(J_t) \quad \text{for} \quad (t = 1,\dots,T), \tag{4}$$

where

$$J_t = (X_t, BR_{t-1}, \dots, BR_1, X_1).$$

Our specification will generate these probabilities from the t-variate normal distribution and can be viewed as a dynamic generalization of the static ordered probit model. To motivate our specification let ΔBR_t^* denote the change in an unobserved 'underlying' Bank Rate that is generated by an ordinary linear regression equation

$$\Delta BR_t^* = X_t'\beta + \epsilon_t, \tag{5}$$

with $\epsilon_t|J_t \sim \text{Niid}(0, \sigma^2)$.

The observed Bank Rate changes whenever it is too far away from BR_t^* according to the rule

$$\Delta BR_t = -50 \quad \text{if } BR_t^* < BR_{t-1} - \alpha_l, \tag{6}$$

$$\Delta BR_t = 0 \quad \text{if } BR_{t-1} - \alpha_l < BR_t^* < BR_{t-1} + \alpha_u, \tag{7}$$

and

$$\Delta BR_t = 100 \quad \text{if } BR_t^* > BR_{t-1} + \alpha_u. \tag{8}$$

The observed rate will decrease by 50 basis points whenever BR_t^* is appreciably less than BR_{t-1}, and increase by 100 basis points whenever BR_t^* is appreciably greater than BR_{t-1}. The definition of 'appreciable' is determined by the constants α_l and α_u.

While our model is broadly similar to the usual ordered probit model, there are two major differences. First, while our equation (5) describes the changes in BR_t^*, the inequalities in (6)–(8) concern its level. This feature introduces stochastic dynamics into BR_t through the accumulation of the disturbance terms ϵ_t. Second, in contrast to the standard ordered probit model, we include in the inequalities (6)–(8) the observed time series, BR_{t-1}. This has implications for the identifiability of parameters in the model.

Equations (5)–(8) can be used to express the probability of Bank Rate movements as functions of the variables in the information set J_t, the un-

Table 4.1: *Definition of variables*

ΔBR	Change in Bank Rate (measured in basis points)
$\Delta G+$	Change in the value of gold and foreign exchange reserves (in millions of £) if the change was positive, zero otherwise
$\Delta G-$	Change in the value of gold and foreign exchange reserves (in millions of £) if the change was negative, zero otherwise
BR_{high}	Value of Bank Rate during the previous week if this rate was greater than 4%, zero otherwise
$(BR - i)+$	Difference between Bank Rate and the market rate over the previous week, if the difference was increasing
$(BR - i)-$	Difference between Bank Rate and the market rate over the previous week, if the difference was not increasing
$(i - i*)$	Difference between the London market rate and the New York rate
ΔU	Monthly rate of change in a 4-week moving average of the number registered as unemployed excluding the effects of the General Strike (in tens of millions)
UGS	Additional number of workers registered as unemployed because of the General Strike (in tens of millions); see text for the construction of this variable
ΔTB	Change in Treasury Bills offered (in hundreds of millions of £)
E	Exchange rate (dollars per pound sterling)

known parameters β, σ^2, α_l, α_u, and the initial value BR_0^*. These probabilities can be used to form the likelihood function of the data, and estimates of the parameters can be found by maximizing this function. While this procedure is straightforward in principle, the dynamic nature of the model makes it quite difficult in practice. In the appendix we derive the likelihood function and present a method for its evaluation. To derive the results presented in Section 4, we used this method to evaluate the function and the Berndt et al. (1974) algorithm to maximize it.

3. Data

In Table 4.1 we present mnemonics and summary descriptions of the variables used in estimation. The remainder of this section discusses the sources and characteristics of these data.

We gathered weekly observations for all variables from the first week of April 1925 through the third week of September 1931. Data on Bank Rate are readily available; our figures are taken from Sayers (1976, volume 3, p. 347). The decision whether to raise, lower, or leave Bank Rate unchanged was made on Thursday mornings at 11.30 a.m. when the Governor of the Bank of England and the Court of Directors met. Although the Governor had the power to raise Bank Rate unilaterally at other times of the week, there were no 'Governor's raises' during our sample period. In contrast to previous studies employing monthly and annual observations, our use of weekly data minimizes the loss of information caused by averaging weekly changes. In addition, the use of weekly data enables us to make realistic assumptions about the latest information available to the Bank.

The value of gold and foreign exchange held by the Bank of England was calculated by the Bank's chief cashier and reported in the Bank's weekly return. The return covered the period from Thursday to the subsequent Wednesday and was available to the Committee of Treasury on the following morning. These figures for gold and foreign exchange reserves are collected by Sayers (1976, volume 3, pp. 349–55), from where our series is drawn. We denote positive and negative changes in reserves as $\Delta G+$ and $\Delta G-$.

Exchange rates were reported daily in the financial press. It is conceivable that members of the Committee could have obtained subsequent information through early morning telephone calls to exchange dealers, but we assume that they relied on quotations up to the Wednesday close-of-business rate reported in the Thursday papers. A number of different bilateral rates could be considered. Here we concentrate on the sterling/dollar rate for cable transactions at the close of business on Wednesday, as published in Thursday's *Wall Street Journal*. When a major holiday fell on a Wednesday and the markets were closed, the previous day's close-of-business rate is used.

The same conventions are used in collecting interest rate data. For the London rate, we employ the rate on 90 day bankers' drafts at the close of business on Wednesday. These figures are taken from weekly editions of the *Economist*. In line with our assumption about exchange rates, as a measure of foreign interest rates we use the rate on 90 day bankers' acceptances in New York, as reported in the *Wall Street Journal*. Again, these figures are for the close of business on Wednesday. Although the New York market closed several hours after the London market, presumably there was time for closing quotations in New York to be cabled across the Atlantic.

The Treasury issued bonds and bills through a weekly tender. Every Friday the sealed tenders were opened at the Bank of England in the presence of the Governor and a Treasury official, at which time the Treasury made public the ('maximum') size of the following week's issues. Our figures are taken from the *Economist*.

As a proxy for the state of domestic economic activity, we use weekly figures for the number of individuals registered as unemployed, not in the belief that this series accurately measures the state of the economy but on the assumption that it provides useful information on internal conditions and that the Committee of Treasury may have thought it relevant.[26] For each Monday the Ministry of Labour recorded the number of individuals registered as out of work at an Employment Exchange. These figures were released weekly, generally on the second Wednesday following the Monday of record. We assume that these figures became available to the Bank of England with a 9 day lag. Our series is drawn from monthly issues of the *Ministry of Labour Gazette*.[27]

The unemployment numbers were smoothed by taking 4-week moving averages. To distinguish the effects of the General Strike of 1926 from other components of unemployment, we replaced the actual values of the series from May 1926 to May 1927 with the average seasonal pattern of the series. This variable is denoted U. (While the strike itself lasted only 2 weeks its effect on the number of unemployed lasted approximately 1 year.) The variable UGS represents the deviation of the actual number unemployed from these average values. Both components of the smoothed unemployment series are plotted in Fig. 4.2.

4. Empirical results

The results of estimating variants of Eq. (1) using OLS and our maximum likelihood procedure are shown in Table 4.2.[28] The fit of the equations is adequate; the standard error is less than 13 basis points. The OLS results are quite plausible: all coefficients but one have the anticipated signs and are of reasonable magnitudes. For example, the negative coefficient on

[26] We do not intend to argue that the Bank attached great importance to weekly fluctuations in unemployment. It is more likely that they considered the most recent figures in light of previous trends. This leads us to use a moving average of the unemployment figures in estimation. See the following discussion.

[27] The limitations of these unemployment figures are well known. The count of the unemployed was not an unbiased estimate but merely a tabulation of the number of persons who chose to register themselves as out of work at an Employment Exchange. The benefits conferred to unemployed persons under the provisions of the Unemployment Insurance Acts provided an incentive to register despite the inconvenience. Therefore, changes in the provisions and administration of the Insurance Acts independently influenced the statistics. R. Garside, *The Measurement of Unemployment, 1850–1979* (Oxford, 1980) discusses six legislative and administrative changes during this sample period with an impact on the recorded figures for numbers employed. The most important changes appear to be those of April 1928, when conditions for the receipt of benefits were relaxed, and May 1930, when the "genuinely seeking work" clause was eliminated.

[28] In all models we have included a constant term because some of the right-hand side variables may not have zero mean whereas the left-hand side variable does.

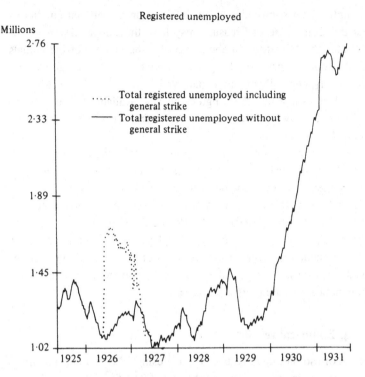

Figure 4.2. Number of registered unemployed.

$\Delta G-$ suggests that the Bank of England responded to a loss of reserves by raising Bank Rate, *ceteris paribus*. However, the Bank does not appear to have lowered Bank Rate upon gaining reserves; the coefficient on $\Delta G+$ is positive rather than negative and small relative to its standard error. The negative coefficient on BR_{high} suggests that the Bank of England did attempt to lower Bank Rate when it exceeded 4%. The negative coefficients on $(BR-i)-$ and $(BR-i)+$, the difference between Bank Rate and the London market rate (when that difference was falling and rising, respectively), suggest that the Bank tended to raise (lower) Bank Rate when it fell short of (exceeded) the market rate in order to insure Bank Rate's effectiveness. The relatively large coefficient on $(BR-i)+$ suggests that this tendency was stronger when Bank Rate was becoming increasingly 'out of touch' with market rates on the upward side. The negative coefficient on $(i-i^*)$, the London–New York interest differential, suggests that the Bank felt able to lower Bank Rate when London rates were rising relative to New York rates, presumably strengthening the capital account. Finally, the coefficients on

Table 4.2: *Estimation results for Bank Rate, 1925–1931*

	OLS	MLE	MLE	MLE
C	−2.217	0.063	−0.028	0.0002
	(3.900)	(0.039)	(0.032)	(0.0004)
$\Delta G-$	−0.046	−0.054	−0.058	−0.064
	(0.005)	(0.017)	(0.014)	(0.011)
$\Delta G+$	0.011	0.012	—	—
	(0.009)	(0.022)		
BR_{high}	−0.008	−0.011	−0.005	−0.001
	(0.004)	(0.003)	(0.004)	(0.004)
$(BR - i)+$	−0.175	−0.216	−0.231	−0.188
	(0.031)	(0.069)	(0.079)	(0.041)
$(BR - i)-$	−0.126	−0.077	—	—
	(0.034)	(0.066)		
$(i - i*)$	−0.009	−0.0003	—	—
	(0.011)	(0.0010)		
ΔU	0.039	−2.012	—	—
	(1.209)	(2.876)		
ΔUGS	1.161	1.316	—	—
	(0.551)	(1.931)		
ΔTB	0.095	—	−0.044	—
	(0.182)		(0.091)	
E	0.470	—	—	—
	(0.803)			
$\hat{\sigma}$	0.128	0.099	0.122	0.118
		(0.029)	(0.035)	(0.030)
$\hat{\alpha}$	—	1.536	1.620	1.549
		(0.163)	(0.206)	(0.170)
BR_0^*	—	5.264	5.134	5.108
		(0.469)	(0.544)	(0.511)
L	—	−43.14	−46.97	−47.64
$\hat{\rho}^a$	—	0.935	0.993	0.992
		(0.090)	(0.021)	(0.018)

[a] Coefficient estimates reported and Likelihood Values are for $\rho = 1$. We reestimated all parameters when we relaxed this constraint on ρ.

the Treasury Bill issue, the two unemployment variables, and the exchange rate (dollars per pound sterling) have signs that are inconsistent with our prior predictions.

While the OLS results seem plausible, their statistical properties are questionable because of the discrete nature of the data. While the maximum likelihood point estimates tell roughly the same story as their OLS counterparts, their asymptotic standard errors (calculated from the inverse of the information matrix) are considerably larger than the standard errors reported by OLS. The OLS standard errors are, of course, biased estimates and their use could lead to invalid inference.

We have estimated the dynamic probit model using a variety of similar specifications. The estimated models tell a consistent story.[29] Results for a model which includes all regressors except ΔTB and E are shown in column 2.[30] The coefficient on $\Delta G -$ is significantly less than zero at standard significance levels, suggesting that the Bank of England responded to a loss of reserves by raising Bank Rate. The coefficient on $\Delta G +$ is positive but small relative to its standard error, suggesting that the Bank was less inclined to lower Bank Rate in response to an increase in reserves. The coefficient on BR_{high} is significantly greater than zero, suggesting that the Bank did in fact become concerned about the impact of Bank Rate on the domestic economy when it exceeded 4%. The results for $(BR - i)+$ and $(BR - i)-$ suggest that the Bank was also concerned with the relationship between Bank Rate and market rates. The relatively large coefficient on $(BR - i)+$ suggests that this influence operated most strongly when Bank Rate was growing increasingly 'out of touch' with market rates on the upward side. The asymmetry in the response to the $(BR - i)$ differential is near statistical significance; the t-statistic for the difference between the two coefficients is 1.8. The coefficient on the London–New York interest rate differential is surprisingly small and insignificantly different from zero at standard levels. The rate of change of the number unemployed appears to have a negative effect on Bank Rate, but the evidence here is far from overwhelming.

The last four rows of Table 4.2 show the likelihood value, L, and the estimates of three parameters, α, BR_0^*, and ρ. α is the sum of the upper and lower threshold parameters α_l and α_u.[31] The estimated value of α in

[29] Although space limitations allow us to report complete results for only three of the specifications, we will mention other relevant results during the course of the discussion.

[30] We present no MLE in the text for models including the dollar/pound exchange rate, E. Results for an equation including ΔTB appear in column 3. When E was added to the ML specification, convergence proved to be very sensitive to the initial values chosen for the parameters. We have estimated a model using the ML procedure and the parameter values shown in column 2 of Table 4.2 as initial values (so that the coefficient on the exchange rate was initialized at zero). The likelihood value increased very slightly and the coefficient on the exchange rate increased only from 0 to 0.0001 with a standard error of 0.0009, while the other parameter estimates changed very little.

[31] In the discussion of the model in the appendix we show that only $\alpha = \alpha_u - \alpha_l$ and the initial value of BR^* is identified.

all of the models is close to 1.5. This confirms that conditions could change quite substantially before causing a discrete change in Bank Rate. BR_0^* is the estimate of the initial value of the underlying Bank Rate; in all cases it is very close to 5%, the initial value of BR. ρ is associated with our equation for the underlying Bank Rate, which we repeat here for convenience:

$$\Delta BR_t^* = \mathbf{X}_t' \boldsymbol{\beta} + \epsilon_t. \tag{5}$$

If we solve this equation backwards for the level of BR^* we find

$$BR_t^* = BR_0^* + \mathbf{S}_t' \boldsymbol{\beta} + \xi_t,$$

where

$$\mathbf{S}_t = \sum_{i=1}^{t} \mathbf{X}_i$$

and the error term ξ_t follows

$$\xi_t = \rho \xi_{t-1} + \epsilon_t \quad \text{with } \rho = 1.$$

For each subset of regressors we have estimated one model including ρ as one of the unknown parameters, and one model constraining ρ to equal 1. While the coefficient estimates shown in the table come from the models where ρ is constrained, we also show the estimate of ρ from the unconstrained model. The estimated values of ρ are close to one, suggesting that the constraint is generally consistent with the data.

In column 3 of the table we eliminate variables with coefficients that are not significantly different from zero and add the change in Treasury Bill issues. The coefficient on ΔTB is negative, though insignificant. This is at best mild evidence in favour of the contention that the Bank was concerned with the attractiveness of new debt issue by the Treasury. In column 4 we present results including only $\Delta G-$, BR_{high}, and $(BR - i)+$. The only change of note is the reduction in the coefficient on BR_{high}.

What do these results imply for the questions posed at the outset? The first question – was policy asymmetric in the sense that the Bank of England was more inclined to raise its discount rate upon losing reserves than to lower it upon gaining them? – can be answered in the affirmative. Our findings suggest that in posing the second question – was the Bank responsive not only to the balance of payments but to internal conditions as well? – it is critically important to distinguish different dimensions of internal conditions and the different constituencies affected by policy. We find only weak evidence that the Bank was responsive in its discount rate policy to fluctuations in the numbers unemployed. In contrast, we infer that the Bank was more sensitive to factors affecting the cost of credit to domestic finance and trade on the basis of the estimated coefficients for the variable BR_{high}. These estimates also suggest a positive answer to our third question of whether the Bank looked beyond balance of payments conditions primarily when the level of Bank Rate exceeded a crucial level.

What do these answers imply for the role of the Bank of England in the operation of the interwar gold standard? They suggest that the Bank's asymmetrical response to international reserve flows shifted the burden of adjustment onto deficit countries during periods when Britain was in surplus, disrupting the symmetric adjustment process posited under the 'rules of the game.' They suggest that the Bank of England's willingness to use Bank Rate to defend its reserves was qualified by its concern with internal economic conditions and with the anticipated impact of its discount rate on the domestic economy. This asymmetrical response and sensitivity to internal conditions reflect the fact that the Bank of England exercized considerable discretion in the formulation of Bank Rate policy. Adherence to 'rules of the game' would seem a particularly inappropriate way of characterizing its actions.

5. Conclusion

In this chapter we have examined the Bank of England's discount rate policy under the interwar gold standard. The historical literature suggests several critical issues concerning both the Bank's operating procedures and the role of internal and external factors in the formulation of Bank Rate policy. These issues are central to the debate over the reasons for the interwar gold standard's unsatisfactory operation and ultimately for its demise. To address these issues we have developed a dynamic model of Bank Rate policy and a maximum likelihood technique for estimating its parameters. Our results reveal an asymmetry in the Bank's response to reserve gains and losses and a sensitivity to domestic economic conditions when formulating Bank Rate policy. Such violations of the 'rules of the game,' here adequately documented for the first time, may have contributed to the instability of the interwar financial system. Documenting the impact of this failure to play by the 'rules of the game' is the next logical step in this inquiry.

Appendix

The probabilities $P_{1t} - P_{3t}$ defined in equations (2)–(4) can easily be generated using (5)–(8). Rewriting (5) in levels yields

$$BR_t^* = BR_0^* + S_t'\beta + \xi_t, \tag{5'}$$

with

$$\xi_t = \sum_{i=1}^t \epsilon_i = \xi_{t-1} + \epsilon_t$$

and

$$S_t = \sum_{i=1}^t X_i,$$

so that

$$\text{Prob}[\Delta BR_t = -50|J_t] = \text{Prob}[\xi_t < BR_{t-1} - \alpha_l - BR_0^* - S_t'\beta|J_t], \tag{6'}$$

$$\text{Prob}[\Delta BR_t = 0|J_t] = \text{Prob}[BR_{t-1} - \alpha_l - BR_0^* - S_t'\beta$$

$$< \xi_t < BR_{t-1} + \alpha_u - BR_0^* - S_t'\beta|J_t], \tag{7'}$$

and

$$\text{Prob}[\Delta BR_t = 100|J_t] = \text{Prob}[\xi_t > BR_{t-1} + \alpha_u - BR_0^* - S_t'\beta|J_t]. \tag{8'}$$

Evaluation of the probabilities in (6')–(8') requires the conditional distribution of ξ_t given J_t. Recall that J_t contains past values of BR_t as well as current and past values of X_t. The past values of BR_t place bounds on past values of ξ_t. Since ξ_t follows a random walk this information on ξ_{t-1}, ξ_{t-2}, etc. has an effect on the conditional distribution of ξ_t. While the process generating ξ_t is Markov, the same is not true for BR_t. The probability that ΔBR_t takes on a certain value will depend not only on ΔBR_{t-1}, but $\Delta BR_{t-2}, \Delta BR_{t-3}, \ldots, \Delta BR_1$, as well. This non-Markov feature arises because ΔBR_{t-1} gives only imprecise information (an interval) concerning ξ_{t-1}; the values of $\Delta BR_{t-2}, \Delta BR_{t-3}$, etc. contain additional useful imperfect information.

The Markov structure of ξ_t does simplify the conditional distribution of ξ_t given J_t. Let l_t and U_t be the bounds placed on ξ_t by the realization ΔBR_t (e.g., $l_t = -\infty$ and $U_t = BR_{t-1} - \alpha_l - BR_0^* - S_t'\beta$ if $\Delta BR_t = -50$) and denote the conditional distribution of ξ_{t-1} given J_t by $g(\xi_{t-1}|J_t)$. The conditional distribution of ξ_t given J_t, say, $h(\xi_t|J_t)$, is given by the convolution

$$h(\xi_t|J_t) = \frac{1}{\sigma} \int_{l_{t-1}}^{U_{t-1}} \phi\left(\frac{\xi_t - \xi_{t-1}}{\sigma}\right) g(\xi_{t-1}|J_t) d\xi_{t-1}. \tag{9'}$$

This can then be 'updated' to find $h(\xi_{t+1}|J_{t+1})$ by noting that

$$g(\xi_t|J_{t+1}) = \begin{cases} [H(U_t|J_t) - H(l_t|J_t)]^{-1}h(\xi_t|J_t) & \text{for } l_t < \xi_t < U_t, \tag{10'} \\ 0 & \text{otherwise,} \end{cases}$$

where $H(\cdot|\cdot)$ is the c.d.f. corresponding to the density $h(\cdot|\cdot)$.

Given the stochastic structure outlined above, the likelihood function is easily derived. The probability of observing $(\Delta BR_1, \Delta BR_2, \ldots, \Delta BR_T)$ is given by

$$P(\Delta BR_1, \Delta BR_2, \ldots, \Delta BR_T | \mathbf{X}_1, \mathbf{X}_2, \ldots, \mathbf{X}_T)$$

$$= \int_{l_T}^{U_T} \int_{l_{T-1}}^{U_T-1} \cdots \int_{l_1}^{U_1} f_T(\xi_1, \xi_2, \ldots, \xi_T) d\xi_1 d\xi_2 \ldots d\xi_T, \quad (11')$$

where f_T is the T-variate normal density with mean vector $\mathbf{o}$, and covariance matrix $\sigma^2 \Omega$, with $[w_{ij}] = \min(i,j)$.

Alternatively, if we define three indicator variables, k_{1t}, k_{2t}, and k_{3t} by

$$k_{1t} = \begin{cases} 1 & \text{if } \Delta BR_t = -50, \\ 0 & \text{otherwise,} \end{cases}$$

$$k_{2t} = \begin{cases} 1 & \text{if } \Delta BR_t = 0, \\ 0 & \text{otherwise,} \end{cases}$$

and

$$k_{3t} = \begin{cases} 1 & \text{if } \Delta BR_t = 100, \\ 0 & \text{otherwise,} \end{cases}$$

then

$$P(\Delta BR_1, \Delta BR_2, \ldots, \Delta BR_T | \mathbf{X}_{T-1}, \ldots, \mathbf{X}_1) = \prod_{t=1}^{T} P_{1t}^{k_{1t}} P_{2t}^{k_{2t}} P_{3t}^{k_{3t}}.$$

The presence of the time varying term BR_{t-1} in the inequalities in $(6')$–$(8')$ makes parameter identification somewhat different than in the static ordered probit model. It allows us to identify the variance of ϵ_t, σ^2. In the dynamic model BR_0^* plays the part of a constant in the level equation and as in the static model only two of the three unknowns α_l, α_u, and BR_0^* are identified. Because of this we normalize $\alpha_l = 50$. The initial condition BR_0^* is then estimated as a nuisance parameter.

It is clear from equation $(11')$ that evaluation of the likelihood function requires, at least implicitly, the evaluation of a T-variate normal distribution. While practical numerical methods exist for T as large as four or five (see Johnson and Kotz, 1970), in our case, $T = 328$. This computational barrier has prevented the use of maximum likelihood estimates in dynamic probit models and led to other, less efficient, but computationally tractable, estimates (see Ruud, 1981, or Avery, Hansen, and Kotz, 1983). Fortunately, the distribution that we must evaluate has a special structure that can be exploited.

Table 4.A: *Approximate log likelihood values (T = 328)*

Number of terms in approximation (k)	L	Seconds of CPU time
5	−44.222	4
10	−42.507	10
20	−42.364	33
30	−42.338	67
50	−42.326	180
80	−42.322	420

We exploit this structure and produce an approximation that can be made arbitrarily accurate at the cost of increased computation. Our approximation appears to be quite accurate and can be used to evaluate any T-variate normal distribution which arises from an underlying density with Markov structure. This approximation replaces the conditional density, $h(\xi_t | J_t)$, by a weighted sum of normal densities. Its accuracy increases with the number of densities in the sum.

The approximation follows directly from the equation

$$h(\xi_t | J_t) = \frac{1}{\sigma} \int_{l_{t-1}}^{U_{t-1}} \phi\left(\frac{\xi_t - \xi_{t-1}}{\sigma}\right) g(\xi_{t-1} | J_t) d\xi_{t-1}.$$

We assume that the expression on the RHS is a definite integral so that if $l_{t-1} = -\infty$ it is replaced by an arbitrarily small number and similarly if $U_{t-1} = \infty$. We will let

$$\Delta_k = (U_{t-1} - l_{t-1})/k$$

and define

$$\tilde{\xi}_i = l_{t-1} + i\Delta_k \quad (i = 1, \ldots, k)$$

and

$$h_k(\xi_t | J_t) = \sum_{i=1}^{k} \frac{1}{\sigma} g(\tilde{\xi}_i | J_t) \phi\left(\frac{\xi_t - \tilde{\xi}_i}{\sigma}\right) \Delta_k.$$

The function $h_k(\xi_t | J_t)$ is the weighted sum of normal densities that serve as our approximation to $h(\xi_t | J_t)$. The probabilities P_{1t}, P_{2t}, P_{3t} can then be approximated by integrating $h_k(\xi_t | J_t)$ which involves only univariate normal densities. The function $g_k(\xi_t | J_{t+1})$ is then formed from equation (10′) with $h_k(\xi_t | J_t)$ replacing $h(\xi_t | J_t)$.

The motivation behind the approximation is quite simple. The multivariate integral in ($11'$) is viewed as an iterated integral. The Markov structure of ξ_t gives the iterated integral a particularly simple form requiring the repeated evaluation of functions like $h(\xi_t | J_t)$. This function arises from an integral which we approximate as a Riemann sum. Clearly as $k \to \infty$ our approximation approaches the value of the likelihood function. This follows directly from the definition of the integral.

In our empirical application we had little *a priori* knowledge of the quality of the approximation for various values of k. Through experimentation we found the $k = 20$ yielded an adequate approximation. Larger values of k produced a slightly better approximation but at a much higher cost. In Table 4.A we present values of the approximate log-likelihood for various values of k. These were formed using all of our data and typical parameter values. We also include CPU time in seconds for one function evaluation on a DEC VAX11/780. These should give some idea of the accuracy/computational cost trade-off. Since the log likelihood had to be evaluated repeatedly during the maximization, our choice of $k = 20$ seemed reasonable.

5. The Bank of France and the sterilization of gold, 1926–1932

The malfunctioning of the interwar gold standard is frequently given much of the credit, or more precisely the blame, for the instability of the world economy in the late 1920s and early 1930s.[1] Accounts of the period typically attribute the monetary standard's unsatisfactory performance to the mismanagement of gold reserves. Due to misguided policy, it is alleged, gold stocks proved insufficient in quantity and elasticity for the system's smooth operation. By reestablishing prewar parities and hence prewar gold prices, governments unwisely depressed the nominal value of metallic reserves. The low level of reserves relative to incomes limited monetary growth, promoted deflation, and complicated the efforts of central banks to maintain convertibility. These difficulties were exacerbated by the uneven international distribution of the available gold. By 1931 the United States and France possessed between them more than 60% of the world's metallic reserves. Their propensity to accumulate gold intensified deflationary pressures operating abroad. With downward rigidity of costs impeding adjustment to these pressures, the shortage of gold caused falling output and employment rather than falling wages and prices. The unemployment which resulted created budgetary difficulties for the authorities, ultimately undermining their ability to maintain fixed parities.[2]

Much of the work on this paper was undertaken during visits to the Institut National de la Statistique et des Études Économiques (Paris) and the Centre for Economic Policy Research (London). I acknowledge the permission of the French Ministry of Finance, the Bank of France, the British Public Record Office, and the United Nations to cite archival materials in their possession. I thank also the Royal Institute of International Affairs for permission to consult the papers of its study group on "The International Gold Problem." This archival work was made possible by a French Government fellowship and a Fulbright grant. I am grateful for discussions with Charles Wyplosz, Jacques Melitz, and Ian McLean, and for the comments of participants in the Brookings Institution's April 1985 program meeting on International Economic Policy Coordination, where an earlier version of this paper was presented.

[1] See, for example, the influential accounts of Brown, *International Gold Standard;* Nurkse, *Currency Experience;* Kindleberger, *World In Depression.*

[2] Perhaps the clearest contemporary statement of this view appears in League of Nations Archives (Geneva), Gold Delegation Paper, R2962/10E/34031/4346, "Report on the Causes

The practice by central banks of offsetting the effects of reserve flows – "sterilization" as it was known in England, "*neutralisation*" as it was known in France – was both a cause and a consequence of this situation. Sterilization by the central banks of surplus countries is seen as a reflection of the desire to accumulate gold; sterilization by the central banks of deficit countries is seen as a reflection of the desire to insulate their economies from deflationary pressures emanating from abroad. If sterilization on the part of surplus countries reinforced the worldwide deflationary trend, sterilization on the part of deficit countries, by undermining confidence in their currencies, hastened the international monetary system's collapse.

The major players in this gold standard game were the Federal Reserve, the Bank of England, and the Bank of France.[3] The Bank of France and the Federal Reserve, as noted, were the principal repositories of metallic reserves. The Bank of England was responsible for managing what remained one of the world's leading reserve currencies and for defending an exchange rate that was viewed as the linchpin of the international gold standard system. While the actions of the British and American central banks have been the subject of considerable recent attention, the activities of the Bank of France have been strangely neglected.[4] In the absence of an historical analysis, it has simply been assumed that the Bank of France was guilty of inducing the inflows of gold which then may have contributed to the unsatisfactory operation of the monetary standard.

The absence of an assessment of the activities of the Bank of France is especially unfortunate given the extent to which accusations of sterilization were disputed at the time. France's critics found evidence of sterilization in its vast accumulations of gold and in the rising ratio of French gold reserves to note circulation. In rebuttal, the French argued that gold inflows simply reflected the normal operation of the price-specie-flow mechanism. They asserted that statutory restrictions together with the unique characteristics of French financial markets rendered the Bank of France incapable of affecting the direction and magnitude of international gold movements.

and Effects of the Recent Increase in the Purchasing Power of Gold," by Professor Gustav Cassel, Sir Reginald Mant, and Sir Henry Strakosch, January 1932. Strakosch's views come in for further discussion, below (p. 93).

3 Chapter 6 analyzes relationships among these central banks in the 1920s and 1930s.

4 On the actions of the Bank of England, see Chapter 4 and the references cited therein. On the activities of the Federal Reserve, see Friedman and Schwartz, *Monetary History*. The only comparable study of the Bank of France, H. Toi-Phang, "L'étalon or en France de 1820 à 1960: Contribution statistique à l'étude de 'Règles du jeu'," *Revue d'économie politique* 72 (1962), 877–90, is ultimately inconclusive.

From their perspective, it was not even sensible to pose the question of whether the Bank of France was engaged in sterilization.

Despite the attention this issue attracted, the debate then remained and still remains unresolved. This chapter therefore reconsiders gold flows into France and the issue of sterilization. The first part considers the sterilization debate itself, with the objective of identifying precisely the issues in dispute and of analyzing the positions of the participants. The point of this analysis is to show that the debate over sterilization revolves around a small number of issues whose historical importance must be determined empirically. The second part reassesses the evidence on international gold flows during the period 1926–1932 in light of the preceding analysis. It presents estimates of the impact of French policy on the extent of gold inflows into France. These estimates are then used in the closing section to reassess the debate over French sterilization and its relationship to the instability of the interwar gold standard.

The conclusions point to the critical role of historical experience in influencing the structure of the financial institutions through which the effects of policy disturbances were mediated. The massive inflows of gold into France in the second half of the 1920s are best understood not as a result of arbitrary or irrational actions on the part of policymakers but rather as a legacy of the inflationary experience of the early years of the decade. The inflow of gold after 1926 resulted from an increase in the demand for domestic credit relative to the supply, a demand stimulated by the decline in interest rates that accompanied price stabilization. Because of new legislation which closed off alternative avenues for expanding the domestic monetary base, supply could be increased only through the conversion of gold imported from abroad. That legislation had been adopted precisely in order to free the central bank from the political pressures which had led it to repeatedly monetize government budget deficits earlier in the decade. The implication is that the maldistribution of world gold reserves, to the extent that they were unnecessarily concentrated in France, should be viewed not so much as a result of arbitrary or irrational actions by policymakers but as a consequence of the economic history of the French nation and the international monetary system in the preceding years.

To appreciate the influence of that historical experience and in particular its implications for the functioning of French asset markets, the main features of the inflation and stabilization must be analyzed. It is to that analysis I now turn.

1. The financial legacy of French inflation

The French inflation of the period 1921–1926 and the franc's depreciation on the foreign exchange market provide the backdrop to the financial
developments of subsequent years. Since this inflationary episode has recently been recounted elsewhere, only its broad outlines need be summarized here.[5] The crucial aspect of this experience from the viewpoint of
the present study is the legacy of the inflation for operation of French financial markets once the gold standard was restored. That legacy can be
considered under three headings: stocks of assets outstanding, attitudes of
investors toward those stocks, and changes in financial regulation adopted
to prevent a recurrence of inflation.

Inflation in France had its origins in the methods of wartime finance.
The government imposed no new taxes during the first 2 years of World
War I, and subsequent tax increases remained relatively small. The first
official long-term loan was only issued 15 months into the war, until which
time military expenditures had been financed almost entirely by the issue
of short-term (floating) debt and by foreign borrowing. One of the largest
components of this debt was the *bons de la défense nationale*, fixed-interest
securities on which the effective cost of debt service varied with the initial
sales price.[6] A substantial fraction of the floating debt served as collateral
for direct advances from the Bank of France to the State, in effect monetizing a portion of the deficit. Between the end of 1914 and the end of 1918,
the Bank's note issue had more than tripled, while the floating debt, which
was negligible before the war, had risen to ff40 billion (ff7 billion of which
was held by the Bank of France).[7]

Postwar reconstruction needs reinforced wartime financial trends. The
situation in 1919, while extraordinary, did much to focus public attention
on the relationship between the budget, the note circulation, and the float-

---

5 The trials and tribulations of successive governments, the tangle over reparations, and other
familiar issues are suppressed here except insofar as they bear on the issues at hand. For
details, see Eichengreen, "Speculation"; Haig, *Public Finances;* J. Kooker, "French Financial Diplomacy: The Interwar Years," in B. Rowland (ed.), *Balance of Power or Hegemony:
The Interwar Monetary System* (New York, 1976); and Rogers, *Process of Inflation.*
6 These securities were issued under the provisions of a decree of 13 September 1914. F. Caron
and J. Bouvier, "Les Années 1914–1930," in F. Braudel and E. Labrousse (eds.), *Histoire
économique et sociale de la France* IV/2 (1980), 633–54; G. Feldman, *Le Franc Français
Depuis 1914* (Paris, 1926).
7 See H. Cheron, *Rapport au Senat,* no. 84, 22 February 1926, Paris, and Feldman, *Franc
Français* for additional statistics and discussion.

ing debt. Some 80% of government expenditure in calendar year 1919 was deficit financed. No more than a tenth of that deficit was funded through the issue of long-term loans, while the remainder was added to the floating debt.[8] With the Bank of France absorbing nearly 20% of the increment to the floating debt, note circulation grew by more than 23% over the course of the year. Consequently, with the termination of support operations in New York in March 1919, the franc began its descent on the foreign exchange market.

Inflation and depreciation were viewed with alarm by both financial interests and the public, who shared a desire to restore the prewar gold standard parity (the *franc germinal*). Hence taxes were raised and long-term loans floated in 1920 to bring inflationary pressures under control. To bolster confidence the government obtained the passage of a law under whose provisions the state was obliged to repay advances from the Bank of France at a rate of ff2 billion per annum. A full repayment was made in 1921 and a partial repayment was made in 1922, temporarily halting the currency's depreciation. However, since the central government budget remained in deficit, these repayments proved possible only through public sales of floating debt, which themselves had potential inflationary consequences.

Thereafter, the franc fluctuated uneasily in response to new information on the fiscal position. In 1923 the budget deficit reached ff18 billion, indicating clearly that the State would again be unlikely to comply with the law requiring it to repay ff2 billion of advances from the central bank. As inflationary expectations were revised upwards, the public grew unwilling to take up long-term loans at rates consistent with the Treasury's debt-management targets. But optimistic that inflationary expectations would eventually moderate, permitting costs of debt service to decline, the Treasury delayed its efforts to fund the debt and in the interim issued short-term bonds to finance the deficit.

Exchange rate depreciation accelerated as the impasse continued. The franc's depreciation reached serious proportions in March 1924 and was halted only when the Poincaré government succeeded in securing foreign loans and in passing new taxes (the "*double décime*" of 13 March). For

[8] Statistics appear in Statistique Générale, *Indices générale du mouvement économique en France de 1910 à 1931* (Paris, 1931). The one long-term loan was issued by the *Crédit National*, an institution formed in 1919 for financing reconstruction of the devastated districts. J. Bouvier, "Monnaie et Banque d'un Apres-guerre a L'autre: 1919–1945," in Braudel and Labrousse, *Histoire*, p. 704.

the present discussion, it is not these measures but rather a less well-known initiative of the Bank of France which is important. At the beginning of the year, the Bank excluded short-term government bills from the list of securities against which it would extend loans on the grounds that funds thereby obtained were being used in operations against the franc.[9] The Bank's action restricted the volume of transactions on the call loan market, a development with implications for the subsequent debate over sterilization.[10]

From March 1924 onward, it was less current budget deficits than volatile expectations of prospective future deficits that were associated with depreciation of the franc. Expectations of future deficits were reinforced by the Poincaré government's replacement in 1924 by the *Cartel des Gauches*, a coalition of radical and socialist parties. These expectations of future deficits had an inflationary impact because of their implications for the public's willingness to hold outstanding government debt and because of the authorities' response. The floating debt ran anywhere from 1 to 12 months to maturity, with a portion maturing each month. When the maturity of an outstanding issue coincided with expectations of future deficits to be financed by additions to the stock of *bons*, the public became unwilling to purchase the existing stock at prices consistent with the Treasury's dcbt management objectives. Rather than attempting to roll over maturing issues at unattractive prices, the Treasury turned instead to Bank of France advances in the hope that inflationary expectations might soon moderate, rendering debt issue more economical. The consequent increase in note issue then validated the inflation that had been anticipated by financial market participants and reinforced expectations of its persistence.

2. The financial legacy of stabilization

None of the expedients of successive governments – proposals for a capital levy, an indexed loan, or appeals to patriotism – eased the financial crisis. To finance its operations, the Treasury repeatedly solicited additional advances from the Bank of France. The franc continued to fall as one finance minister succeeded another in "the waltz of the portfolios," until Poincaré was restored to power in July 1926 at the head of a coalition government.[11]

---

[9] T. Balogh, "The Import of Gold into France: An Analysis of the Technical Position," *Economic Journal* 40 (1930), 442–60.

[10] This point is taken up later.

[11] Perhaps for amusement, A. Sauvy, *Histoire économique de la France entre les deux guerres* (Paris, 1984) provides a page-long list of the finance ministers of the period.

With Poincaré's accession, the currency recovered at once. In fact, Poincaré's government did little more than impose the measures that had been recommended by a Committee of Experts (the Sergent Committee) appointed the previous May. That committee had urged new taxes to balance the budget, establishment of an autonomous Treasury account (the *Caisse d'Amortissement*) to fund and manage the floating debt, and assignment of specific tax revenues to that account. Poincaré allocated the death duties and revenues of the state tobacco monopoly to the *Caisse*.[12] The Bank of France, whose powers had been limited to those specified under the provisions of its 19th century constitution, was newly empowered to purchase gold and foreign exchange at a premium over official gold standard prices.

Each of these changes had lasting implications for French financial markets. The Bank of France's new freedom to conduct open market purchases permitted it for the first time to intervene to prevent any undesirable appreciation of the franc and resulted in its accumulation from December 1926 to June 1928 of vast stocks of convertible foreign exchange. The Bank operated in both American and British currencies, buying dollars at 25 francs and sterling at 122 francs. By the middle of February 1927, the Bank's *masse de manoeuvre*, or reserve of foreign exchange, was ff2,750 million.[13] By the date of de jure stabilization in June 1928, its foreign exchange holdings had soared to ff26,529 million.

The Bank made several attempts to convert this foreign exchange into gold. It was in connection with conversion operations in May 1927 that accusations of sterilization were first voiced. To these complaints, the Bank of France responded that it was not hoarding gold but simply attempting to raise its gold reserves to the point where they would be sufficient, at 35% of sight liabilities, to support the restoration of convertibility.[14] These attempts to purchase gold in London occasioned protracted negotiations, as a result of which the Bank of France ultimately moderated its demands on the Bank of England and shifted its gold purchase operations to New York.[15] Bank of France gold purchases between December 1926 and June

---

[12] P. Frayssinet, *La Politique Monétaire de la France (1924–1928)* (Paris, 1928).

[13] According to the archives of the French Ministry of Finance (Min. Fin.) B32318, "Note sur la liquidation des devises de la Banque de France," 23 May 1932.

[14] See the comments of Charles Rist in Royal Institute of International Affairs, *The International Gold Problem* (Oxford, 1931).

[15] These difficulties and the negotiations to which they gave rise are analyzed by, among others, Clarke, *Central Bank Corporation*, and Eichengreen, "Central Bank Cooperation." The French viewpoint is expressed in Min. Fin. B32318, "Note sur la liquidation."

1928, the date of de jure stabilization, came to just under ff9,000 million.[16]

In contrast to its prominence in international financial markets, the Bank of France's role in the domestic bill market was considerably reduced. In July 1926, at the height of inflation, the central bank discount rate had reached 7½%. But with the level of economic activity running high, the Bank of France remained active in the bill market despite the high price charged for discounts. Bills discounted at the Bank reached a peak for the year 1926 in July.[17] With de facto stabilization and the decline in economic activity that ensued, the demand for Bank of France discounts declined.[18] Discounts fell dramatically in the first half of 1927, despite the reduction in the Bank's discount rate to 5%.

In contrast to the Bank, following the 1926 reforms the French Treasury and the *Caisse d'Amortissement* exercised growing influence over the domestic market. The revenues earmarked for debt retirement and consolidation were accumulated at the Bank of France by the *Caisse*. Since there was often a lag between the receipt of revenues from the death duties and tobacco monopoly and their subsequent dispersal through debt repurchases, these operations were alleged to have had a considerable impact on domestic financial markets. This impact was reinforced by the Treasury's practice of similarly accumulating at the Bank of France surplus revenues to be used to repay advances made in the inflationary era.[19]

Certain of these relationships were again transformed with de jure stabilization in 1928. The law of 25 June 1928, which incorporated conventions between the Bank of France, the Treasury, and the *Caisse*, altered the statutory obligations of the central bank.[20] It defined the new gold standard parity for the franc and obligated the Bank of France to buy all gold offered it at this price, but limited such transactions to minimum amounts agreed

---

16 Min. Fin. B32318, "Note sur la liquidation." Thus, R. Hawtrey's guess, in *The Art of Central Banking* (London, 1932), of 7,000 million francs was something of an underestimate.

17 Dulles, *The French Franc*, p. 493.

18 T. Sargent, "Stopping Moderate Inflations: The Methods of Poincare and Thatcher," in R. Dornbusch and M.H. Simonsen (eds.), *Inflation, Debt and Indexation* (Cambridge, 1983) argues that the stabilization represented a convincing change in monetary and fiscal regime and hence was not followed by a recession of any magnitude or duration. However, both contemporary commentary (viz. *The Economist*, 22 January 1927) and the available statistics (for example, the 20 percent decline in industrial production, or the 3.5 percent fall in Sauvy's estimate of real Net National Product) suggest a sizeable downturn between 1926 and 1927.

19 Balogh, "Import of Gold," pp. 449–51.

20 Bank of France, *Compte Rendu au Nom du Conseil General de la Banque* (Paris, 1928), pp. 11–14.

to by the Minister of Finance and the Bank, thereby placing France, like Britain, not on a pure gold standard but on a gold bullion standard. The law specified that gold alone would be considered the legal reserve of the Bank of France and prohibited the Bank from making further purchases of foreign exchange on the open market. In contrast, it placed no restrictions on the use of foreign exchange already in the Bank's possession.

If the 1928 stabilization law prohibited the purchase of gold at a premium and foreign exchange on the open market. Article 8 of the Bank's 1808 charter similarly prohibited domestic open market operations except where otherwise stated. Under the new conventions, permission to engage in open market operations was limited to two circumstances: first, to facilitate cooperation with other nations, the Bank was empowered to purchase bills and short-term securities on behalf of any foreign banks of issue which maintained current accounts with it; second, the Bank was permitted to repurchase any 3-month bonds of the *Caisse d'Amortissement* which the Bank had previously assisted in placing on the market.

The law of June 1928 also altered the definition of the Bank of France's reserve. Under the new law, the Bank was required to back, at a 35% ratio, not just its note issue but also its deposit liabilities, including even Treasury deposits. At the same time, the practice of permitting advances from the Bank to the Treasury was abolished. The Convention provided that the account of temporary advances from the Bank to the Treasury should be closed.

With the establishment of a new gold standard parity at a price approximately five times the prewar level, capital gains on the order of 500% accrued to the central bank on its gold reserves. These capital gains were the vehicle by which the Treasury's debt to the Bank of France was extinguished. The capital gains were assigned to the Treasury, which used them to repay the Treasury debt to the Bank.[21]

3. Indicators of the external position

Before turning to the debate over sterilization, it is useful to recall the information available to contemporaries on the French balance of payments and on the position of the central bank.

---

[21] In addition to advances to the Treasury, these profits were used to eliminate the Treasury debt to the Bank due to wartime transfers of gold to the Allies for use in foreign exchange market support operations, and to eliminate the asset item on the Bank's balance sheet due to discounting for the Bank of Russia during the War. See A. Neurrisse, *Histoire du Franc* (Paris, 1967).

Table 5.1: *Indicators of the French external position, 1928–1932 (millions of francs)*

	(1)	(2)	(3) Public deposits[c]		(4)	(5)	(6)	(7)
	Trade balance[b]	Note circulation	Treasury	Caisse	Private deposits	Discounts	Gold[d]	Percent gold backing[e]
1928-I[a]	−947	58,816	94	0	8,599	1581	5,543	8.2
1928-II	−4,917	61,496	7552	3893	5,616	2919	30,652	39.0
1929	−8,081	64,719	6333	6139	6,237	6507	37,011	44.4
1930	−9,076	72,906	4773	4972	7,844	5563	45,911	50.7
1931	−11,770	79,209	2036	7910	15,219	6477	58,966	56.5
1932	−10,103	82,131	633	3024	22,624	3807	79,481	73.3

[a] 1928-I denotes first half of 1928. The two halves of the year are distinguished because the mid-year monetary reforms involved revisions of the central bank balance sheet and revaluation of its gold reserve.
[b] *Commerce spécial.*
[c] Sum of Treasury deposits and balances of the *Caisse d'Amortissement.*
[d] Gold is valued at 1913 official par value prices in 1928-I, at June 1928 official prices thereafter.
[e] (6) as a percentage of the sum of (2), (3), and (4).
Source: Tinbergen, *Abstract;* Methorst, *Recueil;* Sauvy, *Histoire;* Bank of France, *Compte Rendu* (various issues). Where figures differ, Sauvy's are taken as definitive.

Data available to contemporaries included the French trade balance, the gold reserve, and the note circulation. These were the figures upon which most inferences about central bank influence were based. They do not uniformly lead to the same presumption about the direction of such influence. Table 5.1 shows that the trade balance was in deficit every year from 1928 through 1932, not exactly prima facie evidence that sterilization of gold inflows was taking place. However, since the readily available figures excluded reexports and since France was known to run a surplus in invisibles (due notably to tourist receipts and foreign interest earnings), the trade balance was interpreted as a lower bound on the current account.[22] With the

22 See Bank of France, *Compte Rendu au Nom du Conseil Général de la Banque* (Paris, 1930), p. 5, and P. Meynial, "La Balance des Comptes," *Revue d'économie politique* 44 (1930), 470–83. Contemporary estimates of the current account of the balance of payments, presented by L. Rist and P. Schwob, "Balance des Paiements," *Revue d'économie politique* 53 (1939), 528–50, support this view, showing a surplus in trade in invisibles in every year of the period. Unfortunately, it was not universally recognized that the French current account had been in persistent surplus before the war, the difference being that prewar surpluses had been more than offset by the volume of foreign lending.

Bank of France accumulating gold throughout the period, French foreign lending was seen as insufficient to offset this current account surplus. Even netting out the acquisition of gold due to conversion of preexisting holdings of foreign exchange, the Bank acquired gold on balance-of-payments account each year from 1928 through 1932. That the balance of payments was taking so long to equilibrate – indeed that the imbalance appeared to be growing – was the principal indication to its foreign critics that the Bank of France must have been engaged in sterilization.

Support for this presumption was found in the central bank balance sheet, extracts from which appear in Table 5.1. The Bank's cover ratio (gold reserves as a share of note circulation and deposits) rose from 38 to 47% between the end of 1928 and the end of 1929, to 53% by the end of 1930, 61% by the end of 1931, and 77% by the end of 1932.[23] Sir Henry Strakosch, in the discussions of a study group on "The International Gold Problem" organized by the Royal Institute of International Affairs, noted that, while the Bank of France's gold reserve had increased by ff37,500 million francs between December 1926 and December 1930, over the same period its note circulation had risen by only ff23,500 million. Strakosch was quite explicit that this was what he had in mind when he accused the French of sterilization. In his words, "Any gold which goes into the Federal Reserve system, and any gold which has gone into the Bank of France since the end of 1928, is no longer monetary gold." The reason it ceased to function as such was that the Bank of France had failed to "build a structure of credit on it."[24]

4. Explanations for gold inflows

Although the dispute between the Bank of France's critics and defenders was partly semantic, there was at its core a substantive point. The point of substance which the two groups disputed was the explanation for gold inflows into France. According to Ralph Hawtrey, the British Treasury expert on matters of international finance, nothing could be more straightforward than the cause of these gold imports. Simply stated, the French government had reduced the supply of currency relative to the demand, and imports of gold and foreign exchange were needed to make up the difference.[25] While

[23] These end-year figures come from the same sources as the annual averages in Table 5.1.
[24] Royal Institute of International Affairs, *Gold Problem*, p. 95.
[25] As described by Hawtrey, *Art of Central Banking*, p. 22. See also PRO T188/22, "The French Gold Imports" (by Frederick Leith-Ross, 3 December 1930).

demand had risen due to the decline in the velocity of circulation that typically accompanies stabilization, the growth of currency supply had been constrained for a number of related reasons. Hawtrey himself emphasized the decision to reimburse the Bank of France for previous advances to the Treasury. Others, such as Frederick Leith-Ross, another British Treasury official, stressed the practice of maintaining Treasury deposits and receipts of the *Caisse d'Amortissement* at the central bank. As Leith-Ross put it, "These balances being taken off the market create a shortage of liquid funds for the French commercial banks which have to obtain further resources from the Banque of France and as explained above can only do so by the importation of gold." [26] The prohibition of open market operations precluded a compensatory increase in the note issue, while the allegedly underdeveloped state of the French bill market impeded the Bank of France's efforts to inject liquidity into the system through this channel. Finally, the demand in France for the notes of the central bank remained high due to the exceptional preference of Frenchmen to transact with currency instead of checks.

French officials and economists rejected this explanation for the extent of gold inflows into France. The nation's gold imports, as one put it, were nothing but "normal commercial transactions." [27] If France continued to import gold, they argued, this merely reflected the operation of the balance-of-payments adjustment mechanism. That the operation of this mechanism happened to be conveying gold to France resulted from a happy combination of national characteristics and historical circumstances, unrelated in the view of the French to the supposed scarcity of currency so emphasized by the British. Among these national characteristics was the innate economy of the Frenchman, who much preferred to save than to spend. A second was the Frenchman's traditional risk aversion, which implied a bias favoring domestic savings over foreign investment, a preference which strengthened the capital account. A third was the sectoral diversification of the French economy between industrial and agricultural production, which was seen as stabilizing the balance of payments during periods marked by economic disturbances.

Other factors strengthening the balance of payments were characterized as a result of historical circumstances. Currency depreciation in the first

26 PRO T188/22, "French Gold Imports."
27 PRO T176/33, "Memorandum by Mr. Pouyanne." See also Min. Fin. B32318, "Note sur la prétendue stérilisation de l'or en France," 25 October 1932; Min. Fin. B32138, "Note sur la liquidation des devises de la Banque de France," 23 May 1932.

half of the 1920s had stimulated activity in France's export trades, many of which, it was suggested, had succeeded in penetrating overseas markets with lasting benefit for the foreign balance. Depreciation had also reduced the burden of the debt, paving the way for investment in productive capacity. The expectations of revaluation which had prevailed in some circles between the end of 1926 and the summer of 1928 had induced substantial capital inflows, especially toward the end of the period.[28] Finally, the Frenchman's inherent aversion to foreign investment on grounds of risk had been heightened by losses recently experienced in connection with the Soviet government's default on French loans to Czarist Russia.

The influence of these domestic factors was reinforced, according to the French, by economic policies and problems abroad. In particular, the Bank of England's tendency to sterilize gold outflows and the failure of British wages and prices to decline to competitive levels had exacerbated Britain's loss of gold to France.[29] As the Bank of France described the situation in a memo to the Finance Ministry, "The monetary difficulties encountered in the course of the last years by England and the United States have been due, in large measure, to the fact that open market policy has been used to sterilize the effects of gold movements."[30] In this view, the uneven international distribution of gold was a result not of insufficient credit creation in France but excessive credit creation abroad. That the British authorities, through their inability or unwillingness to facilitate adjustment to changing market conditions, were undermining confidence in sterling only induced a further flight to the franc, which served as "a refuge for foreign capital desiring to profit from the stability and security" it offered.[31]

Officials of the Ministry of Finance disputed assertions that the Bank of France had provoked gold imports. In their words, the central bank had

---

[28] These capital inflows were of no little concern to the central bank. See Bank of France, "Délibérations du Conseil Général," 7 June 1928.

[29] In response, Ralph Hawtrey of the British Treasury pointed out that the rigidity of wages was by no means peculiar to Britain. PRO T188/21, "The French Memorandum on the English Crisis," 27 November 1931. The French Memorandum in question, by Jacques Rueff, can be found in Min. Fin. B31233, "Note sur les Causes et les Enseignement de la Crise Financière Anglais," 1 October 1931.

[30] Min. Fin. B32323, "Note sur l'open market policy" (note by the Bank of France), 23 May 1933.

[31] Min. Fin. B32138, "Note sur la liquidation des devises." See also Min. Fin. B32318, "Opinion de la 'Délégation de l'or' sur l'afflux de l'or en France et la politique de la Banque de France," 25 October 1932. The French conveyed their view to the British when British and French Treasury officials conferred. See PRO T188/21, Frederick Leith-Ross, "Note of a Discussion with French Treasury Experts," 11 August 1931.

never practiced a deliberate policy of sterilization; rather, it had simply observed the rules of the gold standard game that translated a gold inflow
into a corresponding amount of domestic credit creation.[32] According to
Albert Aftalion, the Bank had done nothing but apply the rules of the gold
standard by automatically extending the right of convertibility to imported
gold.[33] As the Bank of France defended its position in its annual report
for 1929, "We were obliged, in fulfilment of our obligation to regulate the
currency, to accept all gold of foreign origin which was offered to us over
the counter for francs, but we did not at any time intervene in the exchange
market to accelerate the pace of these gold imports."[34]

The French acknowledged that their financial system was uneconomical
in its use of gold. Charles Rist, by this time a former central bank official, argued that the national preference to transact with currency rather
than checks was a reflection of France's rural character.[35] While British
observers acknowledged this difference in habits, they questioned whether
the greater demand for notes in France could not be offset by a lower ratio
of gold backing. As Hawtrey put it, "I do not know why France, with
one-ninth the national income of the United States, should need half the
amount of gold; or why, with half the national income of Great Britain, it
should need three times the amount of gold."[36] As the British saw it, the
only impediment to reform was the French Parliament's failure to amend
the legislation governing the central bank – legislation which the British
presumed could be passed.

Other institutional characteristics peculiar to the French economy further
augmented the demand for gold. Balogh suggested that the narrowness of
the call loan market in France in comparison with other countries contributed to the specie inflow. French banks like the French public held what
were by British standards large amounts of cash. In other countries, economies in the demand for cash reserves could be achieved through interbank
borrowing or central bank rediscounting. In France, interbank borrowing

---

[32] "Note sur la liquidation"; "Opinion."

[33] A. Aftalion, L'or et sa Distribution Mondiale (Paris, 1932), p. 99.

[34] Bank of France, Compte Rendu (1930), pp. 6–7. Similarly, the Governor of the Bank,
Emile Moreau, complained to his colleagues on 1 August 1929 that "contrary to certain
information of foreign origin, the Bank of France has done nothing to provoke imports of
yellow metal." Bank of France, "Deliberations du Conseil General," no. 119 (1929).

[35] Others noted that the ratio of currency to bank deposits was continuing to decline over
time, following much the same pattern in France as previously witnessed in other countries.
R. Marjolin, "Structure Monétaire," Revue d'économie politique 53 (1939), 271–90.

[36] Royal Institute of International Affairs, Gold Problem, p. 208.

was discouraged by the banks' hesitation to deal directly with one another, and there existed no intermediaries like the British discount houses to take up this role. Until 1924 the call loan market had relied almost exclusively for collateral on short-term government bills, and the Bank of France's subsequent unwillingness to accept these securities as collateral is said to have further restricted the market's operation.[37] Charles Rist went further, disputing the claim that the Paris market was inflexible in its use of cash reserves. While admitting that the London market may have had an exceptional ability to economize on the banking system's use of cash, he regarded Paris, Berlin, and New York as approximately equal in this regard.[38]

Observers again cited institutional reasons to explain why rediscounting at the central bank failed to provide the banking system a sufficiently elastic supply of cash reserves. They suggested that the great French banks did not like to borrow at the central bank for reasons of tradition and prestige. Moreover, the Bank of France was a major competitor of the joint-stock banks, promoting an adversarial relationship which discouraged direct dealings.[39] The supply of rediscountable bills was thought to have been quite small in comparison with the banking system's demand for cash reserves, implying that, even insofar as the volume of rediscounting was sensitive to changes in the bank rate, a reduction in the central bank's dis-

---

[37] Balogh, "Import of Gold," p. 453. See also V. Ricard, "Le Marché Monétaire et les Changes," *Revue d'économie politique* 53 (1929), 438–70.

[38] Note was also taken in this connection of how the regulations governing French savings banks and, in particular, a law of 6 August 1895 tended to immobilize gold reserves. The large banks in France were prohibited by statute from paying more than 1.5 percent interest on sight deposits. In contrast, the *Caisse Nationale* was permitted to pay 3.75 percent, and the *Caisses Ordinaires* 2.25 to 3.75 percent. This meant that the French savings banks acquired a large share of national savings (see Bouvier, "Monnaie," pp. 703–5). They in turn were required to transmit these deposits to a government office, which invested the funds in government securities or government guaranteed bonds. The crucial point was that up to 10 percent of these deposits were kept as cash at the Bank of France, which in turn was required to back them in gold. It is not clear in fact whether the emphasis placed on this arrangement by contemporaries was justified. Had the savings banks been permitted to keep their own cash reserves, so long as they deposited them with the Bank of France, the implications for gold backing would have been the same. The argument must hinge therefore either on the savings banks being constrained to hold undesirably large cash reserves under the actual arrangement or on their having been unlikely to deposit their cash at the national bank. In fact, the first argument is implausible, since the Treasury maintained only 6 to 7 percent of savings deposits in the form of cash, a lower figure than the cash reserves held by the great banks.

[39] PRO T188/22, "Notes of Meeting with the French Treasury on February 20th and 21st, 1931"; Balogh, "Import of Gold," pp. 452, 454–5; Royal Institute of International Affairs, *Gold Problem*, p. 100.

count rate was still incapable of producing a sizeable change in the supply of liquid funds.[40] Even Leith-Ross noted that discounts by the Bank of France, which oscillated in the range of ff4,500 million to ff7,500 million, were already as large (by British standards) as a share of the total bills of the four leading banks (roughly ff20,000 million), suggesting that opportunities for expanding domestic credit through further discounts were minimal.[41] Balogh's position was that French gold imports and Bank of France discounts rose and fell together, suggesting that in periods of stringency the banking system turned for cash reserves both to its secondary reserves abroad and to the authorities.[42] That the domestic supply of rediscountable bills was small meant that the largest share of reserves necessarily came from abroad. Even if discounts exhibited some elasticity, the banks still "had to have gold," in the words of Hawtrey, "as there was nothing else to fill the gap." [43]

British Treasury officials responded by expressing disbelief that so powerful an institution as the Bank of France was incapable of influencing domestic money market conditions sufficiently to limit gold imports.[44] They thought it implausible, even given French statutes and market conditions, that it was "impossible for the Bank of France at this moment to do anything but sit down and see its gold accumulate." [45] Neither did the French

---

40 Officials of the Bank of France disagreed with this assessment. They noted that the discount rates of the clearing banks moved in step with Bank Rate, that the Bank of France itself had offices nationwide, and that the Bank discounted bills directly for commerce and industry as well as dealing with the banking system. Together these facts rendered its discount rate a powerful instrument. Min. Fin. B32323, "Note relative aux operations sur le marché libre et a la politique de la Banque de France" (note by the Bank of France), 25 October 1932.

41 See PRO T188/22, "The French Gold Imports" (by Frederick Leith-Ross), 3 December 1930; for the French response, see PRO T188/22, "Note for the Minister" (by the French Ministry of Finance), 13 January 1931. Except for one point in 1932, no information seems to be available on the shares of rediscounts and direct discounts in the Bank of France's discount portfolio. J. Bouvier, "The French Banks, Inflation and Economic Crisis, 1919–1939," *Journal of European Economic History* 13 (special issue, 1984), 29–80. At that point, direct discounts accounted for approximately one-third of the total.

42 Balogh, "Import of Gold," p. 455.

43 Royal Institute of International Affairs, *Gold Problem*, p. 100. A related argument was that the permission granted to the Bank of France to purchase *bons* of the *Caisse d'Amortissement* that it had previously placed on the market was of no use in open market operations because the Bank had never in fact sold any of these bonds. Neurisse, *Histoire du Franc*, chapter 11.

44 See the remarks by Otto Niemeyer in Royal Institute of International Affairs, *Gold Problem*, p. 149.

45 Remarks by Brand in Royal Institute, *Gold Problem*, p. 156.

defense on grounds of statutory limitations and underdeveloped markets satisfy the British. To explain gold imports on such grounds was to admit that they resulted from the operation of "a monetary system of organisation [that] is extremely defective and therefore required modification."

In diplomatic correspondence the British suggested measures the French might adopt to remedy these defects. Leith-Ross criticized the Bank of France's inability to take the initiative by expanding note circulation through open market operations. The Bank, he argued, should be empowered through legislation to undertake such intervention. Leith-Ross also suggested that the central bank's capacity to control domestic credit conditions might be further enhanced if other steps were taken to promote the growth of a more active acceptance and discount market in Paris. The French government was urged to promote foreign lending by liberalizing admission requirements for foreign securities on the Paris Bourse and by promoting the flotation of foreign loans on the Paris market.[46] That the British were willing to overlook the obvious danger that such actions would succeed in capturing for Paris a portion of London's international banking business is an indication of the alarm with which they viewed the accumulation of gold in France.[47]

5. The debate over sterilization

Whether actions dictated by the statutes under which the Bank of France operated or by the peculiar structure of the markets in which it functioned could justifiably be labeled sterilization is where debate on substance shades into semantics. According to Balogh, sterilization implied willful action; the term was appropriate only if a central bank deliberately tried to neutralize the domestic impact of a gold inflow.[48] The implication was that French gold imports should not be considered a result of sterilization if they arose from shortcomings of the French banking system or of the gold standard in general. Others defined sterilization more broadly, so that it encompassed gold inflows which resulted from sins of omission or commission taken not just by the central bank but by all branches of government. Otto Nie-

[46] PRO T160 F12317/1-3, "Conversations with France on Financial Relations" (undated).
[47] To the suggestion by Leith-Ross and others that the French might try to build up an international capital market in Paris in order to promote foreign lending, Balogh responded that such measures could scarcely be expected to provide relief from immediate difficulties. See Balogh, "Import of Gold."
[48] Balogh, "Import of Gold," p. 442.

meyer wondered aloud whether the maintenance of a statute requiring sight liabilities as well as notes to be backed in gold was properly considered as sterilization. He seemed to answer in the negative on the grounds that it was very difficult, for reasons of confidence, to change the laws designating assets to be backed. It could not realistically be argued that the French Parliament in practice possessed the discretion to change the backing rule; its failure to do so was not, therefore, deliberate and should not be characterized as sterilization.[49] There was a similar debate on the question of whether behavior constained by statutes prohibiting open market operations was sterilization. Several British observers argued that it was. To Leith-Ross, changing the statutes governing the Bank of France was merely a matter of extending to the Bank "the same powers as all other central banks enjoy."[50] As Hawtrey put it, "There is no obstacle whatever in the way of the French Parliament and the Bank of France between them allowing the acquisition of French Rentes or the increased accumulation of foreign exchange, and of other devices for enabling the note issue of the Bank of France to be maintained at the required level without so much of it being covered by gold."[51] Lloyd agreed, and put the matter bluntly: "no doubt it is true that technically the Bank of France is not in a position to stop the inflow at the present time, but is not the French nation, or the French Government, really *responsible* [emphasis added] in the sense that it could, by altering the statute of the Bank of France, take the necessary measures?"[52]

It is not easy to distinguish partisan opinion of what should be within the power of the French Parliament to change from objective assessment of the alternatives that were politically feasible. Britain and France had very different histories of price and exchange rate stability in the years preceding the gold standard's resurrection. Since the British had no recent experience comparable to France's inflation and exchange rate depreciation in the period up through 1926, they may have underestimated the ease with which the French Parliament could have extended the discretionary powers of the

---

49 Royal Institute of International Affairs, *Gold Problem*, p. 106. Similarly, Hubert Henderson argued that accusations of misconduct by the French should be dismissed on the grounds that altering the statutes governing the Bank of France involved a "fundamental change in a time honored law." PRO T188/28, H.D. Henderson, "International Cooperation and the Gold Standard," 16 October 1931.
50 PRO T188/22, "The French Gold Imports," 3 December 1930.
51 Royal Institute of International Affairs, *Gold Problem*, p. 159.
52 Royal Institute, *Gold Problem*, p. 185.

Bank. Hawtrey, for instance, argued that the laws in question clearly could be changed, since they had been already "thrown to the winds" during the war and as recently as 1926.[53] This ignores the political and psychological repercussions of these previous suspensions of the Bank of France's statutes. The statutory limitations under which the Bank functioned had been put in place precisely in order to prevent a recurrence of inflation. In particular, the prohibitions on open market operations and on advances to the State were designed, by limiting its discretionary powers, to insulate the central bank from pressure to intervene. Not surprisingly, the discussions of the Royal Institute's study group in 1931 suggest that the assumptions of British participants about options open to French authorities were heavily based on British rather than French experience.

6. The role of French policy in the import of gold

This section estimates the contribution of French policy to the volume of gold imports into France in the period 1926–1932. Four of the actions the authorities took or refrained from taking are considered separately. Analyzing these measures separately enables readers to adopt their preferred definition of sterilization and to construct the appropriate measure of its effects. Since many of the effects considered turn out to be small, my strategy will be to bias the estimates upward as a way of constructing upper bounds.

To assess the effects of policy on French gold reserves, I focus upon four hypothetical actions.

(1) Eliminating balances held by the *Caisse d'Amortissement* at the Bank of France either through immediate purchases of debt or by depositing them instead with the credit banks.
(2) Depositing the Treasury's surplus balances with the credit banks rather than the Bank of France.
(3) Initiating open market operations with the objective of purchasing 2 francs' worth of commercial paper for each franc's worth of gold inflow.
(4) Reducing the central bank discount rate to stimulate discounts.

Quantifying the impact of Treasury and central bank policy on the inflow of gold into France requires a model of the French monetary sector. I start by assuming that the French public maintains stocks of both real cash balances, n, and bank deposits, d. Total note circulation, n_t, expressed

[53] PRO T188/28, Hawtrey to Leith-Ross, 26 October 1931.

in real terms is the sum of the cash held by the public, n, and the notes held by the banking system, $n_b (n_t = n + n_b)$. The public's desired stocks of currency and deposits depend on a scale variable, y, which proxies for the level of transactions, and on an opportunity cost variable, R.

$$n = \alpha_1 + \alpha_2 y - \alpha_3 R, \tag{1}$$

$$d = \gamma_1 + \gamma_2 y - \gamma_3 R, \tag{2}$$

where n denotes real cash balances held by the public and d denotes the real value of bank deposits. In the special case where $\alpha_1 = \gamma_1$, $\alpha_2 = \gamma_2$, $\alpha_3 = \gamma_3$, we have the standard money demand function:

$$n + d = 2(\alpha_1 + \alpha_2 y - \alpha_3 R). \tag{3}$$

Next I consider the banking sector's demand for cash reserves. Banks are assumed to equate the marginal costs and benefits of liquidity. The costs depend on the price of liquid assets obtained from other sources, notably the cost of cash obtained through rediscounts at the central bank, while the benefits decline with the rate of return that would accrue were the funds invested in earning assets.

$$n_b = c_0 - c_1 R - c_2 S + c_3 d, \tag{4}$$

where R is the market interest rate (taken here as the same as the loan rate) and S is the central bank discount rate.

Note that n_b has two components: cash obtained by rediscounting eligible paper at the Bank of France, and other cash on hand obtained via customers' deposits. Cash obtained from the Bank of France equals the value of central bank rediscounts, which is taken as a decreasing function of the discount rate and an increasing function of deposits,

$$n_b' = c_0' - c_2 S + c_3' d, \tag{5}$$

while other cash reserves are taken as a decreasing function of the loan rate R and an increasing function of deposits:

$$n_b'' = c_0'' - c_1 R + c_3'' d. \tag{6}$$

Summing (5) and (6) yields (4) given the identities $c_0 = c_0' + c_0''$ and $c_3 = c_3' + c_3''$.

Finally, the banking system is assumed to maintain, in addition to cash reserves, deposits at the central bank (which appear as private deposits in the Bank of France's balance sheet), and investments and loans to the private sector. The two interest rates, R and S, determine the portfolio shares of cash reserves n_b, deposits at the central bank m_b, and loans l_b. Given equation (4), by specifying the demand for either deposits or loans I can use the adding-up constraints to derive the remaining demand function. For instance, assume:

$$m_b = e_0 - e_1 R + e_2 S - e_3 d. \tag{7}$$

From (4) and (7) and the adding-up constraints:

$$l_b = -(c_0 + e_0) + (c_1 + e_1)R + (c_2 - e_2)S + (1 - c_3 - e_3)d, \tag{8}$$

where l_b denotes net loans and investments (net of those rediscounted at the Bank of France).

Variant I: Eliminating the public deposits of the Caisse d'Amortissement

Tables 5.2 and 5.3 illustrate the effects of eliminating the idle balances held by the *Caisse d'Amortissement* at the Bank of France. The *Caisse* was assigned the revenues of the tobacco monopoly and death duties, which it was empowered to use to retire and service debt. However, these funds were not handed over to the *Caisse* until the revenue accounts were audited well after the end of the fiscal year. In the interim, they sat idly, augmenting the value of Treasury deposits at the central bank.[54] Even with assignment of these balances to the debt management fund, the *Caisse* did not promptly apply them to the extinction of debt; in 1929 the working balances of the *Caisse*, also held on deposit at the Bank of France, rose as high as ff14,000 million.

Assume initially that these balances instead had been used for immediate purchases of government debt. This would have brought about an incipient rise in notes in circulation. By assumption, this incipient rise in note circulation is offset by a matching fall in gold reserves if the demand for notes is unchanged. The figures in Tables 5.2 and 5.3 show some moderation in gold inflows, especially in 1929–1931, but only a marginal decline in the Bank of France reserve ratio.

Variant I calculations, which take the fall in *Caisse* deposits and the decline in gold reserves as offsetting, are based on the assumption that currency demand is unaffected. This will be the case if the arguments of

[54] These Treasury deposits and their effects are considered in more detail later.

Table 5.2: *Change in Bank of France gold reserves, 1928–1932*
(in millions of francs)

	Variant I eliminate *Caisse* d'Amortissement deposits	Variant II eliminate treasury deposits	Variant III open market operations	Variant IV discount rate reduction
1928-I	0	94	0	0
1928-II	−3893	−7552	−2209	0
1929	−6139	−6333	−6406	0
1930	−4972	−4773	−12372	0
1931	−7910	−2036	−20988	0
1932	−3024	−633	−34528	0

Table 5.3: *Bank of France reserve ratio, 1928–1932*
(in percentage points)

	Variant I without *Caisse* d'Amortissement deposits	Variant II without treasury deposits	Variant III with open market operations	Variant IV with discount rate reduction
1928-I	8.2	8.0	8.2	8.2
1928-II	35.8	32.5	36.2	39.0
1929	39.9	39.8	36.7	44.4
1930	47.9	48.0	37.1	50.7
1931	52.9	55.6	36.5	56.5
1932	72.6	73.2	41.5	73.3

equations (1) and (4) remain unchanged. y is held constant on the assumption that output and transactions are unaffected by events in financial markets, S is held constant on the assumption that the central bank does not alter its discount rate, and R is held constant on the assumption that interest rates in France are linked to interest rates abroad by open interest parity. The interest parity condition holds if securities denominated in different currencies are perfect substitutes and if capital is perfectly mobile. Were this condition to fail, purchases of debt would tend to reduce domestic interest rates, increasing the demand for money and causing the injection of notes only to be partially offset by the outflow of gold. Were the decline in interest rates to place upward pressure on y, the demand for money would be further augmented. For these reasons the changes in reserves in Tables 5.2 and 5.3 should be viewed as upper bounds.

An alternative assumption is that the balances of the *Caisse* are not used for immediate purchases of debt but are kept on deposit with credit banks instead of at the central bank. In this case, the gold reserves of the Bank of France would again fall by less than the full amount of the decline in public deposits, for the demand for currency by the banking system will rise by n_b/d times the value of the *Caisse*'s deposits. m_b/d times the value of these liabilities are held by the banking system at the central bank, and these public deposits must be counted when calculating the reserve ratio. During the late 1920s, n_b/d fluctuated in the neighborhood of 10%.[55] For the four largest banks, m_b/d averaged approximately 7.5%.[56] On the basis of these figures, the fall in gold reserves should be multiplied by 0.9, and the fall in deposits at the Bank of France by 0.925. Although the adjustment to reserves is small, again the change in the ratio as presented in Table 5.3 should be viewed as an upper bound. Under each of these assumptions, the relatively small changes in gold inflows and the Bank of France's reserve ratio suggest that the practice by the *Caisse* of maintaining idle deposits at the central bank contributed little to flows of gold into France.

Variant II: Eliminating the public deposits of the Treasury

To consider the effects of eliminating the Treasury's public deposits, assume that they were maintained instead at credit banks. Since the banks' demand for cash reserves rises, the fall in public deposits exceeds the decline in gold reserves; and since the credit banks hold a fraction of the new deposits as reserves at the central bank, the rise in private deposits partially offsets the fall in public deposits to be backed. The effects of the transfer of Treasury deposits are similar in magnitude to the effects of the liquidation of *Caisse d'Amortissement* deposits. There is a decline in the Bank of France's gold stocks and in the reserve ratio. However, these effects moderate only very slightly the observed rise in the reserve ratio.

Variant III: Open market operations

To explore the counterfactual that the Bank of France engaged in open market operations, assume that it expanded the note issue by a total of 3 francs for every franc's worth of gold inflow. This is intended to capture the type

---

[55] Balogh, "Import of Gold," p. 447.
[56] See Loriot, "Les Banques," *Revue d'économie politique* 44 (1930), 538–56.

of intervention rule advanced by the Bank of France's British critics in light of the Bank's 35% reserve ratio.

With the assumption of open interest parity holding interest rates unchanged, the effects of this experiment are straightforward. With domestic and foreign bonds perfect substitutes and capital perfectly mobile, the fall in domestic debt in private sector portfolios resulting from open market purchases is simply offset by a corresponding increase in holdings of foreign debt. One franc of gold is needed on the margin to finance an increase in the demand for currency of three francs, so the net inflow of gold declines substantially. The change in cumulated gold inflows is presented in Table 5.2. Open market purchases in the ratio of three to one largely eliminate the observed rise in the Bank of France's reserve ratio between 1928 and 1932, as shown in Table 5.3. The exceptional increase in the reserve ratio in 1932 reflects the fall in sight liabilities which results from the downturn in economic activity associated with the onset of the Great Depression.

Again, the figures in the tables should be viewed as upper bounds. If interest parity fails to hold, open market purchases of bonds will tend to reduce interest rates, increasing the demand for money and resulting in a smaller reduction in gold stocks than indicated in the table.

Variant IV: Discount rate reduction

Finally, the effects of a two-percentage-point reduction in the Bank of France's discount rate are analyzed. Since for much of the period Bank Rate was below 3%, it makes little sense to consider large reductions, but I consider a perhaps implausibly large two-point reduction so as to again estimate an upper bound. Given the assumption of constant (semi)elasticities, the reader can assess the effects of other reductions by altering the change in reserves proportionately.

The discount rate affects the Bank of France's reserve position through its impact on the credit banks' demand for cash reserves (c_2 in equation (4)) and on the banks' deposits at the Bank of France (e_2 in equation (7)). Changes in the discount rate are also assumed to affect the share of loans in the asset portfolios of the banks, but this does not affect the calculations.

In order to calibrate c_2, I consider econometric evidence on the sensitivity of Bank of France discounts to changes in its discount rate. That in the appendix suggests that the interest semielasticity of demand for discounts was on the order of 0.25 – in other words, that a one-point reduction in the discount rate increases the value of discounts by one-quarter of 1%. Therefore, I assume that the two-point reduction in the discount rate increases rediscounts by 0.50% of the values actually observed. To construct an upper bound on the change in the reserve ratio, I assume that all Bank of France discounts were rediscounts.

Estimates in the appendix suggest also that the interest semielasticity of demand for private deposits is on the order of 0.27 – in other words, that a one-point increase in the discount rate increases the value of private deposits at the Bank of France by slightly more than one-quarter of 1%. I assume that the two-point reduction in the discount rate reduces the value of private deposits by 0.54% of the value actually observed. Note that the two effects of the discount rate on the reserve ratio work in opposite directions.

Since the change in the discount rate does not affect the public's demand for notes or deposits and alters the banking system's demand for currency in exactly the amount supplied by the Bank of France, there is no change in gold reserves. By reducing private deposits and increasing the circulation of notes outside the central bank, two components of the denominator of the reserve ratio are changed. However, the rise in liabilities due to increased rediscounting is both small and offset by the fall in liabilities due to the decline in public deposits. Hence the final column of Table 5.3 is virtually undistinguishable from the actual values in Table 5.1. These calculations therefore support the position that while the Bank of France's discount rate influenced the volume of rediscounts, that volume was insufficient to allow bank rate policy to exercise an economically important influence over the inflows of gold.

In summary, open market operations emerge as the only instrument at the command of the French Treasury or central bank capable of significantly moderating the rise in the Bank of France's reserve ratio. Treasury deposits, the idle reserves of the *Caisse d'Amortissement,* and the level of the discount rate, while all influencing the reserve ratio in the direction suggested by France's British critics, must be relegated to the status of second-order effects. Whether accusations of sterilization were justified is simply a question of whether it is appropriate to attach the term to the French Parliament's refusal to pass legislation permitting open market operations.

Clearly, the calculations of this section all are based on restrictive assumptions. Most fundamental is the assumption that market interest rates and economic activity are exogenous to monetary policy. In a more general model in which domestic and foreign assets were imperfect substitutes or capital was imperfectly mobile internationally, an expansionary monetary initiative would put downward pressure on domestic interest rates, potentially raising the level of domestic production. Significantly, however, these extensions only reinforce the conclusions. Had any of the hypothetical measures described not only expanded note circulation but also reduced market interest rates and increased output, the demand for money would have risen by some fraction of the increase in supply. Any increased currency demand by the public would have had to be met by retaining a portion of the gold reserves which would have otherwise flowed abroad. This reinforces the presumption that the preceding calculations are upper bound estimates, and that only open market operations were capable of making a noticeable dent in the Bank of France's reserve ratio.

7. Conclusion

Of the various explanations proffered by contemporaries for the inter-war gold standard's unsatisfactory performance, none has so permeated the historical literature as the claim that the authorities in France and other surplus countries sterilized inflows of gold. This chapter has reconsidered the debate over sterilization by France. Of the various channels through which France ostensibly influenced gold inflows – Treasury deposits, *Caisse d'Amortissement* reserves, the Bank of France's rediscount policy, and the absence of open market operations – only the last survives scrutiny in the sense of emerging as an economically important determinant of the central bank reserve ratio. The debate over French sterilization may therefore be recast as why expansionary open market operations did not take place. The proximate cause is that the Bank of France was precluded from conducting open market purchases by the statutes under which it operated. To understand why those statutes had been adopted, it is necessary to appreciate the impact on public sentiment and policymakers' attitudes of the traumatic inflationary experience of the early 1920s. Since a necessary if insufficient condition for the initiation of open market operations would have been passage of enabling legislation by the French Parliament, whether the French can be accused of inducing gold inflows in the sense that they failed to exercise their discretionary power to prevent them hinges on the question of whether it was within the power of the authorities to amend the statutes by which the central bank was constrained. Again, forming a judgment on this question requires an appreciation of the traumatic inflationary experience of the previous decade.

In other contexts, commentators have appreciated how the structure and performance of the interwar gold standard was affected by historical experience. Britain's insistence on restoring sterling to parity against the dollar at $4.86 in 1925 is a favorite example of how impressions and presumptions inherited from the prewar era influenced international monetary relations in the 1920s. France's recent economic history also had implications for the operation of the international monetary system, but in this case the implications were of a different nature. France's painful experience with inflation in the early 1920s was directly responsible for the adoption of the stringent regulations which prevented the central bank from intervening to prevent the accumulation of gold. The unwillingness of policymakers to modify those regulations must be similarly attributed to the impact on attitudes of that inflationary episode. This is neither a justification for French policy nor an exception to the view that the international monetary system would have functioned more smoothly had that policy been modified. The point is rather that viewing French attitudes in their historical context sheds more light on the actions of policymakers than do allegations of obstinacy or of failure to understand the workings of the international monetary system.

Appendix

This appendix presents estimates of the discount market elasticities upon which calculations in the text are based. The elasticities of discounts and private deposits at the Bank of France with respect to the discount rate are derived by estimating a three-equation system determining the value of discounts, private deposits, and the discount rate. I hypothesize that the log of discounts is a (negative) function of the discount rate S and a positive function of the volume of activity y.

$$DISCOUNTS = a_0 + a_1 S + a_2 y. \tag{9}$$

The contemporaneous level of activity is by assumption exogenous to the discount rate and the value of discounts. To admit the possibility that the Bank of France responded to events in the discount market by changing its discount rate, I also specify a reaction function for the central bank. I hypothesize that the discount rate chosen by the authorities depends on the value of discounts and on three exogenous or predetermined variables: the market interest rate (R), the lagged percentage change in the authori-

Table 5.A: *The discount rate and the value of discounts, 1927I–1936III: full-information maximum-likelihood estimates*

	a_0	a_1	a_2	b_0	b_1	b_2	b_3	b_4	c_0	c_1	c_2	c_3	Standard errors of regression
(i)	2.527 (0.26)	−0.251 (0.03)	0.002 (0.002)	−47.59 (6.14)	0.590 (0.73)	24.080 (1.72)	4.122 (1.18)	0.349 (11.22)	9.000 (1.15)	−0.010 (0.02)	0.010 (0.02)	0.274 (0.12)	0.454 10.248 0.602
(ii)	2.531 (0.25)	−0.250 (0.03)	−0.002 (0.002)	−47.59 (5.94)	0.595 (0.72)	24.094 (1.70)	4.108 (1.14)	0.790 (10.14)	9.000 (1.16)	−0.010 (0.02)	0.010 (0.02)	0.274 (0.12)	0.454 10.253 0.602
(iii)	2.519 (0.25)	−0.250 (0.03)	−0.002 (0.002)	−47.48 (5.92)	0.583 (0.71)	24.040 (1.70)	4.105 (1.11)		9.000 (1.14)	−0.010 (0.02)	0.010 (0.02)	0.274 (0.12)	0.453 10.229 0.602

Notes: Variables are defined in the appendix. Standard errors of coefficient estimates are in parentheses. The first standard error of the regression is for the equation where discounts is the dependent variable, the second for the equation where the discount rate is the dependent variable, and the third for the equation where private deposits at the Bank of France is the dependent variable. Equations (i) and (ii) differ according to the definition of foreign reserves: (i) includes only gold, while (ii) includes the sum of gold and foreign exchange.

ties' international reserves ($\%\Delta RESERVES_{-1}$), and the lagged discount rate S_{-1}.

$$S = b_0 + b_1 R + b_2 DISCOUNTS + b_3 S_{-1} + b_4 \%\Delta RESERVES_{-1}. \qquad (10)$$

I assume that, over the period when the franc was pegged, the market interest rate is given by world market conditions; in other words, open interest parity holds. If the authorities wish to keep the discount rate in touch with market rates, b_1 will be positive. If they wish to avoid large changes in the discount rate, b_3 will be positive. If they raise the discount rate in response to reserve losses, b_4 will be negative.

The log of private deposits at the Bank of France is assumed to be a function of the discount-rate–market-rate differential and current and lagged values of activity:

$$DEPOSITS = c_0 + c_1 y + c_2 y_{-1} + c_3 (S - R), \qquad (11)$$

where I anticipate $c_3 > 0$.

The discount rate, the value of discounts, and the change in reserves are taken from Bank of France (various issues). Gold and foreign exchange held by the Bank of France are valued at first-half 1928 prices in order to avoid the appearance of a fivefold increase in reserves at the time of de jure stabilization. For the market interest rate I use the call loan or "contango" rate, while as a proxy for activity I use the index of industrial production. Both series are taken from Tinbergen (1934) and Methorst (1938).

The three equations are estimated using full-information maximum-likelihood on quarterly average data from 1927I, the first quarter the franc was pegged, through 1936III, at the end of which it was devalued. There are 39 observations. Since *DISCOUNTS* and *DEPOSITS* are measured as natural logarithms throughout, a_1 and c_3 can be interpreted as semielasticities. The first two sets of estimates reported in Table 5.A differ by the definition of reserves. In the first set only gold reserves are included, while in the second set gold and foreign exchange are summed. In the third set $\%\Delta RESERVES_{-1}$ is omitted.

Results appear in Table 5.A. The critical parameters, a_1 and c_3, are both reasonably well estimated. The point estimates of a_1 are all in the neighborhood of -0.25, with standard errors of approximately 0.03. The value of discounts does not appear to be strongly related to the level of the activity once the level of the discount rate is taken into account. In the Bank of France reaction function, the discount rate depends positively on the market interest rate and on its own lagged value and positively on the value of discounts. The sign of a_2 appears to depend on the way in which the reserves variable is defined. The value of private deposits at the Bank of France, as anticipated, is a positive function of the discount-rate–call-rate differential (with point estimates in the range of 0.275 and standard errors of approximately 0.12) but is only weakly related to the level of activity.

6. International policy coordination in historical perspective: a view from the interwar years

Measures of currency reform will be facilitated if the practice of continuous cooperation among central banks of issue, or banks regulating credit policy in the several countries can be developed. Such cooperation of central banks, not necessarily confined to Europe, would provide opportunities of coordinating their policy, without hampering the freedom of the several banks.

(From Resolution 3 of the Report of the Financial Commission of the Genoa Conference, 1922.)

In the days of the gold standard, it is sometimes said, international policy coordination was a moot point.[1] Popular accounts based more on caricature than on careful historical analysis portray the gold standard as a remarkably efficient mechanism for coordinating the actions of national authorities. Policies were so easily reconciled, it is argued, because those responsible for their formulation, regardless of nationality, shared a belief in balanced budgets and a common overriding objective: pegging the domestic currency price of gold. When central banks intervened in financial markets, it

This paper was written during visits to Stanford University and INSEE. I am grateful to Paul David and Jacques Melitz for helpful discussions, and to the French Ministry of Foreign Affairs, the French Ministry of Finance, and the Controller of H.M. Stationery Office for permission to refer to the Public Records. The French Ministry of External Affairs provided financial support.

[1] For example, according to J.W. Beyen, *Money in a Maelstrom* (London, 1949), 'Under a fully automatic standard,' by which he means the prewar gold standard, 'the need for consultation between central banks was, of course, limited.' He tells a story which illustrates central bankers' attitudes toward policy coordination and consultation. It seems to have been the tradition at the Netherlands Bank for the President and the Directors to personally count the bank notes withdrawn from circulation at a meeting held directly after lunch. One day in 1912 or 1913 two Directors of the Reichsbank paid a visit to Amsterdam, and the President of the Bank had the novel idea of taking them to lunch. The conversation was 'highly interesting,' and the President arrived at the bank note meeting fifteen minutes late with what he thought was an adequate excuse. The oldest of the Directors was unappeased and commented, 'Your work is here, not in coffeehouses.'

is suggested, they did so mechanically, obeying 'rules of the game' which dictated that they only reinforce the impact on domestic money and credit markets of balance of payments conditions. For example, a central bank losing reserves would raise its discount rate while the central bank gaining reserves would lower its discount rate, thereby reinforcing one another's efforts to restore external balance. Hence monetary policy under the gold standard is a favorite example of those who argue that international policy coordination is most readily achieved under a rules-based regime rather than one that depends on discretion.

This naive vision of the days of the gold standard as a simpler, more harmonious era is at best partial and at worst misleading. The very actions of central banks suggest that their objectives were not in fact so easily reconciled by the operation of gold standard constraints. Discount rates tended to move together, not inversely as the 'rules of the game' would suggest.[2] Central banks sterilized international gold flows more often than they intervened to reinforce their impact on domestic markets.[3] These and other actions resemble the outcome of a noncooperative game, in which the participants act to neutralize rather than accommodate the efforts of their counterparts. Yet on occasion central banks and governments managed to achieve cooperative solutions to their problems, such as when they negotiated swap arrangements, earmarked gold, or extended international loans.[4] Both central banks and governments clearly recognized their interdependence, if they did not always succeed in coordinating their actions.

Still, it is fair to say that the interwar period opened the modern era of interdependence. In the 1920s questions of policy coordination and central bank cooperation acquired a new tone of urgency. In part this reflected greater opportunities for coordinating policies in a world with a Bank for International Settlements, an international telegraph, and a trans-Atlantic

---

2 Of course, parallel movements in discount rates could be consistent with the rules of the game if all of the countries considered are either gaining or losing gold to some other country not included in the discount rate comparison. See the discussions in Bloomfield, *Monetary Policy;* O. Morgenstern, *International Financial Transactions and Business Cycles* (Princeton, 1959); and Triffin, "Evolution of the International System."

3 For the period of the classical gold standard (1880–1914), Bloomfield calculates that central banks complied with the rules of the game only 34 percent of the time. Even the Bank of England, thought to be invested with special responsibility for managing the system, adhered to the rules only 47 percent of the time. Bloomfield, *Monetary Policy.*

4 For example, see the discussions of Bank of England–Bank of France loans in J.A. Clapham, *The Bank of England* (Cambridge, 1941), Vol. 2, and R.S. Sayers, *Bank of England Operations 1890–1914* (London, 1936), chapter 5.

telephone.[5] In part it reflected the higher costs of ignoring interdependence in a world of rapid communication, integrated markets, and volatile capital flows. Above all it reflected the widening scope for conflict as governments attached growing importance to domestic economic objectives and put less weight on balance of payments targets.

The interwar period provides examples of various forms of successful collaboration. The League of Nations provided stabilization loans to countries experiencing hyperinflation in return for their accession to protocols which precluded their central banks from monetizing budget deficits and committed them to return to gold. International conferences held at Brussels in 1920 and Genoa in 1922 laid the basis for reconstructing the international monetary system. The United States saw Britain's return to gold as the linchpin upon which the gold standard's resurrection depended, and it provided credits of $300 million to facilitate Britain's restoration of the prewar sterling parity.[6] These efforts were successful in reconstructing the international system: once its renewal had been signaled by Britain's return to gold, some fifty nations joined the United States and the United Kingdom as participants in the interwar gold standard.

Yet the interwar period provides equally dramatic illustrations of failures of cooperation and their costs. The brief duration and early demise of the interwar gold standard is taken to indicate the inability of major participants to effectively coordinate their actions. A prime example is the failure of the countries at the center to harmonize their choice of parities. The important cases are Great Britain, where overvaluation of sterling was associated with unprecedented levels of unemployment and depression in the export trades; and France, where undervaluation of the franc was associated with sustained economic growth and until 1931 insulation from the worst effects

---

[5] The trans-Atlantic telephone was still used sparingly between the wars. The 1936 interchange between Morgenthau and Cochran reported by Clarke suggests that one reason was that it was difficult to hear. S.V.O. Clarke, "Exchange-Rate Stabilization in the Mid-1930's: Negotiating the Tripartite Agreement," *Princeton Studies in International Finance* no. 41 (1977).

[6] Moggridge, *British Monetary Policy*, chapter 3. Thus, for example, in November 1921 the three Scandinavian central banks informed the Bank of England that, however desirous they were of returning to gold, they felt unable to commit to a parity against gold and the dollar unless the UK did so first. The Americans were aware of the problem, since Montagu Norman immediately sent a copy of the confidential Scandinavian memorandum to Benjamin Strong, Governor of the Federal Reserve Bank of New York. It is not surprising, then, that New York saw Britain's return to gold as a joint operation. H. Clay, *Lord Norman* (London, 1957), pp. 141–2.

of the Great Depression. One corollary of this competitive imbalance was an uneven international distribution of gold. Nations such as the United States and France whose international competitive positions were relatively strong acquired and retained a large portion of the world's monetary gold, leaving others such as Britain to defend the convertibility of their currencies on the basis of slender reserves. Another indication of this inability to coordinate policies was the widespread failure to play by the rules of the gold standard game; instead central banks sterilized international reserve flows and hesitated to adjust their discount rates in response to external pressures.

This chapter takes a new look at the financial history of the interwar period to see what light this experience sheds on current concerns over international policy coordination. After a review of the literature and the historical preconditions, it tells a story in three parts. The first part examines the role for policy coordination as envisaged by contemporaries at the start of the period. It takes as a case study the Genoa Economic and Financial Conference of 1922. I will argue that the advantages of policy coordination were in fact well understood in the twenties but that political disagreements impeded efforts to establish a mechanism for cooperative action. Instead, policymakers ultimately pursued noncooperative strategies within the framework of the international gold standard.

The second part considers the effects of noncooperative behavior once the gold standard was again in operation. Identifying these effects requires an explicit model. Yet the idea of strategic behavior by national authorities is wholly incompatible with standard models of the gold standard's operation. The analysis therefore requires the development of an alternative model of the interwar gold standard. While the model developed below bears little resemblance to previous frameworks used to analyze gold standard adjustment, it not only indicates clearly the advantages of coordinated action but suggests why cooperative solutions proved so difficult to achieve.

The final part concerns the question of what the principal participants learned from their pursuit of noncooperative strategies. The lessons of the interwar gold standard as they were understood by contemporaries found reflection in the next attempt to reconstruct the international monetary order: the Tripartite Monetary Agreement concluded by Britain, France, and the United States in the autumn of 1936.[7] The terms of the Tripartite Agree-

---

[7] A comprehensive analysis would consider also the World Economic Conference held in London in 1933. See D. Traynor, *International Monetary and Financial Conferences in the Interwar Period* (Washington DC, 1949).

ment were remarkably similar to the Genoa Resolutions of 1922. Where they differed was in the absence of favorable references to fixed parities and to the gold-exchange standard. They differed as well by more tightly circumscribing the range of issues subject to collaboration. This along with the decline of political obstacles to cooperation permitted the noble sentiments of the Tripartite Agreement to be implemented. Thus, the history of international financial collaboration in the interwar period sheds light not only on the rationale for policy coordination but also on the circumstances conducive to its practice.

1. Leadership and cooperation under a gold standard regime

In theoretical treatments of the gold standard's operation, there is no scope for policy coordination. The adjustment process works automatically, affecting surplus and deficit countries alike. The price-specie-flow variant of the adjustment mechanism emphasizes the role of relative prices in restoring external balance. A gold outflow leads to monetary deflation and falling prices until the international competitiveness of the goods produced by the deficit country is enhanced sufficiently to restore equilibrium to the external accounts. The monetary variant of the adjustment mechanism stresses the role of wealth and real balance effects. A gold outflow reduces absorption through the real balance effect on consumption until the equality of income and expenditure is restored. In each case, the surplus country is affected symmetrically. Beyond standing ready to buy and sell gold at the official price, the only role for central banks is to mechanically reinforce the impact on domestic money and credit markets of incipient gold flows.

Strikingly, these theoretical treatments bear little resemblance to historical analyses of the gold standard's operation either at the end of the 19th century or between the wars. Where theoretical models describe central banks as mechanically reinforcing one another's actions, historical accounts emphasize instead the potential for conflict between national authorities and their strategic interaction. Yet in none of these accounts is the scope for conflict adequately defined, leaving unclear the advantages of leadership and cooperation.

Historical descriptions of the classical gold standard place great weight on asymmetries in the system's operation. Great Britain in particular is seen as possessing unrivaled abilities to manipulate the process of adjustment. Britain's market power is attributed to her position as the world's foremost trading and lending nation. British exports, which had already quadrupled between 1800 and 1850, increased eightfold between 1850 and 1913, and on the eve of the first World War Britain accounted for 14 percent of world exports, a figure far exceeding her share of world production or income. The world's principal organized commodity markets all were centered in England. Not the least of these was the London gold market, which regularly received the bulk of South Africa's gold production. In addition, Britain had no close competitor as the world's preeminent international lender. By 1913, British overseas investments amounted to nearly 45 percent of the external investments of the major creditor countries of the West. Britain's annual capital export was nearly five times that of France, her nearest rival. Never before or since have a nation's overseas investments been such a large share of national income.[8]

Britain's commercial and financial preeminence had profound implications for the international role of sterling, which had implications in turn for the operation of the adjustment mechanism. Sterling was the world's leading vehicle currency in international transactions. Trade that neither touched British shores nor passed through the hands of British merchants overseas might nonetheless be invoiced in sterling. Transactions the world over were settled with the transfer of sterling balances between foreign accounts maintained in London. Securities denominated in sterling were the most popular form of international reserves with which central banks might supplement their stocks of gold.[9]

Under these circumstances, it is argued, the Bank of England exercised powerful leverage over international flows of commodities, capital, and gold – leverage it could employ to manipulate the process of adjustment by which external balance was restored. Changes in Bank Rate (the rate charged by the Bank of England for loans to discount houses and other dealers in Treasury and commercial bills) exerted an influence not shared by foreign discount rates and to a large extent determined credit conditions not merely at home but abroad.[10] A rise in Bank Rate is typically thought to

---

[8] United Nations, *International Capital Movements During the Interwar Period* (New York, 1949), p. 2. International comparisons are provided by M. Edelstein, *Overseas Investment in the Age of High Imperialism* (New York, 1981).

[9] On the composition of international reserves before 1914, see P. Lindert, "Key Currencies and Gold, 1900–1913," *Princeton Studies in International Finance* no. 24 (1969).

[10] A typical statement of this conventional wisdom can be found in H. Cleveland, "The International Monetary System in the Interwar Period," in B. Rowland (ed.), *Balance of Power or Hegemony: The Interwar Monetary System* (New York, 1976), p. 17. As Keynes nostalgically described the prewar system in 1930: "In the latter half of the 19th century,

have forced up the required rate of return on Treasury and commercial bills, and by rendering these assets more attractive increased the opportunity cost to the banking sector of extending loans and overdrafts to borrowers. Given the share of sterling loans and advances in international markets for short-term capital, rates of return on foreign-currency-denominated assets that were substitutes for sterling were forced up as well. Moreover, because the world's most important gold market also was located in London, the Bank of England by altering the cost and availability of short-term credit directly influenced the tendency of nonresidents to purchase and ship abroad gold newly delivered to market.

To paraphrase Walter Bagehot's famous aphorism, raising Bank Rate to a sufficiently high level would succeed in drawing gold from the moon. This leverage over capital flows followed from the fact that no foreign power could match the Bank of England's influence in international financial markets. The United States, without even a central bank, lacked the resources and the expertise to rival Britain in the market. The Bank of France's sphere of influence was limited to Russia and France's colonial possessions. Foreign authorities possessed no feasible alternative but to respond to Bank of England initiatives, as the British understood. Hence, the Bank of England could anticipate with considerable accuracy the response of foreign authorities to a change in Bank Rate in London, and it could frame its policy accordingly. To the Deputy Governor of the Bank of England Keynes described the reaction of foreign governments in the following way: 'In prewar days it used to be maintained – I think truly – that to a large extent we led the world; that is to say, if we reduced Bank Rate it probably brought about a corresponding reduction in the rates in other countries.'[11] As he framed the argument when helping to draft the report of the Macmillan Committee, Britain could 'by the operation of her Bank Rate almost immediately adjust her reserve position. Other countries had, therefore, in the main, to adjust their conditions to hers.'[12]

There is little agreement on the costs and benefits of the Bank of England's exercise of leadership. The benign view of the prewar arrangement

the influence of London on credit conditions throughout the world was so predominant that the Bank of England could almost have claimed to be the conductor of the international orchestra. By modifying the terms on which she was prepared to lend. . .she could to a large extent determine the credit conditions prevailing elsewhere." Keynes, *Treatise*, vol. 2, pp. 306–7.

11 Macmillan Committee evidence of Sir Ernest Harvey, Question 7515, 2 July 1930, reprinted in Sayers, *Bank of England, 1891–1944*, Vol. 3, p. 205.

12 Committee on Finance and Industry, *Report*, p. 125.

is that it operated to the benefit of both the leader and her followers by permitting the participants in the gold standard system to economize in their use of gold. The Bank of England could maintain a slender gold reserve because she had the power to reverse a gold outflow through unilateral initiative. Other central banks, such as those of France, Germany, Austria-Hungary, and Russia, had less leverage over financial flows and were therefore forced to hold larger reserves in order to accommodate wider swings in their reserve positions. But due to the Bank of England's capacity to operate with relatively slender reserves, the gold backing of the world's monetary base could be efficiently reduced. Since the Bank of England's leverage over international capital flows erased any lingering doubts about the convertibility of sterling, other countries were encouraged to supplement their holdings of gold with this key currency, further augmenting international reserves to the benefit of all concerned.

A less sanguine view is that through her exercise of market power Britain was capable of shifting the burden of adjustment abroad. Triffin has argued that, due to London's singular importance as a source of credit for financing international transactions in foodstuffs and raw materials, Britain through the impact of Bank Rate overseas was more than compensated for the economic costs of stringent credit conditions.[13] The argument is that a temporary credit stringency swung the terms of trade in Britain's favor by increasing the cost to foreign producers of carrying stocks of primary products. Given the higher cost of holding inventories, stocks of foodstuffs and raw materials were dumped onto world markets, reducing the cost of British imports. Obviously, carrying costs were important as well to British producers of manufactured exports, who had the same incentive as producers of primary commodities to liquidate stocks in the face of tighter credit conditions. Assuming however that the market for primary products was characterized by exceptionally low price elasticities of demand, Britain's international terms of trade would still have improved on balance.[14]

---

[13] See especially R. Triffin, "The Myth and Realities of the So-Called Gold Standard," in B. Eichengreen (ed.), *The Gold Standard in Theory and History* (London, 1985), pp. 121–40. Also, see the discussion in A.G. Ford, *The Gold Standard, 1880–1914: Britain and Argentina* (Oxford, 1962).

[14] It has proven difficult to extract from the historical record convincing evidence in support of this theory. Attempts to plot the United Kingdom's terms of trade against levels or first differences in Bank Rate have generally proven inconclusive. See Moggridge, *British Monetary Policy*, pp. 12–13; P. Kenen, *British Monetary Policy and the Balance of Payments* (Cambridge, MA, 1960), p. 60; and Lindert, "Key Currencies," p. 44. Moreover,

By the interwar period, it is frequently suggested, circumstances had been transformed. Britain no longer possessed unparalleled influence over the international adjustment mechanism. Other nations had acquired sufficient leverage to formulate if not independent then at least distinctive national policies, leaving the Bank of England in no better position than its rivals to ignore developments abroad. In particular, the interwar period has been characterized as the era when London declined to the benefit of New York.[15] The war and its aftermath had transformed the United States from a net debtor to a net creditor, and she suddenly found herself in possession of a large share of the world's monetary gold. When Britain returned to gold in 1925, U.S. gold reserves were roughly six times those of the Bank of England. The British government owed the United States $4.7 billion in war debts, although their ultimate magnitude and the schedule by which they might be repaid remained very much in doubt. Moreover, Washington was newly equipped with a Federal Reserve Board and New York with a Federal Reserve Bank to direct and carry out financial market intervention.

Through the first part of the twenties New York surpassed London as a source of funds invested abroad. The UK's share of world export value declined from 14 percent in 1913 to barely 12 percent in 1925 and little more than 11 percent in 1928. Before the war, Britain had consistently run current account surpluses; in the century ending in 1913 there had been but two years of deficit. The situation was different between the wars; in the short span from 1925 to 1931 there were already two years of current account deficit.[16] Bankers and merchants, finding themselves to be dealing with both financial centers and running down the balances on sterling accounts maintained in London, increasingly held diversified portfolios of the two key currencies.

The British position was not eased by concurrent developments in France. Unlike Britain, France's share of world trade was stable after 1913. Following de facto stabilization in 1926 at a rate which undervalued the franc,

a number of observers of the London money market have argued that the volume of commercial bills discounted to finance inventory carrying costs was insensitive to interest rate movements: Moggridge, *British Monetary Policy;* Brown, *International Gold Standard.* Hence I make no attempt to incorporate this potential asymmetry into the model I develop below.

15 F. Costigliola, "Anglo-American Financial Rivalry in the 1920s," *Journal of Economic History* 37 (1977), 914 and *passim;* see also C. Parrini, *Heir to Empire: United States Economic Diplomacy, 1916–1923* (Pittsburgh, 1969).

16 Trade statistics can be found in A. Loveday, *Britain and World Trade* (London, 1931), p. 153. Current account estimates are by the Bank of England from Sayers, *Bank of England, 1891–1944,* Vol. 3, pp. 312–13.

France's external position remained strong until Britain's devaluation in 1931. In 1928, when de jure convertibility of the franc was restored, the Bank of France's holdings of liquid sterling assets roughly matched in value the Bank of England's entire gold reserve. Over the next four years, the Bank of France engaged in a persistent effort to convert these balances into gold as part of a conscious policy of elevating Paris to the stature of a first-rank financial center.[17]

The British authorities recognized their heightened interdependence with foreign nations. In particular, the Bank of England found it impossible to neglect the reaction of foreign central banks to a prospective change in Bank Rate. Were the Bank of England to disregard foreign reactions when setting its discount rate, it would 'render itself liable to be flooded with, or depleted of, gold, as the case may be.' As high an official as the Deputy Governor of the Bank of England admitted that 'such leadership as we possessed has certainly been affected by the position which America has gained.'[18]

While policymakers clearly recognized their heightened interdependence, the implications of this recognition remain somewhat unclear. One literature attempts to document the stimulus this recognition of interdependence provided for cooperative action. For example, Clarke (1967) describes instances where central banks extended to one another routine clearing services, shared privileged information, and arranged international stabilization loans. Another literature emphasizes the inability of policymakers to coordinate their actions despite this recognition of interdependence. Thus, Viner (1932, p. 28) and Gayer (1937, p. 29) describe London, Paris, and New York as having worked at 'cross-purposes.' Yet it is not easy to extract from their analyses a sense of how working at cross-purposes affected the operation of the monetary system. In part this is due to the tendency of these authors to argue by analogy rather than specifying the economic model they have in mind. Nevin (1955, p. 12) is typical of this mode when, likening the international monetary system to an automobile, he characterizes Britain and the United States as 'two quite excellent drivers . . . perpetually fighting to gain control of the vehicle.' A system influenced by the actions of two financial centers, like a car with two drivers, will func-

---

17 J. Bouvier, "A Propos de la Stratégie D'Encaisse (or et devises) de la Banque de France de 1928 à 1932," unpublished, University of Paris (1981), pp. 5–6.

18 J.M. Keynes, *Essays in Persuasion* (Cambridge, 1931); Macmillan Committee evidence of Sir Ernest Harvey, Question 7515, 2 July 1930, reprinted in Sayers, *Bank of England, 1891–1944*, Vol. 3, p. 205.

tion only if those centers are capable of cooperating and acting consistently. But, he goes on, 'in the real world, this seldom happens, and the existence of more than one centre with powers of control leads to the existence of more than one policy.' What we would like to know is whether the presence of two chauffeurs causes the car to be driven too fast, too slowly, or too erratically, and what the implications of the chauffeurs' behavior are for the welfare of the passengers.

Arguments by analogy, however appealing, provide no answer to these questions. The historian's instinct is to turn to the documents for guidance. The economist's is to construct a model. We consider these approaches in turn.

2. The Genoa Conference of 1922 and the role for cooperation

When the Genoa Economic and Financial Conference convened in April 1922, European exchange and trade relations were in disarray. Physical devastation in the main theaters of the war created persistent excess demands for foodstuffs and raw materials, particularly in Central and Eastern Europe. Capital goods imports were needed to replace plant and equipment destroyed in the course of the war. Yet the nations of Continental Europe possessed limited resources out of which to finance the required imports. Industrial and agricultural production remained well below 1913 levels.[19] The United States curtailed and quickly eliminated official lending to its European allies, insisted on prompt repayment of its war loans, and constrained Europe's capacity to earn foreign exchange by sharply raising tariff rates. Europe therefore turned to deficit spending to finance economic reconstruction.[20] Some such as the French proceeded on the premise that Reparations payments would eventually permit any new debt to be retired and prewar monetary arrangements to be restored. Others such as the Germans were preoccupied almost entirely by the immediate problem of reconstruction. By the summer of 1920 the mark had already begun its descent; the franc, in contrast, fluctuated uneasily in response to new information about prospects for Reparations.

---

[19] League of Nations, *Course and Phases of the World Economic Depression* (Geneva, 1931), p. 17; I. Svennilson, *Growth and Stagnation in the European Economy* (Geneva, 1954), pp. 233–46.

[20] H.G. Moulton and L. Pasvolsky, *War Debts and World Prosperity* (Washington DC, 1932), p. 431.

In Western Europe and the United States, the Armistice had been followed by a sudden and dramatic boom. Consumers finally were permitted to vent demands that had been pent up during the war, and producers took the opportunity to replenish their stocks. In Britain the pressure of demand led to an inflation of prices unprecedented in peacetime. Employment expanded rapidly, and wages rose in response. In light of these inflationary pressures, the Bank of England raised its discount rate in November 1919 and April 1920. Almost simultaneously, industrial production turned down, and unemployment among trade union members rose from 1.4 to 16.7 percent within a year. Wholesale prices fell by nearly 50 percent between the spring of 1920 and the beginning of 1922. In France wholesale prices turned down in May, falling by 41 percent within a year, while the index of industrial production fell by 8 percent between 1920 and 1921. In the United States fluctuations in industrial production, though not as pronounced as in Britain, followed basically the same pattern, while wholesale prices fell by 46 percent in the 10 months following their May 1920 peak.[21]

As in the 1970s, financial instability impeded efforts to liberalize international trade. Since the major belligerents had imposed trade controls in the course of the war, they had in place the administrative machinery needed to administer import licensing and quota schemes. While some such as Britain rapidly moved to dismantle wartime controls, others such as France, which initially emulated the British example, turned back to tariff protection once their currencies began to depreciate. Trade with Central Europe was further depressed by the slow recovery of these economies. Together with the embargo on Russian trade, the prospects for an export-led recovery appeared dim.

The Reparations question cast a shadow over attempts at monetary reconstruction and impeded efforts to arrange cooperative solutions to Europe's financial problems. The provisions of the Treaty of Versailles designed to provide a mechanism by which realistic Reparations claims might be negotiated were disabled by the refusal of the U.S. Congress to ratify the Treaty. The Treaty itself deferred final determination of the amount of Reparations but required an initial payment of 200,000 million gold marks, the first installment falling due in May 1921.[22] When the Reparations Commission, staffed not by financial experts but by politicians taking instructions from their governments, finally determined the value of Reparations in April

---

21 For monthly statistics, see Tinbergen, *Abstract*.
22 For details, see K. Bergmann, *History of Reparations* (London, 1927).

1921, the amount was fixed at 132 billion gold marks (some $31 billion), three times the sum recommended by the economic experts at Versailles and a much larger amount than the Germans anticipated. In principle, the transfer might be made by payment in gold, payment in services, or payment in commodities. Yet the Reichsbank's gold reserve barely amounted to one semi-annual Reparations payment. German guest workers would scarcely be welcomed in neighboring countries already experiencing high unemployment. Thus, Germany had no alternative but to attempt to finance its transfer through an export surplus. The value of the transfer Germany might have accomplished given the impact of the surplus on her terms of trade has been debated ever since.[23] The only certainty from the point of view of financial market participants was that the magnitude and timing of Reparations payments would remain uncertain, with unknown implications for the public finances of the major creditor countries.

This was the background against which the Genoa Conference of 1922 was convened. Genoa was only one in a series of international monetary and financial conferences held in the 1920s, and negotiations there were not unrelated to previous meetings at Brussels in 1920 and at Cannes in January 1922. For example, the participants in the Brussels Conference had issued declarations which resembled in general terms the resolutions subsequently adopted at Genoa. However, only at Genoa were the particulars of these proposals specified and methods for implementing them through the international coordination of policies given explicit consideration.

The countries with greatest influence over the proceedings at Genoa were the United States, France, and Britain. The three nations approached the Conference with very different objectives. Despite other differences, the Americans and the British shared a common interest in rebuilding the international economy. The leaders of both nations agreed that recovery required the revitalization of foreign trade, for which reconstruction of the gold standard was a necessary prerequisite. Beyond these general goals, however, the two sets of policymakers had little in common. The British were willing to go considerably further than the Americans to promote the expansion of trade. They hoped that diplomatic and commercial relations with the Soviet government could be established and that Reparations could be reduced. To facilitate the renegotiation of Reparations, they suggested

---

[23] The classic references are of course Keynes, *Essays in Persuasion*, and B. Ohlin, "The Reparation Problem: A Discussion," *Economic Journal* 39 (1929), 172–8. Recent discussions include C. Maier, *Recasting Bourgeois Europe* (Princeton, 1976), and D. Silverman, *Reconstructing Europe After the Great War* (Cambridge, 1982).

that the United States forgive at least a portion of its war debt claims. With this groundwork laid, they hoped that the creditor countries would be encouraged to extend loans to the European debtors, promoting economic recovery on the Continent and stimulating international trade.

While restoring sterling's prewar parity was seen as an essential element of monetary reconstruction, the British were wary of the economic costs that the deflation associated with restoration might entail. From their perspective the preferred solution was inflation abroad rather than deflation at home – in particular, inflation in the United States. The British contemplated various schemes to encourage the Americans to inflate, ranging from subtle diplomatic pressure to a far-fetched plan to immediately pay in gold a large share of Britain's war debt in order to drastically expand the American monetary base.[24] This last scheme was dismissed due to the likelihood of American sterilization and its impact on the Bank of England's reserve position. It would be preferable for monetary expansion to be initiated abroad and backed as necessary by reserves of foreign exchange. That a significant portion of foreign exchange reserves would be held in the form of sterling undoubtedly figured in British calculations.[25]

Although the Americans shared Britain's interest in promoting the expansion of world trade, from their vantage point the problem was less pressing. They were willing to participate in discussions of international economic policy only as part of a general settlement. While Warren Harding and his Secretary of State, Charles E. Hughes, expressed an interest in convening in what the President termed a 'real honest-to-God economic conference' designed to reestablish fixed exchange rates, international convertibility, and free international movement of commodities and gold, they evinced little enthusiasm for meetings like those at Genoa which seemed likely to concentrate on stop-gap measures to be adopted in lieu of balanced budgets or Reparations settlements, and whose success appeared to hinge on American concessions regarding war debts.[26] In the end, Hughes agreed only to send to the Conference as an unofficial observer the American Ambassador to Rome, Richard Washburn Child.

In contrast to the Americans, the French sought to define the agenda

---

[24] PRO T160/5, "Export of Gold to America," by R.G. Hawtrey, 5 March 1923.

[25] Certain accounts attribute great foresight to the British, suggesting that their enthusiasm for the gold-exchange standard was part of a conscious strategy of relaxing Britain's balance of payments constraint, rejuvenating the City of London, and enhancing the Bank of England's control over international markets. Costigliola, "Anglo-American Rivalry," p. 917.

[26] Costigliola, "Anglo-American Rivalry," p. 916; Traynor, *International Conferences*, p. 72.

for Genoa as narrowly as possible. The French opposed British proposals for universal adoption of nondiscrimination in trade and the most-favored-nation clause, so they sought to discourage discussion of a general convention on trade policy. In contrast they pressed for discussion of sanctions against the Soviet government on the question of prewar debts.[27] This dispute intensified after January 1922, when Briand's relatively moderate government was replaced by a more nationalistic administration headed by Poincaré, who commenced almost immediately to spar over these issues and Reparations with the equally combative Lloyd George. Poincaré was skeptical about the usefulness of multilateral negotiations and agreed to participate in the conference only on British assurances that France's position on Reparations, the terms of the Treaty of Versailles, and the Russian Imperial debt to France would not be questioned.[28]

The monetary proposals discussed at Genoa originated with the British delegation. In drafting their proposals the British could draw on the First Interim Report of the Cunliffe Committee and on the considerable talents of their monetary specialists, notably Ralph G. Hawtrey, since 1919 Director of Financial Enquires at H.M. Treasury.[29] A number of Britain's Genoa proposals resembled the Cunliffe Committee's recommendations, including the argument that a credible commitment to financial stability required a return to gold.[30] Resurrecting the gold standard, it was stated, required balancing government budgets, insulating central banks from pressure to extend credit to government agencies, and consolidating national debts. Little was novel in these ideas. More novel were the measures first proposed by the Cunliffe Committee and incorporated into the British proposals to economize on the demand for monetary gold: these included eliminating internal circulation of gold coin, concentrating gold reserves at the central bank, and permitting domestic residents to acquire coin and bullion for export only from the authorities. By limiting the use of gold to international settlements, the Cunliffe Committee and the British delegates at Genoa sought to minimize competing demands for reserves.

The British draft was circulated among foreign authorities in February

[27] Archives of the French Ministry of Foreign Affairs (Min. Aff. Etr.) B82/112, "Reunion Interministrielle au sujet de L'Equitable Traitement du Commerce," 28 January 1922.

[28] See the interchange of memoranda between the French and British governments in United Kingdom, *Correspondence Between His Majesty's Government and the French Government Respecting the Genoa Conference* (London, 1922).

[29] PRO T160/5, "The Genoa Currency Resolutions," by R.G. Hawtrey, 4 February 1922. See also R. Hawtrey, *Monetary Reconstruction* (London, 1923).

[30] See Committee on Currency and Foreign Exchanges After the War, *First Interim Report*.

1922, and in March experts from Belgium, France, Italy, and Japan met with British representatives in London to undertake revisions. These proposals were adopted with only slight modification by the Financial Committee at the Genoa Conference in April and by the Conference itself in May.[31]

The Genoa resolutions contained a number of provisions designed to ease the transition to gold. These included the recommendation, ultimately adopted, that governments with significantly depreciated currencies consider stabilizing at a lower rate of exchange. While accepting the argument that prewar parities provided the ideal basis for stabilization, the experts suggested that countries which had experienced sustained inflation might be well advised to avoid the output costs associated with restoring the prewar level of prices. Moreover, they observed that governments would be seriously burdened by the increased real value of internal debt which would result from a substantial reduction in prices.[32] Policymakers were therefore encouraged to stabilize at rates not far distant from those currently prevailing. Significantly for the operation of the interwar gold standard, no sanctions were included to discourage governments from engaging in competitive depreciation.

The Genoa resolutions also contained proposals to economize on the use of gold. The measures proposed by the Cunliffe Committee were altered to

[31] The various drafts can be found in United Kingdom, *Papers Relating to International Economic Conference, Genoa, April–May 1922* (London, 1924). The resolutions of the Financial Commission and the Experts' Report appear in J.S. Mills, *The Genoa Conference* (New York, 1922).

[32] To quote the Report of the Committee of Experts, "The question of devaluation is one which must be decided upon by each country according to its view of its own special requirements. We think it important however to draw attention to some of the considerations which will necessarily weigh with any country in coming to a decision on this question. There is a prevalent belief that a return to pre-war gold parity is necessary or desirable for its own sake. There are undoubtedly advantages to be obtained by such a return, but we desire to point out that for countries where currency has fallen very far below the pre-war parity, a return to it must involve social and economic dislocation attendant upon continuing readjustment of money-wages and prices, and a continual increase in the burden of international debt. Regard being had to the very large debts which have been incurred since the Armistice by many of the countries concerned, we are inclined to think that a return to the old gold parity involves too heavy a strain upon production. We repeat that the decision must be left in each case to the country concerned. . . ." Mills, *Genoa Conference*, p. 369. The French were less enthusiastic than the British about endorsing the option of devaluation, perhaps due to the franc's weakness and the impact of such a position on confidence. They supported devaluation only for cases where it was demonstrably "impossible" to return to the prewar parity. Min. Fin. Etr., B82-16/121, Conference Financière, 11 April 1922.

meet what the British experts regarded as mounting deflationary pressures. Resolution 9 on currency adopted by the Financial Commission urged governments to establish a mechanism to minimize the need for gold by 'maintaining reserves in the form of foreign balances, such as the gold exchange standard, or an international clearing system.'

It was in this connection that the issue of policy coordination was raised. Monetary authorities were encouraged to coordinate their demands for gold and to avoid the wide fluctuations in internal prices that would otherwise result from the 'simultaneous and competitive efforts of a number of countries to secure metallic reserves.'[33] Thus, central banks were for the first time explicitly urged to desist from the competitive struggle for gold. These proposals for international cooperation were predicated upon the establishment of central banks where they did not exist and on their insulation from political influence or control. Thus, at Genoa countries with relatively stable currencies were urged to adopt institutional arrangements similar to those imposed by the League of Nations upon countries undergoing hyperinflation.

The only resolution on international policy coordination acceptable to all the participating countries was one couched in general terms. While consultation and collaboration were encouraged, no formal mechanism for their practice was specified. Instead, the Bank of England was requested to call an early meeting of central bankers to prepare a convention to implement these measures. An accompanying resolution warned that the success of any such plan was contingent upon the participation of the United States. In the words of the Financial Commission, no scheme for stabilizing prices 'can be fully effective without coordination of policy between Europe and the United States, whose cooperation therefore should be invited.'[34]

There is no question that the economic costs of noncooperative behaviour were clearly understood in 1922. Permitting central banks to engage in a competitive struggle for gold was seen as threatening to transmit deflationary pressures to the world economy and delaying recovery from the war. Multilateral negotiations were seen as the most effective technique for achieving agreement on an acceptable international distribution of reserves. Yet it was far from apparent how agreement on this matter might be reconciled with national autonomy on the question of the level at which to stabilize exchange rates, or how these noble sentiments might be institution-

---

[33] Resolution 9, reprinted in Mills, *Genoa Conference*, p. 369.
[34] Ibid., Resolution 10.

alized. But if the participants in the Genoa Conference lacked a coherent view of how policy coordination might be practiced, they agreed on the principle of responding cooperatively to international financial problems. Ultimately, even this modest attempt to provide a framework for cooperation proved to be overly ambitious. To the surprise of the participants, the next step in the process, namely the proposed meeting of central banks, was never held. The Bank of England took the initiative of discussing the proposed meeting with the Federal Reserve, whose participation was endorsed by the U.S. State Department. Once the Bank of England's Committee of Treasury approved the tentative invitation drafted by Norman and Benjamin Strong, a meeting seemed imminent.[35] However, efforts to convene the meeting met with political obstacles, and the prospective conference was soon reduced to a mere bargaining chip to be used in disputes over these other concerns. The French ruled out their participation unless Reparations were again excluded from the agenda. The Americans objected that meaningful progress could not be made unless the Reparations question was reopened. In the autumn of 1922 Britain sent a delegation to Washington to discuss funding the British war debt, and the Bank of England's involvement in these negotiations again postponed the meeting of central bankers. France's occupation of the Ruhr in 1923 cast doubt on German participation, and the financial difficulties of Austria and Hungary were the occasion for further delay. By the summer of 1923, enthusiasm for a general convention of central banks had dissipated. This was not to mark the end of financial collaboration, but subsequent exchanges between central banks took place primarily on a bilateral basis.[36]

With the failure of the Genoa Conference to yield even a general framework for international policy coordination, many of the dangers cited by the financial experts quickly came to pass. There were no sanctions to discourage governments from stabilizing at parities which yielded a system of misaligned exchange rates. There was no mechanism for reconciling the competing objectives of national monetary authorities or to prevent central banks from engaging in what was characterized as a competitive scramble for gold. The implications of noncooperative behavior within the framework of the interwar gold standard would become evident soon enough.

[35] Clay, *Lord Norman*, p. 158.
[36] There were exceptions to this rule, such as the meeting held on Long Island in 1927 among representatives of four major central banks. See Eichengreen, "Central Bank Cooperation."

3. Leadership and cooperation under the interwar gold standard

A. Motivation

Establishing a basis for cooperation among central banks was clearly one of the principal goals of the policymakers who attempted to lay the foundation for the gold standard's resurrection. Yet the gold standard is typically portrayed as a self-equilibrating mechanism under which external balance is restored to deficit and surplus countries alike through the smooth operation of an anonymously functioning international adjustment mechanism. The very concept of conflicting objectives, much less strategies such as leadership and cooperation, are wholly incompatible with familiar attempts to model the gold standard's operation. These familiar models are simply incapable of addressing the questions at hand.

The purpose of this section is to develop an alternative model of the gold standard with which the issues of leadership and cooperation can be addressed. No attempt is made to capture the operation of the international gold standard in all its complexity, for this is not the model's purpose. Its purpose is rather to provide a simple macroeconomic framework which highlights the channels through which the actions of one country's central bank impinge upon the internal and external position of another and the incentives that these repercussion effects provide the second country to respond to the actions of the first. It strips away complications in order to lay bare the dynamics of strategic interaction and to explore the implications of long-standing arguments about the benefits of leadership and cooperation during the interwar period.

The model is based on the notion that the interwar gold standard can be viewed as an 'international struggle for gold.'[37] Simply put, central banks in our model desire incompatibly large shares of the world's gold reserves. This provides the basis for conflicting objectives and for strategic interaction.

Despite its simplicity, the model generates several useful insights. As in

[37] The phrase comes from the interchange between Keynes and Norman before the Macmillan Committee. See Question 3490, reprinted in Sayers, *Bank of England, 1891–1944*, Vol. 3, p. 185. This idea was then adopted in much of the subsequent literature. For example, Cassel, *Downfall*, p. 13, remarks "usually, however, the central banks themselves are responsible for the injurious increase in the demand for gold insofar as they compete with one another in their endeavors to strengthen their reserve."

any strategic game in which the players hold conflicting objectives, non-cooperative behavior has economic costs compared with cooperative solutions.[38] In our model, central banks incapable of coordinating their policies set their discount rates at undesirably high levels, putting downward pressure on the level of prices and depressing incomes at home and abroad. For example, this is the Nash solution to this noncooperative game. While central bank policy was but one factor at work in the world economy in the 1920s, this result is suggestive when applied to a period marked by historically high discount rates, conflicts among central banks, and steady deflation culminating in a Great Depression.

The Stackelberg leader-follower solution to the two-country model provides a halfway point between the Nash and cooperative equilibria. Compared to the Nash solution, the leader-follower solution is less deflationary and yields higher incomes both at home and abroad. Barring cooperation, the exercise of leadership clearly is in the interest of both players; the question is whether either player will choose to exercise it. In fact, there is an incentive for both players to resist the leadership role. It is a standard (and intuitive) property of models of symmetrical countries that both players prefer to adopt the same strategy. We show below that the same holds true in a model of asymmetric countries, where one central bank has exceptional power to influence the direction of international capital flows.

In structure the model has much in common with previous analyses of policy coordination (see for example Hamada, 1976 and 1979). It incorporates the assumption that each central bank has more targets than instruments, forcing it to confront the trade-off between its objectives. This is the assumption of instrument scarcity in whose absence problems of strategy vanish. In addition, it incorporates the assumption that each domestic target variable is affected by the actions of the foreign central bank. This is the assumption of interdependence.

There exists scope for strategic interaction in a model of the gold standard only if central banks can exercise discretion. We will assume that central banks are able to engage in discretionary initiatives to alter the composition of the monetary base through open market operations or changes in fiduciary circulation and to affect the size of the money multiplier through

---

[38] This ranking necessarily holds only when all the players contribute to the cooperative solution. Thus, for example, cooperation between governments can be welfare reducing in the absence of cooperation between a government and the private sector. K. Rogoff, "Can International Policy Coordination Be Counterproductive?" *Journal of International Economics* 18 (1985), 199–218.

changes in discount rates. While the idea that changes in central bank discount rates affect the relationship between the gold reserve and the money supply is a departure from textbook treatments of the gold standard, it captures the fact that the authorities were capable in the short run of either reinforcing the impact of incipient gold flows on domestic financial markets or neutralizing them through sterilization. In fact, under the gold standard there were important sources of slack in the connection between gold reserves and broadly defined monetary aggregates. Central banks could hold gold in excess of that required to back notes in circulation, enabling them to intervene in financial markets with purchases of bonds and bills and to alter the monetary base without any accompanying change in reserves. Only the need to maintain confidence in the convertibility of the currency placed limits on their discretionary actions. Similarly, commercial banks, even if free of statutory reserve requirements, had an incentive to hold precautionary reserves to guard against unanticipated withdrawals. The size of such precautionary reserves was determined in part by the cost of feasible alternatives, including discounting (in the British case, via discount houses) at the central bank. Under the British banking system, there was a conventional ratio between a bank's cash and its liabilities which was basically the same whether those liabilities were demand or time deposits. Nonetheless, the authorities could influence this ratio and hence affect broadly defined monetary aggregates through changes in the deposit multiplier.[39] This was even more true of the countries of the Continent, where there was typically no conventional or legal relation between reserve assets and deposits.

Each central bank in our model minimizes a quadratic loss function defined over gold reserves and domestic prices. Although the historical record suggests that central bankers followed rules of thumb when setting discount rates, we adopt the assumption of optimizing behavior as a simplifying device. The assumption that each bank has an optimal gold reserve is motivated by the observation that, while a central bank could feel more confident of its ability to defend the convertibility of the currency with a larger gold reserve on hand, it was less profitable to hold barren metal than interest-bearing financial assets.[40]

---

[39] British conventions regarding reserve ratios are discussed by Beyen, *Money*, pp. 62–3. See also Balogh, *Studies*. Cairncross and Eichengreen, *Sterling in Decline* provide evidence for Britain on the links between the discount rate and the money multiplier. See especially their table A3.1.

[40] The Bank of England and the Bank of France remained privately held institutions influenced by the desire to pay customary dividends to shareholders. While the extent to which

The idea that central banks maintained a target level for prices is another simplifying assumption. Occasionally it is argued that central banks were concerned ultimately with the domestic-currency price of gold and that they desired only to prevent such fluctuations in prices and economic activity as might threaten convertibility. By this interpretation, the price level is properly viewed not as an independent goal of policy but as an intermediate target whose achievement was helpful for attaining the ultimate objective: maintaining convertibility. Yet central banks were under pressure throughout the interwar years to respond actively to internal conditions. The British case provides an illustration of the pressures brought to bear. British central bankers were publicly cautious when relating their policy to the state of the domestic economy. According to Montagu Norman, the Bank of England's interwar Governor, the ill effects of a high Bank Rate on domestic industry and trade were greatly exaggerated and 'more psychological than real.'[41] Of course, by 1930, when this statement was made, the Bank had been subjected to Treasury criticism for more than half a decade; in 1924, a more relaxed time, Norman had expressed concern for the impact of monetary deflation on the state of the economy.[42] The caution that characterized the Bank's public pronouncements by the end of the decade can be seen as a response to the criticism to which it was subjected. Keynes's articles on monetary policy are the best-known examples of the genre.[43] Surely, however, the Bank of England was more profoundly affected by criticism emanating from H.M. Treasury. The principal goals of Treasury policy in the twenties were to retire outstanding debt and to reduce the burden of debt service charges through conversion of the 5 percent government loans of 1917 at low interest rates. Debt service had risen from 11 percent of central government spending in 1913 to 24 percent in 1920 and more than

the profit motive and public service figured in the authorities' calculations remains difficult to discern, incorporating the profit motive into models of central bank behavior is a step in the direction of realism.

41 See Norman's Macmillan Committee evidence: Committee on Finance and Industry, Questions 3328–3517, 26 March 1930, reprinted in Sayers, *Bank of England, 1891–1944*, Vol. 3, pp. 12–253.

42 For example, see Norman's statements to the Chamberlain-Bradbury Committee in the summer of 1924, cited in D.E. Moggridge, *The Return to Gold, 1925* (Cambridge, 1969).

43 Formal statements of Keynes's view of the relationship of monetary policy to the state of trade appear in Keynes, *Treatise*, while his efforts at pamphleteering are collected in Keynes, *Essays in Persuasion*. Keynes's most accessible account of the channels of transmission came in his private evidence to the Macmillan Committee (Keynes, *Activities, 1929–31*).

40 percent by the end of the decade.[44] Hence between 1925 and 1929 the Treasury consistently objected to Bank of England initiatives which raised the price and reduced the availability of credit. These objections were often communicated to the Bank directly. For example:

The Governor of the Bank called at the Treasury on the 2nd December [1925] about 7:15 pm, and informed me that there was every probability that the Bank Rate would be increased . . . . I reported this to the Chancellor on the following morning and he at once telephoned to the Governor that if the rate were raised, he would have to inform the House that it had been done without his being consulted and against his wishes. It was not fair to the Exchequer that action should be taken which affected all its affairs without an opportunity being given to him to consider it. He expressed an earnest request that action should be deferred at any rate for a week, to enable this to be done.[45]

Whatever the central bankers' beliefs about the effects of monetary policy, it is difficult to dispute that such pressures would have encouraged them to act as if they were concerned about the state of industry and trade. In fact, Bank of England reaction functions for the period 1925–31 indicate some sensitivity of discount rate policy to the state of the domestic economy.[46] In what follows, the target of a stable price level can be thought of as shorthand for stable prices, output, and employment and, depending on the reader's interpretation of the historical literature, different weights can be attached to internal and external targets without greatly affecting the results.

B. Specification

Consider a world of two identical countries, home and foreign.[47] I log-linearize all relationships and use lowercase letters to denote the logs of the variables represented by the corresponding uppercase letters, except for interest rates, which are always measured in levels. Each country has a money supply M, which can be thought of as an M1 or M2 measure. This

---

[44] See B. Eichengreen and F. Giavazzi, "Inflation, Consolidation or Capital Levy? European Debt Management in the 1920s" (unpublished, 1984).

[45] PRO T176/13, Leith-Ross Memorandum, 3 December 1925.

[46] See Chapter 4, especially pp. 75–8.

[47] Extending the model to more than two countries adds generality but alters none of the conclusions that will be presented. See Eichengreen, "Central Bank Cooperation," Appendix B, where a simple three-country model is analyzed. Note also that some implications of relaxing the assumption of identical countries are explored below.

aggregate is the product of the monetary base and the money multiplier V. The base is made up of domestic credit and the central bank's gold reserves. The domestic credit component of the base can be positive or negative, depending on whether central banks hold excess gold reserves or there is a fiduciary issue outstanding. However, to simplify the model we abstract entirely from the domestic credit component of the base.[48]

I assume that a rise in the discount rate, by increasing the cost of re-discounting at the central bank, induces the consolidated banking sector to hold a larger ratio of precautionary reserves to liabilities. Hence the money multiplier depends negatively on the central bank discount rate. Using asterisks to indicate foreign variables, we have:

$$\left.\begin{aligned} m &= -vr + h\overline{g}, \\ m^* &= -vr^* + (1-h)\overline{g}, \end{aligned}\right\} \tag{1}$$

where v is the elasticity of the money supply with respect to the discount rate r. $\overline{g}$ denotes the log of the world stock of monetary gold, of which shares h and $(1-h)$ are held by the domestic and foreign countries. The demand for real balances is a function of output Y and the market interest rate i:

$$\left.\begin{aligned} m - p &= \phi y - \lambda i, \\ m^* - p^* &= \phi y^* - \lambda i^*, \end{aligned}\right\} \tag{2}$$

where p and p^* denote logs of domestic and foreign prices, respectively. Only mathematical complexity is added by assuming that nominal balances are deflated by a consumer price index comprised of domestic and foreign prices.

Aggregate supply in each country is an increasing function of producer prices:

$$\left.\begin{aligned} y &= y(p) = \gamma p, \\ y^* &= y^*(p^*) = \gamma^* p^*, \end{aligned} \quad \gamma, \gamma^* > 0 \right\} \tag{3}$$

---

[48] The model is readily adapted to the analysis of open market operations and many of the same conclusions follow. Again, see Eichengreen, "Central Bank Cooperation." An advantage of adding the domestic credit component of the monetary base to the model is that it would permit domestic assets denominated in one country's currency to be held as international reserves by the other. Again, this adds realism to the model but alters none of the conclusions.

where for convenience we assume constant elasticities of supply (γ and γ^*) and standardize the normal level of output to unity. These functions can be thought of as the short-run supply curves of an aggregation of profit-maximizing firms confronting predetermined wages or material costs. Rather than introducing costs explicitly, we simply note that the classical full employment model ($\gamma = \gamma^* = 0$) and the Keynesian income-expenditure model ($\gamma = \gamma^* \to \infty$) can be treated as special cases. The short-run focus of the model should be borne in mind in the discussion that follows.

Aggregate demand depends positively on the relative price of imports and negatively on the interest rate. The exchange rate is normalized to unity and suppressed.

$$\left.\begin{aligned} d &= \delta(p^* - p) - Bi, \\ d^* &= -\delta(p^* - p) - Bi^*, \end{aligned}\right\} \tag{4}$$

I close the model with the open interest parity condition on the assumption that nonmonetary assets denominated in the two currencies are perfect substitutes and capital is perfectly mobile.

$$i = i^*. \tag{5}$$

The omission of gold production, wealth effects, and dynamics of adjustment, to mention but a few complications, is obvious. Many of these complications could be appended to the model. However, our intent here is not to build a complete model but to present a simple analytical framework containing the essential ingredients for the study of a particular historical episode.

I now posit an objective function for each country of the form:

$$U = -[(p - \bar{p})^2 + \omega(h - \bar{h})^2], \tag{6}$$

where ω is the weight attached to gold reserves relative to prices, output, and employment.[49] Assume $\bar{h} > 1/2$ to capture the idea that the two coun-

---

[49] This formulation, which places the stock of reserves in the authorities' objective function, is in contrast to most previous specifications of policy coordination problems, which typically assume that the authorities have a target balance of payments surplus (i.e., a target for the flow change in reserves). As Niehans points out, the specification here would appear to make more sense in a utility-maximizing framework. J. Niehans, "Monetary and Fiscal Policies in Open Economics under Fixed Exchange Rates: An Optimizing Approach," *Journal of Political Economy* 76 (1968), 893–920.

tries prefer incompatibly large shares of the (log of the) world's stock of monetary reserves – in other words, that the gold standard can be characterized as a competitive struggle for gold. It will be convenient to normalize $\bar{p}$ to zero.

To derive a semi-reduced form expression for h, set each country's money supply equal to its money demand and take the difference of these two relations.

$$h = (1/(2\bar{g}))[\bar{g} + v(r - r^*) + (1 + \phi\gamma)(p - p^*)]. \tag{7}$$

Setting aggregate supply (3) equal to aggregate demand (4) and substituting each country's money supply and money demand equation [(1) and (2)] into its goods market clearing condition yields a semi-reduced form for p:

$$p = \Omega[(v/2)(r + r^*) - \bar{g}/2], \tag{8}$$

where

$$\Omega = \frac{-1}{y + \lambda/B(1 + \phi\gamma)}, \quad \Omega < 0.$$

It is evident that this model provides the minimal ingredients for a study of interdependence. The first element we require for an analysis of interdependence is that each central bank faces a trade-off between its target variables. From (7) and (8):

$$\frac{\partial h}{\partial r} = \frac{v}{2\bar{g}} > 0, \quad \frac{\partial p}{\partial r} = \Omega\frac{v}{2} < 0, \tag{9}$$

and similarly for the foreign country. A rise in the domestic discount rate decreases the domestic money multiplier, putting downward pressure on the price level, and by reducing domestic money supply relative to domestic money demand attracts gold from the foreign country.

The second element we require is that the target variables in the home country are affected by the actions of the foreign central bank. Again from (7) and (8):

$$\frac{\partial h}{\partial r^*} = \frac{-v}{2\bar{g}} < 0, \quad \frac{\partial p}{\partial r^*} = \Omega\frac{v}{2} < 0. \tag{10}$$

An increase in the foreign discount rate reduces the foreign money multiplier and the foreign money supply, attracting gold from the home country and depressing the world price level. Analogous results hold for the foreign country.

It is worth noting that this is a case of positive international transmis-

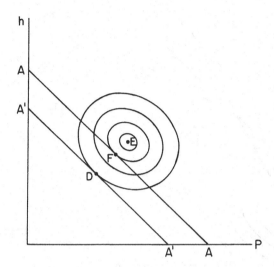

Figure 6.1. The home country's objective function.

sion. Initiating an expansionary policy in one country leads to expansion in the other. This result contrasts with the assumption often made about international transmission between the wars: that policy was 'beggar-thy-neighbor' in the sense that expansion in one country caused contraction in the other. The contrast is due to the way I model the international monetary regime: in this model of the 1920s with fixed exchange rates international transmission is positive, while in a comparable model of the 1930s with flexible rates, transmission might well be negative.

The choices confronting central banks can be illustrated with two familiar diagrams. From (9), we know that, given r^*, the domestic central bank can vary r to attain different combinations of h and p. In Figure 6.1, the frontier of feasible combinations is labelled AA. The optimal setting for r is one which achieves an h-p combination tangent to an indifference curve at the point labelled F.

Consider now a rise in r^*. This shifts the AA frontier inward to $A'A'$. The home country's central bank, faced with a smaller world money supply, is forced to accept lower prices, smaller gold reserves, or a combination of the two. As drawn, it moves to a point such as D tangent to a less desirable indifference curve where both prices and reserves have fallen.

The same exercises can be conducted for the foreign central bank. The analysis becomes interesting once we combine the two banks' problems and consider their interaction. This can be done by transposing the indif-

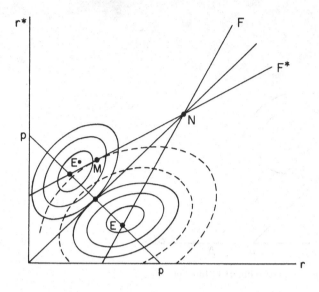

Figure 6.2. Home and foreign policy reaction curves.

ference curves to r, r^* space as in Figure 6.2. We read off from Figure 6.1 the home country's rankings of different combinations of the two discount rates. Thus, point E in Figure 6.2 at the center of the home country's solid indifference curves corresponds to point E in Figure 6.1. The fact that the foreign central bank's indifference curves lie to the northwest of the home central bank's indifference curves reflects the assumption that the two central banks ideally wish to hold incompatibly large shares of the world's gold stock. This is accomplished when each bank's discount rate is high relative to that of its rival.

The downward sloping pp locus depicts combinations of r and r^* for which a price level $\bar{p}$ obtains. Along parallel lines below and to the left of pp, prices are higher, while above and to the right, prices are lower. With symmetry, the two central banks share a common rank ordering over prices and the pp line has a slope of -45 degrees.

The F and F^* curves in Figure 6.2 are the reaction functions of the two central banks. The F curve, representing loss-minimizing discount rates for the home central bank given the foreign discount rate, is the locus of points where the tangent to the home indifference curve is horizontal. Similarly, the F^* curve is the locus of points where the tangent to a foreign indifference curve is vertical. The reaction functions may be positively sloped, as in Figure 6.2, or negatively sloped. The slopes can be derived by substituting the semi-reduced forms for h and p into the objective function, differentiating with respect to each discount rate, and setting the solutions to zero:

$$\left.\frac{\partial r^*}{\partial r}\right|_{F^*=0} = \frac{\omega + \Omega^2}{\omega - \Omega^2}, \tag{11}$$

$$\left.\frac{\partial r^*}{\partial r}\right|_{F=0} = \frac{\omega - \Omega^2}{\omega + \Omega^2}. \tag{12}$$

Both reaction functions will be positively sloped when the weight attached to gold reserves ω is large relative to that placed on prices. Then each central bank responds to a foreign discount rate increase by raising its own rate, attempting to stem the loss of gold reserves at the cost of still lower prices. Conversely, both reaction functions will be negatively sloped when the weight put on gold reserves is relatively small. In this case, each country responds to a discount rate increase abroad by lowering its discount rate, attempting to reduce the fall in prices at the cost of still lower gold reserves. So long as stability is maintained (as can be shown to obtain under symmetry and under other cases considered below), the analysis is essentially the same.

The discussion to follow will concentrate on the configuration depicted in Figure 6.2. The case of upward-sloping reaction functions, in which each country is inclined to respond to a change in the foreign discount rate in the same direction, appears to be the historically relevant case for the 1920s.

C. Solutions

We can now determine the equilibrium values of r and r^* under different solution concepts. After discussing the outcome under different assumptions, we will ask the question of which solution is likely to obtain.

First, consider the model's Nash solution at the intersection of the reaction functions. Note that in the symmetrical model the two discount rates are identical at the Nash solution, so the level of prices and reserves will be the same in each country. In particular, since $p = p^*$ at the Nash solution, we can cancel the second additive term in equation (7) when solving for its characteristics. Differentiating the objective function with respect to each discount rate under the assumption that the other discount rate is invariant, setting each solution to zero and equating them yields:

$$r_N = r_N^* = \frac{1}{v}\left[\frac{1}{2}\bar{g} + \frac{\omega}{\Omega^2}(\bar{h} - \frac{1}{2})\right], \tag{13}$$

where the N subscript denotes the Nash solution.

Second, consider the cooperative solution. Under symmetry, each country holds exactly half the world's monetary gold, and prices are again identical in the two countries. The best they can then do is to set their discount rate equal to one another at the level consistent with $p = 0$. Setting (8) equal to zero yields:

$$r_C = r_C^* = \frac{1}{2v}\bar{g}, \tag{14}$$

where the C subscript denotes the cooperative solution. From (13) and (14), $r_N > r_C$ so long as $\bar{h} > 1/2$.

Under symmetry, the Nash and cooperative solutions yield identical distributions of gold. However, under the assumption of Nash behavior, the desire of rival banks to possess incompatibly large shares of the world's gold stock causes both banks to elevate their discount rates above the level consistent with price level $\bar{p}$. Each is subject to the misapprehension that a marginal increase in its discount rate will secure it larger gold reserves at the cost of a relatively small decline in prices. In fact, each discount rate increase elicits an increase in the foreign discount rate, yielding the initiating bank no additional gold reserves but resulting in still lower prices. Thus, the strategic interaction of central banks imparts a deflationary bias to the world economy, given the assumption that $\bar{h} > 1/2$.

Finally, consider the case where the home country acts as a Stackelberg leader and the foreign country follows. Substituting the foreign country's reaction function into the home country's objective function and minimizing the loss yields the solution depicted at point M in Figure 6.2, where a home indifference curve is tangent to the foreign reaction function. The home country's central bank recognizes that if it lowers its discount rate the foreign central bank will respond in kind. Hence, it is aware that the loss of gold reserves brought about by its discount rate reduction will be partially offset by the reduction in the foreign discount rate, and that the response of the foreign central bank will yield further benefits by reinforcing the tendency of lower discount rates to raise the world money supply and price level. The leader-follower strategy yields a lower domestic discount rate than the Nash solution, resulting in a higher level of utility for the domestic country, whose loss of gold is more than offset by higher prices, output, and employment. The foreign central bank benefits on both counts, since prices are higher and it now obtains a larger share of the world's gold stock.[50]

---

[50] In the case of negatively sloped reaction functions, the details and implications differ. The domestic central bank realizes that a rise in its discount rate will elicit a reduction in the

In this model, the strategic interaction of central banks imparts a deflationary bias to the world economy, assuming only that at the optimum they desire incompatibly large shares of the world's gold stock. Leadership has advantages over other noncooperative strategies: a country which takes its foreign rival's reaction into account can initiate a reduction in discount rates, raising prices and stimulating activity at home and abroad. Cooperation has further advantages over leadership: through cooperation both discount rates can be lowered and the deflationary bias in monetary policy can be eliminated.

D. Sustainable strategies

To this point I have not addressed the question of which solution is likely to obtain. In this section I first consider this question using the symmetrical model of previous sections which is intended to represent the strategic interaction of two or more comparable financial centers during the interwar years. I then extend the analysis to a simple asymmetrical case intended to capture aspects of the prewar situation.

Assuming that cooperative strategies are not feasible, is the Nash solution or the Stackelberg leader-follower solution likely to obtain? I have noted that both countries benefit with movement from the Nash solution to the leader-follower solution. It is clear also that with upward-sloping reaction functions the follower reaps the greater gains: while both countries benefit from higher prices, only the follower benefits from a larger gold reserve. In Figure 6.2, the gains from discount rate reductions are evenly distributed among countries as they move down the 45 degree line toward the origin. Since the leader-follower solution is on the follower's side of that line, the leader reaps the smaller benefits. As Cooper (1984) suggests, the fact that the follower reaps the larger benefits encourages both parties to engage in a game of 'chicken,' each attempting to force the other to accept the role of leader. There may be extended periods when the Nash solution is observed as this game of 'chicken' is played out. Clearly this is one way to interpret statements to the effect that the interwar monetary system was characterized by the absence of leadership.

One might attempt to capture the change in structure of international financial markets between the end of the 19th century and the interwar

foreign discount rate, since the foreign country attaches great weight to the stability of prices. The home country's gain from increased reserves more than offsets any loss due to lower prices. In contrast, the foreign country is worse off and unwilling to play the follower. Since both countries prefer to lead, the configuration will be unstable.

period by adding to the model an asymmetry in the ability of discount rates to influence international capital flows. Assume that the discount rate of the domestic central bank (which might be thought of as the Bank of England) has a larger impact than the foreign discount rate on the domestic money supply (i.e., that $v^* = \theta v$, where $0 < \theta < 1$). In all other respects, including objective functions, the two countries remain the same. Since from (9) and (10) $dh_i/dr_i = -v_i/2\bar{g}$, the domestic discount rate has a larger impact than the foreign discount rate on the international distribution of gold.

Strikingly, introducing this asymmetry into the model does not alter the fact that, in the case of positively sloped reaction functions, each country prefers its foreign counterpart to play the Stackelberg leader. The intuition is straightforward. For simplicity of exposition, consider the case where v is unchanged from subsections B and C above but v^* is now smaller. Since $v^* = \theta v$, we can rewrite equation (1) for the foreign country as:

$$m^* = -v\theta r^* + (1 - h)\bar{g} \tag{1$'$}$$

and leave the rest of the model unchanged. In this case, the model and its solutions are the same, except we can think of the foreign central bank as setting and the domestic central bank as reacting to θr^* rather than r^*. At each solution, the domestic discount rate is the same as in the symmetrical case, while the foreign discount rate is simply θ times its value in the symmetric model. In r, θr^* space, the various solutions could be depicted by the symmetrical diagram of Figure 6.2. In r, r^* space, the slope of each reaction function would have to be multiplied by $1/\theta$. All of the conclusions from the symmetric model concerning the gains to Stackelberg leaders and followers continue to hold.

The simple asymmetrical model suggests, therefore, that to the extent that the Bank of England had more power than its foreign counterparts over the direction of gold flows, this would not have encouraged it to exercise leadership in the Stackelberg sense. If asymmetries in economic structure are to provide an explanation for the Bank of England's leadership role, they must be more subtle than the simple asymmetry considered here.

4. The Tripartite Monetary Agreement of 1936 and the role for cooperation

The devaluation of sterling in 1931 marked the end of the truly international gold standard of the interwar years. The Bank of England had succeeded in holding sterling between the gold points during the period 1925–30 only under considerable duress. The onset of the Great Depression then placed a downward pressure on prices, pushed the government budget into deficit, and by the summer of 1931 raised unemployment rates to 20 percent of the insured labor force. Following financial crises in Austria and Germany and with the Labour and National Governments' inability to take convincing steps either to balance the budget or to initiate economic recovery, defense of the sterling parity was abandoned in September. Against the dollar and the currencies of other countries that continued to peg to gold, the pound depreciated by 25 percent, from $4.86 to $3.75 at the end of the first week of floating.

More than two dozen countries allowed their currencies to depreciate with sterling, among them most of the Empire, Scandinavia, and Eastern Europe.[51] Germany for its part adopted draconian exchange controls and moved increasingly toward a system of bilateral clearing arrangements with its Eastern European trading partners.

The United States broke with gold in 1933. In March, Roosevelt restricted foreign exchange dealings and gold and currency movements, and in April he issued an executive order requiring individuals to deliver their gold coin, bullion, and certificates to Federal Reserve Banks. At this point, the dollar began to float. By setting a series of progressively higher dollar prices for gold, the Administration engineered a significant devaluation. The dollar was finally stabilized in January 1934 at $35 an ounce, 59 percent of its former gold content. The only major currencies that remained freely convertible were those of the Gold Bloc countries: France, Belgium, Holland, Italy, Poland, and Switzerland. These countries were willing to go to great lengths to defend their established parities.

Thus, the international monetary system of the mid-1930s was a hybrid of different regimes. Britain was engaged in a managed float administered by the Exchange Equalization Account (EEA). The United States in January 1934 pegged the dollar to gold at the new $35 price but extended convertibility only to countries on the gold standard. France, under the provisions of the monetary law of 1928, was fully on the gold standard and obligated to buy and sell gold without limit at the prevailing price.

As late as the summer of 1936 the official goal of French policy was to defend and maintain the franc Poincaré. Despite the depth of the Depression, the Bank of France continued to respond to gold losses by raising

---

[51] Hence the movement of the effective exchange rate was somewhat less pronounced; see J. Redmond, "An Indicator of the Effective Exchange Rate of the Pound in the 1930s," *Economic History Review* (sec. ser., 1980), 83–91.

its discount rate. Belgium's devaluation in 1935 served to signal the extent of the franc's overvaluation, and confidence was further undermined by political developments abroad, including Italy's invasion of Ethiopia, Germany's occupation of the Rhineland, and the outbreak of the Spanish Civil War. With the formation of Leon Blum's Popular Front Government in April 1936, pressure on the franc intensified. Blum was pledged to stimulate domestic activity while at the same time maintaining the gold standard parity.[52] Market participants were aware of the incompatibility of these objectives. Blum's proposals had included public works and public employment, a reduction in the length of the work week, paid holidays, universal collective bargaining, and public control of heavy industry and finance. French labor initiated sit-down strikes soon after the election to induce speedy implementation of these measures, and the Bank of France's gold reserves plummeted as a result of capital outflows. The Bank responded by raising its discount rate to 6 percent, three times the Bank of England's rate. Discreet consideration began to be given to the possibility of devaluation.

As devaluation of the franc came to be seen as probable, French policymakers considered how to capitalize on the situation and foreign policymakers how to minimize the damage. Yet the French position was not without difficulties. One French objective was to devalue by a margin adequate to secure a competitive advantage – in other words, devaluation on the 1920s model. At the same time, officials were constrained by the necessity of not arousing the indignation of the electorate or their trading partners. Since the Popular Front had come to power committed to the gold standard, it was desirable that devaluation occur as part of a multilateral system of exchange rate adjustments which laid the basis for a general return to gold. Moreover, given the specter of 1923 and 1926, the French were concerned that a substantial devaluation might cast doubt on the credibility of any fixed parity and set off a vicious spiral of depreciation. To allay speculation the French therefore proposed that realignment be followed by the establishment of new, more realistic gold standard parities by the Bank of England, Bank of France, and Federal Reserve.

In addition to the domestic political situation, the Popular Front had reason to worry about foreign retaliation. Earlier in the decade, France had imposed new commercial restrictions in response to foreign devaluation, leaving her little diplomatic defense against the adoption of comparable

---

52 Opposition on the Left to the option of devaluation was based on a recognition that devaluation would only work by reducing real wages, a result which was viewed as unacceptable. Sauvy, *Histoire*, Vol. 1, p. 246.

measures by the United States and United Kingdom. Equally worrisome was the danger of competitive devaluation. There was no international code of conduct governing the management of exchange rates. The British EEA could intervene with sales of sterling to push the pound down along with the franc, and if 1933 was any indication the American response might be a further devaluation of the dollar. Hence from the French perspective it was essential before proceeding with devaluation to secure an agreement on acceptable margins of adjustment.

For the British and Americans, the danger attached to a French devaluation was that it was beggar-thy-neighbor policy. To the extent that London and Washington viewed one another as inclined to retaliate against a French devaluation, each feared that its own competitive position would be seriously eroded. Moreover, competitive devaluation would only exacerbate exchange-rate instability and uncertainty, with a depressing impact on trade. For the British, the specter of a French devaluation raised the further possibility that London's complete control over the foreign exchange value of sterling would be compromised by French intervention directed at other targets.

The United States and United Kingdom engaged in sporadic negotiations in the spring of 1935, but to little effect since the Americans were primarily concerned to avoid another round of competitive devaluation while the British were primarily concerned to retain their freedom of action. Following the triumph of the Popular Front in 1936, channels of communication between the governments were reopened. The United States continued to press for multilateral negotiations over acceptable margins of adjustment, while the United Kingdom was willing to go no further than to express its hope that the dollar-pound rate could be held steady so long as devaluation of the franc was moderate.[53] Blum and his ministers couched any discussion of devaluation in terms of a fundamental restructuring of the international monetary order. In early September the French proposed an agreement among the three governments which would specify new bands for the franc, dollar, and pound, commit the three governments to collaborative efforts to maintain those rates, bind them not to devalue except by mutual agreement or under exceptional and unforeseen circumstances, and compel them to return to gold convertibility once stability was restored.[54]

The ambitious French proposal was coolly received in London and Wash-

---

[53] On the reopening of negotiations, see Sauvy, *Histoire*, Vol. 1, p. 270. On the different national objectives, see Clarke, "Exchange Rate Stabilization," p. 25.

[54] Clarke, "Exchange Rate Stabilization," p. 34.

ington. The Americans were unwilling to commit to an eventual return to gold or to stabilizing the dollar within a fixed band. Treasury Secretary Morgenthau favored only a mechanism for collaboration among the exchange equalization funds of the three countries and working agreements about the management of rates. The British opposed even more strongly any scheme which threatened to limit their freedom of action.[55] British officials hoped only that Blum and his Minister of Finance Vincent Auriol would devalue the franc in a convincing yet moderate manner, by a margin large enough to induce foreign capital inflows and permit stabilization but small enough to leave unaffected relations between London and Washington.[56]

The French response to these objections was to drop their proposal for fixed bands but to continue advocating an eventual return to gold.[57] However, the Americans and British continued to object to any mention of the gold standard. By the middle of September the French had begun to recognize that the only agreement which might prove acceptable to both London and Washington was one couched in very general terms.[58] Auriol's next proposal was for a single declaration by the three governments pledging to avoid unilateral changes in exchange rates and unnecessary trade restrictions.[59] The Treasuries and central banks of the three countries were to agree to cooperate in managing the exchange markets either through bilateral consultations or multilateral negotiations. This proved an acceptable formula. However, to hasten their appearance, Morgenthau suggested substituting for a document signed by the three governments the simultaneous issuing of separate statements once reference to the particularly contentious issues had been removed.

---

[55] This is precisely the way they put it to the French. Archives of the French Ministry of Finance (Min. Fin.) B32325, Letter from the Chancellor of the Exchequer, 14 September 1936. Another British concern, sometimes now heard in connection with the European Monetary System, was that the establishment of fixed bands for exchange rates would strengthen the position of speculators by increasing the likelihood of adjustments in one direction, and thereby increase rather than diminish speculative pressures. See Clarke, "Exchange Rate Stabilization," p. 36.

[56] Drummond, "London, Washington and the Management of the Franc, 1936–39," *Princeton Studies in International Finance*, no. 45 (November), p. 9.

[57] Min. Fin. B32325, "Projet des note aux gouvernements Americain et Britannique," 8 September 1936.

[58] PRO T177/31, "Sir Warren Fisher for Mr. Morgenthau," 14 September 1936, in Telegraphic Correspondence Respecting the Devaluation of the Franc. Printed for the Foreign Office, September 1936.

[59] "Secretary of State to Chancellor of the Exchequer," 20 September 1936 in ibid.

With all reference to the gold standard and fixed parities eliminated, the Tripartite Declarations, much like the resolutions adopted at Genoa in 1922, amounted basically to three simultaneous statements of willingness to engage in consultations among Treasuries and central banks.[60] No formal mechanism for actually coordinating policies was specified in the documents. Nevertheless, these declarations were seen as essential to insure that the new level for the French franc would be defensible. Otherwise, competitive devaluations would be anticipated by the market and create anticipations of a further devaluation of the franc. In return for extending this expression of cooperation so desired by the French, the Americans and British hoped that they might be able to influence France's choice of parity and prevent an excessive devaluation.

Immediately upon the French devaluation of slightly more than 25 percent and release of the declarations, continuous cooperation among the exchange equalization funds and central banks of the three countries commenced. Belgium embraced the principles of the agreement one day later, and the Dutch and Swiss governments joined within a month. The agreement was hailed by the press. As the *New York Times* put it, 'A streak of sunlight had broken through the dark clouds of nationalism; International cooperation was still possible.'[61]

In contrast to the aftermath of the Genoa Conference, specific arrangements for day-to-day collaboration followed within a month. Under the provisions of the Gold Agreement Act of October 1936, exchange rates were agreed to daily and the three exchange funds cooperated in market intervention, deciding on a common currency to be bought or sold and settling accounts daily in gold.[62] In this respect, the contrast with 1922 was striking. Part of the explanation for the successful implementation of the Tripartite Agreement lies in the fact that by 1936 the major political obstacles to collaboration – notably Reparations and war debts – had largely receded from view. At least as important, however, was explicit recognition that the range of issues subject to collaboration would be circumscribed and

---

[60] For the text of the three declarations, see Bank for International Settlements, *The Tripartite Agreement of September 25, 1936 and Subsequent Monetary Arrangements* (Basle, 1937).

[61] "Restoring Monetary Order," *New York Times,* 4 October 1936.

[62] The exchange funds informed one another each morning of the currency in which they proposed to deal. If the other parties agreed to the currency and the rates, a gold price was specified at which each central bank would exchange foreign currency for gold at the close of the business day. This price was subject to change at the beginning of the next trading day. See PRO T177/33, "Cypher Telegram to Mr. Mallet (Washington)," 7 October 1936.

that nothing in the agreement threatened to undermine each government's independence to formulate domestic policy.

The Tripartite Declarations had warned that although 'in their policy toward international monetary relations [governments] must take into full account the requirements of internal prosperity, the constant object of their policy is to maintain the greatest possible equilibrium in the system of international exchange and avoid to the utmost extent the creation of any disturbance by domestic monetary action.'[63] From this statement it might appear that priority was attached to international policy coordination. In fact, however, internal balance was explicitly recognized as the paramount goal of policy, and the maintenance of international stability was basically a useful ancillary target. As Beyen (1949, p. 112) suggests, policy coordination was seen not as a positive objective of policy but as a negative promise not to indulge in initiatives that might be overly disruptive to the international monetary system.

The international monetary order that emerged from the Tripartite Agreement placed great emphasis on consultation, but beyond efforts to coordinate day-to-day management of the markets placed few restraints on independent action. It provided no mechanism for the formal coordination of monetary or fiscal policies. Nothing in the agreement bound the participating countries to set their exchange rates at current levels. However, under the new arrangement the dollar began to emerge as the link between gold and other currencies, a position it was to hold for more than two decades following the Second World War. The United States was by no means bound to stabilize its currency at $35 to an ounce of gold, a price which could be changed on 24 hours' notice. But with the passage of time the Administration grew increasingly attached to this rate. With the dollar fixed but adjustable in terms of gold and other currencies adjustable at the beginning of each day in terms of the dollar, the system resembled a hybrid of Bretton Woods (in terms of the relation between gold and the dollar) and a crawling peg (in terms of the relationship between the dollar and other currencies).

By the end of 1936, many of the recommendations put forward at Genoa in 1922 had been implemented but, ironically, at the expense of exchange rate stability. Consultation among governments and central banks, so strongly recommended at Genoa, had been institutionalized under the provisions of the Gold Agreement Act of October. Consultation extended

---

63 See Bank for International Settlements, *Tripartite Agreement*.

however only to day-to-day management of exchange markets, national governments retaining complete discretion to set their external rates. The dollar-sterling rate was effectively pegged within a narrow band from the French devaluation in 1936 until the second half of 1939, but the French engaged in several substantial devaluations in the second half of 1937 and again in 1938. The gold economy measures urged at Genoa appeared in the form of restrictions on the internal circulation of gold coin and bullion and measures to limit international flows to transactions between central banks and stabilization funds. With the emergence of currency areas centered upon New York, London and, to a lesser extent, Paris, the reserve currency arrangement proposed at Genoa increasingly became a reality. Indeed, to the extent that the dollar was the currency most tightly linked to gold, it began to exhibit features of the unique role as an international reserve currency it was to take on after World War II. The role for policy coordination lay in lending a semblance of order to the currency markets, insuring that retention of a link to gold was consistent with an adequate level of reserves, and discouraging beggar-thy-neighbor policy. The role for exchange rate flexibility was to provide governments with independence of action. We will never know how long this system would have succeeded in reconciling these objectives.

5. Conclusion

The interwar period witnessed experiments with every modern international monetary arrangement: clean floating in the first half of the twenties and a gold exchange standard in the second, managed floating in the early 1930s, and after 1936 the reintroduction of a link with gold and a form of adjustable peg. Whether the regime was based loosely on a system of rules, as in the case of the gold standard, or placed few limits on the discretion of the authorities, as in the case of floating exchange rates, policymakers harbored no illusions that the international monetary arrangement alleviated the problem of interdependence. In each instance they sought to insure exchange-rate and balance-of-payments stability by establishing a framework conducive to international policy coordination.

A desire for policy coordination is by itself insufficient to insure successful collaboration. The aftermath of the Genoa Conference, when political obstacles impeded efforts to arrange a convention of central banks, illustrates the pitfalls to successful implementation. Ultimately, governments turned to noncooperative strategies within the framework of the gold-exchange standard. The competitive struggle for gold and the deflationary pressures that resulted indicated clearly the advantages of cooperation. Therefore, when France's devaluation in 1936 erased the last vestiges of the interwar gold standard, policymakers once more attempted to establish a framework for coordinated action. On this occasion, not only was the political situation opportune, but in contrast to earlier efforts the negotiators carefully circumscribed the range of issues subject to collaboration and placed relatively few restrictions on each government's freedom of action. Hence the successful conclusion of the Tripartite Agreement and the Gold Agreement Act.

What emerges clearly from this analysis of the interwar period is the tension which pervades all efforts to coordinate economic policies – a tension which is evident also in the 1980s. Then as now the problem for monetary coordination was how to reconcile the need for freedom of action with the desire for order in foreign exchange markets and with the recognition that national policies have international repercussions. Then as now the institutional response was a hybrid international monetary system combining arrangements for exchange market management with autonomy of national policy, and placing a premium on international policy coordination without providing a mechanism for bringing it about.

7. The economic consequences of the franc Poincaré

With Charles Wyplosz

1. Introduction

The macroeconomic performance of the French economy in the 1920s contrasts sharply with cyclical experience in the rest of the industrialized world. French gross domestic product and industrial output grew with exceptional vigor over the first half of the 1920s (see Table 7.1).[1] After a recession in 1926–27 and despite a noticeable deceleration in the rate of economic growth, through the end of the decade the French economy continued to expand at a rate significantly in excess of the international average. Well into calendar year 1930, France remained immune to the effects of the Great Depression, and even in 1931 the downturn remained moderate compared to other parts of the world. But once the full effects of the Depression were felt, its impact in France was exceptionally severe; as late as 1938 gross domestic product had not recovered to 1931 levels.

Accounts of the interwar period attach more weight to the exchange rate than to any other variable affecting the French economy's macroeconomic performance. Histories of the period 1919–26 are dominated by "the battle of the franc," when financial difficulties culminating in the loss of 80 percent of the currency's external value greatly stimulated the export industries and macroeconomy. The period 1926–31 is characterized as the golden era of the "franc Poincaré," when exchange-rate stabilization at an undervalued parity enhanced the competitiveness of French exports, stimulating growth through the end of the decade and insulating the economy from the onset of the Great Depression. Then successive devaluations of other major curren-

Work on this chapter was begun during Eichengreen's visit to the Institut National de la Statistique et des Etudes Economiques. A fellowship from the French Ministry of External Affairs and a Fulbright Grant made this visit possible. We are grateful to INSEAD for financial support, to Robert Levy for exceptionally capable assistance, and to Bradford Lee and participants in the Harvard Economic History Workshop for comments.

[1] Data sources and variable definitions are provided in Appendix A of our 1986 working paper. The country data and weights used to construct "world GDP" in Table 7.1 are the same as in the effective exchange rate calculations to be described.

Table 7.1: *Interwar growth rates*

	France	United States	United Kingdom	Italy	Germany	"World"
Average annual rates of growth of real GDP						
1921–6	10.2	8.4	2.3	2.8	15.1	5.8
1927–30	5.0	−0.9	1.3	1.4	−2.4	−0.3
1930–1	−4.3	−7.7	−5.1	−2.2	−10.9	−7.0
1931–8	−1.6	2.3	3.1	2.8	8.9	−2.8
1921–38	2.8	2.8	2.3	2.0	7.9	2.8
Average annual rates of growth of industrial production						
1921–6	18.9	10.0	6.2	9.1	6.7	9.4
1927–30	8.7	−0.6	−0.7	2.2	−3.8	−1.0
1930–1	−14.8	−19.2	−6.4	−9.4	−18.8	−18.5
1931–8	1.2	7.7	6.1	4.6	14.9	6.9

Source: Eichengreen and Wyplosz (1986, appendix A).

cies starting in 1931 rendered the franc overvalued and greatly exacerbated the impact of the slump on French industry and trade, largely accounting for the singular depth and long duration of the French Depression.

Typically monetary policy is credited with driving the exchange rate and the French economy over the decade ending in 1930. Fiscal policy plays a role only insofar as it influences money supply. In conventional accounts, the period through the summer of 1926 is marked by real and nominal exchange rate depreciation due to excessive money creation. Real depreciation stimulated the French economy for reasons related to both aggregate demand and aggregate supply. On the supply side, the rise in producer prices exceeded the rate of wage inflation, reducing unit labor costs and thereby encouraging firms to increase employment and production. On the demand side, the rate of exchange-rate depreciation exceeded the rate of domestic inflation, enhancing the competitiveness of exports and switching expenditure toward French goods. The period after 1926 is marked by stabilization of the franc at an undervalued rate. Monetary stabilization, by eliminating inflation and reducing nominal interest rates, increased the demand for money, which, under France's gold standard rules, could only be obtained by running a balance-of-payments surplus and importing reserves.[2] Hence the franc's undervaluation continued to stimulate exports

[2] Domestic credit creation was effectively precluded by prohibiting the Bank of France from engaging in expansionary open market operations or monetizing government budget deficits. See Chapter 5, above.

after 1926. In this conventional view, the French economy's expansion in the decade ending in 1930 is a classic instance of export-led growth.

In this chapter we reassess the cyclical performance of the French economy in the 1920s, focusing particularly on the period 1926–31 and on France's resistance to the Great Depression. We find strikingly little support for the export-based explanation of French economic growth after 1926. Although French exports as a share of GDP turn down as early as 1928, the economy continues to expand for several subsequent years. Investment, not exports, emerges as the proximate source of the French economy's resistance to the Great Depression. And fiscal stabilization emerges as the major determinant of French investment spending. In effect, we argue for a more balanced view of the roles of monetary and fiscal policies in French macroeconomic fluctuations over the decade 1921–30.

Whereas our discussion of the links between fiscal policy and investment stresses the resource flow or classic crowding-in effects of budget deficit reductions, an alternative explanation emphasizes instead Poincaré's reputation for financial orthodoxy: Poincaré's return to power removed the specter of financial uncertainty, prospective future budget deficits, and large-scale capital levies, igniting a massive capital inflow that reduced the required rate of return on capital and stimulated investment. In fact, the two hypotheses are compatible, as we shall explain. Our empirical analysis suggests, however, that classic crowding-in due to current budgetary measures, rather than confidence-induced capital inflows due in part to expected future budgetary measures, was the critical determinant of the French investment boom.

In the course of challenging the traditional interpretation of French macroeconomic trends in the 1920s, we touch on several issues of more general interest relevant to contemporary experiences with fiscal stabilization. We provide an explicit analysis of the effects of a fiscal contraction in a perfect-foresight model of an open economy in which the government budget is linked to stocks of productive capital and foreign debt, and in which fiscal policy has an impact on employment due to inertia in labor markets. Previous investigators have studied fiscal policy in the presence of wage and price rigidities but in static models without public sector and economy-wide budget constraints (Mundell, 1963; Fleming, 1962; Sachs, 1980). Dynamic models have been developed but without capital accumulation (Branson and Buiter, 1983; Sachs and Wyplosz, 1984; Cuddington and Viñals, 1986). Investigators working in the disequilibrium tradition combine wage and price rigidities with capital accumulation, but only under restrictive assumptions about dynamics (Neary and Stiglitz, 1983). In these pages, we integrate the essential features of these models into a more general framework.

2. French economic performance, 1921–31

Historical accounts of the French economy in the years 1921–30 typically divide the decade into three segments: the period of inflation from 1921 through mid-1926, the period of stabilization from Poincaré's return to power in July 1926 through the 1927 recession, and the period of renewed growth through the end of 1930. The decline of the franc in the first half of the twenties is credited with subsidizing exports and promoting investment by lightening the burden of fixed charges (Kemp, 1972, p. 97; Bernard, 1975, p. 180; Jackson, 1985, p. 11). Establishment of the franc Poincaré in the second half of the decade, "by slightly undervaluing the currency," is credited with stimulating "an export-led boom to round off the period of postwar prosperity" (Kemp, 1972, p. 84). The Great Depression has relatively little impact on France as late as 1930 chiefly because of exchange-rate undervaluation (Kemp, 1971, p. 89; 1972, p. 100).[3]

To assess the role of the exchange rate in these developments, it is first necessary to have an adequate measure of its movement. We therefore construct quarterly time series for the real and nominal effective exchange rates for the period 1922–37.[4] The nominal effective exchange rate is a weighted

---

[3] These conclusions are representative of an extensive and growing literature. Surveys of the period, such as C. Fohlen, *La France de l'Entre-Deux-Guerres, 1917–1939* (Paris, 1966) and C. Ambrosi, M. Baleste, and M. Tagel, *Economie Contemporaine* (Paris, 1984), convey the same impression of the exchange rate's central role. Kindleberger, *World in Depression*, p. 63, argues that what he refers to as the "French boom" of the second half of the 1920s – an upswing which raised production to impressive levels compared to previous business cycle peaks and did not turn down until the second half of 1931 – was fed by undervaluation of the franc. Even Thomas Sargent, "Stopping Moderate Inflations," not one normally inclined toward nominal variables as explanations for real economic trends, suggests that France remained prosperous in the wake of the Poincaré stabilization partially because of the undervaluation of the franc.

[4] This is not the first nominal effective rate calculated for the interwar years. Redmond, "Indicator," has constructed a nominal effective exchange rate for sterling in the 1930s, whereas he presents nominal effective rates for several currencies, including the franc, for the period from 1929 in J. Redmond, "Effective Exchange Rates in the 1930s: North America and the Gold Bloc," *Journal of European Economic History* 17, 379–409. However, his series for the franc is annual rather than quarterly and does not cover the portion of the twenties of particular interest here. We know of no previous attempt to calculate a real effective exchange rate for this period.

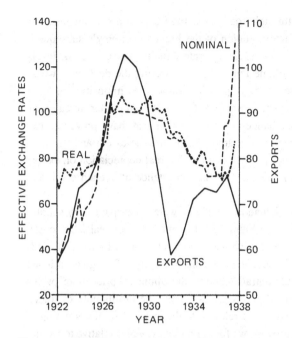

Figure 7.1. Effective exchange rates and exports, 1929 = 100.

average of bilateral rates against France's trading partners, with trade shares serving as weights. The real effective exchange rate is the product of the nominal effective rate and the ratio of foreign to domestic prices. Both effective exchange rates are displayed in Figure 7.1 along with exports in constant 1929 prices.[5] Clearly the real exchange rate had powerful demand-side effects.[6] But although persistent real depreciation was accompanied by

[5] In Table 7.9 we present the effective exchange rate series. Note that the nominal effective rate continues to vary even after France's return to gold because of further exchange-rate change abroad. While small at first, these variations increase in size with sterling's devaluation in 1931 and the dollar's devaluation in 1933.

[6] Both series are measured on an annual average basis. An ordinary least squares regression corrected for first-order serial correlation yields:

$$EXPORTS = -2.17 + 0.74REER + 0.62Y^*, \quad \rho = 0.48, \quad R^2 = 0.83, \quad DW = 1.60,$$
$$(3.89) \quad (3.12) \qquad (3.68) \qquad (1.63)$$

where EXPORTS is *Commerce Spécial* (in millions of tons) from Sauvy, *Histoire*, p. 338, col. 8; REER is the real effective exchange rate (calculated as in Figure 7.1, so that a rise denotes real depreciation); and Y^* is the index of world industrial production (from London and Cambridge Economic Service, *The British Economy*), shown in Table 7.1. The data are annual and the estimation period is 1922–38. In the regression, all variables are entered in logs, with t-statistics in parentheses. ρ is the first order autocorrelation coefficient.

steady export growth through 1926, post-1927 experience is inconsistent with the export-based interpretation of the French economy's subsequent expansion. Despite the real exchange rate's maintenance at peak levels through 1930, export volume fell in 1929, reflecting the decline in world incomes due to the onset of the Depression followed by imposition of trade restrictions abroad.[7] The export share of GDP fell even earlier, in calendar year 1928. Although exchange-rate depreciation may have prevented exports from declining even more rapidly than this, the extent and the very fact of their decline suggests that the impact of real depreciation on export demand cannot by itself account for the persistence of French economic growth after 1928.[8]

To see whether these demand-side effects were accompanied by supply-side stimuli, we consider in Figure 7.2 two measures of real labor costs: the nominal wage deflated by wholesale and retail price indices, labeled, respectively, the real producer and real consumer wage. Though each index includes both traded and nontraded goods, the wholesale price index places a heavier weight on traded-goods prices.[9] Since the profitability of traded goods production is particularly relevant to the export-led interpretation of the French economy's growth, we focus on money wages relative to whole-sale prices as a measure of the real wage. Although Figure 7.2 confirms that nominal wages lagged behind wholesale prices during the 1922–26 inflation, it indicates also that much of this reduction in real producer wages was eroded within a year of stabilization.[10] Once inflation was halted in

---

7 The pattern we describe in the text holds for exports of foodstuffs, raw materials, and manufactured goods alike, except that raw materials exports fall in 1928, foodstuffs in 1929, and manufactures in 1930. The early downturn in exports of materials reflects the worldwide slump in primary commodity markets, which even an "undervalued franc" was apparently unable to overcome. See Lewis, *Economic Survey*.

8 Another channel through which the exchange rate conceivably might have influenced demand was import substitution. Even if the volume of exports fell after 1928 and the export/GNP ratio fell after 1927, depreciation could have stimulated domestic demand had expenditure on imports been switched toward home goods at an even faster rate. In fact, the trade balance deteriorates rather than improves over the period, indicating that imports declined less quickly than exports, which casts doubt on the import-substitution hypothesis.

9 For example, such nontraded goods as housing, the prices of which moved in a very different fashion due to rent control, are included only in the retail price index. See Hawtrey, *Art of Central Banking*. On the construction of these indices, see INSEE, *Annuaire Statistique de la France: Résumé retrospectif* (Paris, 1966).

10 The one exception to the general erosion of real wages during the inflationary era – the rise in real wages between the first and second quarters of 1924 – is itself explicable in terms of wage lag: the exceptional real wage increase of early 1924 took place in a period when the authorities succeeded in temporarily stabilizing the franc and actually engineering a price decline.

Figure 7.2. Real consumer and producer wages and unemployment.

1926, the franc appreciated over the second half of the year and prices declined, albeit more slowly than the exchange rate recovered. As prices fell, money wages lagged behind, and by 1927:3 the relationship between wages and wholesale prices had been restored to 1923 levels. By 1928 the franc no longer provided the producers of traded goods an incentive to expand export supplies. It does not appear, therefore, that the franc's depreciation had long-lived supply-side effects.

This emphasis on supply-side considerations is predicated on the notion that the real producer wage influenced the level of employment, because employers adjusted hiring to equate the cost of labor and the value of its marginal product. As evidence of this relationship, Figure 7.2 also presents Galenson and Zellner's (1957) estimate of French unemployment. Though this estimate of the unemployment rate is far from definitive, even with a generous margin for error it would appear that the real producer wage and unemployment tended to move in the same direction. Although the 1927 recession, when firms apparently were demand constrained, is a notable exception, the correspondence between the real producer wage and unemployment is generally consistent with our interpretation.

The finding that the franc's depreciation failed to have long-lived supply-

Table 7.2: *Decomposition of French national income*
(as percentage of GNP)

	Consumption	Investment	Government spending	Current account
1922	.533	.139	.312	.016
1923	.606	.140	.240	.014
1924	.599	.167	.216	.019
1925	.648	.152	.176	.023
1926	.645	.174	.152	.029
1927	.670	.143	.163	.023
1928	.643	.180	.159	.017
1929	.658	.183	.147	.013
1930	.608	.209	.182	.001
1931	.629	.193	.190	−.012
1932	.645	.165	.214	−.023
1933	.646	.156	.213	−.015
1934	.656	.146	.205	−.007
1935	.631	.147	.225	−.004
1936	.634	.153	.230	−.016
1937	.634	.156	.232	−.022
1938	.637	.141	.221	.001

Source: Calculated from Carré, Dubois, and Malinvaud, *French Economic Growth.*

side effects contrasts with experience elsewhere in Europe both in the first half of the 1920s and after 1931. In both instances, nominal depreciation tended to reduce real wages and have a sustained impact on unit labor costs.[11] Only in France in the mid-1920s was the impact of nominal depreciation on real wages not sustained. The reason for the contrast, Figure 7.2 suggests, is not necessarily any exceptional flexibility of the French labor market, but that the Poincaré stabilization initiated a large fall in the nominal exchange rate and prices that largely neutralized the implications for aggregate supply of the preceding depreciation. Thus, if the franc Poincaré insulated France from the initial effects of the Depression, it must have worked through different channels than those emphasized in simple aggregate-supply/aggregate-demand analyses.[12]

[11] On the early 1920s in Europe, North America, Japan, and the Antipodes, see B. Eichengreen, "The Australian Economic Recovery of the 1930s in International Comparative Perspective," in N.G. Butlin and R.G. Gregory (eds.), *Recovery From the Depression* (Sydney, 1989). On European experience in the 1930s, see Chapter 9.

[12] One possibility is that it had major sectoral effects. It is true that all sectors of the economy did not share equally in France's initial immunity to the Great Depression. Textiles and

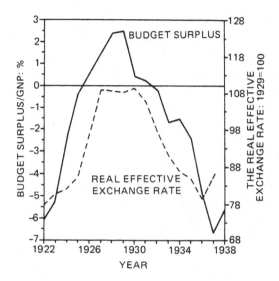

Figure 7.3. The budget surplus and the real effective exchange rate.

To shed further light on the behavior of investment-goods industries, Table 7.2 decomposes GNP into consumption, investment, government spending, and the current account of the balance of payments. The share of investment in GNP rises rapidly toward the end of the 1920s, from 14 percent in 1927 to nearly 21 percent in 1930 and 19 percent in 1931. In comparison, the current account moves only slightly, from a surplus of 3 percent of GNP in 1926 to balance in 1930. Clearly, the "French boom" of the second half of the 1920s was investment-led expansion, not export-led growth. Insofar as France resisted the onset of the Depression, credit lies with the buoyancy of investment rather than with exports.

The shifts in the composition of demand between exports, investment, and government spending emerge as a key feature of the period. Figure 7.3 further documents the dramatic evolution of the government budget. It moves from substantial deficit in the immediate postwar years to balance by 1925–26 and then into surplus, which peaks as a share of GNP in 1929. These shifts should have been promoted by the changes in relative prices

autos did relatively poorly whereas engineering machinery did relatively well. The general pattern seems to favor investment-goods over consumer-goods industries. (We used here industrial production indices from various issues of League of Nations, *Monthly Statistical Bulletin*.) Existing accounts provide no guidance, however, as to why exchange-rate changes should have had such differential effects.

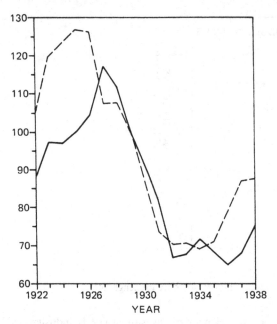

Figure 7.4. Export performance and relative prices, 1929 = 100. *Key:* solid line, share of exports/GNP; dashed line, wholesale/retail prices.

displayed in Figure 7.4 (and implicit in Figure 7.2). The rise in the ratio of retail to wholesale prices after 1927 implies an increase in the relative price of nontraded goods that should have shifted resources out of the production of exportables and into the home goods sector. This explains how the French economy accommodated the fall in export demand associated with the onset of the Depression abroad without significantly reducing the level of economic activity. At approximately the same time as the onset of the Depression was reducing foreign demand for French exports, the rise in the relative price of nontraded goods at home was transferring resources out of the production of exportables and into the production of nontradables.

This reallocation of resources cannot be viewed simply as a response to the Depression, however. Were this the case, one would expect the traded-nontraded goods price ratio to move concurrently with or to follow the decline in export demand. In fact, Figure 7.4 shows that the fall in the relative price of traded goods led by a year the decline in the export share of French GNP. This suggests the need to analyze supply conditions at a more disaggregated level.

This review of French economic performance in the 1920s identifies two central questions. First, why did the price and production of French exports fall after 1927 despite the maintenance of a depreciated exchange rate? Second, what accounts for the surge in domestic investment? We take up these questions one at a time in the next two sections.

3. Export growth and stabilization: a Franco-Scandinavian model

Clearly, a one-sector model that fails to distinguish between the production of traded and nontraded goods is incapable of capturing key aspects of French economic performance in this period.[13] The distinction between traded and nontraded goods has been popularized by Scandinavian economists (e.g., Aukrust, 1977; Edgen, Faxen, and Odhner, 1969). In the Scandinavian model, wages are tied to the prices of traded goods.[14] Figure 7.2 suggests, however, that in the 1920s French wages were more closely linked to the cost of living inclusive of the prices of nontraded goods. Our model therefore departs from the Scandinavian approach in its specification of wage determination, and in addition by allowing the level of employment to be endogenously determined.[15]

We start with the small country assumption, which implies that rest-of-world prices of traded goods P^* together with the exchange rate determine the domestic price of traded goods P_T (we relax the assumption of parametric export prices in the next section):

---

[13] The importance of this distinction did not escape contemporary French economists such as Dessirier, who calculated indices of profitability separately for industries producing traded and nontraded goods. In addition, Dessirier distinguished a third sector comprised of firms engaged in the provision of public services. See J. Dessirier, "Secteurs 'abrités' et 'non abrités' dans le Déséquilibre Actuel de l'Économie Française," *Revue d'économie politique* (July–August 1935), 1330–61.

[14] It is this focus on wage formation that leads us to emphasize our model's resemblance to the Scandinavian Model rather than the Dependent Economy Model in W. Salter, "Internal and External Balance: The Role of Price and Expenditure Effects," *Economic Record* XXXV (1959), 226–38; and T. Swan, "Economic Control in a Dependent Economy," *Economic Record* 73 (1960), 51–66, which also distinguishes traded and nontraded goods.

[15] To our knowledge, no previous model incorporates both these features, although the framework developed here bears some resemblance to those of R. Dornbusch, "Real and Monetary Aspects of the Effects of Exchange Rate Changes," in R.Z. Aliber (ed.), *National Monetary Policies and the International Financial System* (Chicago, 1974), 64–81; J. Frenkel and C. Rodriguez, "Exchange Rate Dynamics and the Overshooting Hypothesis," *IMF Staff Papers* 29 (March 1982), 1–30; and R. Dornbusch, *Open Economy Macroeconomics* (New York, 1980), 97–115. Dornbusch's Dependent Economy Model implicitly maintains the assumption of full employment, however, whereas in Frenkel and Rodriguez output depends only on relative commodity prices.

$$P_T = eP^*, \tag{1}$$

where the exchange rate e is the domestic price of one unit of foreign currency. P^* is normalized to unity. Throughout, T and N subscripts denote traded and nontraded goods, respectively.

We assume that the production of nontraded goods is less capital intensive than the production of tradables. For simplicity, nontraded goods are characterized as Ricardian commodities, requiring inputs of labor alone. (All our conclusions carry over to the general case, so long as nontraded goods remain labor intensive.) Perfect competition, constant returns to scale, and marginal cost pricing together imply that the price of nontraded goods is proportional to the wage W. Normalizing labor productivity to unity gives

$$W = P_N. \tag{2}$$

Traded goods, in contrast, are Heckscher-Ohlin commodities, produced using both labor and an exogenously fixed stock of capital. (We relax the assumption of a fixed capital stock in the next section.) Given a production function $f(L, K)$ and the assumption of perfect competition, employment in the traded goods sector is adjusted to equate the wage with the value marginal product of labor (VMPL$_T$):

$$W = P_T f_L(L) = e f_L(L), \quad f_L < 0, \tag{3}$$

where $f_L = \partial f / \partial L$. Inverting (3) yields the derived demand for labor in the traded goods sector:

$$L_T = f(W/e), \quad f' < 0. \tag{4}$$

Under the small country assumption, domestic producers of traded goods are not constrained in the quantities they sell; though domestic demand depends on relative prices and income, any excess of domestic supply over demand can be exported to foreign markets. Domestic producers adjust production and hiring to be on their labor demand curves. In Figure 7.5, employment in the production of traded goods is the distance PL_T. This distance is determined by the intersection of the employment schedule VMPL$_T$ with the wage.

In contrast to the demand for traded goods, which is perfectly elastic at world prices, the demand for nontraded goods depends on domestic income (which is proportional to total employment L_T and L_N) and on their relative price P_N/P_T. The (uncompensated) price elasticity of demand for

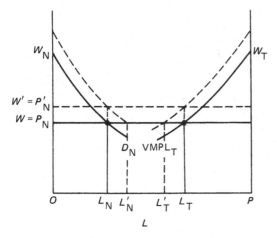

Figure 7.5. Labor market equilibrium.

nontraded goods appears in Figure 7.5 as the D_N schedule, which (under the Ricardian assumption) is also the derived demand for labor in the non-traded goods sector. Employment in the production of nontraded goods is the distance OL_N:

$$L_N = g(P_N/P_T) = g(W/e), \quad g' < 0. \tag{5}$$

Aggregate labor supply is constant and represented in Figure 7.5 by the length OP. Unemployment is the distance L_TL_N. Taking the exchange rate as exogenous, the model is closed by a wage determination rule. We assume that labor mobility equates wages across sectors and, as suggested by Figure 7.2, that economy-wide wages respond with a lag to the cost of living:[16]

$$W_t = \gamma e_{t-1} + (1 - \gamma)P_{N,t-1}. \tag{6}$$

We can use this model to analyze the effects of a permanent, unanticipated depreciation of the exchange rate.[17] Depreciation raises the VMPL$_T$ schedule in Figure 7.5. Given the lagged response of nominal wages to the cost of living, the real producer wage in the traded goods sector (W/e) falls, and employment in that sector expands to OL'_T. Since $W/e = P_N/P_T$

---

[16] Equation (6) is a linear approximation around an initial position in which W, e, and P_N all equal unity and γ is the share of traded goods in consumption.

[17] A limitation of this framework is the absence of explicit treatment of the monetary sector. Depreciation of the exchange rate therefore must be taken as exogenous.

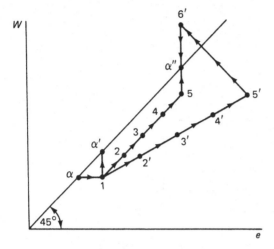

Figure 7.6. Response to a depreciation.

(from equations (1) and (2)), depreciation switches domestic demand toward nontraded goods. Both the relative price and the income effects shift the D_N schedule upward, increasing the demand for labor in the nontraded goods sector. In the period of the depreciation, unemployment falls from $L_T L_N$ to $L'_T L'_N$. In the subsequent period, wages respond to the initial rise in the cost of living, restoring the equality $W = P_N = P_T = e$ and returning employment to its initial level. In Figure 7.5 this is shown as an upward shift in the $W = P_N$ schedule.

These dynamics are depicted in Figure 7.6. A one-time depreciation moves the system from α to 1; with the economy to the right of the 45° line, the real wage has been reduced and the level of employment has been correspondingly increased. With no further change in the exchange rate, the wage rises in the next period to α', restoring employment to its initial level.

The model can be used to interpret several macroeconomic features of the 1920s. According to leading accounts of the period (e.g., Sauvy, 1984), the years 1921–6 were dominated by a series of unanticipated depreciations.[18] Each time the exchange rate depreciated, domestic prices initially

---

[18] The lack of foresight regarding the evolution of the exchange rate, inflation, and the money supply is justified on the grounds that changes in the rate of money growth were related to unanticipated changes in governments and Ministers of Finance. There were 11 cabinets in the period 1921–6. See Sauvy, *Histoire*, Vol. 3, pp. 388–92.

lagged behind. Prices and wages subsequently responded, however, to increases in the exchange rate. In Figure 7.6, the path α-1-2-3-4-5 is meant to capture these aspects of French experience. As in Figure 7.2, the real wage (nominal wage deflated by the cost of living) initially falls but remains stable in the face of successive depreciations. (In contrast, the path α-1'-2'-3'-4'-5' shows the effects of accelerating depreciation.) As in Figure 7.4, the CPI falls relative to the WPI, and depreciation is associated with a decline in unemployment. As in Figure 7.1, depreciation is accompanied by a rise in exports.

The effects of terminating inflation and permitting the exchange rate to appreciate before returning the franc to the gold standard (the course of events between Poincaré's return to power in the summer of 1926 and the de facto stabilization at the end of the year) are depicted in Figure 7.6 by the path 5'-6'-α''. Due to the response of wages to lagged prices, real wages rise above their initial level following stabilization, and employment temporarily falls. As in Figure 7.2, stabilization is associated with transitional unemployment, and, as in Figure 7.1, the volume of exports falls.

Thus, a simple model provides a coherent explanation for many of the dominant macroeconomic characteristics of the French economy in the 1920s, including the declining role of exports in the French economy following the Poincaré stabilization. What remains to be explained is the buoyancy of investment in the poststabilization era.

4. Investment and fiscal stabilization: a dynamic model

In this section, we explore the links between the 1926 stabilization, the subsequent decline in the export share of GNP, and the surge in investment spending that was the proximate source of the French economy's resistance to the onset of the Great Depression. The previous section explains the decline in the export share as a delayed effect of exchange-rate stabilization. In this section, we integrate that explanation with an analysis of the investment response.

The model providing the basis for the analysis is summarized in Table 7.3. As in our Franco-Scandinavian model, the domestic economy produces both traded and nontraded goods, traded goods using capital and labor, nontraded goods using labor alone, with the price of nontraded goods proportional to the wage. But in contrast to that model, three distinct commodities are consumed: importables, exportables, and nontraded goods (with the domestic economy specialized in the production of the last two).

Table 7.3: *Model of the French economy*

$Y = Y^E + \lambda^N Y^N$	(9)
$D = D(Y - T, \Omega), \quad D_1, D_2 > 0$	(10)
$\Omega = B + \lambda B^* = qK$	(11)

Nontraded goods sector

$Y^N = D^N + G^N$	(12)
$D^N = \alpha_N D / \lambda_N$	(13)
$G^N = \alpha^N G / \lambda_N$	(14)
$\lambda_{N,t+1} = \lambda_{N,t} + \gamma[Y_t^N - f^N(\lambda_N)], \quad f_{\lambda_N}^N < 0$	(15)

Exportables sector

$Y^E = f^E(K, \lambda_N), \quad f_K^E > 0, \; f_{\lambda_N}^E < 0$	(16)
$Y^E = D^E + G^E + I + X$	(17)
$D^E = \alpha^E D$	(18)
$G^E = \alpha^E G$	(19)
$X = X(\lambda), \quad X_\lambda > 0$	(20)

Investment

$K_{t+1} - K_t = \psi(q_t), \quad \psi_q > 0$	(21)
$I_t = K_{t+1} - K_t + \delta K_t$	(22)
$r_t = (q_{t+1} - q_t)/q_t + f_{K,t}^E$	(23)

Portfolio balance

$r_t = r^* + (\lambda_{t+1} - \lambda_t)/\lambda_t + \theta(B_t + q_t K_t, \lambda_t B_t^*), \quad \theta_1 > 0, \; \theta_2 > 0$	(24)

Government budget

$G_t = T_t - r_t B_t + (B_{t+1} - B_t)$	(25)

Demand depends on two relative prices, the price of nontradables relative to exports (P_N/P_E), and the price of imports relative to exports (eP^*/P_E). (Exportables are the numeraire throughout.) We adopt the semi-small-country assumption that the world price of imports is given exogenously, but that domestic supplies are capable of influencing the world price of exports. We define the real exchange rate as

$$\lambda = eP^*/P_E \qquad (7)$$

and the relative price of nontraded goods as

$$\lambda_N = P_N/P_E. \qquad (8)$$

The real exchange rate, investment, and the adjustment of government spending are now endogenously determined. Real GDP is given by (9) in Table 7.3. Real expenditure, given by (10), is a function of real disposable income and real wealth Ω. Disposable income as a determinant of expenditure can be justified on the basis of liquidity constraints; thus, our expenditure function incorporates both Keynesian and permanent income features.[19] As in the previous section, the supply of traded goods is perfectly elastic at the prevailing wage (12), with the wage adjusting gradually to eliminate excess supply or demand in the labor market (15). Domestic expenditure is the sum of the demands of the private (13) and public (14) sectors, whose allocations across commodities are derived from instantaneous Cobb-Douglas utility functions.

The real exchange rate λ adjusts instantaneously to clear the market for exportables (17). The demand for exportables is the sum of private (18), public (19), and foreign (20) consumption plus domestic investment (17). Capital accumulation is a function of Tobin's q (21). Gross investment spending differs from capital accumulation by an allowance for capital depreciation at rate δ (22).

Domestic debt and equity are assumed to be perfect substitutes for one another but imperfect substitutes for foreign assets. Foreigners do not hold domestic assets. These assumptions highlight the role of the (exchange) risk premium in rendering domestic residents willing to hold increasing quantities of domestic assets. They are designed to capture the idea that increases in public debt raise the danger of a capital levy on all domestic assets, a policy option much discussed in France in the 1920s. Portfolio balance determines the relationship among the domestic real interest rate, foreign real interest rate, and real exchange rate (23), where B_t is the real value of public debt (in units of exportables) and B_t^* the net real value of foreign assets held by domestic residents. We assume perfect foresight regarding the evolution of the real exchange rate λ and equity prices q. The perfect substitutability of domestic debt and equity implies that the real yield on one-period bonds r_t equals dividends plus capital gains on shares. This arbitrage condition is given by (24) with dividends assumed to equal the marginal productivity of capital.

Equation (25) is the government budget constraint. The growth of public debt equals the excess of government spending G over the sum of net taxes T and debt service rB. Changes in fiscal policy take the form of changes in government spending, holding taxes constant.

Our neglect of the monetary sector in general, and of money financing of the deficit in particular, in our analysis of the post-1926 situation can

---

[19] In the limiting case of perfect substitutability, $db/dz = \infty$. The analysis which follows is based on the general case of imperfect substitutability. In the interest of simplicity, we suppress the Laursen-Metzler effect. However, permitting saving to be positively related to λ would have no effect on our simulation results.

be justified on two grounds. First, under the gold standard the supply of money was determined, in principle, exclusively by money demand. Given a credibly pegged exchange rate, nominal interest rates were determined exclusively by interest rates in the rest of the world; changes in the domestic credit component of the monetary base therefore should have had no implications for total money supply. Second, after 1926 the Bank of France functioned under new regulations which prohibited it from monetizing government budget deficits.

To analyze the post-1926 situation in France, we perform the following experiment. Starting from steady-state equilibrium in period zero, we cut government spending so as to reduce the steady-state value of public debt from B_0 to $\overline{B}$. The real debt is assumed to evolve according to

$$B_t = B_{t-1} + \mu(\overline{B} - B_{t-1}). \tag{26}$$

Since taxes are held constant, (25) and (26) together determine the path of public spending.[20]

Given its size, the model in Table 7.3 cannot be solved analytically. Instead, we calibrate it using data for the 1920s, linearize it around the steady state, and simulate it under the assumption of perfect foresight. Parameter values and initial conditions for endogenous variables are given in Tables 7.3 and 7.4. Although we have attempted to use historical data to guide the selection of parameter values, any attempt at calibration can only approximate the properties of the economy being modeled. The simulation results only illustrate the properties of the model and indicate the general orders of magnitude of the results of our fiscal policy experiment.

The simulation generates a real depreciation on impact followed by a relatively flat real exchange rate path, both of which resemble Figure 7.1. As the fiscal contraction reduces domestic demand, an incipient excess supply of exportables develops and is eliminated through a fall in their relative price, which increases export sales. The brevity of the 1927 recession may be explicable in part on the basis of this expenditure-switching effect.

Thus, we find that not only monetary policy but fiscal policy as well is critical for understanding the post-1926 real exchange rate path. Had the real depreciation of the period 1922-6, so prominent in Figure 7.1,

---

[20] Alternative deficit closing rules are discussed in Sachs and Wyplosz, "Exchange Rate Effects." Nothing of importance hinges on the particular specification adopted here since it is assumed that government spending falls on exportables, nontradables, and imported goods in the same proportions as private spending.

Table 7.4: *Simulation results* ($B_0 = 800$, $\overline{B} = 700$)

	B	λ	λ_N	q	I	G	X	Y
Initial steady state	800	100.0	100.0	1.000	9.5	38.0	25.1	145.0
Period 1	800	109.1	100.0	1.026	10.8	23.8	26.8	137.9
Period 2	781	108.3	99.4	1.018	10.4	29.0	26.7	141.6
Period 3	773	108.2	99.1	1.017	10.4	30.1	26.7	142.7
Period 4	766	108.2	99.0	1.016	10.3	30.7	26.6	143.3
Period 5	759	108.1	98.9	1.014	10.2	31.3	26.6	143.8
Period 10	735	108.3	98.6	1.011	10.1	33.3	26.7	145.4
Period 20	712	109.2	98.2	1.008	10.0	35.4	26.8	147.4
Period 30	704	110.3	97.9	1.005	9.8	36.0	27.0	148.3

Note:

Initial values: $Y_0 = 145$, $Y_0^N = 69$, $Y_0^E = 76$, $G_0 = 38$, $I_0 = 9.5$, $D_0 = 100$, $X_0 = 25.1$, $B_0 = 800$, $B_0^* = 500$, $K_0 = 1900$, $q_0 = \lambda_0 = \lambda_{N0} = 1$. $r_0 = 0.01$.

Parameter values: $x^E = 0.3$, $x^N = 0.5$, $\delta = 0.1$, $\mu = 0.1$, $r^* = 0.05$.

Production functions: exportables, Cobb-Douglas with share of capital $= 0.25$; nontraded goods, $(\partial Y^N/\partial \lambda)(\lambda/Y^N) = 0.2$.

Consumption function marginal propensities to spend: out of income, 0.9; out of wealth, 0.1.

Portfolio balance: $\partial r/\partial(B + \cdots /\lambda B^*) = 0.001$.

Investment function: $\partial(K_{t+1} - K_t)/\partial q_t = 4$.

resulted simply from nominal exchange rate overshooting in response to monetary expansion and inflation prior to the Poincaré stabilization (the Dornbusch, 1976, mechanism), one would expect the real exchange rate to recover following monetary stabilization; instead, the real exchange rate remains high, suggesting that the domestic expenditure effects of fiscal contraction played a dominant role in its post-1926 path. (The correlation between the government budget deficit and the real exchange rate is evident in Figure 7.3.) Thus, the real depreciation of the franc, rather than a clever ploy by French monetary policymakers, should be seen as a consequence of the fiscal reforms which eliminated the budget deficit.

The simulation also generates a surge in investment as a result of a jump in Tobin's q.[21] Following its initial rise, q declines continuously toward its steady-state level, and investment falls gradually. The behavior of q is a consequence of the public debt reduction. The real exchange rate depreci-

---

[21] By specifying investment solely as a function of q and eliminating any accelerator mechanism, the danger is reduced that an investment response to an autonomous recovery could be misconstrued as a cause of that recovery.

ates on impact, after which it rises slowly; so long as it is rising the domestic interest rate must fall relative to the yield on foreign assets. Over time, a fall in the outstanding stock of domestic debt reduces the interest rate domestic residents require in order to hold that debt, reinforcing this effect. Since arbitrage equalizes the rates of return on domestic debt and equity, the lower interest rate on debt implies capital losses on equity, causing q to fall over time. For q to fall over time, it must rise on impact, providing the initial stimulus to investment. Thus our model exhibits the crowding-in effect of fiscal stabilization familiar from simple income-expenditure models. But there are two important differences. First, the short-run crowding-in results from the relationship among real interest rates, real exchange rates, and Tobin's q. Second, whereas the fiscal multiplier is positive in the short run, leading to a contraction following stabilization, it is negative in the long run, leading to more real growth. This is because the larger capital stock, which results from higher investment, sustains an increased volume of production. Over the span of time of concern to us here, 1926 to 1931, the reduction in government spending probably remained contractionary, reducing the rate of growth of the French economy. This is consistent with the deceleration in the rate of French economic growth between 1921–6 and 1927–30. At the same time, the fiscal stabilization switched demand toward domestic sources, namely, investment, reducing the economy's dependence on foreign demand and insulating the economy from the initial effects of the Great Depression.

The one aspect of the simulation at variance with historical experience is the simulated decline in the price of nontraded goods relative to the price of exports. The reason for this result is our assumption that investment spending falls exclusively on exportables whereas government spending is distributed among exportables, importables, and nontraded goods. In the simulation, as government spending falls and investment rises, expenditure tends to be switched away from nontraded goods, resulting in a modest decline in their relative price. It would be straightforward to alter the specification of the composition of investment spending to better track this aspect of historical experience.

5. Further evidence

Our specification of investment in the previous section highlights the role of Tobin's q. Figure 7.7 illustrates the close correlation between q and French investment during the interwar years, but suggests that investment

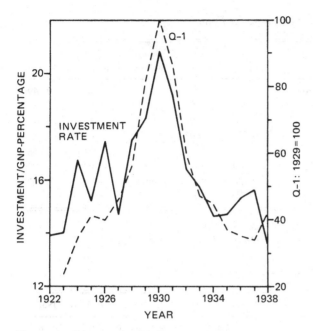

Figure 7.7. Investment and q_{-1}.

depended not on current but on lagged real share prices.[22] This is inconsistent with early formulations of the q theory of investment, as proposed by Tobin (1969) and developed by Abel (1980) and Hayashi (1982), in which current q encapsulates all relevant information about the current and expected future profitability of additions to the capital stock. However, a variety of studies of the postwar period have found, as in Figure 7.7, that lagged q has more explanatory power than current q, leading Fischer (1983), Kydland and Prescott (1982), and Ueda and Yoshikawa (1986) to incorporate order and delivery lags into the q theory of investment and to derive estimating equations in which current investment depends on lagged q. Empirical versions of our investment equation appear in Table 7.5.

---

[22] Note that the dependence of investment on real equity prices need not suggest that the stock market was a significant source of liquidity for firms wishing to fund investment. (In fact, this was generally not the case in interwar France.) Rather, it reflects the impact on investment of assessments of the current and future profitability of additions to the capital stock relative to the cost of those additions, assuming only that the expectations of stock market participants are positively correlated if not necessarily representative of the expectations of investors as a whole.

Table 7.5: *Investment equations for France*

	Constant	q	q_{-1}	dY/Y	Capital inflows	ρ	ξ
1	0.66 (27.58)	-0.08 (-0.79)	0.52 (5.22)	0.53 (2.31)		-0.55 (-1.93)	0.049
2	0.66 (28.02)		0.45 (10.77)	0.41 (2.41)		-0.52 (-1.90)	0.048
3	0.67 (24.47)		0.43 (8.56)			-0.43 (-1.58)	0.056
4	0.63 (21.74)		0.49 (9.74)	0.31 (1.80)	-0.36 (-1.34)	-0.56 (-2.17)	0.047

Note: Annual data: 1923–38. Dependent variable: I/Y.
Source: Sauvy, *Histoire; Statistique Générale de la France* (various issues).

Table 7.6: *Rates of growth of investment*

	1922–6	1922–7	1928	1929	1930	1931	1928–31	1932–8
Total economy	7.8	3.9	23.4	18.7	9.3	-15.0	9.1	-3.6
Agriculture	4.0	3.2	9.2	23.5	-0.8	-8.9	5.8	-1.2
Metallurgy	24.9	18.9	24.6	21.9	4.2	-30.3	5.1	-3.5
Chemical industry	18.4	11.1	37.9	29.8	4.6	-19.7	13.1	-0.9
Textile industry	5.9	3.5	12.0	7.8	-2.1	-28.5	-2.7	-5.1
Buildings	58.2	42.4	43.1	28.2	4.9	-17.1	14.8	-8.9
Transport	-9.2	-9.4	23.5	12.9	44.6	11.5	23.1	-3.9
Services	6.9	1.5	25.2	15.0	7.8	-8.9	9.8	-4.3
Commerce	14.2	8.7	21.5	14.0	-0.5	-13.0	5.5	-8.2

Note: Investment is in constant prices.
Source: INSEE.

The results confirm that lagged q dominates current q as a determinant of investment.[23]

Lagged q plays a central role in our interpretation of French macro-economic performance on the eve of the Great Depression. The buoyancy of the French economy in calendar year 1930 is primarily a buoyancy of investment spending, which remains high in 1930 because q was high in 1929. The investment boom continued into 1930 because of lags in the

---

[23] Our preferred specification, Equation (2), provides support for a hybrid investment equation which combines the q theory with the accelerator. Such equations are sometimes justified on the grounds that some firms are liquidity constrained and are able to increase investment only when profits rise as a result of increased output.

Table 7.7: q and the government budget,
annual data, 1922–37: dependent variable, q

Constant	Budget surplus	λ	Capital inflows	ρ	ξ
0.57	0.10			0.63	0.117
(6.88)	(2.33)			(3.25)	
−0.54	0.02	1.25		0.40	0.104
(−1.20)	(0.54)	(2.51)		(1.63)	
0.57	0.10		0.15	0.62	0.121
(6.72)	(2.25)		(0.17)	(3.08)	

Note: t-statistics in parentheses. The budget surplus variable
is defined as the ratio of the surplus to GNP.
Source: See Eichengreen and Wyplosz (1986, appendix A).

ability of firms to order, receive, and install capital goods and equipment
that they would have wished to obtain in 1929 when stock prices peaked.
The French economy was exceptionally resistant to the onset of the Depression because demand had been switched toward this domestic source –
investment – and away from foreign sources precisely when foreign markets
collapsed.

How general was this surge in investment spending? Table 7.6 displays
investment trends in agriculture, three leading manufacturing industries,
construction, transportation, services, and commerce. Investment rose in
all sectors but transportation in 1927 and across the board in 1928 and 1929.
In 1930 investment fell significantly only in the textile industry (which produced luxury goods for export and therefore was overwhelmed by the onset
of the Depression abroad) and declined marginally in agriculture and commerce as well. In 1931, in contrast, there was a dramatic fall in investment
in every sector except transportation, which was dominated by the relative
stability of government spending. Thus, the investment surge highlighted
in our account of post-1926 French macroeconomic trends is impossible to
explain in terms of shocks to particular sectors, and surely resulted from
economy-wide developments such as changes in the stance of fiscal policy.

In our model, investment is linked to fiscal policy via Tobin's q. Table 7.7
documents the linkage. In the first two equations, q (and, according to
Table 7.5, investment) responds positively to the budget surplus. Evidence
of serial correlation led us to add additional regressors. Neither the money
supply nor its rate of growth (in real or nominal terms) significantly influenced real share prices or reduced the autocorrelation. In contrast, the

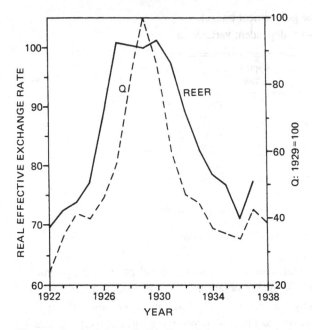

Figure 7.8. q and the real effective exchange rate.

real exchange rate was statistically significant, reduced the autocorrelation, and dominated the fiscal policy measure, as shown in the third line of Table 7.7. The close correlation between Tobin's q and the real exchange rate is evident in Figure 7.8. Yet this correlation is evidence against the fiscal policy–q relationship only if the real exchange rate is not itself a function of fiscal variables. Our model predicts that Tobin's q and the real exchange rate should be jointly determined by fiscal policy. Table 7.8 confirms that this was the case: that fiscal contraction led to real exchange rate depreciation. We enter as additional regressors the rate of real money growth and the rate of real money growth interacted with a dummy variable for the fixed exchange rate period to allow the real exchange rate to respond to both monetary and fiscal policies. Adding monetary policy confirms that both monetary and fiscal policies influenced the path of the real exchange rate, but does nothing to undermine the real exchange rate's dependence on the budget surplus.

Finally, we attempt to test our explanation for the post-1926 investment surge against a competing interpretation. While our explanation for the investment boom stresses observed reductions in the budget deficit and the classic crowding-in effects of contractionary fiscal policy, the alternative

Table 7.8: *The French real exchange rate*

Constant	Budget surplus	Real money growth	Real money growth times FIX	Capital inflows	ρ	ξ	DW
0.88	0.058	—	—	—	0.64	0.054	—
(22.65)	(2.96)				(3.37)		
0.87	0.045	0.17	—	—	0.64	0.052	—
(22.18)	(2.14)	(1.37)			(3.03)		
0.83	0.066	−0.28	0.90	—	—	0.039	1.66
(47.62)	(5.21)	(−1.67)	(4.18)				
0.84	0.066	−0.30	0.88	0.11	—	0.040	1.63
(40.28)	(5.03)	(−1.65)	(3.88)	(0.39)			

Note: Annual data, 1922–37. See Table 7.3. FIX is a dummy variable that takes a value of unity during the fixed exchange rate period (1927–35), and zero elsewhere. Money supply is from Saint-Etienne, "L'offre et la demande."

emphasizes the impact on confidence of Poincaré's reputation for financial orthodoxy. According to the reputational argument, Poincaré's return to power removed the specter of continued financial uncertainty, future budget deficits, and capital levies. Once confidence was restored, capital flight came to an end, reducing the required rate of return on capital and stimulating investment. Thus, confidence – in particular, confidence-induced capital inflows – rather than the resource flow or classic crowding-in effects of contractionary fiscal policy explains the investment boom. Since Tobin's *q* captures market expectations, the confidence interpretation is not incompatible with ours; it differs by asserting that the rise in stock prices cannot be explained solely by contemporary observable policy measures.

Attempts to test the confidence argument lend it little support. Capital inflows, under the alternative view, should be comprised of both a component reflecting observed policy measures and a residual component reflecting confidence. Since the equations estimated in Tables 7.7 and 7.8 include both observed policy measures and capital inflows, the confidence argument can be tested by examining the coefficient on the capital inflows variable.[24] In both tables, the capital inflows proxy uniformly enters insignificantly. Thus, we find no support for the alternative view.

[24] Alternatively, we included a dummy variable for the years of Poincaré's government as another proxy for confidence effects. This variable failed to undermine the significance of the fiscal policy measure, was itself statistically insignificant, and generally entered with a negative sign.

Table 7.9: *Nominal and real effective exchange rates, 1921–1929*

	Nominal	Real		Nominal	Real
1921:4	41.1	75.3	1930:1	98.6	103.4
1922:1	38.3	71.2	1930:2	98.3	107.5
1922:2	37.3	66.4	1930:3	97.5	100.3
1922:3	41.1	71.4	1930:4	97.1	102.1
1922:4	45.1	75.2	1931:1	96.5	100.5
1923:1	49.8	73.7	1931:2	96.5	99.9
1923:2	48.0	71.8	1931:3	94.8	101.6
1923:3	51.4	75.6	1931:4	88.6	96.4
1923:4	53.0	75.1	1932:1	88.3	91.2
1924:1	62.2	78.3	1932:2	89.4	90.4
1924:2	52.6	72.1	1932:3	88.6	92.1
1924:3	57.6	75.2	1932:4	87.6	91.4
1924:4	59.0	75.8	1933:1	87.8	89.7
1925:1	60.6	76.9	1933:2	85.9	86.5
1925:2	63.6	77.0	1933:3	82.9	81.7
1925:3	67.3	77.6	1933:4	81.2	80.7
1925:4	79.1	83.6	1934:1	79.0	78.3
1926:1	88.5	84.2	1934:2	77.7	78.6
1926:2	96.0	87.0	1934:3	77.1	80.7
1926:3	108.2	88.7	1934:4	77.1	83.3
1926:4	107.3	102.1	1935:1	76.1	82.3
1927:1	98.8	100.1	1935:2	72.1	75.9
1927:2	100.3	101.0	1935:3	72.1	78.3
1927:3	100.4	104.2	1935:4	72.1	77.3
1927:4	100.3	107.1	1936:1	72.1	72.9
1928:1	100.1	103.8	1936:2	72.4	72.9
1928:2	100.2	102.5	1936:3	72.6	70.4
1928:3	100.3	102.5	1936:4	94.4	74.5
1928:4	100.2	102.1	1937:1	94.3	71.5
1929:1	100.0	100.0	1937:2	97.8	74.8
1929:2	99.6	100.4	1937:3	118.3	81.6
1929:3	99.5	103.6	1937:4	131.2	88.2
1929:4	99.2	104.6			

Note: 1929: 1 = 100.

6. Conclusion

In this chapter we have critiqued the standard view that the undervalued franc Poincaré, by boosting exports, succeeded initially in insulating
France from the Great Depression. Our own explanation emphasizes instead the role of investment growth as the proximate source of France's
resistance to the onset of the slump. The traditional interpretation has also

tended to stress monetary factors, attributing undervaluation of the franc even after 1929 to a sustained period of inflation terminated by an abrupt monetary stabilization in 1926. We consider such a long-lasting monetary nonneutrality unplausible and focus instead on fiscal stabilization, which transformed the government budget from a large deficit in the early 1920s to surplus after 1926. Real depreciation, the surge in stock prices, and the attendant crowding-in of investment spending are all shown to follow from fiscal stabilization. We do not intend to belittle the role either of monetary factors in the nominal depreciation or of monetary finance of budget deficits. But we wish to emphasize that the independent effects of fiscal policy have not been adequately acknowledged.

These effects are analyzed here using a model relevant to current policy discussions in countries attempting to curb their government deficits and reduce their public debts in the course of stabilization. Although we have not estimated the model, its key assumptions are supported by the data. In particular, the links among fiscal policy, the real exchange rate, and Tobin's q are sufficiently well established that we see no need to invoke the purely psychological effects of Poincaré's return to power when attempting to understand the macroeconomic sequel to that event. What mattered were Poincaré's policies, not just his reputation.

8. Sterling and the tariff, 1929–1932

1. Introduction

In February of 1932, less than six months after leaving the gold standard, Great Britain adopted a 10 percent *ad valorem* tariff on imports from foreign countries.[1] For nearly two years, a number of politicians and economists had argued that Britain should abandon her traditional commitment to free trade and impose a general tariff, initially as a means of reducing unemployment and raising prices without driving herself off the gold standard, and later as a way of balancing her external accounts in order to defend the gold standard directly. Yet it was only *after* Britain was forced off the gold standard in September of 1931 by a combination of domestic and foreign events, and a floating exchange rate was adopted, that a general tariff was finally imposed.

With the demise of the gold standard, a tariff would seem to have retained no special advantage over increased public spending, a reduction in Bank Rate, or other remedies for domestic unemployment. Furthermore, with the adoption of a floating exchange rate, there was a sense in which

I am grateful to the many individuals who have commented on previous versions of this study. I owe special thanks to Carol Gurvitz, Susan Howson, Donald Moggridge, and William Parker, each of whom rendered detailed comments on successive drafts of the manuscript. I would also like to thank Alec Cairncross, N. F. R. Crafts, Carlos Díaz-Alejandro, Richard Kahn, Jorge de Macedo, Lionel Robbins, Robert Skidelsky, Donald Winch, and participants in the Economic History Seminar at All Souls College, Oxford. Remaining errors are my own.

Financial support has been provided by SSRC and Fulbright-Hayes grants. St. Antony's College and the Federal Reserve Board supplied research facilities in Oxford and Washington, D.C., respectively. For permission to cite documents, I acknowledge the Controller of H. M. Stationery Office and the Librarians of the London School of Economics, the Modern Records Centre at the University of Warwick, and the Trades Union Congress.

[1] The standard nominal rate of protection was quickly raised to 20 percent. Effective rates varied widely. See Capie, "British Tariff." It has been estimated that between 1930 and 1932 the percentage of British imports entering duty-free declined from 83 to 25. See Pollard, *Development of British Economy*, p. 197. Duty-free imports under the Import Duties Act of 1932 included most Empire exports and raw materials.

there no longer remained a balance-of-payments "problem."[2] Thus, the decision to impose a tariff in 1932 has remained an unsolved mystery in the history of British economic policy.

Some historians have argued that this decision was ill-conceived and counterproductive. For example, Drummond (1974, pp. 178–9) writes:

> As Professor Mundell has shown, when a country has a floating exchange rate a new tariff is likely to be contractionary – that is, it will increase the number of unemployed, reducing national output and income, other things being equal. . . . The National Government itself believed that it was following an anti-unemployment policy. With respect to its own goals, therefore, we must find its measures inconsistent.[3]

According to this view, at the very time when their concern with unemployment reached its peak, British policy-makers adopted the one policy guaranteed to make unemployment even worse. Their decision is seen as an undiscerning action – an example of the British tendency, when two courses have long been urged, to adopt both (see Skidelsky, 1967).[4]

This chapter tells the story of the circumstances leading to the imposition of the General Tariff of 1932 and offers a new explanation for its adoption.

It is argued that the General Tariff was not imposed as an anti-unemployment policy but rather as an attempt to strengthen the trade balance and prevent the exchange rate from depreciating excessively. Policy-makers were not convinced that Britain's departure from the gold standard had solved the balance-of-payments problem. They had little faith in the curative power of flexible exchange rates. Specifically, they feared that exchange-rate depreciation would set off a "vicious spiral" of inflation, wage increases, and further depreciation, with no improvement in the external accounts. The

---

[2] Even with a floating exchange rate, however, Britain continued to intervene in the foreign-exchange market in the 1930s. Though sporadic at first, this intervention became systematic once the establishment of the Exchange Equalisation Account relieved the Bank of England of the obligation to buy and sell foreign exchange on its own account. The EEA, endowed initially with £175 million, held a portfolio composed of gold, foreign exchange, and British Treasury bills. These assets were controlled by the Treasury, but day-to-day operations were undertaken by the Bank of England on the Treasury's behalf. See Sayers, *Bank of England, 1891–1944;* S. Howson, "The Management of Sterling, 1932–1939," *Journal of Economic History* 40 (1980), 53–60; S. Howson, *Sterling's Managed Float: The Operations of the Exchange Equalisation Account, 1932–1939* (Princeton, 1980). For purposes of the present argument, however, the important fact is that the exchange rate did float.

[3] For an analysis of the generality of Mundell's result, see Eichengreen, "Dynamic Model."

[4] Drummond's assessment is cited in S. Howson and D. Winch, *The Economic Advisory Council, 1930–1939* (London, 1977), p. 97.

General Tariff was designed to accomplish what exchange-rate depreciation would not: the restoration of external balance.

Uneasiness about the stability and corrective power of a floating exchange rate was not the only influence behind the decision to impose the General Tariff in 1932. Special interest groups affected the outcome, and objectives such as the promotion of imperial preference and "rationalisation" in key industries shaped the tariff's structure. (On these questions, see Capie, 1981, and Drummond, 1974.) Party, ideology, and personality determined how politicians responded to the pressures that were applied, and other authors have emphasized factors such as these (see, e.g., Drummond 1972, 1974; Abel, 1945; Lowe, 1942; and Tiwari, 1942). This chapter emphasizes instead the role of the exchange-rate regime in the debate over tariff protection as macroeconomic policy. In contrast to most previous studies, which conclude that the British authorities' adoption of the tariff was a misguided employment policy, the evidence presented here suggests that the authorities' distrust of the effects of a floating exchange rate formed the basis for their decision to impose the General Tariff in 1932.

2. Commercial policy and the gold standard, 1929–1931

By 1929 Britain had endured nearly a decade of sustained unemployment at levels unprecedented in the twentieth century. In every year between 1921 and 1929, the number of workers recorded as unemployed exceeded one million, a level that had been reached only three times in the first twenty years of the century. While figures for the unemployment rate are not directly comparable across decades, the probability of being unemployed in the 1920s appears to have been at least twice as high as it was during the preceding twenty years. The persistence of unemployment can be traced, at least in part, to the decision to return to the gold standard in 1925, which saddled the economy with high interest rates and falling prices, and to the reduced flexibility of wages that characterized the British economy in the 1920s.[5]

---

[5] Statistics are drawn from London and Cambridge Economic Service, *Key Statistics*, pp. 8, 20. On the debate over the causes of interwar unemployment, see J.M. Keynes, *The Economic Consequences of Mr. Churchill* (New York, 1925) and R.S. Sayers, "The Return to Gold, 1925," in S. Pollard (ed.), *The Gold Standard and Employment Policies Between the Wars* (London, 1970), 85–98. For a recent contribution that argues that the dole played an important part in interwar unemployment, see Benjamin and Kochin, "Searching for an Explanation."

Proposals for reducing the level of unemployment by expansionary monetary policy and large-scale public works programs were advanced outside the Government but were rejected by the authorities. In 1923, when the Conservatives advocated the imposition of a tariff as a response to the unemployment problem, the party suffered such a decisive electoral defeat that it campaigned thereafter on the basis of a pledge not to impose new duties.[6]

When the second Labour Government took office under Prime Minister Ramsay MacDonald in June of 1929, the British economy finally appeared to have embarked on the road to recovery. The percentage of insured persons registered as unemployed had fallen from 12.2 to 9.6 since the beginning of the year. The value of total imports and exports was rising, while the level of retail prices and the Bank of England's gold and foreign-exchange reserves appeared to be holding steady.

Initially, the members of the Labour Cabinet were united in their opposition to a tariff. They considered protection to be a regressive method of indirect taxation that would impoverish the working class. Free trade symbolized the labor movement's commitment to internationalism and was justified by the principles of classical political economy. The most committed free trader was Philip Snowden, who based his views on moral, intellectual, and political precepts. The Government's initial attitude toward the tariff question was signaled by the appointment of Snowden as Chancellor of the Exchequer, and of Snowden's disciple Willie Graham as President of the Board of Trade. The Government announced that it would not consider applications for protection, nor would it renew the safeguarding duties, which had been imposed in 1921 to shelter a limited number of key industries against foreign competition. Instead, the Government put its faith in a campaign for an international tariff truce. Graham submitted to the League

---

[6] On a number of occasions, Keynes advocated public works or expansionary monetary policy. See Keynes, *Tract*, chap. 4; J.M. Keynes and H. Henderson, *Can Lloyd George Do It?* (London, 1929). The Bank of England's view is expressed by Governor Norman in his 1930 Macmillan Committee evidence, reprinted in P. Einzig, *Montagu Norman* (London, 1932), pp. 179–255. Recent analyses include Moggridge, *British Monetary Policy;* S. Howson, *Domestic Monetary Management in Britain, 1919–1938* (New York, 1975); and Sayers (1976). On the Treasury view of public works, see R. Hawtrey, "Public Expenditure and the Demand for Labour," *Economica* 13 (March 1925), 38–48. Academic opinion is analyzed by K.J. Hancock, "Unemployment and the Economists in the 1920s," *Economica* 17 (November 1960), 305–21, and Hancock, "The Reduction of Unemployment as a Problem of Public Policy, 1920–1929," *Economic History Review*, new ser., 15 (December 1962), 329–43. For details on the 1923 General Election, see K. Middlemas and J. Barnes, *Baldwin: A Biography* (London, 1969).

of Nations a proposal for a two-year moratorium on commercial initiatives, to be followed by a round of multilateral tariff reductions. The final version of this plan that emerged from Geneva, however, was highly diluted, and by the time the Cabinet at last agreed upon ratification, rapidly deteriorating economic conditions had destroyed foreign support for the truce.[7]

The subsequent development of Labour attitudes toward protection was influenced by a variety of individuals, among the most prominent of whom was John Maynard Keynes. While one must take care not to exaggerate the impact of Keynes's views, since in some quarters they were received with considerable skepticism, Keynes frequently dominated the deliberations of the Government's economic advisors, and he had the ear of the Prime Minister. Furthermore, the way in which his views on the tariff question evolved is representative of the response of other influential economists to changing economic conditions.

For much of the Labour Government's term in office, Keynes was the principal advocate of innovative policies for dealing with Britain's economic problems. When he first came to advise the Labour Government, he was widely perceived as a proponent of free trade, a reputation he had acquired as a result of his activities during the 1923 General Election. In an article published that year in the *Nation and Athenaeum* (Dec. 1, p. 336), Keynes distinguished between a tariff's ability to stimulate production in protected industries and its inability to influence the overall level of activity. His analysis was based upon the classical presumption that, under full employment, any reduction in import demand will be offset by a fall in export supply. In a remark that returned to haunt him in 1930, Keynes labeled the claim that a tariff can be used for employment purposes "the Protectionist fallacy in its grossest and crudest form."[8]

It was the recognition that the British economy was behaving differently in 1930 than it had in 1923 that led Keynes to modify his position on the tariff question. Keynes's first rehearsal of his new espousal of tariff protection came in his private evidence before the Macmillan Committee in February

---

[7] Public Record Office (hereafter, PRO) T172/1713, "Tariff Truce," March 1930. See also T.N. Graham, *Willie Graham* (London, 1948); League of Nations, *Commercial Policy in the Interwar Period: International Proposals and National Policies* (Geneva, 1942); and W.H. Janeway, *The Economic Policy of the Second Labour Government, 1929–1931,* unpublished Ph.D. dissertation, Cambridge University (1971).

[8] For Lionel Robbins's subsequent resurrection of Keynes's 1923 views, see PRO C58/150 EAC (E.) 13, "Answers by Professor L. Robbins to Questionnaire Prepared by the Chairman," 23 September 1930. Keynes's own reflections on his 1923 views appear in J.M. Keynes, *The General Theory of Employment, Interest and Money* (London, 1936).

of 1930.[9] This Committee, set up to carry out Labour's electoral pledge to investigate the relations between finance and industry, heard Keynes present a variety of unconventional proposals for dealing with unemployment. These included import duties, export bounties, import boards (to be empowered to issue import licenses), tax cuts, public investment, subsidies on private investment, an embargo on foreign loans, and bold action by the Bank of England to lower interest rates. These proposals reflected the conclusions to which Keynes had been drawn while putting the finishing touches on his *Treatise on Money*.[10] To the bankers, industrialists, and labor leaders who made up the Macmillan Committee, Keynes explained that output responded to changes in the ratio of prices to costs, which in turn depended on the relationship of saving to investment. Britain's economic malaise could be traced to the high interest rates that the Bank of England maintained to defend the gold value of sterling. High interest rates encouraged saving and depressed investment. High levels of saving reduced the demand for consumer goods, while low levels of investment depressed the demand for producers' goods. The result was downward pressure on commodity prices, which, in conjunction with the limited flexibility of wages, gave rise to unemployment.[11] Each of Keynes's proposals was designed to stimulate employment by raising investment relative to saving. A tariff, for example, would increase domestic profits and improve Britain's trade balance, enabling the Bank of England to reduce Bank Rate and thereby stimulate investment without undermining the stability of the exchange rate.

The limited flexibility of wages was a critical component of Keynes's analysis. In his view, the single most significant change in the structure of the British economy was in the labor market's response to price changes. While wages had been far from fully flexible in a downward direction in previous decades, it appeared that the degree of flexibility had declined over the course of the 1920s. Between 1921 and 1922, wages and prices

---

[9] The report of the Committee on Finance and Industry was almost two years in appearing. Keynes's Macmillan Committee evidence is contained in PRO T200/4 and T200/6.

[10] When the *Treatise* finally appeared later in 1930, it too contained an admission that the author was coming around to the view that it might be advisable to use commercial policy to reduce unemployment. Keynes, *Treatise*, Vol. 2, p. 189.

[11] The *Treatise* framework is analyzed in detail in D.E. Moggridge, *Keynes* (London, 1975), and D. Patinkin, *Keynes' Monetary Thought* (Durham, 1976). But see also J. Robinson, "What Became of the Keynesian Revolution?," in M. Keynes (ed.), *Essays on John Maynard Keynes* (London, 1975), pp. 124–5. Keynes's fullest exposition of the framework came before the Macmillan Committee on 21 February 1930. See PRO T200/4, especially pp. 38–46.

both fell by more than 20 percent, in part because 55 percent of all wage reductions that took place in 1921 and 38 percent of those occurring in 1922 were a result of sliding-scale agreements of the sort adopted during the war. Thereafter, however, indexation fell out of favor, and by 1930 Keynes recognized that the flexibility of the economy in general and the labor market in particular had somehow been reduced. Wage reductions could be achieved only "as a result of a series of struggles ensuing on business losses and unemployment." [12] This rigidity of wages was a source of unemployment that warranted governmental action. One possible response was the imposition of a tariff, which could stimulate employment by raising prices relative to wages.

Two aspects of Keynes's Macmillan Committee evidence are relevant to the tariff debate. First, his support for a tariff was extremely hesitant. Although firmly convinced that there was a case for tariff protection as short-run employment policy, Keynes described himself as "frightfully afraid of Protection as a long run policy" (T 200/4, Mar. 6, 1931, p. 2). He warned of the danger that a temporary tariff would become permanent, entrenching inefficient firms behind high protective barriers. Eventually, Keynes came to downplay his fears about a tariff's long-term effects, but many who were otherwise convinced by his arguments retained reservations on precisely these grounds.

A second, and striking, aspect of Keynes's evidence was his rejection of devaluation as a solution to the unemployment problem. Although Keynes had opposed Britain's return to the gold standard in 1925, arguing that the proper target for monetary policy was internal price stability rather than exchange-rate stability, in 1930 he was unwilling to recommend going off gold (T 200/4, Feb. 21, p. 29). [13] Keynes saw the gold standard as the linchpin of the international finance system. London's status as an international financial center and Britain's earnings from financial services rendered to foreigners depended on the gold standard's survival. Abandoning that standard would lead to a flurry of competitive devaluations abroad and panic flights of short-term capital, creating uncertainty that would further dis-

---

12 Although much British unemployment was related to international problems, Keynes still attributed a "large residuum (to) the greediness of the factor of labor." See PRO T200/6, 21 September 1930, p. 1.

13 See also Keynes, *Tract* and Moggridge, *Return to Gold*, pp. 9–10. As late as the summer of 1931, only a few iconoclasts such as Ernest Bevin were openly willing to entertain the prospect of devaluation. See A. Bullock, *The Life and Times of Ernest Bevin* (London, 1960), pp. 426–41; F. Williams, *Ernest Bevin* (London, 1952); and D. Winch, *Economics and Policy* (New York, 1969), p. 137.

rupt international trade. This would be particularly devastating to Britain, where unemployment was already concentrated in the export industries.

As a result of the gold standard's supposed indispensability, any measure for combatting unemployment that threatened the stability of the exchange rate could not command widespread support. Keynes, himself, placed little emphasis on his proposals' implications for exchange-rate stability. Although he realized that increased public spending or Bank of England initiatives to reduce interest rates might force the balance of payments into deficit and undermine confidence in sterling, he suggested that complementary measures by American and French authorities could neutralize the potentially damaging impact of domestic reflation on the stability of the exchange rate.[14] Nonetheless, Keynes was attracted to the idea of a tariff as a response to the unemployment problem precisely because a tariff was the one measure consistent with both the target of lower unemployment and the constraint of remaining on the gold standard.

The debate in the Economic Advisory Council

The first Government agency in which the virtues of a tariff were actively debated was the Economic Advisory Council. Established by Prime Minister Ramsay MacDonald in February of 1930 to provide the Cabinet with expert economic advice, the Council was made up of a disparate collection of economists, trade-union leaders, and businessmen.[15] Soon thereafter, an EAC Committee of Economists was established to consider the causes of Britain's industrial difficulties. This committee, under Keynes's chairmanship, included among its members A. C. Pigou, Lionel Robbins, and Hubert Henderson. Precisely how influential the advice tendered by the EAC proved to be is a matter of dispute (see, e.g., Winch, 1969, p. 124). However, the body's deliberations are noteworthy if only because this was the first instance in which British politicians systematically solicited the

---

[14] Keynes and Hubert Henderson disagreed on this point. Henderson argued that the probability of international cooperation was low, so that, in the interest of exchange-rate stability, recommendations for reflation should be limited to fiscally responsible proposals. Henderson argued that public works programs should be financed "in ways which will not do more harm to industrial activity by depressing business confidence than the stimulation of capital expenditure will do good." Henderson's own scheme for public investments entailed an import duty on manufactured goods to provide the necessary finance and maintain balance-of-payments equilibrium. See Henderson's memo, PRO C24/212 CP196(30), 3 June 1930, "Unemployment Policy–Industrial Reconstruction Scheme."

[15] A definitive history of the EAC is provided by Howson and Winch, *Economic Advisory Council*.

theoretical and empirical analyses of economists. Moreover, the minutes of the EAC document the evolution of opinion on the tariff question.

As early as the summer of 1930, the idea of imposing a general tariff to reduce unemployment had considerable support within the EAC. Several of its members, while still contending that protection could not affect employment under normal circumstances, admitted that a tariff might reduce unemployment insofar as present conditions resulted from the abnormal rigidity of wages. The idea that wage rigidities impeded adjustment in the labor market was still unfamiliar in 1930, as is evident in the work of William Beveridge, the reigning British expert on unemployment. In his earlier writings on the causes of unemployment, Beveridge (1909, pp. 197–214) had emphasized the impact of part-time employment, impediments to the exchange of information between employers and workers, and the imperfect mobility of labor. By 1930, Beveridge (1930, pp. 368–9) had come to stress the tendency of money wages to lag behind prices during periods of deflation.[16] This drove up production costs, providing an important part of the explanation for the unemployment of the 1920s. Beveridge thought the change in the behavior of the labor market resulted from the spread of collective bargaining and the extension of unemployment-insurance coverage. That he did not devote the same systematic attention to the question of whether money wages tended to lag behind prices during periods of inflation is understandable in light of the decade of persistent price deflation Britain had just experienced. Yet the question of whether wages were equally inflexible in the upward and downward directions was to prove central to the subsequent debate over a tariff.

As they became aware that the labor market was not functioning normally, the members of the Committee of Economists began to reassess their attitudes toward a tariff. Evidence of this reassessment appears in their responses to the series of questionnaires submitted to the Committee in 1930. In July, Prime Minister MacDonald asked for views of the causes of the slump and recommendations for Government action. Among the options mentioned were a general tariff, selective import duties, import boards, and import prohibitions. The realization that the international character of the depression limited the prospect for basing recovery on the export trade moved several respondents to consider measures for restricting imports. Together these memoranda reflected a desire to promote what

---

[16] The evolution of Beveridge's views is described by J. Harris, *William Beveridge: A Biography* (Oxford, 1977).

Hubert Henderson described in his summary as "a new orientation in our economic life in which the export trade plays a smaller part and production for the home market a larger part." They also reflected a recognition that the traditional argument that a tariff merely diverts labor from the production of exports to the production of import substitutes "loses much of its force when a large number of workers are, not merely temporarily, but permanently unemployed." [17]

Keynes's response to the Prime Minister's queries provided a taxonomy of the benefits to be derived from a tariff. Keynes began by reminding MacDonald of a central implication of the *Treatise* framework: a solution to the unemployment problem could be found in any measure that succeeded in raising investment relative to saving. After dismissing as "overdone and irrecoverable" objections to tariffs on the grounds that they encourage political nationalism and are incompatible with sound financial principles, Keynes repeated the list of remedies he had presented to the Macmillan Committee in February. The weight of the argument for a tariff was increased by his admission that many of the other alternatives, such as a lower Bank Rate, might prove incompatible with the maintenance of the gold-standard parity.[18] Keynes framed this argument in terms of the relatively straightforward impact of a tariff on output prices and costs, rather than basing it on the more complex transmission mechanism that ran from savings and investment to prices and production, and from there to employment. Presumably, the simpler explanation was designed to appeal to the politicians in the Labour Cabinet.

Although it was never used, a second questionnaire drawn up by the Committee of Economists' secretary, Richard Kahn, is significant because it indicates that the discussions of the Committee were beginning to move away from the full-employment framework. Particularly revealing is Kahn's emphasis on the rigidity of money wages and his assertion that a tariff "is a direct method of securing primary employment, and secondary employ-

---

[17] The economists' analyses were not based on Keynes's saving and investment approach but upon the simpler proposition that, if money wages are sticky, a tariff can stimulate production by raising prices and increasing profits. The Prime Minister's questions can be found in PRO Cab 58/10 EAC (H.)98, "The State of Trade," 8 July 1930, p. 417. See also PRO Cab 58/11 EAC (H.)120, "Revised Summary by the Staff of Replies to the Questions Circulated by the Prime Minister," 13 August 1930; PRO Cab 58/150 EAC (E.)2, "The State of Trade," 28 August 1930.

[18] Keynes invoked a tariff's favorable terms-of-trade effects and its contribution to balancing the government budget as further reasons for considering protection. PRO, Cab 58/150 EAC (E.)15, "Memorandum by Mr. J.M. Keynes, C.B.," 23 September 1930.

ment follows in the same ways as when the primary employment occurs in the form of home investment." [19] At the same time, the absence of unanimity is apparent. Robbins's announcement that he was prepared to submit an alternative list of topics for discussion indicates his fundamental dissatisfaction with the direction in which the debate was moving.

A shorter questionnaire drawn up by Keynes and used in lieu of Kahn's instructed the members of the Committee to consider how "(a) British output (b) British prices (c) British wages [would] be affected by (i) an increase in investment . . . (ii) a tariff (iii) a reduction of British money wages." [20] The members' responses indicate that – with the exception of Keynes, who was unambiguously in favor, and Robbins, who was unambiguously opposed – the economists supported with certain reservations a general tariff to combat unemployment. Henderson, for one, warned that protection would hinder the recovery of the export trades and emphasized that he supported a tariff only as part of a comprehensive program for economic retrenchment. Pigou lent cautious support to the concept of a tariff but suggested that, in practice, the higher retail prices created by a tariff were likely to generate increased wage demands, thereby destroying the tariff's ability to stimulate profits. [21] This was a theme that appeared again and again in the debate over the macroeconomic effects of a general tariff.

Keynes's response to this questionnaire summarized the case for a tariff as it stood in the autumn of 1930. He found the principal justification for a tariff in the rigidity of nominal wages. A tariff would succeed in stimulating employment if it raised prices relative to wages. Along with a general tariff, Keynes presented a number of alternative remedies for British unemployment. Among these were measures designed to restore flexibility to the labor market. In 1930 Keynes still believed that, in principle, money-wage reductions provided a way out of Britain's economic predicament. Raising prices rather than lowering wages might have the larger effect to the extent that saving out of profits exceeded saving out of wages, but, in theory, money-wage reductions would still increase employment. In practice, the situation was different. Price increases were preferable to wage

---

[19] The quotation provides evidence that the multiplier was already part of the thinking of some of the economists by early September. PRO Cab 58/150 EAC (E.) 7, "Draft Heads for Discussion," 6 September 1930.

[20] PRO Cab 58/150 EAC (E.) 8, "Questionnaire Prepared by the Chairman," 15 September 1930.

[21] PRO Cab 58/150 EAC (E.) 12, "Answers by Professor A.C. Pigou, M.A., to Questionnaire Prepared by the Chairman," 15 September 1930.

reductions on grounds of both equity and feasibility. As Keynes put it to the Committee of Economists, the "almost complete rigidity of our wage-rates since 1929" rendered inflationary tactics such as tariff protection the expedient course.[22]

It was when Keynes referred to the "almost complete rigidity" of wage rates that he and his critics parted company. Pigou and Robbins both argued that, if wages were flexible in an upward direction, a tariff would have no effect on profits or employment. Keynes's response to this objection came in two parts. He first suggested that a tariff was less likely than alternative measures to provoke union demands for wage increases, but he left the claim unsubstantiated. Owing perhaps to his own doubts about the validity of this argument, Keynes went on to claim that even if money wages rose along with import prices and left real wages unchanged, a tariff would still increase domestic employment. Keynes reasoned that a tariff which improved the current account of the balance of payments would give rise to increased foreign investment. This investment eventually would raise the foreign demand for British goods.[23] Beveridge and his colleagues at the London School of Economics countered this argument with the suggestion that a tariff would impoverish foreigners by depressing the British demand for their exports and reducing foreign consumption of British goods.[24]

Robbins was quick to capitalize on the weaknesses of Keynes's argument. He admitted that in some hypothetical society in which money wages remained constant, "it is theoretically possible that a tariff might reduce unemployment." Robbins judged, however, that conditions in Britain were completely different. In reality, a tariff would stimulate the import-competing sectors, where there was comparatively little excess capacity and unemployment, and impede the recovery of the export industries, where there was considerable unemployment but wages were already as low as they could be pushed. Hence wage rates had nowhere to go but up. The workers, Robbins wrote, would soon be demanding "a share of the loaves

---

22 Keynes also mentioned the danger of offsetting wage reductions abroad as another argument against wage cuts. PRO Cab 58/11 EAC (H.) 106, "The State of Trade: Answers by Mr. J.M. Keynes, C.B.," 21 November 1930, p. 5.

23 PRO Cab 58/150 EAC (E.) 13, "Memorandum by Mr. J.M. Keynes, C.B.," 23 September 1930.

24 Beveridge's analysis appears in W.H. Beveridge, *Tariffs: The Case Examined* (London, 1932). Harris, *William Beveridge*, p. 319, reports Keynes's rejoinder. A theoretical analysis of the employment effects of a tariff under conditions of real-wage rigidity appears in B. Eichengreen, "Protection, Real Wage Resistance and Employment," *Weltwirtschaftiches Archiv* 119 (1983), 429–52.

and fishes." He asserted that Keynes's arguments were merely the "hackneyed slogans of a thousand controversies elsewhere."[25]

Robbins resisted Keynes's attempts to force a unanimous conclusion upon the Committee.[26] Ultimately, he refused to sign the Committee's report, which included substantial portions of his own draft, because of objections to the section on tariffs. Miraculously, Keynes managed to paper over the dispute. The final document endorsed measures to lower wages through such means as reforms of unemployment insurance, as well as measures to raise wages and prices through any one of a number of expansionary initiatives. Keynes, Henderson, and Sir Josiah Stamp reaffirmed their support for a general tariff. Pigou was not sympathetic to this course and attached reservations, while Robbins rejected the proposal outright.

The debate in the Cabinet

It is difficult to assess the impact of the Committee of Economists' report on the opinions of the Cabinet Ministers. The recommendations of the economists were discussed in December of 1930 and again the following summer at the height of the financial crisis. The Ministers were disturbed by an analysis which concluded that either raising or lowering wages was preferable to leaving things as they were, and some detected what they took to be internal inconsistencies in the report.[27]

Influencing the Ministers' responses to the report were considerations of party, politics, and doctrine. Free trade continued to symbolize the Labour Government's commitment to international solutions to Britain's economic problem. Snowden, Graham, and their colleagues Lords Parmoor and Passfield, Lord President and Colonial Secretary, respectively, adamantly opposed any compromise of what they considered to be a moral and intellectual principle of the first order. In their view, at stake was not

---

25 PRO Cab 58/150 EAC (E.) 13, "Answers by Professor L. Robbins to Questionnaire Prepared by Chairman," September 23, 1930. Robbins's own solution to the unemployment problem was to increase labor-market flexibility. He recommended curbing the power of the unions and reforming the system of unemployment compensation. See L. Robbins, *Autobiography of an Economist* (London, 1971), pp. 151–165.

26 Robbins to Cannan, Cannan Papers, London School of Economics, n.d., vol. 1, 3030, 197.

27 Henderson's plan to combine a general tariff with a program of industrial reorganization to be financed out of tariff revenues appears to have impressed the Cabinet as much as the report of the Committee of Economists. See D. Marquand, *Ramsay MacDonald* (London, 1977), p. 524. Henderson describes his scheme in PRO Cab 24/212 (CP196/30), "Unemployment Policy-Industrial Reconstruction Scheme," 3 June 1930.

only the welfare of the unemployed but also the living standards of the four-fifths of the work force still employed, to whom a tariff-induced rise in the cost of living would be a serious blow.

As the year 1930 progressed, Snowden more than ever came to symbolize the financial competence of the Labour Government. His resignation as Chancellor of the Exchequer would have seriously undermined confidence in the City of London. Snowden's opposition to a tariff was incontrovertible, and the Cabinet's receptivity to the Committee of Economists' report fluctuated along with his health.[28] On November 7, when the EAC took up the report, Snowden was fit, and his characterization of a revenue tariff as regressive taxation incapable of stimulating employment ended discussion of the matter. Next, a small Cabinet Committee on Trade Policy, chaired by Snowden, was created to consider the economists' recommendations in more detail. At its first meeting on December 1, the members agreed that the report was a disappointing document – inconsistent, impractical, and containing too many general suggestions.[29] At the second meeting, Snowden asserted that the report's analysis of commercial policy was not worthy of consideration, and no further discussion of the matter ensued. However, Snowden's ill health undermined his campaign against protection. In February of 1931, he was unable to attend meetings of the EAC, permitting Prime Minister MacDonald to express his sympathy with some of the proposals of the Committee of Economists. Soon thereafter, Snowden attempted to reassert his influence by hosting a series of luncheons for prominent free traders.[30]

Snowden had two formidable allies in this campaign. One was the Liberal contingent in the House of Commons. Toward the end of 1930, the Government had begun to move toward closer cooperation with the official Liberal Party, obtaining support for its programs in return for promises of electoral reform and continued opposition to a tariff. A second source of support was a group of economists affiliated with the London School of Economics. This group, which included Lionel Robbins and Frederic Ben-

---

[28] Snowden reaffirmed his position before the House of Commons in July 1930 and again in a speech delivered at Free Trade Hall in Manchester in October. See also C. Cross, *Philip Snowden* (London, 1966), p. 254; Skidelsky, *Politicians*, pp. 68–9; P. Snowden, *An Autobiography* (London, 1934).

[29] PRO Cab 27/435 T.P.C (30), "Minutes of the First Meeting of the Cabinet Committee on Trade Policy," 1 December 1930, p. 1.

[30] Even in his absence, Snowden's lieutenants at the Treasury were preparing ammunition for use upon the Chancellor's return. See PRO T175/52(5), Forber to Fergusson, 26 March 1931, and PRO T175/52(5), "Some Notes on Revenue Tariffs," 26 March 1931.

ham, agreed in October of 1930 to produce a book under the editorship of William Beveridge. Their volume, entitled *Tariffs: The Case Examined*, presented a detailed, if not always transparent, restatement of the classical analysis of trade policy.[31] Beveridge's chapter on the employment effects of a tariff emphasized the belief that any fall in import demand would induce a decline in foreign demand for Britain's exports. Beveridge admitted that the net employment effect of stimulating the import-competing sectors and depressing the export-oriented sectors was uncertain in theory. But the existence of substantial excess capacity in Britain's export industries along with relatively little slack in the import-competing sectors led Beveridge to conclude that the overall employment effects were likely to be unfavorable. In addition, he argued that because of the tendency of wages to rise with the cost of living, a tariff should not be expected to raise profits and thereby stimulate investment. Beveridge stated bluntly the argument Robbins had put to the Committee of Economists: the utility of a tariff as employment policy depends on the assumption that money wages will continue to be rigid in both an upward and a downward direction. If money wage rates are flexible downward, a tariff is unnecessary; if they are flexible upward, it is useless.

While Snowden made use of these sources of support in his Cabinet-level campaign to defend free trade, his position was under attack from several directions. His campaign was undermined when the Prime Minister expressed willingness to support a 10 percent tariff under certain conditions, as he did in January and again in July of 1930 (Marquand, 1977, pp. 554–5). MacDonald was above all a pragmatist, willing to consider whatever economic policy the circumstances might warrant. His new views on the tariff question were sympathetically received by J. H. Thomas, initially Lord Privy Seal with special responsibilities for dealing with unemployment, and by Noel Buxton, the Minister of Agriculture. In part, MacDonald may have adopted this new stance out of concern about the Conservative Party's increasingly protectionist position. Neville Chamberlain, Conservative son of Joseph Chamberlain and heir to the tariff reform tradition, did much to promote protectionist sentiment while the Conservatives were in opposition. In the interest of party unity and in response to the campaign for Empire free trade led by the press lords Beaverbrook and Rothermere, Stanley Baldwin, leader of the Conservatives, moved toward the protectionist wing of his Party.

Chamberlain had encouraged the protectionists within his Party by help-

---

31 As it happened, the book appeared only after Britain's departure from gold.

ing to establish a research department and a shadow-cabinet subcommittee to prepare a plan for adopting an across-the-board tariff. He advocated protection on many grounds but found it particularly useful to suggest that a tariff might be used to promote industrial "rationalisation." "Rationalisation" was the code word for national industrial policy, which entailed consolidating existing operations and installing new plant and equipment. Chamberlain suggested that protection could be used to promote investment in industries requiring rationalization, and he argued that it was necessary to impose import duties in order to protect sectors undergoing rehabilitation from the predatory tactics of foreign competitors.[32]

However, the single factor that did most to strengthen the case for a tariff was the deteriorating state of the economy. Over the course of 1930, unemployment rose from 12 to 20 percent of the insured labor force. Deflation accelerated, led by the collapse of primary commodity prices. Even more disturbingly, Britain's balance-of-trade deficit grew; the sterling value of imports fell by approximately 14 percent, but export value fell by nearly 50 percent. The only reassuring development was the stability of the Bank of England's gold and foreign-exchange reserves.[33]

The worsening state of the economy led a number of prominent figures previously identified with the Labour Government's approach to trade policy to announce their defection. In May of 1930, with the unemployment rate for insured persons at 15 percent, Oswald Mosley, an outspoken member of the Cabinet unemployment task force, resigned from the Government following its rejection of his proposal for an ambitious program of home development supported by a comprehensive set of import controls. In June, the General Council of the Trades Union Congress, an organization traditionally opposed to import duties, adopted a rather ambiguous position on protection. Another blow came in March of 1931, when Keynes announced publicly his support for a 10 percent tariff.[34]

Soon thereafter, in July of 1931, the Macmillan Committee's report

---

[32] Chamberlain's moves are discussed in Howson and Winch, *Economic Advisory Council*, p. 96.

[33] Monthly statistics on unemployment, prices, and the trade balance appear in Tinbergen, *Abstract*, pp. 114–24. Information on the Bank of England's position appears in Moggridge, *British Monetary Policy*, pp. 148–9.

[34] R. Skidelsky, *Oswald Mosley* (New York, 1975), pp. 177–220; Trades Union Congress (TUC) Economic Committee, *Minutes*, 18 June 1930; A. Bullock, *The Life and Times of Ernest Bevin* (London, 1960), pp. 442–3. Trade-union attitudes are discussed in detail by S. Pollard (ed.), *The Gold Standard and Employment Policies between the Wars* (London, 1970), pp. 146–61; *New Statesman and Nation*, 7 March 1930, pp. 53–4; Marquand, *Ramsay MacDonald*, pp. 590–1.

finally appeared. The report effectively publicized the case for imposing a general tariff as a way of reducing domestic unemployment. A variety of measures designed to increase international liquidity and raise the domestic price level were discussed, but devaluation was ruled out because Britain's "international trade, commerce and finance are based on confidence" (Committee on Finance and Industry, 1931, par. 256, pp. 110–11). The body of the report contained no suggestion that recommendations for reflation and for defense of the gold standard might prove incompatible. However, awareness of this problem led Keynes and other Committee members to attach an addendum to the report. In it they revived Keynes's argument that wage reductions could not be relied upon to solve the unemployment problem because money wages had proven themselves "less elastic" of late. With devaluation ruled out, a scheme for uniform import tariffs and matching export bounties was presented as a way to raise the price level without undermining confidence in the currency. The signatories to the addendum argued that employment was likely to rise more in the import-competing sectors than it would fall in the export-producing industries. Keynes's contention that a tariff, unlike a devaluation, could be used to raise prices without eliciting increased wage demands made another appearance. Only Ernest Bevin and Sir Thomas Allen, who represented organized labor, did not share their colleagues' fears of devaluation. In a reservation to the addendum, they stated their preference for devaluation instead of a tariff, but their decision to sign the addendum may be an indication that they realized the impractability of their position (Addendum I and reservation to Addendum I, pp. 190–210).

The impact of the 1931 financial crisis

Under different circumstances, the Macmillan Committee's report might have swayed Cabinet-level opinion toward advocacy of a tariff as a way of combatting unemployment, but the problem of unemployment and the report itself were soon overshadowed by other events. The rapid deterioration of Britain's external position in the summer of 1931 forced policy-makers to turn their attention to the balance-of-payments problem. In 1931, Britain's current-account balance moved into deficit for the first time in five years. This deficit was due not so much to the excess of commodity imports over commodity exports, which was little worse in the early months of 1931 than in earlier years, as to the insufficiency of invisible earnings. The depression cut into Britain's invisible balance, because declining international trade reduced incomes from shipping and financial services and falling interest rates lowered the return on foreign investments. Superimposed on the deteriorating current account were the effects of Continental liquidity crises. The collapse of the Austrian and German banking systems and French procrastination regarding Hoover's proposed debt moratorium created a scramble for liquidity. As foreigners liquidated their deposits in London, Britain's capital-account position worsened.

The publication of the May Committee's report on July 31 (Committee on National Expenditure, 1931) provided many with their first inkling that the budget was seriously out of balance. The May Committee, set up in March to consider the Government's budgetary position, predicted in its report that the budget deficit for the year 1932–33 would approach £120 million. While the accuracy of this figure was disputed, the basic premise was correct. The depression had aggravated the budgetary problem both by reducing revenues and by increasing expenditure, especially on the dole.[35] From the French experience in the 1920s, the public had learned that there was a correspondence between government budget deficits and balance-of-payments deficits. Thus the May report, which revealed the magnitude of Britain's budget deficit, severely undermined confidence in sterling. From the beginning of August, the Bank of England began to lose gold at a rate that could be sustained for perhaps a month, and the Cabinet became totally preoccupied with the defense of the exchange rate.

The financial community believed that sterling's strength could be restored only by balancing the budget, and the Cabinet-level debate centered upon what combination of higher taxes and lower expenditure should be adopted. Most Conservatives demanded reduced spending on unemployment relief and public services. Since Labour backbenchers opposed any proposal that would reduce support or raise the cost of living for the unemployed, the Government found it difficult to agree on a measure designed to balance the budget either by reducing spending or by increasing taxes. As Bank of England gold losses continued to mount, however, it became vital to do something to restore confidence. One option was to reduce unemployment benefits by 10 percent. Another was to impose a 10 percent revenue tariff. A tariff was seen as the most desirable way to balance the budget because, besides raising tax revenues it would discourage consumption of

[35] The 1931 financial crisis is considered by J.S. Davis, *The World between the Wars: An Economist's View* (Baltimore, 1975); D.E. Moggridge, "The 1931 Financial Crisis–A New View," *The Banker* 120 (August 1970), 832–9; D. Williams, "The 1931 Financial Crisis," *Yorkshire Bulletin of Economic and Social Research* 15 (November 1963), 92–110; and "London and the 1931 Financial Crisis," *Economic History Review*, sec. ser., 15 (April 1963), 513–28.

imports and thus directly strengthen the trade balance. Under normal circumstances, a tariff would not have been acceptable to the Trades Union
Congress or to Labour Members of Parliament. But the specter of substantial reductions in unemployment payments created a considerable change
of opinion in trade-union circles on the question of tariffs.[36]

Thus, by midsummer of 1931 a tariff was no longer being advocated as
a means of reducing unemployment but, rather, as the least objectionable
method of balancing the budget and restoring confidence in sterling. The
question of whether a tariff should be used to defend the exchange rate
came to a vote before the Cabinet on August 19. Five Ministers apparently
blocked adoption of the measure. Four days later, the Cabinet split again,
with nine Ministers opposing the alternative of a 10 percent reduction in unemployment benefits. Incapable of marshaling support for a response to the
flight from sterling, the Labour Government was dissolved the following
morning.

The new National Government, formed on August 24, quickly broke the
impasse over macroeconomic policy. The four Labour, four Conservative,
and two Liberal Ministers who served under MacDonald agreed to austerity measures. These included lowering the salaries of public employees,
cutting the standard rate of unemployment benefits, reducing public borrowing and support for local-authority expenditure, raising unemployment-
insurance contributions, and adding new taxes. These measures were introduced in the House of Commons on September 10.

While some, such as Snowden, argued that these economies completely
destroyed the case for a tariff, others remained unconvinced that the Government's actions had in fact solved the confidence problem. Keynes, for
one, predicted that the new budget would have little immediate impact on
the balance of trade and would only worsen unemployment. He argued that,
for both reasons, the imposition of a tariff was still in order. Henderson,
in his September 18 evaluation of the balance-of-payments position, came
to the same conclusion.[37] Even some members of the General Council of
the Trades Union Congress continued to press the National Government to
adopt a general tariff as a way to defend the exchange rate (*Times*, Sept. 4,
1931, p. 10).

[36] Although the General Council of the TUC reached no final decision, support for a tariff increased considerably during the second and third weeks of August (TUC Economic
Committee, *Report on Fiscal Policy*, 1932, pp. 3–4; see also *Times*, 19 August 1931, p. 10,
and 20 August 1931, p. 10; R. Bassett, *Nineteen Thirty-One: Political Crisis* (London,
1958), p. 75.

[37] Keynes, "Mitigation by Tariff," in *Essays in Persuasion* (London, 1931), pp. 271–87; PRO
T172/1746(6), "The Balance of Payments," 18 September 1931.

The more vocal advocates of protection were not deterred by the announcement of the new budget. The Board of Directors of the Manchester Chamber of Commerce adopted a resolution of support for a tariff, and the President of the Federation of British Industries (F.B.I.), the leading employers' group, recommended imposing a tariff for balance-of-trade purposes (F.B.I./C/32 Box 75, University of Warwick). The imperial preference lobby continued to press its case for a tariff. While applauding the Government's budgetary economies, the editors of the *Times* suggested that a balanced budget and a tariff were but two indispensable components of a comprehensive scheme to restore economic stability and stated that "there is an enormous preponderance of opinion in the country behind [a tariff] already" (*Times*, Sept. 16, 1931, p. 16).

The events of the following week were to prove correct those who had warned that budgetary measures would not stem the run on sterling. On September 18 and 19, the Bank of England's gold and foreign-exchange losses reached crisis proportions, and the Government was forced to suspend convertibility on September 21. Almost immediately the pound fell toward $4.00. On September 24, the Bank of England intervened with sales of sterling to push the pound down still further to what it estimated was the equilibrium level. By the end of September, sterling had reached $3.75. This drop was followed by a brief recovery and a period of stability lasting through the end of October. Then sterling fell again, and once more the Bank of England did little to slow the adjustment. The pound fell to $3.24 at the beginning of December but began to recover soon thereafter. It reached $3.40 by the end of 1931, and Treasury officials eventually decided that this was not an undesirable neighborhood in which the exchange rate might float.[38]

3. Commercial policy and the floating pound sterling, 1931–32

The fall of the exchange rate and the continued weakness of the trade balance reinforced the impression that the crisis was not yet over. Thus it proved unrealistic to anticipate an early dissolution of the National Government. Perceiving the disarray in which the opposition had been left by the collapse of the Labour Government, the leaders of the Conservative Party pressed for an early election. They hoped that the new Government's

---

[38] Sayers, *Bank of England, 1891–1944*, p. 419; Howson, "Sterling's Managed Float," pp. 5–6. For bilateral exchange rates against the major currencies, see P. Einzig, *The Theory of Forward Exchange* (London, 1937), pp. 470–1.

mandate to balance the budget and defend the exchange rate could be extended to encompass protectionist measures. Parliament was dissolved on October 7, 1931, and MacDonald went forth to campaign for a "doctor's mandate" to apply any necessary remedy to Britain's economic ills. Each party issued its own election manifesto. The Labour manifesto stated that "in the circumstances produced by our departure from the gold standard, [tariffs] have no relevance to economic need" (*Times*, Oct. 10, 1931, p. 7). The Conservative manifesto, as enunciated by Stanley Baldwin, advocated the imposition of a tariff as a way to strengthen the trade balance and stabilize the exchange rate:

At home, the paramount question is that of the adverse balance of trade, the redress of which is essential to secure our financial stability. This can be accomplished only by reducing imports, by increasing exports, or by a combination of both. I am prepared to examine any method which can effect what is required. I recognize that the situation is altered by the devaluation of the pound, but in my view the effect of that devaluation can be no valid substitute for a tariff. . . . We must shrink from no step to prove the stability of our country and to save our people from the disasters attached to a currency fluctuating and falling through a lack of confidence at home and abroad (Royal Institute, 1932, pp. 20–1).

The election resulted in a resounding victory for the National Government and a substantial increase in Conservative influence in the Cabinet and the House of Commons. Prime Minister MacDonald transferred Snowden to the post of Lord Privy Seal and replaced him with Neville Chamberlain, who came to dominate the formulation of economic policy in this Cabinet much as Snowden had dominated it under the Labour Government (Feiling, 1946, p. 201; Walker-Smith, 1939, pp. 173–4). Resistance to a tariff within the National Cabinet of twenty came only from Snowden and three free-trade Liberals: Sir Herbert Samuel, Sir Archibald Sinclair, and Sir Donald Maclean. The issue of overriding importance for the new National Government, succinctly stated in the King's speech on November 10 (*Hansard*, Nov. 10, 1931, p. 46), was to establish confidence in Britain's financial stability by ensuring a favorable balance of trade. Whether a general tariff was needed to accomplish this goal became a question for heated debate.

By November it was generally recognized that the suspension of the gold standard was permanent. Even those who desired a return to the traditional parity recognized that the Bank of England lacked the resources to bring it off. Most politicians and economists were aware that the advent of a floating rate had altered the policy environment, although whether for the better was subject to considerable disagreement. Some, like Lionel

Robbins and Frederic Benham, argued that exchange-rate flexibility provided a complete solution to Britain's problem of external balance. In their view, the current-account deficit no longer represented an economic problem, for exchange-rate adjustments would lead automatically to balance-of-payments equilibrium. The misguided individuals who continued to call for a tariff to balance the external accounts simply did not realize that circumstances had changed.

Yet others, like Hubert Henderson and Henry Clay, had less faith in the corrective power of a floating exchange rate. They worried that depreciation would be incapable of restoring balance to the external accounts or that, even if it could, the social costs of the required depreciation would be prohibitively high. To some, this meant that external balance could be restored only if Britain imposed a tariff. To others, it implied that, while exchange-rate adjustments were capable of balancing the external accounts, a tariff could do so at a lower social cost.

Some of the participants in the debate altered their views on the desirability of a tariff once Britain left the gold standard, but two of Britain's political parties remained unswayed. For the Liberals free trade and for the Conservatives protection constituted the central issue uniting party members. Indeed, by 1931 defense of free trade had become the primary rationale for the Liberal Party's survival. The Conservative Party, which had suffered the effects of several years of internal dissension, united behind Baldwin's protectionist election manifesto. The 1922 Club of Conservative backbenchers declared unanimously that "the suspension of the gold standard had in no way modified the need for immediate imposition of an emergency tariff" (*Times*, Oct. 10, 1931, p. 7). The position of the Labour Party was more difficult. Although the Party opposed protection throughout the 1931 electoral campaign, the credibility of its position was undermined by the public's knowledge that in August a majority of the Labour Cabinet had been willing to support a general tariff as an alternative to spending reductions.

Employers and employees were on opposite sides of the tariff question. The Trades Union Congress was convinced that the adoption of a floating exchange rate had destroyed the force of the argument for a tariff. Tariffs, its Economic Committee stated, were of "no relevance to economic need" (*Times*, Sept. 22, 1931, p. 12; TUC Economic Committee *Report*, p. 4). Ernest Bevin, the most prominent of Britain's labor leaders, had argued for months that depreciation was sufficient to resolve the balance-of-payments problem, and he had said as much in his own addendum to the Macmillan Committee report. In October and November, Bevin admitted of no doubts that depreciation was having its anticipated effect. The Federation of British Industries expressed the opposite opinion. On September 25, its Economic Emergency Committee was told that "the mere departure from the gold standard could not of itself correct our adverse trade balance; the imposition of a tariff – advocated for a long time past by the F.B.I. – was also necessary" (F.B.I./C/32 Box 75). A declaration to this effect (F.B.I./ C/32 Box 74) was submitted to the Board of Trade, which passed it on to Treasury officials.[39]

Editorial opinion could be predicted on the basis of past performance. Publications catering to the export trade boldly stated the case for a floating exchange rate. In the words of the *Manchester Guardian Commercial*, "Losing the gold standard we gain an opportunity. There is now no need to devote our attention to our adverse trade balance, for this will be quickly adjusted by the exchanges" (Oct. 15, 1931, p. 339). The *Manchester Guardian* labeled demands for a tariff "parrot cries" and suggested on September 28 (p. 8) that there was no reason to doubt that the trade balance had already righted itself. On October 19 (p. 9) it published an article by Frederic Benham and Lionel Robbins restating the case for floating exchange rates. The *Economist* made the same point some four months after Britain's departure from the gold standard: "For it cannot be too often repeated," its editors wrote, "that, with the pound no longer tied to gold, the balance of payments cannot do otherwise than adjust itself automatically" (Feb. 6, 1932, p. 283). The *Times* continued to argue that a floating exchange rate alone would not restore external balance and that a tariff was needed to bring imports and exports into line (Sept. 24, 1931, p. 13; Nov. 5, 1931, p. 13).

Neither the Treasury nor the Bank of England played a major role in the public debate. Montagu Norman, Governor of the Bank of England, described the desirability of a tariff as a purely political question and refused to make public his opinion. The Treasury view of protection, naturally, fluctuated with the inclination of the Chancellor of the Exchequer. When Chamberlain replaced Snowden as Chancellor, Treasury analyses of the protectionist case became increasingly sympathetic. Even so, there were some in the Treasury, such as R. G. Hawtrey, willing to disagree with Chamberlain on this issue.

---

[39] PRO T172/1768, "Statement of Policy of the Federation of British Industries," 15 January 1932.

Elasticity pessimism and the case for a tariff

Within the National Government, it was widely feared that the depreciation that would ultimately be required to balance the external accounts would be unacceptably large. Henry Clay had warned the Ministers that Britain's price elasticity of demand for imports was low because it imported more than half its foodstuffs and a large part of its raw materials. This pessimism about the size of demand elasticities implied that residents would economize on their consumption of imported goods only if import prices rose considerably. The elasticity pessimists drew on evidence from Britain's experience with floating rates in 1919, when a 20 percent depreciation had been followed by a negligible improvement in the trade balance. Hubert Henderson argued that the French experience with a floating exchange rate between 1923 and 1926 had shown that a sizable depreciation was necessary to effect an improvement in the trade balance.[40] Keynes counseled that the Government should not attempt to stabilize the exchange rate at more than 75 percent of its gold-standard parity, and Hawtrey, writing the week following devaluation, recommended aiming for an exchange rate of approximately $3.40.[41]

The National Government's Cabinet Committee on the Financial Situation, with its familiar cast of characters (Keynes, Henderson, and Lord Macmillan among them), considered this question as early as September 24. Chamberlain attempted to exploit the fears of the elasticity pessimists; on those occasions when he admitted that there existed a value of the pound at which the trade deficit would be eliminated, he selected an alarming figure like $2.[42]

Fear about the extent of the depreciation that would be required to restore balance to the external accounts was reinforced by expectations of competitive devaluation abroad. The assumption that any depreciation of sterling would be accompanied by similar movements of other currencies was correct. To some extent, of course, devaluation abroad was encour-

---

[40] PRO T188/29, "Comment on Mr. Hawtrey's Memorandum by H.D. Henderson," October 1931.

[41] PRO T175/56, "Pegging the Pound I," 28 September 1931, pp. 64–6; Marquand, *Ramsay MacDonald*, p. 610.

[42] PRO T172/1768, "Capital Items in the International Balance of Payments," 15 December 1931. Note that the Economic Advisory Council Subcommittee on Financial Questions was constituted as the Prime Minister's Advisory Committee on Financial Questions. See Cab 58/169 EAC (S.1(31)), "Minutes," and Cab 58/169 EAC(H.)147, "Report on Sterling Policy," 15 December 1931.

aged by the British themselves. In the Economic Advisory Council, it was recognized that depreciation would stimulate production only insofar as output prices rose relative to costs. In light of Britain's dependence on imported raw materials, officials hoped that sterling would depreciate relative to the currencies of Britain's industrial competitors, but they encouraged the principal raw-material suppliers to link their currencies to the pound at the traditional parity.[43] A total of twenty-five countries followed Britain off the gold standard. Foremost among these were the British Commonwealth nations, all of which, except for Canada, tied their currencies to sterling. Other countries to which the British export market was important, such as Portugal, immediately devalued in order to maintain their exchange rates against the pound. Still others, such as Argentina, whose currencies had already depreciated took the opportunity to establish a peg against the pound. All the countries of Scandinavia and much of Eastern Europe eventually joined in the decision to devalue.

Robbins, Benham, and others were quick to point out that under floating exchange rates there was no reason to worry about the effects on the trade balance of foreign devaluation. Competitive devaluation would be offset automatically by further depreciation of the pound, bringing Britain's external accounts back into balance. "Our balance of trade must balance," they stated bluntly and simplistically, given the importance to Britain of invisibles and capital transactions (Benham and Robbins, 1931). Yet the public and a dominant contingent within the National Government were unwilling to entertain the prospect of a large depreciation. Depreciation would lower the real value of British foreign investments denominated in sterling. Moreover, it would reduce the real value of the earnings on fixed-interest sterling securities. Not only would depreciation reduce the real value of British wealth, but it would contribute to deterioration of the invisible component of the current account. The Treasury, in particular, was concerned that excessive depreciation would increase the cost of repaying that portion of Britain's external debt denominated in U.S. dollars relative to the income from British foreign investments denominated in sterling. Britain's war debt to the United States was an obvious example of a liability denominated in dollars, while interallied debts owed the United Kingdom were denominated largely in sterling. When both public and private assets were considered, perhaps half of Britain's foreign-investment income

---

[43] This strategy is discussed in PRO T172/1768, "Note by the President of the Board of Trade prepared for the Committee on the Balance of Trade" (undated, but apparently December 1931); see also Clay, *Lord Norman*, pp. 410–11.

was denominated in sterling. On Sept. 24, the Cabinet Committee on the Financial Situation took note of this fact.[44]

The concern that a large depreciation would lead to a costly reduction in the value of Britain's external assets provided a rationale for the imposition of a tariff. Although both exchange-rate depreciation and the imposition of a tariff would reduce real wealth by raising the price level, some felt that a tariff was preferable because it would not raise the cost of repaying the American debt relative to the interest income accruing on Britain's sterling-denominated loans to foreigners.

A second reason why many politicians were unwilling to countenance a large depreciation was that higher import prices would impoverish the working class. If the cost of living rose by 25 or 50 percent, living standards would decline as long as wages lagged behind prices. The *Times* (Nov. 5, 1931, p. 13) warned that a depreciation resulting in a calamitous rise in the cost of living would intensify class conflict. While concern for workers' living standards provided an argument against excessive depreciation, it did not provide a rationale for an across-the-board tariff, since both import taxes and lower exchange rates would raise the cost of living. Indeed, the effect of a tariff on the cost of living was the basis of Snowden's opposition to commercial restrictions. However, there was considerable dispute about the realism of the assumption that wages would continue to lag behind higher import prices.

The exchange rate and the vicious spiral

It seems curious that policy-makers were preoccupied by fears of uncontrollable inflation during a period of pronounced price deflation. By the reckoning of the Board of Trade, wholesale prices fell by 34 percent between 1925, when Britain returned to the gold standard, and 1931. They fell by 23 percent between 1929 and 1931 alone, and the cost of living fell by 8 percent over the same two-year period (Methorst, 1938, pp. 200–14). Yet the gold-standard system was seen as the only restraint on the government's innate tendency to spend more than it took in. Once Britain abandoned the gold standard and allowed the exchange rate to float, policy-makers considered the way opened for runaway inflation. Thus Henry Clay advised the National Government in August 1931:

---

[44] "A Crisis of the £," *Times*, 17 October 1931, p. 13; PRO Cab 58/169 EAC (H.) 147, "Minutes," 24 September 1931.

Above all, the abandonment of the gold standard would remove the chief obstacle to inflation. The Government could incur expenditure without thought of covering it by taxation and expand the floating debt to cover the deficit. This would cause a fall of sterling on the exchanges and a rapid rise in prices at home. This is advocated as the simplest way of cutting real wages and other charges. But it might stimulate demands for wage increases which would lead to further inflation and further sterling depreciation. In other words, the process of inflation is a vicious circle. . . . This was the experience of England during the war and of most Continental countries since the war.[45]

Not only the policy-makers but also the public were haunted by memories of the Central European inflations of the 1920s. In particular, the fear that exchange-rate depreciation would lead to uncontrollable inflation was rooted in recollection of the German hyperinflation of 1923. The fear of inflation with which this episode imbued a generation of policy-makers is a recurrent theme in the history of British economic policy in the interwar years. But even before 1923, similar concerns had been foremost in the minds of members of the Cunliffe Committee. When recommending in 1919 that Britain return to the gold standard at the pre-war parity, the Committee cited the danger of inflation, and this phobia was reinforced by the post-war inflation that accompanied the unpegging of sterling (Winch, 1969, p. 89). The German hyperinflation was fresh in the public mind in 1925, when Britain's return to the gold standard met with widespread support. Winston Churchill referred to the danger of runaway inflation under floating exchange rates in the debate over the return to gold. Snowden voiced similar fears in 1927 and again whenever the gold standard came under attack during his reign as Chancellor of the Exchequer (Howson, 1975, p. 76).

In announcing that Britain was being forced off the gold standard, the Government referred obliquely to previous episodes by mentioning reassuringly the enormous financial resources of the nation. This did not prevent members of the government from using fears of hyperinflation to their advantage. In a famous incident of the election campaign, MacDonald brandished a handful of German currency from the 1920s and warned of what the combination of a floating exchange rate and irresponsible financial management could entail.[46]

In part, fears of hyperinflation were based upon a simple "confidence"

---

[45] "The Pound and the Gold Standard" (A Note Prepared by Henry Clay for the Guidance of the National Government, Lothian Papers, Box 219), quoted in Skidelsky, *Politicians*, pp. 414–15.

[46] *Manchester Guardian*, 21 September 1931, p. 9; *News Chronicle*, 29 September 1931, p. 1.

argument. Any large depreciation would convince the public that sterling was no longer a stable store of value, and further depreciation would ensue as individuals lost faith in the currency. To a considerable extent, however, the fear of hyperinflation was based upon the unions' presumed response to a rise in the cost of living. Officials within a number of Government ministries anticipated that a sizable depreciation that led to an unmistakable rise in the cost of living would stimulate increased wage demands. Costs would rise along with prices, so that depreciation would not stimulate output and employment. More to the point, depreciation would not restore balance-of-payments equilibrium. If domestic costs rose, the price of home goods would not fall relative to the price of imports. There would be no incentive for consumers to redirect their spending from imports toward domestic goods, so that no reduction in the size of the trade deficit would take place. Since Britain was running a trade deficit at the time of devaluation, the sterling value of that deficit would be increased, assuming little or no change in the volume of trade. Further depreciation would result, followed by another round of wage increases and ever-accelerating depreciation. This was the "vicious circle of inflation" of which Clay warned (Skidelsky, 1967, pp. 414–15).

Concern with this problem was voiced at the Treasury and the Board of Trade. "Depreciation will only work if prices rise relative to wages," read an internal Treasury communiqué.[47] Arthur Loveday, the British economist in charge of the League of Nations Economic Intelligence Service, warned Sir Arthur Salter of the Treasury, who had served previously as Britain's representative to the League of Nations Economic Commission, of the danger that substantial depreciation would lead to escalating wage demands. Henderson issued a blunt warning that wage demands would offset any large depreciation, and Chamberlain alluded to the "insoluble problems" that would be created by a very great rise in the cost of living.[48] Not everyone agreed that wages would rise in step with import prices. Hawtrey, for example, argued that in the past wages had always lagged behind prices. Even if the unions had acquired increased market power, he saw no reason to anticipate that they would exert it during the present crisis.[49]

---

[47] PRO T188/29, "Comments on Mr. Hawtrey's Memorandum by H. D. Henderson," 6 October 1931. Sentiment within the Board of Trade is reported by the *Times,* 14 October 1931, p. 7.

[48] PRO T175/56, Loveday to Salter, 26 September 1931, pp. 102–5; T175/56, Henderson to Hawtrey, 16 October 1931; Cab 27/467 BT(31)8, "Capital Items in the Balance of International Payments," 15 December 1931.

[49] PRO T188/29, "Pegging the Pound II," 16 October 1931.

The British had learned from the German experience that inflation is fueled by the government's printing presses. Therefore, the discussion of inflation focused on two issues: the effect of exchange-rate depreciation on the Government budget and the authorities' response to the growth of the deficit. Depreciation would force up Government expenditure by adding to the cost of the goods purchased by Government agencies and raising the wages paid in the public sector. So long as there was no decline in the unemployment rate, expenditure on the dole would not be relieved. With some sources of revenue fixed in nominal terms, Government receipts would lag behind outlays. Together, these factors meant that depreciation would add to the burden of deficit finance. If the Government financed the deficit by expanding the floating debt, higher wages would be accommodated and no ceiling would be placed on the wage-price spiral.

Advocates of a tariff suggested that the Government could abort the wage-price spiral by relying on commercial policy rather than exchange-rate depreciation to restore external balance. If a tariff were added to depreciation, the import-tax revenues accruing to the Government could be used to balance the budget. The authorities would not be forced to expand the floating debt, wage increases would not be accommodated, and the vicious spiral would be halted. If workers continued to demand higher wages, the unemployment problem might be exacerbated but hyperinflation would not ensue.

The protectionists had additional arguments. They suggested that offers of protection could be used to promote investment and modernization. Industries characterized by scale economies would be able to produce at lower cost if provided with tariff protection. In addition, they argued that only through the imposition of a tariff could Britain force foreign countries to reduce their own trade barriers.[50] However, the vicious-spiral argument was the essence of their case for a tariff.

[50] Oddly, the question of possible foreign retaliation did not play a major role in the debate over a tariff, perhaps because many foreign countries had already imposed trade barriers of their own. The Subcommittee on Financial Questions did point out that foreign authorities would perceive the imposition of a tariff so soon after exchange-rate depreciation as a heavy economic blow and a violation of the code of international comity. However, Cabinet Ministers disagreed about whether it would be more effective to impose a tariff first and then bargain for foreign concessions or merely to threaten imposition unless foreign restrictions were lifted. Samuel felt that, by merely threatening to use the powers of retaliation, Britain could obtain immediate concessions from Germany and the Scandinavian countries. Once imposed, he suggested, a tariff would be useless for bargaining purposes. Chamberlain argued the opposite, asserting that the British threat would be made credible only by the passage of a tariff bill and that foreign concessions could be extracted only following the actual imposition of trade restrictions.

While doubts about the ability of a freely floating exchange rate to bring the external accounts into balance were pervasive in official circles, they were treated skeptically by the academic community. Keynes submitted a letter to the *Times* a week after the departure from gold in which he argued that the case for a tariff had ceased to be urgent. Salter suggested that there remained a case for a tariff under a regime of floating exchange rates only if foreign countries pursued a policy of competitive depreciation. He was confident that Britain would escape the vicious spiral simply because the authorities were unwilling to see the value of the nation's external assets reduced to naught. Beveridge argued that since Britain had gone off the gold standard, the case for a tariff had been "killed entirely." [51] The 1932 edition of *Tariffs: The Case Examined,* again edited by Beveridge, contained a new chapter in which Benham analyzed the virtues of a tariff in light of Britain's departure from gold. A floating exchange rate, he wrote, "is a solution, and a complete solution, of the problem of restoring external equilibrium. . . . The case for a tariff on these grounds is dead" (p. 253). Benham could detect no evidence that there remained an adverse trade balance, no tendency of wages and other costs to rise in step with import prices, and no indication that sterling would depreciate at an ever-accelerating rate.

Most economists were aware that the imposition of a tariff was likely to exacerbate the unemployment problem. Henderson reminded Treasury officials in October that any tariff-induced appreciation of sterling would offset the favorable effects of depreciation on domestic economic activity. Robbins composed for Beveridge an elaborate memorandum in which he argued, "If, when the exchanges are free, we impose a tariff, not only do we do what is unnecessary, we also do what is immediately harmful." Loveday made the same point in a letter to his friend Sir Richard Hopkins at the Treasury.[52]

Yet the employment effects of a tariff were a concern of only secondary importance in the Government. Many Ministers were not convinced that the depressing effects of the price deflation induced by exchange-rate appreciation were as important as the reduction of uncertainty that would result from the restoration of balance to the external accounts and the stabilization of the exchange rate at a new equilibrium level. They saw the alternative to protection as persistent current-account and budget deficits, with

---

[51] *Times,* 29 September 1931, p. 15, 2 October 1931, p. 14, and 17 October 1931, p. 13.

[52] PRO T175/56, Henderson to Hawtrey, 16 October 1931; T175/56, Loveday to Hopkins, 26 October 1931; L. Robbins, "How to Balance the Balance of Trade," Beveridge Papers, BP/II/B London School of Economics, undated.

wages and prices spiraling ever upward and the exchange rate depreciating without end.

The decision to impose a tariff

The continuing concern with the international accounts and skepticism that a floating exchange rate alone was sufficient to restore external balance were reflected in Parliamentary debate. While traditional free-trade and protectionist sentiment and the special problems of certain industries made their inevitable appearance, several Members of the House of Commons focused upon the role of a tariff in correcting the adverse balance. On November 11, Mr. Mander presented the view that, under a floating exchange rate, the balance of trade must balance. This Mr. Entwistle labeled the "most arrant nonsense" (*Hansard*, Nov. 11, 1931, pp. 202–3, 221–2). Entwistle's objections were based on the vicious-spiral argument. Entwistle's view was echoed the following month by a number of Conservative Members, who argued that a tariff was the only weapon capable of correcting the adverse trade balance and preventing the pound sterling from falling further (*Hansard*, Dec. 9, 1931, pp. 1976–82).

As this debate progressed, it became obvious that importers were increasing their inventories in anticipation of possible future import levies. To deter anticipatory importing, the Abnormal Importations Act was introduced in the House of Commons on November 17 while the desirability of permanent measures was still under consideration. This Act conferred on the Board of Trade temporary power to impose duties of up to 100 percent *ad valorem* on imports judged to be entering the country in abnormal quantities. Three orders were quickly issued, imposing duties of 50 percent *ad valorem* on a variety of products.[53]

At this point the debate reached the Cabinet. The Cabinet Committee on the Balance of Trade, constituted on December 11, 1931, provided the arena within which the final battle over the General Tariff was fought. With the Abnormal Importations Act already in effect, Liberal members of the Cabinet hoped that the new Committee would undertake a comprehensive analysis of permanent measures. In this they were disappointed. The Committee met only five times, under the chairmanship of Chamberlain,

---

[53] In addition, a Horticultural Products (Emergency Provisions) Act was introduced to provide the Minister of Agriculture with temporary power to impose specific duties on products that were difficult to value and tax on an ad valorem basis. For details, see R. Findlay, *Britain under Protection* (London, 1934).

who resisted proposals to call upon outside experts. Snowden no longer attempted to influence the course of the proceedings, satisfying himself with a harshly worded memo of dissent from the Committee's report. Samuel, the Home Secretary, was the principal spokesman for the anti-tariff view, but Chamberlain neutralized his efforts by giving ground on minor points and ruling Samuel's major objections out of order.

When the Committee first met on December 17, it possessed a considerable amount of information on the economic situation. In September, the Economic Advisory Council Committee on Economic Information had been forced to admit the difficulty of making "even an approximate estimate" of how the balance of trade responded to exchange-rate changes. Now the Cabinet Ministers possessed preliminary estimates of trade in November. Between September and October, the sterling value of both imports and exports had risen, but the increase in the value of imports had been four times as great. In November, the increase in the value of imports had been substantially smaller, but export value had actually fallen relative to the preceding month. December would show the first signs of improvement, with imports falling and exports rising in value. The cost of living had begun to climb slowly, but wage rates were holding firm for the time being.

Chamberlain set the tone of the meeting on January 2, 1932, by turning first to his own memorandum on the external position. The Chancellor argued that the trade balance was the critical component of the external accounts; the stability of the pound could still be undermined by capital outflows, and the announcement of further deficits in merchandise trade might be sufficient to undermine foreign confidence. He argued that relying on exchange-rate adjustments to eliminate the trade deficit would entail an unacceptably large depreciation. The members of the Committee generally agreed with Chamberlain on the dangers of depending on exchange-rate depreciation to solve the problem of external balance. But when Chamberlain invoked Keynes as an authority who favored tariff protection, Samuel did not let this slip by. He pointed out that Keynes no longer favored a tariff now that Britain had left the gold standard.[54]

The third meeting of the Committee, on January 12, was notable for the presentation of Chamberlain's own proposal for a general tariff. This plan entailed a 10 percent duty on all imports plus selective surtaxes on luxury

---

[54] PRO T172/1768, Samuel to Chamberlain, Chamberlain to Samuel, 17 December 1931. See also Cab27/467 BT(31)8, "The Balance of Trade: Memorandum by the Chancellor of the Exchequer," 12 January 1932.

items. When Samuel pointed out that the imposition of taxes on imported raw materials would constitute a burden for the export industries, Chamberlain yielded on this issue. The Committee reconvened the following day, and the Chairman expressed his willingness to meet Samuel's objections by drawing up a plan for a 10 percent tariff that excluded raw materials. Chamberlain then summarized the case for a general tariff. Along with its effects on the external accounts, Chamberlain emphasized a tariff's contribution toward balancing the Government budget. Again, the only discordant note was sounded by Samuel, who reported that Keynes was no longer concerned about Britain's balance of payments and retained complete confidence in what the other members of the Committee referred to derisively as the "automatic equilibrium theory." [55]

The Report of the Cabinet Committee on the Balance of Trade, issued on January 19, predicted continued weakness in Britain's trade balance.[56] A 10 percent general tariff was proposed as a means of reducing imports by 25 percent and balancing the budget. Memoranda of dissent by Snowden and Samuel were attached. Snowden's expressed its author's undiminished faith in the power of a floating exchange rate to rectify any imbalance in Britain's external accounts. Samuel's contained a blanket rejection of the majority's views.

Snowden and Samuel, along with Sinclair, the Secretary of State for Scotland, proved equally intractable in the debates that took place at the Cabinet level. On January 21, Sir E. Hilton Young, the Minister of Health, put forth the vicious-spiral argument on behalf of the majority.[57]

Previous experience showed that in a large country with a highly developed economic organisation what was likely to happen with such an adverse balance as ours was not that the £ would balance exports and imports by slow movements, but that there would be a gradual fall to a danger point, at which there would be a catastrophic fall, with far more serious consequences to the cost of living than those attending a tariff.

---

55 Samuel also reported Keynes's mysterious remark that a tariff might be appropriate in the future for political or social reasons. PRO Cab 27/467 BT(31), "Conclusions of the Third Meeting of the Cabinet Committee on the Balance of Trade," 12 January 1932, pp. 39–48. See also Howson and Winch, *Economic Advisory Council*, p. 98; R. Harrod, *The Life of John Maynard Keynes* (London, 1951), p. 431. Keynes developed these views in an article first delivered as the Findlay Lecture at University College, Dublin, 19 April 1933, and published as "National Self-Sufficiency," *Yale Review*, new ser., 22 (1933), 755–69.

56 PRO Cab 27/467 CP25(32), 19 January 1932, pp. 3–18.

57 PRO Cab 23/70 Cabinet 5(32), "Conclusions of a Cabinet Meeting," 21 January 1932, p. 111.

Prime Minister MacDonald responded that he had been forced to reconsider his position on a policy that he believed to be unsound under normal international conditions. He agreed that the Government must find some means of protecting the pound. He was prepared to contemplate a tariff under "these exceptional circumstances." [58] Sinclair raised the question of tariff retaliation abroad and expressed his belief that it would be impossible to dispense with the tariff once circumstances had returned to normal.

Without the cooperation of the dissenting members, the Government was faced with the alternatives of abandoning plans for a tariff or restructuring the Cabinet. The Conservative majority was unwilling to adopt the first course, but the second would have destroyed MacDonald's pretensions of leading a government of national unity. In fact, a third alternative was invented: the celebrated agreement to differ, whereby the free-trade members of the Cabinet could continue to serve in the Government while speaking out against its tariff proposal (Beer, 1965, pp. 287–92).[59] Thus Snowden, Samuel, Sinclair, and Maclean, the Education Minister, dissociated themselves from the decision to approve the Report of the Cabinet Committee on the Balance of Trade.

These members of the Cabinet also dissociated themselves from the Import Duties Bill, which was introduced in Commons on February 4, 1932. This bill provided for three types of duties: a general 10 percent import levy, additional duties and exemptions for special commodities, and retaliatory duties. Imports from the Empire were exempted, pending negotiations with the Empire at the Ottawa Conference. Imports of many raw materials were excluded, among them wheat and maize, meat and animals, iron and tin ores, scrap steel, zinc, lead, rubber, pulp and newsprint, cotton, wool, flax, and hides and skins. An Import Duties Advisory Council was created to receive applications for modifications of existing duties and to frame recommendations for new and modified duties for presentation to Parliament.

The introduction of the Import Duties Bill was widely perceived as the culmination of a series of momentous events in the evolution of British commercial policy. The *Times* (Feb. 5, 1932, p. 12) noted the festive and attentive appearance of the House of Commons and remarked that it reflected the fact that "the business at hand marked a turning point in British policy." The unusually moving character of Neville Chamberlain's speech

[58] Ibid., pp. 114–15.
[59] See also ibid., 22 January 1932, pp. 2–5.

of introduction was widely commented upon. Its substance was that a tariff was needed to improve Britain's adverse trade balance and "to effect an insurance against a rise in the cost of living which might easily follow upon an unchecked depreciation of our currency." Chamberlain concluded that "really the essential point is the value of sterling" (Royal Institute, 1932, pp. 25–6).

4. Conclusion

No single factor was responsible for the British decision to adopt the General Tariff in 1932. The familiar shibboleths of protection and free trade continued to dominate the opinions of many politicians, although Britain's immediate economic problems forced some to reconsider their views. Recently, it has been suggested that the policymakers' dominant concern was unemployment, and that, because they waited to impose a tariff until Britain had adopted a floating exchange rate, their actions magnified the dimensions of this problem. The evidence presented here supports another interpretation. The politicians' outlook was conditioned by the European inflations of the 1920s, and few had faith that a floating exchange rate represented a solution to the problem of external balance. They supported the imposition of the General Tariff in order to guard against the dangers of hyperinflation and unbounded exchange-rate depreciation, and they made this choice knowing that the tariff might exacerbate the problem of domestic unemployment. This possibility, however, was the price to be paid for exchange-rate and price stability.

In retrospect, it is difficult to assess the realism of the politicians' fears. Whether, in the absence of a tariff, the British economy would have been launched into a vicious spiral of inflation and depreciation is a matter for conjecture. To many, this possibility now seems unlikely. But, justified or not, the authorities' fears and their distrust of the effects of a floating exchange rate formed the basis for their decision to impose the General Tariff.

9. Exchange rates and economic recovery in the 1930s

With Jeffrey Sachs

Whether they are concerned with the magnitude of the initial contraction or the retardation of the subsequent recovery, most analyses of the Great Depression attach considerable weight to the effects of economic policy. The misguided actions of the Federal Reserve and the unfortunate commercial initiatives of the executive and legislative branches are blamed for transforming the American recession into an unprecedented depression.[1] Perverse monetary and fiscal responses in such countries as Germany and France are blamed for reinforcing the deflationary pressures transmitted from the United States to the rest of the industrial world.[2] In desperate attempts to promote recovery, or at least to provide insulation from destabilizing foreign shocks, national authorities had recourse to currency devaluation and tariff escalation. Such initiatives are typically characterized as beggar-thy-neighbor policies. Individually they are seen as attempts to better a country's position at the expense of its neighbors; together, it is argued, they disrupted international economic relations and, by impeding foreign trade, destroyed one of the only remaining sources of autonomous demand.[3]

An earlier version of this paper was presented to seminars at New York, Queen's, and Yale universities, and Nuffield College, Oxford. We thank Charles Kindleberger, Ian McLean, and Peter Temin for comments, while noting that the normal disclaimer applies with special force.

[1] The classic indictment of the Fed is of course Friedman and Schwartz, *Monetary History*. For analyses which emphasize also the effects of protectionist initiatives, see Alan Meltzer, "Monetary and Other Explanations for the Start of the Great Depression," *Journal of Monetary Economics* 2 (1976), 455–72; and Christian Saint-Etienne, *The Great Depression, 1929–1938: Lessons for the 1980s* (Stanford, 1984).

[2] Kindleberger, *World in Depression;* Karl Hardach, *The Political Economy of Germany in the Twentieth Century* (Berkeley, 1976); and Sauvy, *Histoire*. This is not to imply that the Great Depression in Europe was solely a reflection of the downturn in the United States. (On Europe's difficulties in the 1920s, see Svennilson, *Growth and Stagnation*, or Peter Temin, "The Beginning of the Depression in Germany," *Economic History Review*, sec. ser., 24 (1971), 240–8.) All that is necessary for the argument is that the Depression in Europe was heavily affected by concurrent developments in America. Space limitations do not permit us to formally address the causes of the Depression.

[3] For a statement of this view, see Nurkse, *Currency Experience*.

215

With notable exceptions, such as "cheap money" in Britain after 1931, fiscal expansion in Sweden, and industrial policy giving way to central control in Germany, public policy receives little credit for helping the economies of Europe find their way out of the Great Depression.[4] One can conceive of various policies these nations might have pursued: devaluation, protection, monetary expansion, and fiscal stimulus. In practice, however, there was little scope for significant policy initiative within the institutional and intellectual framework inherited from the 1920s. Fiscal policy, except in Sweden, would continue to be guided by the principle of balanced budgets until the adoption of Keynesian approaches to taxation and spending.[5] Even had there existed a belief in the efficacy of countercyclical fiscal policy, it might have been of little practical consequence on the national level so long as the fixed parities of the gold-exchange standard served as an external constraint. The potential of monetary initiatives, although more widely recognized and acknowledged, was equally inhibited by the gold standard constraint.

The critical decision for national economic authorities therefore concerned the stance of external policy. Not only might currency devaluation, exchange control, tariff protection, and quantitative trade restrictions have macroeconomic effects of their own, but by changing the external constraints they could open the way for initiatives on other fronts. Some have argued, however, that such policies provided a country relief from the Depression only at the expense of its neighbors, and that by eliciting retaliation they only exacerbated the global crisis. Thus, many studies of the Depression which do not dismiss the effects of policy as negligible condemn them as positively harmful.

A proper understanding of the role of external economic policy must begin with a sharp analytical distinction between protectionist measures (such as tariffs and quotas) and exchange rate management. Tariffs and de-

---

4 Even these cases have been disputed. Lars Jonung, "The Depression in Sweden and the United States: A Comparison of Causes and Policies," in Karl Brunner, ed., *The Great Depression Revisited* (Boston, 1981), pp. 286–315, has questioned the role of fiscal policy in Swedish growth. Beenstock, Griffiths, and Capie, "Economic Recovery," have attempted to show that policy had little role in Britain's recovery. The German situation is in many ways special and will be given relatively little attention here.

5 An extensive literature analyzes the extent to which public officials, especially in Britain, were or were not converted to Keynesian views in the 1930s. See, for example, Howson and Winch, *Economic Advisory Council;* G. C. Peden, "Keynes, the Treasury and Unemployment in Later Nineteen-Thirties," *Oxford Economic Papers*, n.s., 32 (1980), 1–18; and Alan Booth, "The 'Keynesian Revolution' in Economic Policy-Making," *Economic History Review*, sec. ser., 26 (1983), 103–23.

valuation are often spoken of as two sides of the same coin, both being policies designed to shift demand from foreign countries to the domestic economy. But in fact the general equilibrium implications of the two sets of policies are very different. Tariff changes inevitably create output price distortions, while a series of devaluations in many countries can leave relative output prices unchanged.[6] A tariff increase in one country is likely to reduce economic welfare in other countries and provoke retaliation; and a global round of tariff escalation is likely to reduce welfare in all countries.[7] The implications of exchange rate management are far more complex. One country's devaluation need not beggar the remaining countries, and a series of devaluations can easily leave all countries better off.

This chapter offers a new interpretation of the effects of currency depreciation in the 1930s. We will argue that depreciation was clearly beneficial for the initiating countries.[8] We then establish that there is in fact no theoretical presumption that depreciation in the 1930s was a beggar-thy-neighbor policy. While there is evidence that the foreign repercussions of individual devaluations were negative – that policy had beggar-thy-neighbor effects – the finding does not support the conclusion that competitive devaluations taken by a group of countries were without benefit for the system as a whole. Although it is difficult to determine whether

6 Exchange control is effectively a combination of tariff and devaluation policy, in the sense that it both changes the relative prices of national currencies and causes distortions in output prices.

7 See Harry G. Johnson, "Optimum Tariffs and Retaliation," *Review of Economic Studies* 21 (1953/54), 145–53, for one of the original game-theoretic analyses of tariff wars. Johnson shows that all countries suffer from a tariff war with retaliation if their economies are symmetric, whereas some countries may be better off, relative to free trade, in an asymmetric environment.

8 In this respect, our work supports the findings of E. Choudri and L. Kochin, "The Exchange Rate and the International Transmission of Business Cycle Disturbances," *Journal of Money, Credit and Banking* 12 (1980), 565–74. Choudri and Kochin document the relationship between exchange depreciation and relative national price levels and outputs for several European countries. An analysis almost identical to theirs appears in George F. Warren and Frank A. Pearson, *Prices* (New York, 1933). Neither set of authors, however, works with a formal macroeconomic model, as in this chapter, and thus they do not attempt to describe the structural mechanisms linking exchange rates with other aggregate variables, nor do they discuss the foreign repercussions of exchange rate changes. The conclusion that currency depreciation in the 1930s benefited the initiating country is itself controversial, since it has recently been argued, in the spirit of the new classical macroeconomics, that the effects of depreciation were in some instances negligible. Beenstock, Griffiths, and Capie, "Economic Recovery." The new classical macroeconomics insists that purely monetary changes, such as changes in the price of gold, can have no real effects since other nominal values will adjust proportionately to the monetary change. We argue that the experience of the 1930s is clearly inconsistent with this doctrine.

the devaluations which actually took place had on balance an expansionary
or contractionary impact on the world economy, there is little doubt that
similar policies, had they been adopted even more widely and coordinated
internationally, would have hastened economic recovery from the Great
Depression.

1. Currency depreciation in the 1930s

Table 9.1 sets out the basic chronology of departures from the gold standard in the ten European countries whose macroeconomic experience is
considered here.

Britain's departure from the gold standard in 1931 is often taken to signal the beginning of the "devaluation cycle" of the 1930s.[9] It is important
to recognize therefore that the start of the cycle preceded Britain's departure from gold by nearly two years. Argentina and Uruguay suspended
gold payments in December 1929, while Hungary, Paraguay, and Brazil
found themselves unable to maintain their currencies at par.[10] In 1930 the
exchanges of Chile, Venezuela, Peru, Australia, and New Zealand fell and
remained below the gold export point. Most of these countries were both
primary producers and international debtors. The reasons for their difficulties will have a familiar ring to modern observers: first, the decline in
foreign lending by the United States starting in 1928; second, the fall in primary commodity prices which accelerated dramatically in 1929; and third,
the imposition of protective tariffs by industrial countries, notably on their
imports of food.[11]

The international system, then, had already shown signs of weakness
when financial difficulties surfaced in Europe and America in 1930. Bank-

---

[9] The phrase is from Nurske, *Currency Experience.* We elaborate on its meaning below.

[10] In addition, at the end of 1929, Canada, which like the United States until 1914 adhered
to the gold standard without the benefit of a central bank, introduced new restrictions on
the operation of the gold standard in response to its deteriorating economic position.

[11] U.S. foreign lending began to contract in 1928 as the New York stock exchange boom
drove up interest rates and diverted funds from foreign lending to domestic financial markets, and this contraction accelerated as the Federal Reserve failed to accommodate the
rising demand for credit. The decline in primary commodity prices following the downturn
in the United States was not an entirely new development, as commodity prices had been
trending downward for much of the decade owing to the vast expansion in non-European
productive capacity that had taken place during World War I. See Svennilson, *Growth and
Stagnation.* The same can be said of the move toward protection, which was well under-
way before the onset of the Depression. See, for example, H. Liepman, *Tariff Levels and
the Economic Unity of Europe* (London, 1938); or J. B. Condliffe, *The Reconstruction of
World Trade* (New York, 1940).

Table 9.1: *Principal measures affecting exchange rates as of 1937 (month and year of introduction)*

Country	Official suspension of gold standard	Exchange control	Depreciation or devaluation
Belgium	3.35	3.35	3.35
Denmark	11.31	11.31	11.31
Finland	12.31	—	10.31
France	—	—	9.36
Germany	—	7.31	—
Italy	—	5.34	3.34
Netherlands	9.36	—	9.36
Norway	9.31	—	9.31
Sweden	9.31	—	9.31
United Kingdom	9.31	—	9.31

Source: League of Nations, *Monetary Review* (Geneva, 1937), appendix table 1.

ing crises in the United States at the end of 1930 and in Austria and Germany the following summer led to the introduction of exchange control by Germany, in July 1931. By undermining the credibility of the gold standard the controls helped to set the stage for Britain's departure from gold, in September.[12] Britain was forced to devalue, but many of the countries that followed sterling off the gold standard were not. Their reasons for depreciation varied, but the fear that export market share would otherwise be lost to countries with depreciated currencies surely bulked large. In this sense their actions have been viewed as competitive depreciations. By the end of October 1931 all of the British Dominions (except South Africa), the rest of the British Empire, the Scandinavian countries, and Portugal, Egypt, Bolivia, and Latvia had turned to depreciation.[13] They were followed within six months by Japan, Greece, Siam, and Peru.[14]

[12] The Austrians followed the Germans with a lag, imposing exchange control in October 1931. Britain's devaluation has been examined recently by Cairncross and Eichengreen, *Sterling in Decline*. There is some dispute over the importance of financial difficulties such as the Continental bank failures relative to the development of Britain's balance of payments position. See also Moggridge, "1931 Financial Crisis."

[13] South Africa's decision must be understood in terms of its unusually strong external position and exceptional attachment to a stable gold price, attributable to its position as a gold producer.

[14] By December 1931, when sterling reached a trough, it had depreciated by 40 percent relative to the currencies which remained on gold. This raises the question of how countries

The next round of depreciation commenced with the fall of the U.S. dollar in 1933. In March of that year President Roosevelt unexpectedly restricted foreign exchange dealings and gold and currency movements, and the following month he issued an executive order requiring individuals to deliver their gold coin, bullion, and certificates to Federal Reserve Banks. From this point the dollar began to float. By setting a series of progressively higher dollar prices of gold the Administration engineered a substantial devaluation. When the dollar was finally stabilized in January 1934 at $35 an ounce it retained but 59 percent of its former gold content.[15] The U.S. action is typically viewed as a clear instance of beggar-thy-neighbor policy, since on the eve of the decision the American balance of payments was already strong; depreciation represented a further shift of demand away from the products of the rest of the world.

The dollar's depreciation set off another wave of retaliatory devaluations. South Africa joined the emerging Sterling Area, and the South American currencies, many of which established links with the floating dollar, fell at accelerating rates. The Japanese yen, which had remained relatively stable in terms of sterling, now moved lower, rupturing its de facto link with the Sterling Area. The only major currencies that remained freely convertible were those of the Gold Bloc countries: France, Belgium, Holland, Italy, Poland, and Switzerland.

The international financial history of the subsequent two years was dominated by the battles fought by the Gold Bloc countries against the forces threatening to undermine their parities. The devaluation of the dollar weakened their international competitive positions and induced a reflux of capital to the United States.[16] The need for increased public expenditure on rearma-

which did not engage in depreciation could ignore such a large relative price effect. The answer is that they concluded almost universally that the costs of a loss of competitiveness were more than outweighed by the benefits of avoiding the inflation that devaluation might provoke. This was clearly the basis for the French decision: see Marguerite Perrot, *La Monnaie et l'opinion publique en France et en Angleterre, 1924–1936* (Paris, 1955). Despite the popularity of competing explanations, Kindleberger, *World in Depression*, pp. 163–4, concludes that this was the basis for the German decision as well.

15 There is considerable dispute over the extent to which the U.S. administration understood the relationship of its gold-buying program to the exchange rate and the price level. See John Morton Blum, *From the Morganthau Diaries, vol. I: Years of Crisis, 1928–1938* (Boston, 1959), p. 73; or Kindleberger, *World in Depression*, pp. 226–7.

16 These difficulties were reinforced by the downward movement of sterling and its allied currencies, the tightening of exchange control by countries that used this device to reconcile expansionary initiatives with the balance-of-payments constraint, and by growing social resistance to further reductions in wages and nominal incomes.

ment compromised the fiscal position of even the countries most committed to a deflationary policy in defense of the gold standard. The financial positions of the Gold Bloc countries deteriorated seriously beginning in 1934, culminating in May 1935 in a marked loss of confidence in the sustainability of their parities and flight of international capital. Belgium, which suffered exceptionally because of unusual dependence on foreign trade, and which had experts studying the devaluation option as early as 1933, was the first Gold Bloc country to leave the fold, in March 1935.[17] Similar difficulties were experienced in all of the other Gold Bloc countries except Poland. In each of these countries, as the burden of deflation mounted, working-class resistance grew, and devaluation was increasingly discussed.[18]

By the second quarter of 1936 the external situation in the Gold Bloc countries had reached a crisis. Poland in April 1936 imposed exchange control for the first time. France, Holland, and Switzerland resisted exchange control, and suffered heavy gold losses. In France, the Popular Front, which came to power in April 1936, committed itself to a vigorous reflationary policy and to defense of the gold standard. Within months of its accession, the incompatibility of the two goals was recognized. Currency depreciation was postponed to September, with considerable difficulty, while the French negotiated with the British and Americans to prevent competitive depreciations.[19] But once the franc was allowed to begin its descent the other Gold Bloc currencies followed without delay. Devaluation had come full circle.

[17] In addition, the deterioration of economic conditions in its colonial possessions further undermined Belgium's budgetary position. Moreover, late in the summer of 1934, the government turned to a reflationary program, lowering the central bank discount rate and expanding credit in an effort to revitalize the economy. These efforts were sufficient to undermine confidence in the currency but inadequate to stimulate recovery. See van der Wee and Tavernier, *Banque Nationale*.

[18] These difficulties were least pronounced in Holland, whose trade was heavily concentrated in its seven colonies and hence immune to the effects of foreign tariffs, and whose coal, electricity, and cement industries actually continued to expand between 1929 and 1933. See Fernand Baudhuin, "Europe and the Great Crisis," in Herman van der Wee, ed., *The Great Depression Revisited* (The Hague, 1972). The French case bears a remarkable resemblance to that of Belgium. In September 1935, the French government, which had previously remained firm in its commitment to deflation, demanded new constitutional powers to enable it to carry through its program, which were ultimately denied. This government fell and was replaced by another which included a policy of domestic credit expansion as part of its program. See Sauvy, *Histoire*.

[19] These negotiations culminated in the Tripartite Agreement of September 1936. See Clarke, "Exchange Rate Stabilization," and Chapter 6 for details.

2. Forms of currency depreciation

Currency depreciation in the 1930s took a number of forms, with differing implications for domestic and foreign economies. The precise character of the devaluations hinged on the domestic and international financial policies that accompanied the change, including the allocation of profits on revalued central bank reserves, the restrictions on dealings in foreign exchange, and the mechanisms to control fluctuations in the exchange rate.

Not all countries wrote up the book value of foreign reserves to reflect the higher domestic-currency price at which gold would now be traded. The United Kingdom and many members of the Sterling Area, for example, continued to value gold reserves at par. Revaluation profits were put to various uses. One option was to use them to support an expansion of the money supply, without reducing the proportionate backing of the currency by international reserves. Revaluation profits were transferred directly to the fiscal authorities (the method used in Argentina, Italy, and to a limited extent in Romania), or else were allocated to special funds designated for purchases of government securities (the method used in Belgium starting in April 1935 and in France starting in July 1937). The alternative of using revaluation profits to extinguish government debt held by the central bank – adopted wholly or in part by France in October 1936, Czechoslovakia, Romania, and Japan – had no direct effect on the money supply.[20]

Another alternative was to allocate the revaluation profits to newly established exchange stabilization funds, as was done in the United States, Belgium, Switzerland, and France in 1936. In these cases, the profits on revalued gold reserves were reflected neither in the book value of the central bank's reserves nor in its reserve ratio. But to the extent that a fund was entitled to use the currency it got to purchase securities held by the public, through the intervention of the fund the revaluation profits might ultimately support an expansion in the money supply.

The ostensible purpose of these funds was to smooth short-term fluctuations in the exchange rate. If they restricted their intervention to damping temporary fluctuations, their operations would have no lasting impact on the money supply. Yet in practice many such funds intervened to defend the competitive advantage conferred by devaluation, preventing any subsequent appreciation of the exchanges. The actions of the British Exchange Equalisation Account, for example, among the most active funds, have re-

---

[20] In France, some 35 percent of the profits were so applied.

cently been interpreted in this light.[21] The American Exchange Stabilization Fund, in contrast, bought and sold dollars only occasionally, as required to maintain the $35 gold price.[22]

The other way in which exchange rates were regulated following devaluation was through the imposition of exchange control. In many cases exchange control had first been adopted during the 1931 financial crisis as a way of stemming capital flight. In nearly every instance the restrictions adopted then were retained after the immediate convertibility crisis subsided (for details, see Table 9.1). Restrictions on capital exports ranged from attempts to impose a complete prohibition, as in Austria and Estonia, to relatively moderate disincentives such as the 4 percent tax imposed by Mexico on all remittances not of commercial origin. In order to prevent disguised capital transfers, countries imposing tight exchange control adopted new regulations on commercial transactions.[23] In many countries the authorities nonetheless proved incapable of preventing the development of black markets in foreign exchange.[24] Potential international borrowers attempted to discriminate in the treatment of new and old loans in such a way as to encourage further capital imports. Thus, provisions were included in several exchange control laws to guarantee the free transfer of service on new foreign investments.[25]

3. Single-country effects of depreciation

There are four principal channels through which the currency depreciations of the 1930s could have affected domestic and foreign economies: real wages, profitability, international competitiveness, and the level of world interest rates. Our analysis makes use of a simple two-country model, drawing on the work of Mundell and Fleming, but extended to encompass the determinants of aggregate supply and the gold-standard constraints. The model, whose elements appear in the note to Table 9.2, incorporates

---

21 For qualitative evidence see Howson, "Sterling's Managed Float," and for econometric support see Cairncross and Eichengreen, *Sterling in Decline*.

22 The Fund instituted in Belgium was abolished once the exchange rate was stabilized. Similar funds were also created by Canada and China.

23 In many cases this need to increase oversight of commercial transactions reinforced the tendency toward increased trade restrictions.

24 See Bank for International Settlements, *Annual Report* (Basle, 1934), for examples.

25 For example, a regulation was adopted in Poland in November 1937 under which the transfer of principal and interest on new foreign loans was exempted from exchange control. Similar measures were adopted in Italy and elsewhere.

Table 9.2: *Impact of exchange-rate depreciation on endogenous variables, 1929–1935*

| | Variable | | | | |
Case	Domestic output	Foreign output	Domestic reserves	Foreign reserves	Interest rate
I. Sterilized devaluation	+	−	0	0	−
II. Unsterilized devaluation	+	+/−	+/−	+/−	+/−
III. Simultaneous devaluation, unchanged gold backing	+	+	0	0	−
IV. Simultaneous devaluation, unchanged monetary base	0	0	0	0	0

Note: A plus or minus indicates the sign of the comparative statics result. $+/-$ indicates that the direction of the effect cannot be signed.

These results are derived from a model of two symmetrical countries, in which each country is characterized by relationships of the following form. (Lowercase letters denote logs of variables, and asterisks denote foreign values.)

Aggregate supply is a negative function of the real product wage:

$$q = -\alpha(w - p),$$

where q is the log of GDP, w is the log wage (taken as fixed), and p the log price of domestic goods. Under a gold standard, each country fixes the domestic price of gold, where G is ounces of gold per unit of domestic currency. The foreign price of domestic currency is G/G^* and the log exchange rate $g - g^*$. Aggregate demand is a decreasing function of the relative price of domestic goods and of the nominal interest rate:

$$q = -\delta(p + g - g^* - p^*) - \sigma i,$$

where the domestic interest rate i equals the foreign rate by open interest parity. The demand for money takes the form:

$$m - p = \phi q - \beta i,$$

where m is the log of nominal money balances. Money supply is defined as the value of gold reserves R/G (where R is the volume of reserves) times the reciprocal of the gold-backing ratio $\psi = (R/G)/M$.

$$m = r - g - \psi.$$

Since the (fixed) world gold stock is divided between the two central banks:

$$\gamma dr + (1 - \gamma)dr^* = 0,$$

where γ is the domestic bank's initial share of the world total. Comparative statics results are derived in Eichengreen and Sachs, "Competitive Devaluation."

Keynes's characterization of labor and output markets; in each country nominal wages adjust only slowly, but prices adjust with sufficient speed to clear commodity markets. Aggregate supply in each country depends on profitability, as measured by the ratio of product prices to wages. Aggregate demand in each country depends on competitiveness (or the ratio of domestic to foreign prices) and on interest rates (which determine the division of spending between present and future). Money demand depends on output and interest rates, where interest rates are linked internationally by the open interest parity condition. Expectations of exchange rate changes are neglected; domestic and foreign interest rates can therefore be taken as equal, and no distinction need be made between real and nominal interest rates.

The effects of a depreciation depend on its form, and in particular on the accompanying monetary measures. In "sterilized devaluation" the depreciating country expands the domestic component of its money supply sufficiently to leave gold reserves unchanged. In "unsterilized devaluation" the depreciating country adjusts domestic credit only enough to keep unchanged the ratio of gold backing to money in circulation. Gold reserves may rise or fall. Two other cases useful for analyzing competitive depreciation are simultaneous unsterilized devaluation, when both countries leave the ratio of gold backing unchanged but allow the total base to fall; and simultaneous devaluation in which both countries leave their monetary base, and money supply, unchanged. Following the notation in Table 9.2, sterilized devaluation is when $dg < 0$ but gold backing is adjusted to permit reserves to remain unchanged ($dr = 0$). Unsterilized devaluation is when $dg < 0$ and the gold backing remains unchanged ($d\psi = 0$).

The effects of depreciation are summarized in Table 9.2. In all cases of unilateral devaluation, currency depreciation increases output and employment in the devaluing country. By raising the price of imports relative to domestic goods, depreciation switches expenditure toward domestic goods. The increased pressure of demand will tend to drive up domestic commodity prices, moderating the stimulus to aggregate demand and (by reducing real wages) stimulating aggregate supply, until the domestic commodity market clears. The same effect switches demand, of course, away from foreign goods, exerting deflationary pressure on the foreign economy. But the extent of the change in domestic production and the beggar-thy-neighbor outcome depend not only on adjustments in commodity markets; they depend also on conditions in asset markets. Devaluation, if accompanied by sufficient monetary expansion to cause gold to flow abroad, will tend to reduce *world* interest rates and thereby stimulate demand in *both* countries. The stimulus from lower interest rates can exceed or fall short of the contractionary shift of demand away from foreign goods and toward the devaluing country. Thus foreign output may rise or fall after the devaluation. Necessary though not sufficient conditions for foreign output to increase are that the foreign country gain gold reserves after devaluation in the home country, or that the foreign country allow its own ratio of gold backing to decline.

The change in foreign output and employment depends, therefore, on the home-country measures that accompany depreciation. For example, the devaluing country could expand the domestic credit component of its monetary base sufficiently to prevent any international movement of reserves, the case of sterilized devaluation. Output rises at home and falls abroad, while world interest rates decline. Alternatively, the devaluing country might refuse to initiate any change in domestic credit. Since the volume of gold remains linked to the quantity of money at the initial ratio, the impact on the foreign country will be more contractionary than with sterilized devaluation. Domestic output rises, foreign output falls, and, in the case of symmetrical countries, world interest rates are unchanged.

A third possibility is that the devaluing country recognizes the existence of capital gains on its gold reserves and expands the monetary base by the percentage devaluation, leaving the gold backing of the base unchanged (with gold valued at the new parity).[26] This is the case of unsterilized devaluation. The gold reserves of the devaluing country can either rise or fall. The decline in world interest rates may swamp the expenditure-switching effect, causing foreign output to rise.

This analysis is premised on a framework in which monetary variables are nonneutral. One may ask whether this is an appropriate premise. Figure 9.1 provides an example of the relationships which led to it. The figure shows the percentage change in the exchange rate between 1929 and 1935 and the percentage change in industrial production. The terminal date of 1935 is chosen to permit depreciations as much time as possible to work their effects.[27] We include all the economies of western Europe for

---

[26] To keep the percentage of gold backing unchanged, open market operations are required not just to inject into circulation currency in the amount of the capital gains on gold reserves but also to increase the domestic credit component of the monetary base by the proportion of devaluation. Compare Gottfried Haberler, *Prosperity and Depression* (Geneva, 1937), chap. 12.

[27] Still later dates are undesirable because by 1936 all countries had devalued and, hence,

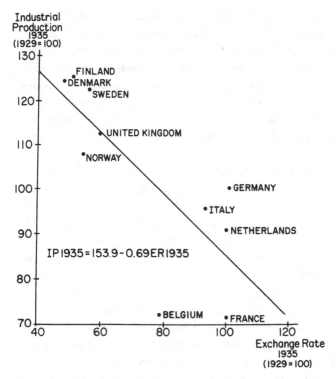

Figure 9.1. Changes in exchange rates and industrial production, 1929–1935.

which comparable data could be obtained.[28] A depreciation, plotted along the horizontal axis, is expressed as the gold price of domestic currency in 1935 as a percentage of the 1929 parity; a value of 100 for France indicates no depreciation, while a value of 59 for the United Kingdom indicates a 41 percent depreciation. The change in industrial production, plotted along the vertical axis, is the ratio of production in 1935 to 1929 multiplied by 100.

There is a clear negative relationship between the height of the exchange rate and the extent of recovery from the Depression. The countries of the Gold Bloc, represented here by France, the Netherlands, and Belgium, had

there remain no gold standard countries with which to compare, but also because the course of recovery becomes increasingly dominated by rearmament expenditure.

[28] We purposely excluded the United States on the grounds that the Depression to a large extent originated there rather than being imported from abroad and therefore would have had very different implications for the characteristics of both the downturn and the recovery. We did no experimentation with different samples of countries but intend to increase the size of the sample in future work.

by 1935 failed to recover to 1929 levels of industrial production. Countries which devalued at an early date (the United Kingdom, Denmark, and the Scandinavian countries) grew much more rapidly; and there appears to be a positive relationship between the magnitude of depreciation and the rate of growth. Germany and Belgium are outliers, Belgium presumably because it devalued only at the end of the period, leaving relatively little time for exchange rate changes to influence growth, and Germany presumably because of the influence of capital controls whose effects were analogous to an explicit depreciation.[29]

The first regression in Table 9.3 shows the reduced-form relationship between changes in industrial production and the exchange rate. As explained above, the United States was excluded from the sample on the grounds that the Great Depression to a large extent originated there, rendering the downturn unusually severe and differentiating the course of the subsequent recovery. In fact, including the United States weakens the relationship only slightly, as shown in the second line of Table 9.3. Moreover, if the distinguishing characteristics of the Depression in the United States had their greatest impact on the depth of the initial decline rather than on the effects of subsequent exchange-rate changes, then the relationship should be stronger when growth between 1932 and 1935 is compared with the extent of depreciation. Since the German economy becomes tightly regulated after 1931, it is necessary to add a dummy variable for Germany. The regression appears in the third line of Table 9.3.

It can be objected that both the exchange rate and industrial production are endogenous variables, so that we should not attribute variations in economic growth to movements in exchange rates rather than vice versa. We prefer our interpretation for several reasons. First is a matter of timing. In all cases, devaluation preceded the beginning of recovery, judged on the basis of annual data. Second is a matter of logic. It is hard to make a case for reverse causation, that faster growing countries were pushed into devaluation. Indeed, we will demonstrate that the faster growing countries were absorbing, not losing, gold, so that it would be tricky indeed to make the case that fast growth forced countries off their gold parities. Third is a matter of history. Exchange rates in the 1930s depended not merely on economic pressures but on national attitudes toward the monetary standard, where the attitudes towards the standard were predetermined relative

---

[29] Belgium's participation in the Gold Bloc and its decision to leave in 1935 are discussed in detail by van der Wee and Tavernier, *Banque Nationale*. A detailed description of German exchange control is provided by Howard S. Ellis, *Exchange Control in Central Europe* (Cambridge, 1941).

Table 9.3: *Reduced-form regression results, 1929–1935*

Dependent variable	Period	Constant term	Exchange rate term	Dummy variable for Germany	R^2
1. Industrial production	1929–35	153.9 (10.06)	−0.69 (3.51)		.56
2. Industrial production (including U.S.)	1929–35	142.9 (7.61)	−0.59 (2.32)		.32
3. Industrial production (including U.S.)	1 32–35	2.04 (7.40)	−0.97 (2.96)	0.58 (4.10)	.62
4. Real wage	1929–35	0.73 (3.00)	−0.0065 (2.07)		.27
5. Export volume	1929–35	1.39 (8.30)	−0.0075 (3.46)		.55
6. Discount rate	1929–35	−4.29 (4.26)	0.031 (2.25)	−1.86 (1.95)	.47
7. Tobin's q	1929–35	136.8 (5.62)	−0.933 (2.96)		.46
8. Gold reserves	1931–35	2.40 (4.84)	−0.018 (2.79)		.43

Notes and Sources: t-statistics in parentheses. All variables are normalized to 100 in 1929 and defined as follows:

1. *Industrial production:* National indices of industrial production, from Mitchell, *European Historical Statistics,* and Methorst, *Recueil.*

2. *Exchange rate:* Gold value of currencies as a percentage of 1929 gold parity, from League of Nations, *Monetary Review* (Geneva, 1938).

3. *Real wage:* Nominal wage deflated by wholesale price index. Wages, from Mitchell, *European Historical Statistics,* measure hourly, daily, or weekly wages, depending on country. Note that wages for Belgium are for males in transport and industry only, that wages in France are for men only. Wholesale price indices are from Mitchell, *European Historical Statistics.*

4. *Export volume:* Special trade, merchandise only, measured in metric tons, from League of Nations, *Monthly Bulletin of Statistics* (Geneva, July 1936); League of Nations, *Review of World Trade* (Geneva, 1938).

5. *Discount rate:* From League of Nations, *Review of World Trade* (Geneva, 1936).

6. *Gold reserve:* Gold stock valued in constant dollars of 1929 gold content, as of December of the year. From Hardy, *Is There Enough Gold?* and Federal Reserve Bulletin (various issues).

7. *Security prices:* Indices of industrial share prices. From League of Nations, *Monthly Bulletin of Statistics,* and Methorst, *Recueil.*

to the events of the early 1930s. The allegiance of nations to their gold standard parities appears to have been largely dependent on their stabilization experiences in the early 1920s. Ironically, those nations which made the most concerted efforts to restore prewar gold standard parities in the early 1920s showed the least hesitation to devalue in the early 1930s. The

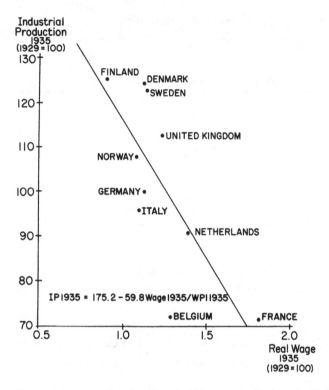

Figure 9.2. Changes in real wages and industrial production, 1929–1935.

obvious contrast is between Britain and France, although the point applies generally. French opinion was so traumatized by the successive "battles of the franc" that took place between 1922 and 1926 that it was hesitant even to contemplate the option of devaluation before 1936.[30] In Britain, where the decision to return to the prewar parity was little questioned in 1925, there was nearly no mention of a return to the gold standard once convertibility was suspended.[31] The important point is that the decision of whether to devalue in the 1930s was heavily influenced by considerations

[30] French opinion on monetary and financial questions, along with British comparisons, is reviewed by Perrot, *La Monnaie*. Political aspects of the French debate are summarized by Sauvy, *Histoire*.

[31] The definitive analysis of the decision to return to par in 1925, which highlights the role of the few dissenters such as Keynes, is Moggridge, *Return to Gold*. An account which emphasizes the implications of the 1925 decision for attitudes toward depreciation in 1931 is Cairncross and Eichengreen, *Sterling in Decline*.

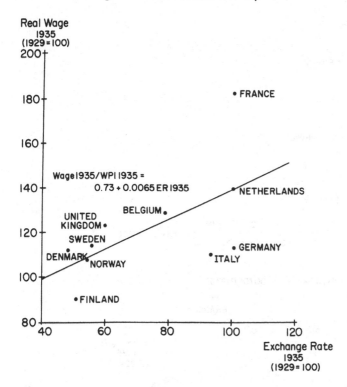

Figure 9.3. Changes in exchange rates and real wages, 1929–1935.

exogenous to our macroeconomic model, namely, the historical experience of the 1920s.

Figures 9.2 through 9.5 show various aspects of the mechanism linking exchange rates to economic activity. In Figure 9.2 the change in real wages (on the horizontal axis) is plotted along with the change in industrial production (on the vertical axis). The clear negative relationship indicates that supply considerations strongly influenced the rate of economic recovery.[32] Countries which succeeded in reducing real wages enhanced profitability

---

[32] Although both industrial production and the real wage are endogenous variables, we report the regression for completeness.

$$IP1935 = 175.2 - 59.8 \; (WAGE1935/WPI1935) \quad R^2 = .50.$$
$$ (7.39) \quad (3.14)$$

Similar relationships are reported by Sheila Bonnell, "Real Wages and Employment in the Great Depression," *Economic Record* 57 (1981), 277–81.

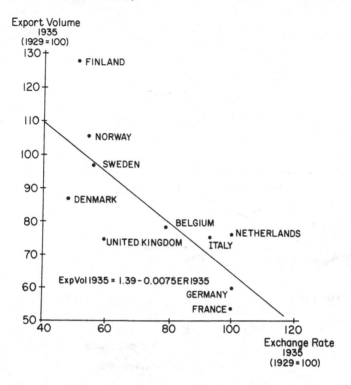

Figure 9.4. Changes in exchange rates and export volume, 1929–1935.

and boosted aggregate supply. Again, Belgium appears as something of an outlier, perhaps because the late date of devaluation there left little time for its effects. Figure 9.3 and Table 9.3 show the relationship between the change in the exchange rate and the change in the real wage, suggesting that depreciation, by putting upward pressure on prices, contributed to the reduction in the real wage which stimulated supply in devaluing countries. Of course, other factors in addition to exchange-rate policy influenced the evolution of real wages. These other factors appear to have played relatively large roles in Germany, Italy, Finland, and France. In Italy and especially in Germany the labor market came under increasingly strict government regulation as the 1930s progressed; it is not surprising that the change in real wages only moderately reflects the market forces considered.[33]

---

[33] Control of the German labor market has been analyzed by Otto Nathan, *The Nazi Economic System* (Durham, 1944).

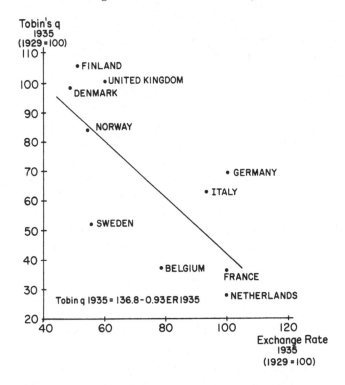

Figure 9.5. Changes in exchange rates and Tobin's q, 1929–1935.

The impact of depreciations on demand is apparent in Figure 9.4, where they are plotted against the change in export volume. The fifth regression in Table 9.3 documents the statistical relationship: countries which depreciated succeeded in promoting the recovery of export volume compared with countries that remained on gold.[34] The result may or may not be consistent with the beggar-thy-neighbor characterization of exchange-rate policy, but it indicates that a single depreciation, taken in isolation, did increase demand in the depreciating country. In Figure 9.4, France and Finland are the noticeable outliers, presumably reflecting the impact of the same supply-side factors causing these countries to be outliers (in Figure 9.3) in terms of wage performance.

[34] The same picture would emerge were we to construct measures of the real exchange rate and plot them against export volume, since each country's real exchange rate is dominated by the movement of its nominal exchange rate.

A second major channel through which depreciations could have influenced demand is through the world level of interest rates. Countries that devalued could have taken advantage of the relaxation of gold-standard constraints and engineered a reduction in interest rates through the adoption of accommodative money and credit policies. In the formal model, depreciation and accompanying monetary initiatives affect only the overall level of world interest rates. In a more general model, depreciation might give rise to interest-rate differentials among countries, creating not only the expenditure-increasing effect but also an expenditure-switching effect. In practice it is difficult to marshall evidence concerning the impact of exchange-rate policy on interest rates. Interest rates on assets with even approximately comparable maturities and risk characteristics are available for only a subset of European countries. In the sixth line of Table 9.3 we therefore report a regression of the change in the exchange rate against the change in the central bank discount rate. The discount rate is an administered price rather than a direct measure of market conditions. Yet in market economies the discount rate could not diverge markedly from freely determined rates, since central banks which discounted the eligible paper of the private sector could not afford to do so at rates far out of line from market levels (see p. 41). The regression indicates a positive relationship between the height of the exchange rate and the discount rate once account is taken of the extent of capital controls in Germany.[35] When currencies were devalued, central banks were able to capitalize on the increased strength of the external position by reducing interest rates.

A third major channel through which exchange-rate changes could have stimulated demand was by promoting domestic investment. Increased competitiveness, by raising current sales, could have enhanced profitability and provided an incentive to invest. To the extent that central banks were able to utilize the leeway provided by depreciation to reduce the level of interest rates, the present value of expected future profits also would have been raised, further increasing perceived profitability, while the reduction in interest rates at the same time lowered the cost of investment. Adequate data on the volume of domestic investment are available only for a few European countries. We therefore examine the behavior not of investment itself but

---

[35] The relationship is strengthened when a further dummy variable is added for Italy, the other country with stringent capital and exchange market controls.

$$\Delta CBDR = -4.77 + 0.040\Delta ER - 2.31 GERMANY - 1.55 ITALY \quad R^2 = .51$$
$$(5.37) \quad (4.19) \qquad (2.73) \qquad (1.92)$$

of a measure of the incentive to invest: Tobin's q. In theory, q – the ratio of security prices to output prices – incapsulates all the information relevant to the investment decision.[36] Figure 9.5 plots the change in the exchange rate along with the change in the ratio of security prices to wholesale prices. Again, a negative relationship is evident: countries which depreciated their currencies in the 1930s succeeded in raising Tobin's q and increasing the incentive to invest. The result is consistent with the view that both domestic investment demand and foreign export demand promoted their economic recovery.

4. International repercussions of depreciation

Together this evidence on the structural relationships linking exchange rates to economic recovery suggests that the cross-section pattern depicted in Figure 9.1 is not a spurious correlation. Exchange-rate policy promoted growth not through one but through each one of the major channels: by reducing real wages, enhancing competitiveness, promoting exports, and permitting a reduction of interest rates. Whether the gain to devaluing countries had as its counterpart a loss to those which remained on gold – in other words, whether this policy was beggar-thy-neighbor – depends on the precise form of the devaluations. If the devaluing country increases its money supply sufficiently to induce an outflow of gold, the stimulus to demand of lower interest rates abroad may be sufficient to expand the foreign economy. As mentioned earlier, gold outflow is a necessary but not sufficient condition for the foreign expansion. Thus, the direction of gold flows provides an indicator of whether devaluation was necessarily beggar-thy-neighbor. The final equation in Table 9.3, therefore, regresses the exchange rate against the change in gold reserves. The negative relationship is apparent: depreciating countries gained rather than lost gold reserves. Further evidence to this effect appears in Table 9.4. Currency depreciation, while beneficial from the individual country's point of view, was in fact beggar-thy-neighbor.

Whether the gain to the devaluing countries outweighed the loss to their neighbors is an extremely difficult question. It remains true, however, that had such policies been adopted even more widely and in a coordinated fashion, they could have been beneficial for all the countries involved. In our model, a simultaneous devaluation taken by all countries may have no

---

[36] See Tobin, "General Equilibrium Approach."

Table 9.4: *Gold reserves and gold cover ratios of central banks*

Country	Ratio of gold reserves to notes and other sight liabilities (%)		Amount held (in millions of 1929 U.S. dollars)	
	1929	1936[a]	1929	1936
Belgium	38.1	67.8	163	373
Denmark	39.6	50.8	46	32
Finland	19.0	61.3	8	21
France	47.4	59.1	1,631	1,769
Germany	36.1	1.0	560	16
Italy	27.5	22.0	273	123
Netherlands	49.9	81.4	180	289
Norway	36.0	74.2	39	58
Sweden	29.0	63.8	66	142
United Kingdom	27.4	78.3	711	1,529

[a] With gold at market prices.
Source: League of Nations, *Monetary Review* (Geneva, 1937), table 6.

immediate effects; simply raising the domestic-currency price of gold in each country affects none of the equilibrium conditions in goods or asset markets.[37] But if money supplies are expanded to reflect the capital gains on gold reserves (thus holding the gold cover ratio constant), then the reduction in interest rates stimulates activity both at home and abroad.

The cogent criticism of exchange-rate depreciation in the 1930s, therefore, is not that it was used unfairly but that the policy was pursued sporadically, and was avoided altogether by some major countries. Often, exchange rates were adjusted in the wake of a crisis, although this was not uniformly the case.[38] Financial crises shifted from one country to another, because each time a country known to be in a delicate position devalued, a new country was elevated to the position of being the next one expected to fall. Nurkse labels this sequential pattern the "devaluation cycle." The resulting uncertainty about exchange rates may have had the depressing impact on

[37] We stress *immediate* effects. By raising the price of gold in terms of commodities, an increased flow supply of new gold could be elicited in the long run. For contemporary discussion of this mechanism, see League of Nations, *Report of the Gold Delegation* (Geneva, 1932).

[38] An obvious contrast is between the successive financial crises in Austria, Germany, and Britain in the summer of 1931, which gave rise to either devaluation or the imposition of exchange control, and the voluntary decisions of many of the countries which decided to follow Britain off gold in the course of subsequent months.

trade so emphasized by contemporaries but also may have led international investors (including central banks) to liquidate a portion of their foreign exchange holdings and replace them with gold. In our model the effects of such actions are captured by a rise in the gold cover ratio.[39] The same world stock of gold can then support only a smaller money supply, raising interest rates and exerting deflationary pressure. To the extent that demands for gold were increased by the "sequential" or "successive" nature of the devaluations of the 1930s, the benefits of an "all-round" devaluation were reduced.[40]

Protection, like devaluation, also is capable of exerting expansionary effects at home. But the adoption of tariffs by all countries (reducing producer prices and lowering output and employment) may leave everyone worse off; coordinated devaluation both at home and abroad together with accommodative monetary measures is likely to leave everyone better off.[41] Too often competitive devaluation and tariff protection have been viewed as interchangeable. They are not.

5. Conclusions

Given the number of unanswered questions posed along the way, this chapter has been as much an agenda for research as a statement of results. The main limitation of the present analysis is the subset of policies on which it focuses. Currency depreciation was only one of several instruments of external economic policy, along with exchange controls and trade restrictions. Moreover, internal economic measures – notably fiscal policy – can and should be incorporated into the model, although their empirical analysis awaits construction of adequate measures of fiscal stance.[42] Above all, we

[39] This experiment is analyzed as Case V in Eichengreen and Sachs, "Competitive Devaluation."

[40] It is conceivable that this could yield the outcome suggested by Kindleberger, namely that devaluation could lower prices abroad while leaving home-country prices unchanged. Note, however, that the mechanism is very different from his argument concerning a ratchet effect in commodity markets. Kindleberger, *World in Depression*, chap. 4.

[41] For a formal analysis of the effects of commercial policy, see Eichengreen, "Dynamic Model," and Eichengreen, "Political Economy."

[42] To date, constant employment measures of the government budget have been constructed only for the United States and Britain. See E. Cary Brown, "Fiscal Policy in the Thirties: A Reappraisal," *American Economic Review* 46 (1956), 857–79; and Roger Middleton, "The Constant Employment Budget Balance and British Budgetary Policy, 1929–39," *Economic History Review*, sec. ser., 34 (1981), 266–86. For an extension to the analysis of commercial policy, see Eichengreen, "Australian Recovery."

have taken the formulation of policy as exogenous to our analytical frame-work. A full understanding of the role of policy in the economic recovery of the 1930s requires an integrated analysis of both policy's formulation and effects.

This much, however, is clear. We do not present a blanket endorsement of the competitive devaluations of the 1930s. Though it is indisputable that currency depreciation conferred macroeconomic benefits on the initiating country, because of accompanying policies the depreciations of the 1930s had beggar-thy-neighbor effects. Though it is likely that currency depre-ciation (had it been even more widely adopted) would have worked to the benefit of the world as a whole, the sporadic and uncoordinated approach taken to exchange-rate policy in the 1930s tended, other things being equal, to reduce the magnitude of the benefits.

10. The gold-exchange standard and the Great Depression

Two broad approaches dominate the literature on macroeconomics of the Great Depression. One, associated mainly with studies of the United States, emphasizes misguided policy responses at the national level as an explanation for the Depression's singular depth and long duration. The other, with a long tradition but associated prominently with the work of Charles Kindleberger, emphasizes instead the malfunctioning of the international system. The strength of the first approach is the transparency of the propagation mechanism, usually taken to be deflationary monetary trends. The weakness of the second is precisely the opposite, that the propagation mechanism tends to be opaque. It is not clear what dimension of the international system malfunctioned after 1929, nor through what channels its malfunctioning contributed to the Depression.

A prime suspect is surely the gold-exchange standard of the interwar years. That system was a hybrid, neither a pure gold standard like that which prevailed in various countries prior to World War I nor a fiat money system like that which succeeded the breakdown of Bretton Woods. As under a gold standard, countries were required to maintain convertibility between domestic currency and gold and to leave international gold movements unfettered. But they were permitted – indeed encouraged – to hold international reserves in the form of foreign exchange. This introduced into the operation of the gold standard "a new psychological element never present before the war."[1] When financial crisis culminating in currency inconvertibility struck the system in 1931, central banks alarmed by fluctuations in the foreign-exchange value of reserve currencies rushed to liquidate their foreign asset positions. It is argued that the consequent reduction in global reserves constrained money supplies in countries required to maintain statutory ratios of reserves to notes and deposits, heightened the difficulties of gold bloc countries attempting to defend their gold stan-

For helpful comments I thank Michael Bordo, Peter Kenen, Charles Kindleberger, and Bradford Lee.
[1] The phrase is from Brown, "International Gold Standard."

dard parities, and exacerbated the monetary deflation associated with the deepening of the post-1929 slump. As a result of this experience, the gold-exchange standard has come to be viewed as inherently unstable due to its susceptibility to the operation of Gresham's Law, and its instability has come to be viewed as an important part of the explanation for the severity of the Great Depression.

The gold-exchange standard was adopted in response to the widely perceived danger of an international shortage of gold.[2] Between 1915 and 1925, prices had risen worldwide due to the inflation associated with wartime finance and postwar reconstruction. These higher prices combined with economic growth to increase the transactions demand for money. Yet world money supply was constrained by the availability of reserves. Statutory regulations prevented central banks from reducing the reserve backing of their money supplies, while recent experience with inflation deterred politicians from moving to revise those statutory regulations. The output of newly mined gold had been depressed since the beginning of World War I, and experts offered pessimistic forecasts of future supplies. The alternative to increasing either the supply of monetary gold or the intensity of its utilization, namely, forcing a reduction in the world price level, was viewed as undesirable since it would only add to the difficulties of an already troubled world economy.

The solution to this problem was to permit central banks to supplement the gold backing of their currencies with exchange reserves. Much was done to encourage the habit. Observers preoccupied by the specter of a worldwide gold shortage argued, however, that this practice was never systematized sufficiently or carried far enough. According to their interpretation of events, when deflation set in starting in 1929, the gold shortage had come home to roost.

There are analytical difficulties with the explanation for interwar monetary problems that emphasizes a global gold shortage. For one, the danger of a shortage of gold constraining the volume of transactions was alleviated by the all but complete removal of gold coin from circulation.[3] Hence,

---

[2] The leading exponent of the gold shortage theory was Gustav Cassel. A summary of his views is Gustav Cassel, *The Crisis in the World's Monetary System* (Oxford, 1932). The interpretation summarized in the remainder of this paragraph is elaborated in Charles Hardy, *Is There Enough Gold?* (Washington DC, 1936). Many of these propositions are scrutinized below.

[3] Between 1913 and 1926 the circulation of gold coins in Europe shrank from 9.9 to 0.2 million marks. Feliks Mlynarksi, *Gold and Central Banks* (London, 1929), p. 72.

the supply of monetary gold backed a considerably increased volume of central bank liabilities and supported a relatively stable price level through 1928. The percentage gold cover of the short-term liabilities of all central banks was little different in 1928 than it had been in 1913.[4] It is unclear why a gold shortage, after having exhibited only weak effects in previous years, should have had such a dramatic impact starting in 1929. As the Gold Delegation of the League of Nations concluded, "The world's total stock of monetary gold, apart from any considerations as to its distribution among different countries, has at all times in recent years been adequate to support the credit structure legitimately required by world trade and . . . the rapid decline in prices which began in 1929 cannot be attributed to any deficiency in the gold supply considered in this sense."[5]

As this quotation presages, the alternative characterization of the monetary problem associated with the operation of the gold-exchange standard emphasizes mismanagement of gold and foreign-exchange reserves rather than their overall insufficiency. There exist two versions of this argument, one which focuses on the distribution of gold, the other which focuses on the demand for foreign exchange. The first posits a maldistribution of gold, blaming France and the United States for imposing deflation on the rest of the world by absorbing disproportionate shares of global supplies. As the point was expressed by Britain's Macmillan Committee in the summer of 1931, "The present distribution of gold is very generally held to be unsatisfactory; a maldistribution to which is to be attributed a large measure of responsibility for the heavy fall in prices in recent years."[6] Between the ends of 1928 and 1932 French gold reserves rose from $1247 million to $3257 million of constant gold content, or from 13 to 28 percent of the world total. The gold backing of the notes and public deposits of the Banque de France rose from 47 to 78 percent.[7] In the United States' case, critics complained not of the rate of increase of gold reserves, which was 8 percent over the period, but of their high level. In contrast to the period 1925–8, when the Federal Reserve facilitated the reconstruction of the international gold standard by releasing substantial quantities of gold, after 1928 the United States persistently maintained 35 to 40 percent of

---

4 This statement refers to short-term liabilities. Melchior Palyi, *The Twilight of Gold* (Chicago, 1972), p. 125.
5 League of Nations, *Report of Gold Delegation*, p. 190.
6 Committee on Finance and Industry, *Report*, cited in Palyi, *Twilight*, p. 179.
7 League of Nations, *Monetary Review* (Geneva, 1937), tables V–VI; see also Chapter 5.

global gold reserves.[8] As shown in Table 10.1, by the end of 1932 France and the United States together possessed nearly 63 percent of the world's central monetary gold.

The second version of this argument blames the collapse of fixed parities and central banks' systematic liquidation of foreign assets for reducing the availability of international reserves just when they were most desperately needed. Since even those central banks that devalued their currencies were obliged to back their notes and (in many cases) sight liabilities, the shift out of foreign exchange, by reducing the available stock of reserves, could have reduced the money supplies that could be supported. Any one central bank might succeed in importing additional gold to be used to back an expansion of its note circulation but only at the expense of heightened monetary stringency abroad. Between 1928 and 1932 the share of foreign exchange in the reserves of 24 European countries fell from 42 to 8 percent (see also Table 10.2). In large part this liquidation reflected the persistent efforts of the Banque de France to convert its foreign assets into gold.[9] But when France is excluded, the share of foreign exchange in the reserves of the remaining 23 countries still declines dramatically, from 36 percent in 1928 to 11 percent in 1932.[10]

The major portion of the decline in the share of foreign exchange in global reserves took place between the ends of 1930 and 1931. Prior to 1931, the share of exchange in the reserve portfolios of 23 European countries, excluding France, remained steady, varying only between 35 and 40 percent.[11] Between 1930 and 1931, it fell from 37 to 13 percent. Because of its timing, this dramatic decline is blamed on the 1931 financial crisis, the imposition of exchange control in Europe, and the devaluation of sterling, which combined to undermine faith in the stability of the two reserve currencies, sterling and the dollar, and induced central banks to substitute gold

---

[8] Mlynarksi, *Gold*, chapter 3.

[9] Under the monetary law of 1928 which marked France's official return to the gold standard, the Banque de France was no longer permitted to purchase foreign exchange. When the law was passed, the Bank already possessed contracts for foreign exchange for forward delivery. As these contracts matured late in 1928, the Bank's foreign exchange holdings rose substantially and, given the dubious legal status of these reserves, the French authorities engaged in persistent efforts over the subsequent year to convert them into gold. These efforts were renewed following sterling's depreciation in September 1931.

[10] These are the calculations of Nurkse, *Currency Experience*, p. 41 and Appendix II.

[11] Nurkse, *Currency Experience*, pp. 34–5. This stability was especially pronounced among countries that stabilized either very early or very late – that is, among those which stabilized before or together with Britain in 1925 and those which did not carry out stabilization programs before 1929. Brown, *International Gold Standard*, p. 737.

Table 10.1: *Central monetary gold reserves, 1929–1934 (in millions of U.S. dollars of constant gold content)*

	Dec. 1929	Dec. 1930	Dec. 1931	Dec. 1932	Dec. 1933	Dec. 1934
1. Gold bloc	2,240	2,734	3,983	4,632	4,275	4,399
France	1,631	2,099	2,683	3,257	3,015	3,218
Switzerland	115	138	453	477	386	368
Belgium	163	191	354	361	380	348
Netherlands	180	171	357	415	371	338
Poland	79	63	67	56	53	56
Other[a]	72	72	69	66	70	71
2. United States and Philippines	3,903	4,228	4,054	4,046	4,013	4,866
3. European countries with exchange control in 1935	987	988	724	700	670	548
Germany	560	544	251	209	109	36
Italy	273	279	296	307	373	306
Other[b]	154	165	177	184	188	206
4. British Empire and sterling bloc	1,344	1,380	1,223	1,216	1,584	1,610
United Kingdom[c]	711	722	590	587	933	938
British Dominions and colonies[d]	444	469	430	402	398	419
Egypt and Siam	19	20	44	61	33	32
European countries with currencies linked to sterling[e]	170	169	159	166	220	221
5. European countries with fluctuating currencies not included in 4[f]	527	508	472	465	487	488
6. Latin America	715	555	370	363	360	376
Argentina	405	411	252	248	238	238
Brazil	150	11	—	—	—	4
Other[g]	160	133	118	115	122	134
7. Japan	542	412	234	212	212	232
World total, excluding Soviet Union	10,258	10,805	11,060	11,634	11,601	12,519
8. Soviet Union	147	249	328	na	416	439

[a] Danzig, Lithuania, Albania, Algeria, Morocco, Belgian Congo, Netherlands Indies.
[b] Czechoslovakia, Romania, Hungary, Bulgaria, Latvia, Turkey, Yugoslavia. [c] Including Irish Free State. [d] India, Canada, Union of South Africa, New Zealand, Australia, Straits Settlements. [e] Sweden, Norway, Denmark, Portugal, Finland, Estonia. [f] Spain, Austria, Greece.
[g] Uruguay, Venezuela, Mexico, Colombia, Chile, Peru, Bolivia, Ecuador, and other countries.
na: Not available.
Source: League of Nations, *World Economic Survey, 1934/35* (Geneva, 1935), p. 250.

Table 10.2: *Foreign assets as percentage of total gold and foreign asset holdings of twenty-nine central banks, 1929–1935*

End of:	1929	1931	1934	1935
Australia	30.2	55.9	98.7	98.4
Egypt	88.1	81.5	72.7	76.7
Albania	90.5	75.5	61.4	60.2
India	67.4	42.1	65.3	65.5
Finland	69.3	65.9	81.6	73.7
Sweden	52.0	19.2	61.2	60.7
Ecuador	84.1	63.6	38.3	7.9
Austria	79.7	42.5	22.1	38.9
Hungary	32.9	18.8	30.8	47.5
Norway	31.1	12.6	23.2	20.0
Union of South Africa	46.8	na	32.1	30.9
Bulgaria	45.5	14.5	7.3	22.0
Portugal	66.3	64.3	21.7	24.9
Latvia	70.1	31.7	7.9	13.7
Estonia	78.9	70.8	22.5	14.3
Colombia	40.7	33.7	11.7	14.2
Romania	42.5	3.2	10.6	15.3
Czechoslovakia	64.3	39.1	7.9	2.9
Spain	3.8	11.0	11.1	11.1
Lithuania	69.2	39.8	13.8	32.8
Peru	11.2	28.3	10.1	16.4
Poland	42.8	26.2	5.3	5.7
Danzig	100.0	53.9	11.0	30.7
France	38.5	23.9	1.2	2.0
Switzerland	37.2	4.2	0.4	0.5
Chile	85.9	48.7	1.1	0.9
Italy	49.8	27.8	1.2	10.8
Netherlands	32.9	8.9	0.1	0.3
Belgium	33.0	0	0	0

Note: na = not available.
Source: League of Nations, *Monetary Review* (Geneva, 1937).

for foreign exchange in the effort to avoid capital losses on their reserves.[12] To some extent, the liquidation of exchange reserves was a consequence of central bank statutes, many of which required the liquidation of sterling reserves once the pound was rendered inconvertible. But in addition, the

---

[12] Withdrawing sterling balances remained straightforward even once the pound was rendered inconvertible. Countries simply sold sterling for convertible currencies on the London foreign exchange market at the current rate and, if they wished, proceeded to convert those currencies into gold.

newly introduced element of risk due to foreign devaluation discouraged central banks from holding exchange reserves. Countries holding London balances which had previously harbored no doubts about the stability of reserve currencies learned an expensive lesson from sterling's devaluation and altered their behavior accordingly. For example, after having lost 25 percent of the domestic value of its £12 million sterling reserve, the National Bank of Belgium quickly moved to liquidate its dollar balances.[13] When speculative pressure shifted from sterling to the dollar, such Eastern European countries as Poland, Czechoslovakia, and Bulgaria also shifted their balances out of New York.[14] As one contemporary expert observed, "The risks involved in currency depreciation have been very forcibly – and for some gold exchange central banks, disastrously – demonstrated during the recent period."[15]

In this chapter I provide the first systematic analysis of the international distribution of gold- and foreign-exchange reserves under the interwar gold-exchange standard with which these issues can be addressed. I analyze both the exceptional behavior of the United States and France and the shift out of foreign exchange after 1930. While both U.S. and French gold policies and systemic weaknesses of the gold-exchange standard emerge as important factors in explaining the international distribution of reserves, the first of these factors turns out to play the more important role in the monetary stringency associated with the Depression.[16]

---

[13] For example, the Netherlands Bank, in its Annual Report for 1931–2, defended its failure to avoid losses on its London balances by joining the run on sterling on the grounds that "Management were of opinion that they should not do this because they were convinced that the British Government and the Bank of England firmly intended to maintain the gold standard and to make the gold stock of the said Bank entirely available for this purpose. This conviction was based on the conversations which Dr. Vissering and Dr. Tetrode had with the Management of the Bank of England on August 26, 1931, when anxiety concerning the financial position of England began to prevail." Cited in Brown, *International Gold Standard*, pp. 1170–1. On the National Bank of Belgium, see Kindleberger, *World in Depression*, pp. 161–8.

[14] Nurkse, *Currency Experience*, pp. 39–40.

[15] L. Pasvolsky, *The Necessity for a Stable International Monetary Standard* (Paris, 1933), p. 49.

[16] In this chapter I do not analyze the causes of the initial downturn, as opposed to reasons for its singular depth and long duration; my central concern is to analyze instead the response to that event. The argument that follows is compatible with both real and monetary explanations for the initial contraction, as advanced by Temin, *Monetary Forces*, and Friedman and Schwartz, *Monetary History*. Nor do I explore the bases of the French and U.S. gold policies that emerge as critical, not because they are unimportant but because, unlike the issues addressed here, they are fully analyzed elsewhere. Chapter 5 analyzed the reasons

It is important to bear in mind the implications of this analysis for the literature on the Great Depression. A number of authors have emphasized international aspects of the Depression, arguing that the boom and slump are properly understood not simply as an outcome of misguided U.S. policy but as a result of an unstable international system subjected to a shock to confidence.[17] One way in which "international interactions across boundaries" could have magnified an initial disturbance was through the collapse of the international monetary system. Convertibility crises, forced devaluations, and a loss of confidence in the stability of reserve currencies, by inducing central banks to shift out of foreign assets, reduced the stock of international reserves available to back domestic liabilities. If the availability of reserves remained a constraint on monetary authorities' willingness to increase national money supplies, then the collapse of the gold-exchange standard and the liquidation of foreign-exchange reserves would have limited the scope for reflation and exacerbated the money stringency that contributed to the severity of the Depression.[18]

Alternatively, if Federal Reserve and Banque de France policies leading to the concentration of gold in the United States and France rather than the scramble for gold unleashed by the gold-exchange standard's disintegration were primarily responsible for exacerbating monetary stringency throughout the world, then responsibility for the Depression should be assigned not to systemic weaknesses of the gold-exchange standard system but to misguided national policies. Note, however, that the national policies blamed for the Depression need not be limited to the United States and still may be transmitted across national borders by the international monetary system.

Finally, it is possible that this entire emphasis on international monetary forces is misplaced. If the collapse of the gold-exchange standard, the liquidation of foreign assets, and the advent of exchange-rate flexibility

for France's post-1928 import of gold. U.S. policy is the subject of a considerable literature, including Elmus Wicker, *Federal Reserve Monetary Policy 1917–1933* (New York, 1966), Friedman and Schwartz, *Monetary History,* and Kindleberger, *World in Depression.*

17 See Kindleberger, *World in Depression.* The phrase in the next sentence, "international interactions across boundaries," is from Charles Kindleberger, "International Capital Movements and Foreign Exchange Markets in Crisis: The 1930s and the 1980s," in Ivan Berend and Knut Borchard (eds.), *The Impact of the Depression of the 1930s and Its Relevance for the Contemporary World* (Budapest, 1986), p. 437.

18 The role of monetary stringency in the Depression is discussed, for example, by Friedman and Schwartz, *Monetary History,* and, more recently, by James Hamilton, "Monetary Forces in the Great Depression," *Journal of Monetary Economics* 19 (1987), 145–61, for the United States, Temin, "Beginning of the Great Depression," for Germany, and Jonung, "The Depression," for Sweden.

offered central banks the opportunity to free their monetary policies from the reserve constraint, they could have chosen to initiate an expansionary response to the Depression regardless of the state of international reserves. Were this the case, international aspects of the Depression would have had to operate through different channels than those emphasized in the literature on international monetary forces.

This focus on external constraints on domestic monetary policies is not new.[19] However, previous studies which have acknowledged the role of external constraints have analyzed them on a national basis rather than considering global monetary conditions and the global availability of reserves as factors in the global Depression. Even if national policies rather than systemic failures ultimately prove dominant in the explanation for the Great Depression, an implication of this chapter is that their effects can only be fully understood when analyzed in an international setting.

I. The mechanics of the gold-exchange standard

Had the interwar gold-exchange standard possessed a birth certificate, it would have read "born in Genoa during the Economic and Financial Conference of 1922." The distinguishing feature of the new monetary regime was not the practice by central banks of holding foreign currency reserves, for many countries, particularly smaller ones and members of the British Empire, had done so on a substantial scale prior to 1913.[20] The significance of Genoa lay rather in the effort to institutionalize and encourage the practice. The Financial Commission of the Genoa Conference proposed the adoption of an international monetary convention, formally entitling countries "in addition to any gold reserve held at home, [to] maintain in any other participant country reserves of approved assets in the form of bank balances, bills, short-term securities, or other suitable liquid resources."[21] Participating countries were required to fix their exchange rates against one another, with any failing to do so losing the right to hold the reserve bal-

---

[19] Recent studies emphasizing the external constraint on monetary policy include Chapter 4 for the United Kingdom, Gerald Epstein and Thomas Ferguson, "Monetary Policy, Loan Liquidation and Industrial Conflict: The Federal Reserve and the Open Market Operations of 1932," *Journal of Economic History* XLIV (1984), 957–84 for the United States and Temin, "Beginning of the Great Depression," for Germany.

[20] Nurkse, *Currency Experience,* pp. 28–30; Lindert, "Key Currencies."

[21] The text of the resolutions and related correspondence, from where this paragraph's quotations are drawn, are to be found in United Kingdom, "Papers Related to Economic Conference."

ances of other participants. Foreign exchange would be used in the same manner as gold to settle accounts and defend exchange rates. The principal creditor nations were encouraged to take early steps to "establish a free market in gold and thus become gold centres" where the bulk of foreign-exchange reserves would be held.

If the official convention advocated by the Financial Committee failed to materialize, it nonetheless exercised considerable influence over the practices of central banks.[22] The first effect of the Genoa resolutions was to encourage the adoption of statutes permitting central banks to back notes and sight deposits with foreign exchange as well as gold. Central banks of countries that stabilized their currencies with League of Nations assistance, including Austria, Hungary, Bulgaria, and Greece, were empowered to hold the entirety of their reserves in convertible foreign bills and balances. The newly created Latin American central banks designed by Kemmerer Commissions were permitted to hold both gold and foreign exchange, generally in proportions of their choosing. Various restrictions were placed on the form of eligible exchange reserves: the reserve of the new Central Bank of Chile, for example, was to consist of gold coin and bars in the vaults of the Bank, earmarked gold abroad, and deposits payable in gold on demand in banks of high standing in London and New York. In the later 1920s, the statutes adopted by newly created or reformed central banks tended to require that a specified minimum proportion of total reserves be held in the form of gold; these proportions ranged from 33 percent in Albania to 75 percent in Belgium, Poland, and Germany.[23] Finally, a number of the older central banks retained long-standing regulations requiring them to back their liabilities exclusively with gold. Central banks whose eligible reserves were limited to gold included those of Denmark, France, Japan, the Netherlands, Norway, and, of course, the two reserve currency countries, the United States and the United Kingdom.[24]

Statutes regulating central banks also differed in the amount of backing required. Most of the older central banks, exemplified by the Bank of England and the Norges Bank, were required to back only notes in circulation but, after an exemption for the fiduciary issue (a certain fixed quantity of

---

22 Nurkse, *Currency Experience,* p. 28.
23 In August 1930 the National Bank of Belgium shifted from a gold to a gold bullion basis. Royal Institute, *Gold Problem,* p. 134. This did not prevent it from holding foreign exchange outside its eligible reserve, as described in what follows.
24 This is a partial list. For a complete list of countries legally permitted to hold only gold reserves and countries permitted to hold foreign exchange, see League of Nations, *Legislation on Gold* (Geneva, 1930).

notes), to maintain 100 percent cover on the margin. Newer banks, as well as such older institutions as the Netherlands Bank and Banque de France which had modernized their statutes, typically had no fiduciary issue but were required instead to hold proportional backing against liabilities, on the order of 35 or 40 percent. This was viewed as a useful method of economizing on the use of gold. But the statutes requiring proportional reserves often extended the definition of liabilities to be backed to include not only notes but in addition sight deposits at the central bank, an amendment which tended to increase the use of reserves.[25] According to one expert, the move to proportional backing and the requirement to back sight liabilities other than notes had roughly offsetting effects on the global demand for international reserves.[26]

The upshot of these regulations was that there existed under the gold-exchange standard a stable if somewhat flexible relationship between international reserves and the domestic monetary base. Although that relationship differed across countries and was more elastic than under a gold coin or even a gold bullion standard, it existed nonetheless. It existed as much because of convention as official regulation, since statute provided only a general guide as to the relationship between money supplies and reserves. The minimum gold cover, for example, was under normal circumstances never employed. Banks of issue attempted to maintain excess reserves over their minimum legal requirements, typically on the order of 7 to 10 percent of liabilities.[27] Not only was this prudent banking practice, but it provided leeway for open market operations designed to insulate the domestic economy from the impact on domestic money supplies of gold outflows.[28] Moreover, the minimum was not always binding. Some banks of issue, including those of Austria, Chile, Czechoslovakia, and Hungary,

[25] The origin of these ratios is "somewhat obscure," in the words of C. H. Kirsch, quoted in Royal Institute, *Gold Problem*, p. 151. The regulations emulated what legislators viewed as prudent banking practice, often taken to be Bank of England practice prior to Peel's Act of 1844, when it was the Bank's convention to maintain a 33 percent cash reserve against notes and deposits. Or as the League of Nations, *Interim Report of the Gold Delegation of the Financial Committee* (Geneva, 1930), p. 19, put it, "But the minimum reserves which are required by law today are to a large extent the outcome, not of these considerations, but of past tradition, of convention and habit, of the natural fear which each individual legislature has that a departure from general practice may impair confidence in the currency."

[26] Palyi, *Twilight*, p. 125.

[27] League of Nations, *Legislation on Gold*, p. 14.

[28] The major central banks, with the notable exception of the Banque de France and National Bank of Switzerland, all possessed the power to undertake open market operations. League of Nations, *Monetary Review* (Geneva, 1938), p. 86.

were entitled, upon payment of a special tax, to temporarily reduce their gold cover ratios below the statutory minimum. Denmark and South Africa required only a special government permit. In Salvador the central bank was merely required to raise its discount rate by half a percentage point for each point by which its reserve fell below 30 percent.[29] Similarly, the proportions in which central banks held gold and exchange reserves only loosely followed statutory regulation. Some central banks entitled to hold foreign exchange chose not to do so. Others without this right chose to maintain large amounts of exchange outside their legal reserve.

Critics of this system noted the wide variation across countries in the relation of gold reserves to money supplies, arguing that in principle "the gold which a central bank holds ought to have no particular relation to its note issue."[30] They were especially critical of the practice of holding excess reserves. They admitted, however, that so long as other central banks maintained conventional backing ratios, public confidence in any one country's currency hinged upon its continuing to do the same. A solution to this problem was to arrange an internationally coordinated reduction in cover ratios which would not undermine confidence in any particular currency.[31] In practice, the major central banks could not be brought to cooperate in such action.

Even most of those countries which went off the gold standard following the onset of the Great Depression maintained gold cover ratios not far different from those which had traditionally prevailed, either because of statutory requirements or out of concern to prevent depreciation due to loss of confidence. Some countries, including of course the members of the gold bloc, simply left their cover regulations unchanged. In contrast, Germany and Italy suspended central bank reserve requirements in 1932 and 1935, respectively. Although four countries with a fixed fiduciary system varied the amount of the maximum uncovered issue, most of those variations were small. The Bank of England's limit was raised from £260 million to £275 million on August 1, 1931, in response to pressure on sterling, and returned to £260 million on March 31, 1933, when the dollar was under attack. The Bank of Sweden's was raised from 250 to 350 million kroner in 1933 to facilitate an expansion of the domestic money supply. The most dramatic change was that of Japan, where the limit was raised in 1932 from

[29] Nurkse, *Currency Experience*, p. 95.
[30] J. M. Keynes, quoted in Royal Institute, *Gold Problem*, p. 186.
[31] This solution was suggested by the League of Nations, *Report of Gold Delegation*, and the Committee on Finance and Industry, *Report*. See also Keynes, "Is There Enough Gold?"

120 to 1000 million yen. Of the proportional reserve countries, legal cover ratios were lowered by Austria in 1932 (from 24 to 20 percent), by Danzig in 1935 (from 40 to 30 percent), and in 1936 by Denmark, Bulgaria, and Latvia (from 33⅓ to 25 percent, from 33⅓ to 25 percent, and from 50 to 30 percent, respectively).[32]

An implication of the preceding discussion is that the positive association between domestic money supplies and international reserves depended ultimately on central bank preferences rather than the mechanical linkages posited by theoretical models of the gold standard. What then determined the preferences of central banks? Contemporary observers such as Keynes, Gayer, and Nurkse argued that the basic motivation for holding reserves was precautionary, deriving from the desire to smooth the impact of temporary fluctuations in export earnings on the capacity to purchase imports. They suggested that deviations of the reserve proportion from the 33 to 40 percent norm were explicable in terms of costs and benefits of financing instead of adjusting to temporary disturbances to the balance of payments. As Charles Hardy put it, "The size of the gold stock which a country needs depends on the size and also on the character of the probable gold movements out of the country."[33] Arthur D. Gayer termed this "the magnitude of the probable external drain, the amount a country is likely to require for equalising the balance of its international payments in the interval during which corrective measures are being applied internally to remove the causes of the gold export and thus restore equilibrium."[34]

Observers agreed that agricultural producers, particularly those whose exports were heavily concentrated in a single crop, were especially vulnerable to fluctuations in export earnings and therefore were in need of additional reserves to ensure their ability to purchase imports.[35] They noted that, along with countries with highly variable exports, those with large shares of exports and imports in GNP had reason to maintain additional reserves, since the costs of responding to an export shortfall by foregoing imports were highest where trade was most important. At the same time, they acknowledged that precautionary reserves were a luxury good. Nurkse likened the demand for reserves to the individual's demand for cash bal-

---

[32] League of Nations, *Monetary Review* (Geneva, 1938), pp. 87–9. The League mentions four other countries which adopted more complicated measures to effect small reductions in their cover ratios.

[33] Hardy, *Enough Gold?* p. 96.

[34] A. D. Gayer, *Monetary Policy and Economic Stabilisation* (London, 1937), pp. 78–9.

[35] J.M. Keynes, cited in Royal Institute, *Gold Problem*, p. 186; Nurkse, *Currency Experience*, p. 90.

ances. "A rich man can afford and will probably want to hold a large idle cash reserve, while a poor man will not. In the same way a poor country is less likely than a rich one to sacrifice potential imports and to tie up some of its limited wealth in an international cash reserve." [36]

Readers will note the resemblance of these interwar analyses to modern discussions of optimal international reserves.[37] Attempts to estimate models of optimal reserves specify the demand for reserves as a function of income, openness, and some measure of balance-of-payments variability. The specification estimated by Frenkel (1974) is typical:

$$r = \alpha_0 + \alpha_1 t + \alpha_2 s + \alpha_3 y, \tag{1}$$

where r is reserves, t is the import-to-GNP ratio, s is balance-of-payments variability measure, y is GNP, and the α_i are parameters to be estimated. The expectation is that α_1, α_2, α_3 are positive. The specification suggested by the above discussion differs only by the addition of a measure of domestic monetary base h:

$$r = \alpha_0 + \alpha_1 t + \alpha_2 s + \alpha_3 y + \alpha_4 h, \tag{2}$$

where α_4, the cover ratio, is positive.[38] Variants of this specification are estimated below.

The internal consistency of inferences about the effects of a decline in willingness to hold exchange reserves and/or a rise in the central bank demand for gold can be analyzed theoretically by embedding equation (2) in a model like that which is used in Nurkse's (1944) discussion. Since I am concerned with the impact of global reserves on global money supply and global income, the framework for analysis is, as in Barro (1979), a model of the world economy under fixed exchange rates. Although it is straightforward to analyze the impact of changes in the supply and demand for reserves in a multicountry setting, as in Eichengreen and Sachs (1986), for present purposes the multicountry analysis is unnecessarily elaborate.

---

[36] Nurkse, *Currency Experience*, p. 90.

[37] Contributions to this literature include Jacob Frenkel, "The Demand for International Reserves by Developed and Less-Developed Countries," *Economica* 41 (1974), 14–24; H. Robert Heller, "Optimal International Reserves," *Economic Journal* 76 (1966), 296–311; Peter Kenen and E. Yudin, "The Demand for International Reserves," *Review of Economics and Statistics* 47 (1965), 242–50.

[38] The monetary variable used to explain movements in the demand for reserves should be treated as endogenous since, unless gold and foreign exchange flows are completely sterilized, disturbances affecting the stock of reserves are likely to result in a change in the base. This, however, is a matter of estimation rather than specification, and will be considered below.

The first equation, the demand for reserves, is equation (2). r now measures global reserves, y global income, and so forth, and all variables are expressed in nominal terms. (For simplicity, remaining equations will also be expressed in nominal form.)

Total reserves are the sum of gold g and foreign-exchange f:

$$g = \sigma_0 + \sigma_1 t + \sigma_2 s + \sigma_3 y + \sigma_4 h, \tag{3}$$

$$f = \gamma_0 + \gamma_1 t + \gamma_2 s + \gamma_3 y + \gamma_4 h, \tag{4}$$

where $\alpha_i = \sigma_i + \gamma_i$ ($i = 0, 1, 2, 3, 4$) and $r = g + f$. Whereas the global supply of monetary gold g is exogenously fixed (hence ignoring mining and nonmonetary uses of gold), the supply of exchange reserves f is demand determined.[39]

The demand for nominal money balances is assumed to take Cambridge transactions demand form:

$$m = \lambda y. \tag{5}$$

The broadly defined money supply can be decomposed into the base and the multiplier,

$$m = \psi_0 + \psi_1 h. \tag{6}$$

Equations (3) through (6) and the identity $r = g + f$ (equivalently (2) and the coefficient restrictions) determine five endogenous variables: r, f, h, m and one to be selected. It is not obvious why openness or export variability might be affected by financial market conditions, and in any case such effects are remote from the questions at hand. Income is therefore the logical remaining endogenous variable.

It is useful to consider how this approach compares to conventional models of the money supply process under the gold standard. The textbook model of the gold standard, as in McCloskey and Zecher (1976) or Barro (1979), assumes that the money supply m bears a fixed relationship to the stock of reserves r:

$$m = \theta r. \tag{7}$$

---

[39] Ignoring the impact on stocks of the flow supply of new gold is appropriate only given a short time horizon. G. Fremling, "Did the United States Transmit the Great Depression to the Rest of the World?" *American Economic Review* 75 (1985), 1181–5, notes that there was in fact considerable flow supply of new monetary gold in the 1930s. Since the issue of whether that new supply was or was not a response to deflation-induced changes in the real price of gold is distinct from the issues with which this paper is concerned, the exogeneity assumption is maintained throughout.

In contrast to (7), equations (1) and (2) focus on the relationship of reserves to the monetary base rather than to the broadly defined money supply. They introduce other variables affecting the link between reserves and the base and leave open the possibility that other factors may influence the relationship between the base and broad monetary aggregates. In addition, equation (2) differs from conventional treatments of the monetary base by not explicitly mentioning that the base is the sum of domestic credit and foreign reserves. This difference is apparent rather than real, however, since domestic credit is simply the difference between h and r, and the implicit central bank reaction function determining credit can be derived by solving (2) for $h-r$.[40] In treating foreign exchange as a component of international reserves, this paper differs from Fremling (1985, p. 1183), who questions this procedure on the grounds that "what is a foreign reserve asset for one country is an equally sized liability for another." As the framework of this section makes clear, the import of this observation hinges on the form in which foreign reserves were held. When they were held as government securities, they do not need to be netted out of the money supply available to domestic residents, and the argument has no force. When they were held as deposits in commercial banks, they should be subtracted from m. But since m is a multiple of h and h is a multiple of r, any such adjustment has only minor implications for the analysis conducted here.

I consider the impact on income of two exogenous shocks: a shift out of foreign exchange into gold ($d\gamma_0 = -d\sigma_0 < 0$), and a decline in the willingness to hold foreign exchange *not* accompanied by a rise in the demand for gold ($d\gamma_0 < 0$).

The effects of the latter are particularly simple. Since the stock of exchange reserves is demand determined whereas the stock of gold reserves is exogenously given, the monetary base is determined by equation (3) alone. The base determines the money supply through (6), which determines nominal income through (5). Changes in γ_0, that is, in the willingness to hold foreign-exchange reserves, have no impact on h and therefore

---

[40] Denoting domestic credit as c,

$$c = (1 - \alpha_4)h - \alpha_0 - \alpha_1 t - \alpha_2 s - \alpha_3 y.$$

Alternatively, domestic credit can be written as a function of reserves and other variables:

$$c = \frac{1 - \alpha_4}{\alpha_4}r - \frac{\alpha_0}{\alpha_4} - \frac{\alpha_1}{\alpha_4}t - \frac{\alpha_2}{\alpha_4}s - \frac{\alpha_3}{\alpha_4}y.$$

Since the sign of dc/dr is theoretically ambiguous, no implicit assumption is necessarily made about whether central banks play by the "rules of the game."

no implications for m or y. A decline in the demand for foreign exchange not accompanied by a rise in the demand for gold therefore has no direct effect on money supply or income, since the supply of foreign exchange simply adjusts to accommodate it.

In the case of a shift out of foreign exchange into gold, the results are dramatically different:

$$\frac{dy}{d\gamma_0} = \frac{-\psi_1}{\lambda\sigma_4 - \psi_1\sigma_3},$$ (8)

which is negative, assuming the denominator to be positive (a necessary condition for an increase in gold to be expansionary). The shift into gold $(d\sigma_0 > 0)$ reduces the monetary base that can be supported by a given gold supply. The consequent decline in income increases with the elasticity of money supply with respect to the base ψ_1 and the income elasticity of demand for gold σ_3, and falls with the income elasticity of money demand λ and the elasticity of gold demand with respect to the base σ_4. Thus, what is crucial is not whether the demand for foreign exchange fell significantly after 1929 but whether any such fall was accompanied by a rise in the demand for gold.

2. Empirical analysis

Despite the popularity of the explanation that ascribes the concentration of gold reserves to the beggar-thy-neighbor policies of the United States and France and the growing reliance on gold rather than foreign exchange to the uncertainties created by the gold standard's collapse, it is not obvious that observed movements in the distribution of reserves reflect these factors rather than the effects of changes in incomes, balance-of-payments variability, and openness which normally affect the demand for reserves, especially since the Great Depression was marked by dramatic fluctuations in all three variables. Merely to note, as did the Gold Delegation of the League of Nations, that in 1928 a mere 15 countries held over 90 percent of the world's monetary gold reserves does not establish the existence of a problem. As Nurkse expressed the point somewhat later, "the fact that the distribution of reserves was highly unequal in the later thirties does not itself prove that it did not represent an equilibrium position from the point of view of the individual countries concerned, given the existing structure of basic conditions."[41]

[41] Nurkse, *Currency Experience*, p. 93.

In order to analyze the international distribution of reserves and its determinants, I estimate demands for gold and foreign exchange by 24 countries using a specification based on equation (2). To test the hypothesis that the United States and France held reserves in excess of those which can be ascribed to the normal determinants of reserve demand, I introduce dummy variables for these countries. To test the hypothesis that the years after 1930 witnessed a liquidation of foreign-exchange reserves, with or without an accompanying shift into gold, I introduce dummy variables for individual years.

The sample of countries included in the econometric analysis was dictated by data availability. Some countries were excluded because of the lack of reasonable national income estimates, others because the absence of a central bank meant that information on money and foreign reserves was not provided on a compatible basis. Nonetheless, most of the important repositories of gold and foreign assets are included in the sample.[42] Note that the sample of countries is not the same as in Table 10.2.

Data on reserves are taken from the *Statistical Bulletins* and *Monetary Reviews* of the League of Nations, which draw in turn on published returns of central banks.[43] I utilize figures on the book value of gold and exchange reserves of central monetary institutions (apart from Exchange Equalization Funds) at the end of calendar years. Gold reserves are valued at legal parities. Although the paper value of gold exceeded its book value in countries which continued to value that specie at par despite having depreciated their exchange rates, I only revalue these reserves when this was done by the central bank itself, since this was when capital gains on gold were reflected in the central bank's backing ratio.[44]

In contrast to gold, foreign assets are valued at market rates, since this was the practice of central banks. As already noted, a number of central banks functioned under restrictions on what type of foreign assets qualified

---

[42] To facilitate the pooling of time-series and cross-section data, in the final analysis I included only those countries for which data were obtained for all years. Hence, Belgium is excluded because income estimates are available only for selected years. The countries analyzed are Austria, Hungary, Czechoslovakia, Argentina, Colombia, Mexico, Australia, Japan, Chile, the United Kingdom, Bulgaria, Denmark, Finland, France, Germany, Italy, the Netherlands, Norway, Romania, Spain, Sweden, Guatemala, El Salvador, and the United States.

[43] The main sources are League of Nations, *Monetary Review* (Geneva, 1938) and League of Nations, *Statistical Yearbook* (Geneva, 1939).

[44] Attitudes toward the revaluation of reserves and toward the disposition of capital gains are discussed in Chapter 9.

for backing liabilities. Most of these countries held their foreign assets exclusively in eligible form. But for a small minority, there was a difference between the total and eligible foreign assets of the monetary authorities. Since total foreign assets is the more encompassing measure of exchange reserves, in those few cases where the two figures differed, the total was used. The two exceptions are Germany and Denmark, which reported negative total foreign assets (but positive eligible assets) for selected years.[45] Since it is impossible to analyze these negative figures using the standard specification which takes as its dependent variable the log of foreign reserves, for those years where total foreign assets were negative, eligible foreign assets were used instead.

Except for data for the United States and United Kingdom, which are drawn from U.S. Department of Commerce (1976) and Feinstein (1972), respectively, the remaining variables are assembled from sources described in the appendix to Eichengreen and Portes (1986). The share of imports in GNP is used as the measure of openness, note circulation as the measure of the monetary base, and the variance of exports over three years (centered upon the year for which the dependent variable is defined) as the measure of balance-of-payments variability.

Since the controversy surrounding the international distribution of gold centers on the years 1931–3, the period spanned by the 1931 devaluation of sterling and the 1933 devaluation of the dollar, I estimate the model for a period bracketing those years: 1929–35. 1929 is the first year following the revaluation of the Banque de France's gold stock and France's official return to gold, events commonly taken to indicate that reconstruction of the international monetary system was complete, whereas 1935 is the last year before the collapse of the gold bloc and final demise of the gold-exchange standard.

Equation (2) is estimated using two-stage least squares to account for the endogeneity of money. The appropriate instruments are the arguments of the demand-for-money function, taken to be income, the opportunity cost of holding money, and lagged money balances.[46] Results for individual

---

45 In the case of Germany, the difference is due to the $100 million loan made in 1931 by the Bank for International Settlements, the Bank of England, the Bank of France, and the Federal Reserve Bank of New York, which was fully repaid only in 1933. In the Danish case the discrepancy is due to an item listed in the National Bank's balance sheet as correspondents abroad. The results proved insensitive to the exclusion of these observations.

46 Since the variable to be instrumented is nominal money supply, the instruments are nominal income and lagged nominal balances, along with the opportunity cost variable. In the

Table 10.3: *Demand for reserves, 1929–1935: equilibrium model*

Year	Constant	Log GNP	Import share	Export variability	Log money	R^2	n
1929	−3.498	0.777	3.431	7.517	0.266	.94	22
	(3.83)	(6.79)	(3.23)	(1.52)	(3.43)		
1930	−4.098	0.861	2.815	1.040	0.283	.97	22
	(5.77)	(8.93)	(3.76)	(1.20)	(4.55)		
1931	−4.008	0.849	2.893	1.437	0.255	.95	22
	(4.55)	(7.33)	(2.29)	(1.79)	(3.43)		
1932	−3.576	0.849	4.005	4.516	0.192	.94	22
	(3.94)	(7.14)	(1.81)	(1.78)	(2.45)		
1933	−3.485	0.866	4.520	7.188	0.161	.92	22
	(3.96)	(6.63)	(3.20)	(0.22)	(1.89)		
1934	−4.386	0.918	7.602	12.10	0.151	.86	22
	(2.91)	(4.94)	(2.32)	(1.71)	(1.26)		
1935	−3.769	0.875	5.849	15.57	0.150	.88	22
	(2.89)	(5.43)	(1.89)	(1.97)	(1.46)		
1929–35	−3.936	0.877	3.592	1.672	0.213	.90	154
	(11.05)	(17.91)	(6.74)	(2.58)	(6.52)		

Notes: Dependent variable is log of gold plus foreign exchange reserves. Two-stage least squares estimates. t-statistics in parentheses. All variables are measured in millions of units of domestic currency. Instruments for log money are inflation and log money lagged. Variable definitions: import share = imports/GNP; export variability = variance of exports over $t − 1, t, t + 1$.
Source: See text.

years and for the entire period 1929–35 are reported in Table 10.3. The demand for reserves is an increasing function of log GNP, the import share, and export variability, as in modern estimates of models of optimal international reserves. With the exception of export variability, the coefficients consistently exceed zero at the 90 percent confidence level or better. Even the coefficient on export variability is consistent with modern estimates, in which the coefficient on balance-of-payments variability tends to be unstable.[47]

absence of market interest rates for the entire sample of countries, the inflation rate is used to measure the opportunity cost of holding money.

[47] See the discussion in Peter Kenen, *Financing, Adjustment and the International Monetary Fund* (Washington, DC, 1986). A possible explanation for this problem is that export variability is only one component of balance-of-payments variability. But studies which have used more comprehensive measures of the balance of payments such as the variance of re-

Changes in money consistently exhibit the anticipated positive association with the demand for reserves. The pooled time-series cross-section estimate suggests for the entire period a gold- and foreign-exchange cover of 21 percent on the margin, confirming that, despite their maintenance of excess reserves, central banks were concerned to increase their reserves when increasing money supplies. However, both the size of the coefficient and its statistical significance tend to decline over time, suggesting that once countries began to leave the gold standard in 1931 the links between money supplies and international reserves were loosened. This is consistent with the steps, described above, to alter but not eliminate legal cover ratios. I consider below whether the link between money supplies and international reserves loosened significantly as the period progressed, and whether shifts in this linkage were sufficient to neutralize the potential impact on money supplies of factors constricting the availability of reserves.

These four economic characteristics of countries explain a large share of the international distribution of reserves, ranging from 86 to 97 percent depending on year and averaging 90 percent over the period. In other words, it may be unnecessary to appeal to exceptional French and American appetites for gold or to the collapse of the gold-exchange standard to account for the observed distribution.

This specification does not explicitly test the hypothesis that the observed distribution of reserves was an equilibrium allocation. This may be a significant omission since, in a period marked by convertibility crises and unanticipated devaluations, countries may have been unable to maintain their desired reserve stocks. To test this hypothesis, the rate of change of the exchange rate over the preceding period is added to the model.[48] The

cent changes in the level of reserves or the variability of detrended reserves are marked by the same instability of coefficient estimates. A notable aspect of the results in Table 10.3 is that the point estimate of the income elasticity of the demand for reserves tends to be less than unity, rather than greater than unity as in modern estimates and as suggested by the luxury good argument. This result is attributable to the inclusion of log money as an additional explanatory variable. The total elasticity of the demand for reserves with respect to national income is the direct elasticity plus the income elasticity of money demand times the coefficient on log money. If the income elasticity of money demand is unity, the two coefficients simply can be added, yielding a total income elasticity of demand for reserves on the order of 1.1.

48 Sebastian Edwards, "The Demand for International Reserves and Exchange Rate Adjustments: The Case of LDC's," *Economica* 50 (1983), 269–80, estimates a similar specification, including a dummy variable for years preceding a devaluation, and interprets the coefficient estimate of −0.3 as suggesting that, prior to devaluation, reserves were some 30 percent below desired levels.

Table 10.4: *Demand for reserves, 1929–1935: disequilibrium model*

Year	Constant	Log GNP	Import share	Export varia-bility	Log money	Percent appre-ciation	R^2	n
1929	−3.633	0.804	3.828	9.406	0.219	6.435	.96	22
	(4.42)	(7.77)	(3.94)	(2.08)	(3.03)	(2.21)		
1930	−4.027	0.874	2.852	1.243	0.251	4.616	.97	22
	(5.84)	(9.34)	(3.94)	(1.46)	(3.94)	(1.45)		
1931	−3.921	0.844	2.869	1.439	0.252	0.367	.95	22
	(4.08)	(7.02)	(2.21)	(1.74)	(3.31)	(0.27)		
1932	−3.508	0.837	3.803	4.641	0.199	−0.238	.94	22
	(3.60)	(6.34)	(1.56)	(1.74)	(2.33)	(0.24)		
1933	−3.494	0.872	4.596	4.858	0.156	0.119	.92	22
	(3.85)	(6.33)	(3.03)	(0.14)	(1.710)	(0.17)		
1934	−4.387	0.918	7.600	12.100	0.151	−0.005	.86	22
	(2.55)	(4.78)	(2.11)	(1.66)	(1.22)	(0.002)		
1935	−3.612	0.865	6.217	15.540	0.146	5.492	.89	22
	(2.75)	(5.35)	(1.99)	(1.96)	(1.42)	(0.99)		
1929–35	−3.944	0.876	3.597	1.675	0.215	−0.114	.90	154
	(11.01)	(17.90)	(6.76)	(2.58)	(6.54)	(0.30)		

Note: Dependent variable is log of gold plus foreign exchange reserves. Two-stage least squares estimates with t-statistics in parentheses.
Source: See text.

exchange rate is measured as a percentage of its 1929 gold parity, so negative values signify depreciation.[49] The sign of its coefficient is theoretically ambiguous: If devaluation were forced, as was the case for several primary producers in 1929–30, then depreciation should be associated with reserve losses and the coefficient should be positive; but if devaluation were voluntary, as in the case of the U.S. depreciation of 1933–34, then depreciation should be associated with reserve gains and the coefficient should be negative.

The results of estimating the disequilibrium model are reported in Table 10.4. The only year for which the coefficient on depreciation differs significantly from zero is 1929, when countries forced to depreciate held reserves

---

[49] This follows Chapter 9. More precisely, it is measured as the change in the annual average exchange rate between the current and preceding years. Since reserves are measured at the end of the year, the use of annual average exchange rates should minimize simultaneity bias due to the impact of changes in reserves on changes in the exchange rate.

Table 10.5: *Demand for gold reserves, 1929–1935*

Year	Constant	Log GNP	Import share	Export variability	Log money	R^2	n
1929	−2.762	0.644	0.709	7.118	0.343	.91	24
	(2.42)	(4.50)	(0.53)	(1.15)	(3.55)		
1930	−3.597	0.762	0.823	1.176	0.335	.97	24
	(5.28)	(8.23)	(0.53)	(1.41)	(5.61)		
1931	−4.167	0.797	2.095	1.176	0.329	.94	24
	(4.60)	(6.88)	(1.66)	(1.47)	(4.48)		
1932	−4.176	0.814	3.718	3.660	0.294	.94	24
	(4.60)	(6.86)	(1.68)	(1.44)	(3.76)		
1933	−5.360	0.967	4.680	−18.73	0.244	.89	24
	(4.48)	(5.44)	(2.44)	(0.43)	(2.10)		
1934	−6.659	1.042	8.739	8.57	0.245	.84	24
	(3.62)	(4.59)	(2.18)	(0.99)	(1.67)		
1935	−5.730	0.993	6.915	13.22	0.198	.83	24
	(3.14)	(4.40)	(1.59)	(1.19)	(1.38)		
1929–35	−3.961	0.789	2.605	1.514	0.305	.88	168
	(10.13)	(14.31)	(4.21)	(1.93)	(7.75)		

Note: Dependent variable is log of gold reserves. Two-stage least squares estimates with t-statistics in parentheses.
Source: See text.

significantly less than desired.[50] In general, the results tend to support the equilibrium specification.

In Tables 10.5 and 10.6 I estimate separately the demand for the two components of international reserves: monetary gold and foreign assets. Consider first the pooled time-series cross-section results. Both demands depend positively on income, openness, and export variability. Although the coefficients on export variability again exhibit instability, their movement displays no obvious pattern. However, only gold and not foreign exchange reserves are consistently related to the size of national money supplies at standard significance levels, especially after 1930. This result

---

[50] In contrast, in 1931, a year marked by major convertibility crises, the disequilibrium model adds nothing to the explanation provided by the equilibrium version. A plausible interpretation of this failure is that the variable conflates the effects of Britain's convertibility crisis, which should yield a positive coefficient, and the effects of simultaneous devaluations by countries attempting to protect their shares of British markets, which should yield a negative coefficient. However, adding a dummy variable for Britain interacted with the rate of depreciation does not change the result.

Table 10.6: *Demand for foreign exchange reserves, 1929–1935*

Year	Constant	Log GNP	Import share	Export variability	Log money	R^2	n
1929	−5.605	0.930	5.992	11.01	0.127	.94	20
	(5.64)	(7.45)	(5.10)	(2.04)	(1.51)		
1930	−6.207	0.955	5.481	1.335	0.221	.91	20
	(4.77)	(5.40)	(4.02)	(0.84)	(1.98)		
1931	−5.509	0.916	4.855	2.626	0.083	.88	20
	(3.95)	(4.98)	(2.40)	(2.05)	(0.72)		
1932	−3.617	0.806	2.773	6.306	0.001	.74	20
	(2.08)	(3.51)	(0.63)	(1.27)	(0.01)		
1933	−3.352	0.853	−0.682	9.80	−0.114	.59	20
	(1.63)	(2.80)	(0.21)	(1.32)	(0.58)		
1934	−4.361	0.951	3.197	8.74	−0.187	.51	20
	(1.62)	(2.86)	(0.54)	(0.69)	(0.87)		
1935	−5.427	1.021	2.771	6.85	−0.056	.60	20
	(2.03)	(3.06)	(0.42)	(0.42)	(0.26)		
1929–35	−5.298	0.960	5.055	3.513	0.001	.70	140
	(7.99)	(10.53)	(5.06)	(2.93)	(0.02)		

Note: Dependent variable is log of foreign exchange reserves. Two-stage least squares estimates with t-statistics in parentheses.
Source: See text.

is broadly consistent with the views of Nurkse (1944): since the primary objective of backing the note circulation was "to maintain confidence in the currency," Nurkse suggested that backing for notes would tend to be held in the confidence-inspiring form of gold, whereas reserves maintained for other purposes would be held in the form of foreign exchange as well.[51] The Table 10.5 coefficients on money supplies are significantly greater than zero at the 90 percent level or better for every year except the last and tend to decline over time. Though in Table 10.6 there appears to be no association between exchange reserves and money supplies after 1930, contrary to Nurkse there is weak evidence of an association in the gold standard years 1929–30. It appears that both gold and foreign exchange were used to smooth external transactions and, to a greater extent for gold than foreign exchange, to back the central bank's domestic liabilities during the period of the global gold-exchange standard; once that standard began to collapse, however, whereas gold was still held both to smooth external transactions

[51] Nurkse, *Currency Experience*, p. 96 and passim.

Table 10.7: *Demand for reserves, 1929–1935: U.S. and French effects*

Independent variables	Dependent variable						
	Log reserves			Log gold			Log foreign exchange
Constant	−3.666	−3.854	−3.556	−3.687	−3.879	−3.578	−5.368
	(10.42)	(10.92)	(10.25)	(9.53)	(10.08)	(9.44)	(7.87)
Log GNP	0.857	0.863	0.840	0.771	0.774	0.753	0.966
	(18.03)	(17.72)	(17.87)	(14.36)	(14.21)	(14.28)	(10.47)
Import share	3.335	3.819	3.575	2.307	2.879	2.588	5.114
	(6.43)	(7.14)	(6.93)	(3.81)	(4.68)	(4.34)	(5.06)
Export variability	0.148	1.819	0.228	−0.326	1.713	−0.231	3.895
	(0.19)	(2.84)	(0.31)	(0.35)	(2.21)	(0.25)	(2.67)
Log money	0.201	0.211	0.198	0.290	0.302	0.285	0.005
	(6.33)	(6.54)	(6.35)	(7.55)	(7.81)	(7.61)	(0.08)
France	1.262		1.343	1.504		1.605	−0.321
	(3.51)		(3.80)	(3.43)		(3.74)	(0.46)
U.S.		0.657	0.745		0.929	1.024	
		(2.30)	(2.71)		(2.70)	(3.08)	
R^2	.91	.91	.91	.89	.88	.89	.70
n	154	154	154	168	168	168	140

Note: Pooled time-series cross sections. Two-stage least squares estimates with t-statistics in parentheses.
Source: See text.

and to provide backing for money supplies, foreign assets were held only for the first of these purposes.

Table 10.7, where dummy variables for the United States and France are added, can be used to assess the contention that the Federal Reserve and the Banque de France held reserves in excess of those explicable by their economic characteristics and normal patterns of central bank behavior.[52] It is not clear that the proper interpretation of this contention is that the two countries held disproportionate quantities of global reserves or disproportionate quantities of gold. The results lend support to both interpretations.

[52] It might be argued that a dummy variable for the UK should also be included to pick up any effects associated with its (and America's) reserve currency roles (and their liabilities to the outside world). Adding such a variable yields a uniformly insignificant coefficient, with a t-statistic of 0.45 in the pooled equation in Table 10.4 and one of 0.27 in the third equation of Table 10.7, for example. In the latter instance the coefficients on individual years remain uniformly insignificant.

From the third equation, U.S. gold reserves were fully 110 percent and
French gold reserves 280 percent above levels that can be accounted for
by their economic characteristics and the behavior typical of the sample
of countries.[53] From the sixth equation, U.S. monetary gold stocks were
nearly three times and French gold stocks nearly five times those predicted
by the international cross section.[54]

These magnitudes are economically important in the context of the Great
Depression. Recall that in 1931 France and the United States possessed between them some 60 percent of the global stock of monetary gold. The
results in Table 10.7 suggest that, had France and the United States adhered
to the same patterns as other countries, their combined share would have
been less than one-quarter, almost exactly doubling the gold reserves of
other countries. Assuming that central banks were concerned to retain some
proportion between their reserves and domestic liabilities, like that shown
in Tables 10.4 and 10.5, and that they were constrained in their desire to
reflate by the availability of gold, this redistribution of reserves would have
provided considerable scope for an expansion of money supplies.

Table 10.8 adds dummy variables for years subsequent to 1929 to analyze
shifts over time in the willingness to hold reserve assets. The interpretation
of reserve movements which emphasizes the shift out of exchange and into
gold due to the collapse of the gold-exchange standard predicts negative
coefficients for later years in the demand-for-exchange-reserves equations
and significant positive coefficients in the equations for gold. Only the first
of these predictions receives strong support. Except in 1932, the demand
for exchange reserves is significantly lower in every year after 1930 than
in 1929.[55] As before, the orders of magnitude are striking: by 1931 the demand for foreign assets has fallen by almost exactly 50 percent compared
to 1929.[56] This is more than a restatement of the fact that between 1929 and

---

[53] Since the dummy variables for France and the United States are 1.343 and 0.743, respectively, the gold reserves are $e^{1.343} = 3.83$ and $e^{0.743} = 2.11$ times those predicted by their
characteristics and the average behavior of other countries.

[54] In contrast, French exchange reserves differ insignificantly from those of other countries
with similar characteristics.

[55] An alternative specification is to interact the dummy variables for years with money, under
the assumption that what shifted over time was not the average propensity to hold reserves but their elasticity with respect to the money supply. Since the results of estimating
this alternative specification, shown in Table 10.9, are virtually indistinguishable from the
results of estimating the basic specification, only the latter are discussed in the text.

[56] The coefficients differ significantly from zero at the 95 percent level for the one-tail test
and at the 90 percent level for the two-tail test.

Table 10.8: *Demand for reserves, 1929–1935: U.S., French, and year effects*

Independent variables	Dependent variable					
	Log reserves		Log gold		Log foreign assets	
Constant	−4.209	−3.845	−4.343	−3.962	−4.455	−4.484
	(10.08)	(9.48)	(9.30)	(8.80)	(5.81)	(5.69)
Log GNP	0.885	0.848	0.803	0.766	0.935	0.937
	(17.80)	(17.34)	(14.26)	(14.24)	(10.28)	(10.18)
Import share	3.956	3.919	3.969	2.920	4.042	4.073
	(6.89)	(6.97)	(4.50)	(4.56)	(3.80)	(3.76)
Export variability	1.087	0.483	1.537	−0.239	3.332	3.488
	(2.80)	(0.62)	(1.90)	(0.25)	(2.73)	(2.31)
Log money	0.209	0.194	0.300	0.280	0.014	0.245
	(6.33)	(6.19)	(7.50)	(7.39)	(0.22)	(0.25)
France		1.246		1.573		−0.123
		(3.44)		(3.59)		(0.18)
United States		0.775		1.044		
		(2.79)		(3.12)		
1930	0.128	0.161	0.153	0.193	−0.065	−0.069
	(0.59)	(0.78)	(0.60)	(0.80)	(0.16)	(0.16)
1931	−0.030	0.020	0.192	0.253	−0.700	−0.705
	(0.14)	(0.10)	(0.74)	(1.03)	(1.67)	(1.67)
1932	0.258	0.263	0.411	0.417	−0.479	−0.477
	(1.16)	(1.24)	(1.57)	(1.69)	(1.13)	(1.12)
1933	0.328	0.304	0.326	0.298	−0.821	−0.816
	(1.48)	(1.44)	(1.25)	(1.21)	(1.94)	(1.92)
1934	0.248	0.227	0.237	0.210	−1.019	−1.014
	(1.10)	(1.05)	(0.91)	(0.85)	(2.38)	(2.35)
1935	0.312	0.293	0.361	0.338	−0.679	−0.674
	(1.39)	(1.37)	(1.38)	(1.37)	(1.59)	(1.57)
R^2	.91	.92	.88	.89	.72	.72
n	154	154	168	168	140	140

Note: Pooled time-series cross sections. Two-stage least squares estimates with t-statistics in parentheses.
Source: See text.

1931 the share of foreign exchange in the reserves of 24 countries fell from 37 to 19 percent (37 to 13 percent when France is excluded). It establishes that the decline in income, contraction of trade, and changes in money supplies associated with the Depression cannot by themselves account for this development.

The results do not provide equally compelling support for the contention that this liquidation of foreign exchange was at the same time a shift into gold. Although in the equations for gold the coefficients on 1930 and subsequent years are uniformly positive (as they should be according to the "scramble into gold" hypothesis), they tend to differ insignificantly from zero at standard confidence levels. Neither do the dummy variables for years differ from zero as a group when their significance is tested jointly. On the basis of these estimates one cannot reject the null hypothesis that the demand for gold rose insignificantly at the same time the demand for foreign exchange fell.

These findings should be treated cautiously, since the coefficients on the dummy variables for years in the equations for gold are not particularly robust. Though it is not possible to reject the hypothesis that these coefficients equal zero, neither is it possible to reject the alternative hypothesis that they take on a range of positive values. To better gauge the robustness of the coefficients, the equations were estimated under a variety of alternative specifications. First, the dummy variables for years were interacted with log high-powered money, under the assumption that what shifted over time was not the average propensity to hold reserves but the elasticity of demand for gold reserves with respect to the money supply. The results using this specification (reported in Table 10.9) are virtually indistinguishable from those reported in the text. In only one instance was one of the dummy variables for years, that for 1932, significantly greater than zero at the 90 percent confidence level. Thus, there is some evidence that the propensity to back monetary liabilities with gold increased in 1932, but even so that shift did not persist into subsequent years.

Second, the dummy variables for years were redefined to equal unity not only in a given year but in succeeding years as well. The individual coefficients can be used to test that demands for reserves shifted not just temporarily but permanently. These equations show that the demand for foreign exchange declined once and for all in 1931. Only the coefficient for 1931 is significantly less than zero (at the 90 percent confidence level) in the demand-for-foreign-exchange equations. But once again, none of the

Table 10.9: *Demand for reserves, 1929–1935: U.S., French, and interactive year effects*

Independent variables	Dependent variable					
	Log reserves		Log gold		Log foreign assets	
Constant	−3.983	−3.611	−4.090	−3.701	−4.970	−4.952
	(10.85)	(10.06)	(10.16)	(9.47)	(7.63)	(7.38)
Log GNP	0.881	0.845	0.803	0.766	0.931	0.929
	(17.58)	(17.53)	(14.25)	(14.25)	(10.46)	(10.33)
Import share	3.799	3.714	2.947	2.852	3.862	3.840
	(6.63)	(6.61)	(4.47)	(4.44)	(3.75)	(3.65)
Export variability	1.882	0.294	1.610	−0.349	2.902	2.790
	(2.69)	(0.35)	(1.92)	(0.35)	(2.33)	(1.77)
Log money	0.191	0.176	0.263	0.242	0.115	0.115
	(4.67)	(4.51)	(5.37)	(5.22)	(1.58)	(1.56)
France		1.312		1.609		0.080
		(3.51)		(3.58)		(0.12)
United States		0.755		1.037		
		(2.70)		(3.09)		
1930 * log money	0.019	0.029	0.022	0.033	−0.002	−0.001
	(0.61)	(0.94)	(0.60)	(0.94)	(0.02)	(0.01)
1931 * log money	−0.006	0.009	0.027	0.044	−0.104	−0.103
	(0.17)	(0.28)	(0.71)	(1.20)	(1.72)	(1.68)
1932 * log money	0.028	0.030	0.059	0.061	−0.093	−0.093
	(0.88)	(1.00)	(1.53)	(1.70)	(1.56)	(1.54)
1933 * log money	0.030	0.025	0.048	0.043	−0.159	−0.159
	(0.93)	(0.82)	(1.28)	(1.20)	(2.69)	(2.68)
1934 * log money	0.025	0.019	0.041	0.035	−0.183	−0.184
	(0.75)	(0.62)	(1.06)	(0.96)	(3.04)	(3.03)
1935 * log money	0.032	0.027	0.051	0.045	−0.114	−0.114
	(0.99)	(0.89)	(1.33)	(1.26)	(1.90)	(1.90)
R^2	.90	.92	.88	.89	.73	.73
n	154	154	168	168	140	140

Note: Pooled time-series cross sections. Two-stage least squares estimates with t-statistics in parentheses.
Source: See text.

dummy variables for years is significantly greater than zero in the demand-for-gold equations. The largest coefficient is that for 1932 and subsequent years, but its t-statistic is less than 1.25.

Third, the dummy variables for years were constrained to be equal in magnitude but opposite in sign in the demand-for-gold and demand-for-foreign-exchange equations. This was designed to test the special case considered at the end of Section 1, that each time a central bank liquidated $1 of gold it attempted to acquire $1 of foreign exchange. Testing this hypothesis required entering the dependent variables (along with GNP and money) in levels rather than logs and limiting the sample to those 20 countries (and seven years) for which both gold- and foreign-exchange data are available. The only year for which there is any evidence of a shift between gold and foreign exchange was 1935 (for which year the shift is statistically significant at the 90 percent level). And that shift was, paradoxically, out of gold and back into foreign assets, presumably reflecting the fact that the devaluations of sterling and the dollar were receding into the past, reducing the perceived riskiness of holding foreign exchange, rather than a shift out of foreign exchange and into gold that would have been destructive of the reserve base.

Perhaps the strongest evidence against the hypothesis that there occurred in the course of the 1930s an upward shift in the global demand for gold is that the coefficients for 1930 and 1931 in the gold equations, however specified, are virtually indistinguishable from one another. 1931 was the year of the most serious uncertainty due to Continental financial crises, Central European exchange control, sterling devaluation, and competitive depreciation, the year over which the share of foreign exchange in the reserves of European central banks fell most dramatically. If uncertainty ever increased the demand for gold, it should have been between the ends of 1930 and 1931. That the point estimates of the dummy variables for those years indicate increases of no more than five percent is difficult to reconcile with the gold-exchange-standard-liquidation view.

The conclusion that the demand for gold reserves rose insignificantly is entirely consistent with the finding that the demand for foreign exchange fell. Together, these results suggest that what happened starting in 1931 as a result of the gold-exchange standard's collapse was that countries reduced their propensity to hold exchange reserves as backing for their money supplies without substituting additional gold (aside from a temporary 1932 increase). The devaluations which led to the scramble out of exchange reserves at the same time loosened the reserve constraint on national money supplies. Rather than substituting gold for recently liquidated foreign assets, some central banks appear to have simply reduced their excess reserves. There is little evidence, to reiterate, of a wholesale scramble for gold induced by the liquidation of foreign-exchange reserves.

This conclusion contrasts with the implications of the analysis of French and American behavior. When the dummy variables for years are added to Table 10.8, the coefficients on the dummy variables for France and the United States remain positive and significant at the 99 percent level in the equations for both gold and total reserves. Because the practice of backing money supplies with gold remained, the exceptional demands for gold by the Federal Reserve and Banque de France placed downward pressure on global money supplies. This effect is large relative to any which might be ascribed to the liquidation of the gold-exchange standard.

3. Summary and implications

This chapter has presented the first systematic analysis of the distribution of international reserves under the gold-exchange standard. The demand for reserves has been shown to depend on, among other variables, national money supplies. That dependence changed, however, in important ways after 1930. Where it had previously been the practice of gold-exchange-standard countries to back their money supplies with both foreign assets and gold, the instability of reserve currencies caused central banks to liquidate that portion of their reserve portfolios which had taken the form of foreign assets. Had no other change in behavior occurred, this would have placed downward pressure on money supplies. Yet the results of empirical analysis do not permit us to rule out other changes sufficiently important to eliminate any such effect. Instead of attempting to maintain the overall reserve backing of their money supplies by substituting gold for foreign exchange, central banks may have reduced their cover ratios to permit the maintenance of previously established relations between money supplies and gold reserves. It is not clear that the deflationary linkage running from international monetary instability to domestic financial stringency was operative.

But since central banks attempted on average to maintain previously established ratios between money supplies and gold, any factor which reduced the availability of gold reserves served as an impediment to monetary expansion. Here the gold policies of the Federal Reserve and the Banque de France emerged as crucial. According to the estimates provided here, the exceptional policies of these two countries reduced the gold reserves available to other countries by fully one half, an effect larger than any which can be ascribed to the liquidation of the gold-exchange standard.

As noted in the introduction, these findings have clear implications for the literature on monetary forces in the Great Depression. These implications only emerge, however, when the demand for reserves and supply of money are viewed on a global basis. Since central banks generally maintained a relatively stable relationship between their money supplies and gold reserves, any factor which constrained the availability of gold constrained their ability, given regulations and attitudes, to engage in monetary reflation. U.S. and French gold policies must therefore share the blame for exacerbating the monetary aspects of the Great Depression.

These findings also have implications for the dichotomy between explanations for the Great Depression which emphasize national policies and those which emphasize the international system. They suggest that the distinction is overdrawn. The conclusions of this chapter are entirely consistent with the view that the Depression can only be fully understood as a global phenomenon. They support the notion that international considerations were significant determinants of national monetary policies. But they suggest that national monetary policies, rather than systemic features of the international regime, were the source of the most important destabilizing monetary impulse transmitted by the international system.

Another way of looking at these results is in terms of the debate over the exchange-rate devaluations of the 1930s. Chapter 9 argued, in contradistinction to the existing literature, that the devaluations of the 1930s were useful reflationary initiatives when taken individually, although as executed they had beggar-thy-neighbor effects abroad.[57] Had they been undertaken more widely, it was suggested, they would have had at worst no effects and at best extremely favorable effects, depending on accompanying monetary measures.[58] The only caveat to this conclusion lay in the possibility that the uncoordinated manner in which devaluation was undertaken created uncertainty which led to a shift out of exchange reserves and into gold, putting downward pressure on global reserves and national money supplies. The results reported here confirm the shift out of exchange reserves, but provide no compelling support for the implication of deflationary consequences.

[57] $e^{-0.7} = .496$.
[58] See pp. 235–8 above.

11. Hegemonic stability theories of the international monetary system

An international monetary system is a set of rules or conventions governing the economic policies of nations. From a narrowly national perspective, it is an unnatural state of affairs. Adherence to a common set of rules or conventions requires a certain harmonization of monetary and fiscal policies, even though the preferences and constraints influencing policy formulation diverge markedly across countries. Governments are expected to forswear policies that redistribute economic welfare from foreigners to domestic residents and to contribute voluntarily to providing the international public good of global monetary stability. In effect, they are expected to solve the defection problem that plagues cartels and – equivalently in this context – the free-rider problem hindering public good provision.[1] Since they are likely to succeed incompletely, the public good of international monetary stability tends to be underproduced. From this perspective, the paradox of international monetary affairs is not the difficulty of designing a stable international monetary system, but the fact that such systems have actually persisted for decades.

Specialists in international relations have offered the notion that dominance by one country – a hegemonic power – is needed to ensure the smooth functioning of an international regime.[2] The concentration of eco-

An earlier version of this paper was prepared for the Centre for Economic Policy Research Conference on International Regimes and the Design of Macroeconomic Policy. I thank my conference discussant, Peter Kenen, as well as Dilip Abreu, Ralph Bryant, Robert Gilpin, Joanne Gowa, Robert Keohane, Charles Kindleberger, and Kala Krishna for comments and discussion.

[1] See Mancur Olson, Jr., and Richard Zeckhauser, "An Economic Theory of Alliances," *Review of Economics and Statistics* 48 (August 1966), 266–79.

[2] I refer to this as "the theory of hegemonic stability," a phrase coined by Robert O. Keohane, "The Theory of Hegemonic Stability and Changes in International Economic Regimes, 1967–1977," in Ole R. Holsti, Randolph M. Siverson, and Alexander L. George, eds., *Change in the International System* (Boulder, CO, 1980), 131–62. In Keohane's words, the theory of hegemonic stability posits that "hegemonic structures of power, dominated by a single country, are most conducive to the development of strong international regimes whose rules are relatively precise and well obeyed" (p. 132). See Robert Gilpin, *U.S. Power*

nomic power is seen as a way of internalizing the externalities associated with systemic stability and of ensuring its adequate provision. The application of this "theory of hegemonic stability" to international monetary affairs is straightforward.[3] The maintenance of the Bretton Woods System for a quarter century is ascribed to the singular power of the United States in the postwar world, much as the persistence of the classical gold standard is ascribed to Britain's dominance of international financial affairs in the second half of the nineteenth century. "The monetary systems of the past

and the Multinational Corporation: The Political Economy of Foreign Direct Investment (New York, 1975); Stephen D. Krasner, "State Power and the Structure of International Trade," World Politics 28 (April 1976), 317–47; Peter F. Cowhey and Edward Long, "Testing Theories of Regime Change: Hegemonic Decline or Surplus Capacity?" International Organization 37 (Spring 1983), 157–88; Joanne Gowa, "Hegemons, IOs, and Markets: The Case of the Substitution Account," International Organization 38 (Autumn 1984), 661–83; Charles Lipson, "The Transformation of Trade: The Sources and Effects of Regime Changes," International Organization 36 (Spring 1982), 417–56; Duncan Snidal, "The Limits of Hegemonic Stability Theory," International Organization 39 (Autumn 1985), 579–614; Arthur A. Stein, "The Hegemon's Dilemma: Great Britain, the United States, and the International Economic Order," International Organization 38 (Spring 1984), 355–86; and Beth V. Yarbrough and Robert M. Yarbrough, "Free Trade, Hegemony, and the Theory of Agency," Kyklos 38 (1985), 348–64.

3   Attempts to test the applicability of hegemonic stability theory have considered international trade policy. See Krasner, "State Power"; John A. C. Conybeare, "Tariff Protection in Developed and Developing Countries: A Cross-Sectional and Longitudinal Analysis," International Organization 37 (Summer 1983), 441–67; Fred Lawson, "Hegemony and the Structure of International Trade Reassessed: A View from Arabia," International Organization 37 (Spring 1983), 317–37; T. J. McKeown, "Hegemonic Stability Theory and 19th Century Tariff Levels in Europe," International Organization 37 (Winter 1983), 73–91; and D. A. Lake, Power, Protection and Free Trade: International Sources of U.S. Commercial Strategy, 1887–1939 (Ithaca, NY, 1988). Attempts to do such testing also have considered international investment. See, for example, Gilpin, U.S. Power and the Multinational Corporation. For attempts to test applicability to international monetary arrangements, see Robert O. Keohane, "Inflation and the Decline of American Power," in Raymond E. Lombra and Willard E. Witte, eds., Political Economy of International and Domestic Monetary Relations (Ames, IA, 1983), pp. 7–24; John S. Odell, "Bretton Woods and International Political Disintegration: Implications for Monetary Diplomacy," in Lombra and Witte, Political Economy, pp. 39–58; and Kenneth A. Oye, "The Sterling-Dollar-Franc Triangle: Monetary Diplomacy 1929–1937," in Kenneth A. Oye, ed., Cooperation under Anarchy (Princeton, 1986), pp. 173–99. Finally, such attempts have also considered international administration of world oil prices. See Keohane, "The Theory of Hegemonic Stability," and Robert O. Keohane, After Hegemony: Cooperation and Discord in the World Political Economy (Princeton, 1984). The theory's popularity was stimulated by Charles Kindleberger's argument, following William Adams Brown, that the international financial system and macroeconomic environment of the interwar years were destabilized by lack of leadership by a dominant economic power willing to provide the public good of international monetary stability by acting as international lender of last resort. See Kindleberger, World in Depression; and Brown, International Gold Standard.

were relatively stable when a single currency dominated: sterling through most of the nineteenth century, the dollar in the early postwar period."[4] By contrast, the instability of the interwar gold exchange standard is attributed to the absence of a hegemonic power, due to Britain's inability to play the dominant role and America's unwillingness to accept it.

The appeal of this notion lies in its resonance with the public good and cartel analogies for international monetary affairs, through what might be called the carrot and stick variants of hegemonic stability theory. In the carrot variant, the hegemon, like a dominant firm in an oligopolistic market, maintains the cohesion of the cartel by making the equivalent of side payments to members of the fringe. In the stick variant, the hegemon, like a dominant firm, deters defection from the international monetary cartel by using its economic policies to threaten retaliation against renegades. In strong versions of the theory (what Snidal refers to as the benevolent strand of the theory), all participants are rendered better off by the intervention of the dominant power. In weak versions (what Snidal refers to as the coercive strand of the theory), either because systemic stability is not a purely public good or because its costs are shunted onto smaller states, the benefits of stability accrue disproportionately or even exclusively to the hegemon.[5]

Three problems bedevil attempts to apply hegemonic stability theory to international monetary affairs. First is the ambiguity surrounding three concepts central to the theory: *hegemony,* the *power* the hegemon is assumed to possess, and the *regime* whose stability is ostensibly enhanced by the exercise of hegemonic power. Rather than adopting general definitions offered previously and devoting this paper to their criticism, I adopt specialized definitions tailored to my concern with the international monetary system. I employ the economist's definition of economic – or market – power: sufficient size in the relevant market to influence prices and quantities.[6] I define a hegemon analogously to a dominant firm: as a country whose market power, understood in this sense, significantly exceeds that of all rivals. Finally, I avoid defining the concept of regime around which much debate has revolved by posing the question narrowly: whether hegemony is conducive to the stability of the international monetary system

---

4 C. Fred Bergsten, *Toward a New International Economic Order: Selected Papers of C. Fred Bergsten, 1972–1974* (Lexington, MA, 1975), p. 31.

5 See Snidal, "Limits of Hegemonic Stability Theory," pp. 581–2.

6 Alternatives to this definition are offered by Jeffrey Hart, "Three Approaches to the Measurement of Power in International Relations," *International Organization* 30 (Spring 1976), 289–305.

(where the system is defined as those explicit rules and procedures governing international monetary affairs), rather than whether it is conducive to the stability of the international regime, however defined.[7]

The second problem plaguing attempts to apply hegemonic stability theory to international monetary affairs is ambiguity about the instruments with which the hegemon makes its influence felt. This is the distinction between what are characterized above as the carrot and stick variants of the theory. Does the hegemon alter its monetary, fiscal, or commercial policies to discipline countries that refuse to play by its rules, as "basic force" models of international relations would suggest?[8] Does it link international economic policy to other issue areas and impose military or diplomatic sanctions on uncooperative nations?[9] Or does it stabilize the system through the use of "positive sanctions," financing the public good of international monetary stability by acting as lender of last resort even when the probability of repayment is slim and forsaking beggar-thy-neighbor policies even when used to advantage by other countries?[10]

---

[7] The concept of regime was introduced into the international relations literature by John Gerard Ruggie, "International Responses to Technology: Concepts and Trends," *International Organization* 29 (Summer 1975), 557–83. For critical analyses of its uses, see Oran R. Young, "International Regimes: Problems of Concept Formation," *World Politics* 32 (April 1980), 331–56; and Susan Strange, "Still an Extraordinary Power: America's Role in a Global Monetary System," in Lombra and Witte, eds., *Political Economy*, pp. 73–93. Keohane, "The Theory of Hegemonic Stability," p. 132, defines a regime as "the norms, rules, and procedures that guide the behavior of states and other important actors." Since my method of analysis does not hinge on a particular definition of the international monetary regime, it is compatible with a range of alternative definitions. I prefer to distinguish between the monetary system, which is made up of a set of explicit rules and procedures (pegging rules, intervention strategies, and IMF statutes governing reserve availability, for example), and the international monetary regime as a broader framework that incorporates the explicit rules comprising the system but embeds them within a set of implicit understandings about how economic policymakers will behave (promises to coordinate macroeconomic policies or to provide loans in time of convertibility crisis, for example). Thus, whereas the compass of the international monetary system is limited to matters that impinge directly on monetary affairs, the international monetary regime may involve issues that impinge indirectly, such as trade policy or diplomatic action. In effect, I am distinguishing between the monetary "system" and "regime" in the same way that the monetary "system" and "order" were distinguished by Robert A. Mundell, "The Future of the International Financial System," in A. L. K. Acheson, J. F. Chant, and M. F. J. Prachowny, eds., *Bretton Woods Revisited* (Toronto, 1972), pp. 91–104.

[8] See James March, "The Power of Power," in David Easton, ed., *Varieties of Political Theory* (Englewood Cliffs, NJ, 1966), 39–70.

[9] For discussions of issue linkage, see Richard N. Cooper, "Trade Policy Is Foreign Policy," *Foreign Policy* 9 (Winter 1972–3), 18–36; and Ernst B. Haas, "Why Collaborate? Issue Linkage and International Regimes," *World Politics* 32 (April 1980), 357–405.

[10] See Kindleberger, *World in Depression*, p. 28; and Keohane, "Theory of Hegemonic Stability," p. 136.

The third problem is ambiguity about the scope of hegemonic stability theories. In principle, such theories could be applied equally to the design, the operation, or the decline of the international monetary system.[11] Yet in practice, hegemonic stability theories may shed light on the success of efforts to design or reform the international monetary system but not on its day-to-day operation or eventual decline. Other combinations are equally plausible a priori. Only analysis of individual cases can throw light on the theory's range of applicability.

In this chapter, I structure an analysis of hegemonic stability theories of the international monetary system around the dual problems of range of applicability and mode of implementation. I consider separately the genesis of international monetary systems, their operation in normal periods and times of crisis, and their disintegration. In each context, I draw evidence from three modern incarnations of the international monetary system: the classical gold standard, the interwar gold exchange standard, and Bretton Woods. These three episodes in the history of the international monetary system are typically thought to offer two examples of hegemonic stability – Britain before 1914, the United States after 1944 – and one episode – the interwar years – destabilized by the absence of hegemony. I do not attempt to document Britain's dominance of international markets before 1914 or the dominance of the United States after 1944; I simply ask whether the market power they possessed was causally connected to the stability of the international monetary system.

The historical analysis indicates that the relationship between the market power of the leading economy and the stability of the international monetary system is considerably more complex than that suggested by simple variants of hegemonic stability theory. Though one cannot simply reject the hypothesis that on more than one occasion the stabilizing capacity of a dominant economic power has contributed to the smooth functioning of the international monetary system, neither can one reconcile much of the evidence, notably on the central role of international negotiation and collaboration even in periods of hegemonic dominance, with simple versions of the theory. Although both the appeal and limitations of hegemonic stability theories are apparent when one takes a static view of the international monetary system, those limitations are most evident when one considers

[11] For example, Kindleberger, *World in Depression*, is primarily concerned with the role of hegemony in ensuring the smooth operation of an extant system, whereas Gilpin, *U.S. Power and the Multinational Corporation*, and Krasner, "State Power and the Structure of International Trade," focus instead on the role of hegemony in system design and formation. Similar distinctions are emphasized by Stein, "The Hegemon's Dilemma."

the evolution of an international monetary system over time. An international monetary system whose smooth operation at one point is predicated on the dominance of one powerful country may in fact be dynamically unstable. Historical experience suggests that the hegemon's willingness to act in a stabilizing capacity at a single point in time tends to undermine its continued capacity to do so over time.

The notion that a concentration of economic power may be intrinsic to the smooth operation of the international monetary system, while intuitively appealing to political scientists for whom the concept of power is bread and butter, may seem to economists as strange as the ideas of the Pareto optimality of free trade or the efficiency of perfect competition are to nearly everyone but economists.[12] The point of departure of this chapter is necessarily different, therefore, from that which characterizes most work in economics, and requires of economists in the audience, like theater goers, a willing suspension of disbelief.

The genesis of monetary systems and the theory of hegemonic stability

My analysis begins with an examination of the genesis of three different monetary systems: the classical gold standard, the interwar gold exchange standard, and the Bretton Woods system.

The classical gold standard

Of the three episodes considered here, the origins of the classical gold standard are the most difficult to assess, for in the nineteenth century there were no centralized discussions, like those in Genoa in 1922 or Bretton Woods in 1944, concerned with the design of the international monetary system.[13] There was general agreement that currencies should have a metallic basis

---

12 In *U.S. Power and the Multinational Corporation*, p. 5, Gilpin's characterization is a bit strong: "Economists do not really believe in power; political scientists, for their part, do not really believe in markets."

13 A limited parallel is the International Monetary Conference of 1881, which brought together the members of the Latin Monetary Union. Another candidate is the conference that resulted from the U.S. Bland-Allison Act of 1878, which instructed the president to invite members of the Latin Monetary Union and other European countries to a conference intended to result in mutual adoption of a bimetallic system based on a common ratio of silver to gold. See A. Barton Hepburn, *A History of Currency in the United States*, rev. ed. (New York, 1924).

and that payments imbalances should be settled by international shipments of specie. But there was no consensus about which precious metals should serve as the basis for money supplies or how free international specie movements should be.

Only Britain maintained a full-fledged gold standard for anything approaching the century preceding 1913. Although gold coins had circulated alongside silver since the fourteenth century, Britain had been on a de facto gold standard since 1717, when Sir Isaac Newton, as master of the mint, set too high a silver price of gold and drove full-bodied silver coins from circulation. In 1798 silver coinage was suspended, and after 1819 silver was no longer accepted to redeem paper currency. But for half a century following its official adoption of the gold standard in 1821, Britain essentially remained alone. Other countries that retained bimetallic standards were buffeted by alternating gold and silver discoveries. The United States and France, for example, were officially bimetallic, but their internal circulations were placed on a silver basis by growing Mexican and South American silver production in the early decades of the nineteenth century. The market price of silver was thus depressed relative to the mint price, which encouraged silver to be imported for coinage and gold to be shipped abroad where its price was higher. Then, starting in 1848, gold discoveries in Russia, Australia, and California depressed the market price of gold below the mint price, all but driving silver from circulation and placing bimetallic currencies on a gold basis. Finally, silver discoveries in Nevada and other mining territories starting in the 1870s dramatically inflated the silver price of gold and forced the bimetallic currencies back onto a silver basis.

The last of these disturbances led nearly all bimetallic countries to adopt the gold standard, starting with Germany in 1871.[14] Why, after taking no comparable action in response to previous disturbances, did countries re-

[14] Although German politicians had previously perceived the country's silver standard as beneficial to the development of its Eastern European trade, by 1870 most of that region had suspended convertibility. Germany used the proceeds of the indemnity received as victor in the Franco-Prussian War to purchase gold on the world market, thereby contributing to the ongoing rise in its price. Silver inflation led to the suspension of silver coinage and convertibility by Holland, Denmark, Norway, Sweden, France, and the countries of the Latin Monetary Union (Belgium, Switzerland, Italy, and Greece), making gold the basis for the monetary standard in every European country except those that retained inconvertible paper. In 1879 the United States ended the greenback period, and Russia and Japan restored gold convertibility. Although neither Italy nor the Hapsburg monarchy adopted formal convertibility, from the turn of the century both pegged their currencies to gold. Further details may be found in Eichengreen, *Gold Standard in Theory and History*.

spond to post-1870 fluctuations in the price of silver by abandoning bi-metallism and adopting gold? What role, if any, did Britain, the hegemonic financial power, play in their decisions?

One reason for the decision to adopt gold was the desire to prevent the inflation that would result from continued silver convertibility and coinage. Hence, the plausible explanation for the contrast between the 1870s and earlier years is the danger of exceptionally rapid inflation due to the magnitude of post-1870 silver discoveries. Between 1814 and 1870, the sterling price of silver, of which so much was written, remained within 2 percentage points of its 1814 value, alternatively driving gold or silver from circulation in bimetallic countries but fluctuating insufficiently to raise the specter of significant price level changes. Then between 1871 and 1881 the London price of silver fell by 15 percent, and by 1891 the cumulative fall had reached 25 percent.[15] Gold convertibility was the only alternative to continued silver coinage that was judged both respectable and viable.[16] The only significant resistance to the adoption of gold convertibility emanated from silver-mining regions and from agricultural areas such as the American West, populated by proprietors of encumbered land who might benefit from inflation.

Seen from this perspective, the impetus for adopting the gold standard existed independently of Britain's rapid industrialization, dominance of international finance, and preeminence in trade. Still, the British example surely provided encouragement to follow the path ultimately chosen. The experience of the Latin Monetary Union impressed upon contemporaries the advantages of a common monetary standard in minimizing transactions

---

[15] See Marcello De Cecco, *The International Gold Standard: Money and Empire*, 2d ed. (London, 1984), p. 239.

[16] A third option, maintaining bimetallism but raising the relative price of gold, had been discredited by the difficulties of the Latin Monetary Union and evoked little enthusiasm when advocated by the United States at the international conference convened under the provisions of the Bland-Allison Act of 1878. Contemporaries recognized that international cooperation was necessary for the successful functioning of a bimetallic system. The more countries that participated in a bimetallic system, the greater the probability that their common mint ratio would dominate the market ratio. But of the major countries, only the United States and Italy favored immediate adoption of a global bimetallic standard. Though France, Holland, and Austria also favored bimetallism, they viewed its immediate implementation on a global basis as impractical. Germany, Belgium, and the Scandinavian states favored immediate adoption of the gold standard, Germany so strongly that it boycotted the conference. The record of conference proceedings is found in *International Monetary Conferences Held in Paris, in August 1878*, Senate Executive Doc. 58, 45 Congress, 3 sess. (Washington, DC, 1879). Also see Henry B. Russell, *International Monetary Conferences* (New York, 1898).

costs.[17] The scope of that common standard would be greatest for countries that linked their currencies to sterling. The gold standard was also attractive to domestic interests concerned with promoting economic growth. Industrialization required foreign capital, and attracting foreign capital required monetary stability. For Britain, the principal source of foreign capital, monetary stability was measured in terms of sterling and best ensured by joining Britain on gold. Moreover, London's near monopoly of trade credit was of concern to other governments, which hoped that they might reduce their dependence on the London discount market by establishing gold parities and central banks. Aware that Britain monopolized trade in newly mined gold and was the home of the world's largest organized commodity markets, other governments hoped that by emulating Britain's gold standard and financial system they might secure a share of this business.

Britain's prominence in foreign commerce, overseas investment, and trade credit forcefully conditioned the evolution of the gold standard system mainly through central banks' practice of holding key currency balances abroad, especially in London. This practice probably would not have developed so quickly if foreign countries had not grown accustomed to transacting in the London market. It would probably not have become so widespread if there had not been such strong confidence in the stability and liquidity of sterling deposits. And such a large share of foreign deposits would not have gravitated to a single center if Britain had not possessed such a highly articulated set of financial markets.

But neither Britain's dominance of international transactions nor the desire to emulate Bank of England practice prevented countries from tailoring the gold standard to their own needs. Germany and France continued to allow large internal gold circulation, while other nations limited gold coin circulation to low levels. The central banks of France, Belgium, and Switzerland retained the right to redeem their notes in silver, and the French did not hesitate to charge a premium for gold.[18] The Reichsbank could at

---

[17] In 1850 Belgian and Swiss silver coins were new and full-bodied, in contrast to French coins, which had lost up to 8 percent of their silver content through wear. Hence, French coins were exported to Belgium and Switzerland, while Belgian coins were exported to Germany and the Netherlands. In 1862 Italy adopted a bimetallic standard, but the country's silver coins were only 0.835 percent pure and hence ended up being shipped to France. The confusion that resulted convinced the countries involved to adopt a common standard that entailed the French parity of 15½ ounces of silver per ounce of gold and silver coins that were 0.835 percent pure. See Henry Parker Willis, *A History of the Latin Monetary Union: A Study of International Monetary Action* (Chicago, 1901).

[18] Harry D. White, *The French International Accounts, 1880–1913* (Cambridge, MA, 1933), pp. 182–200.

its option issue fiduciary notes upon the payment of a tax.[19] In no sense did British example or suggestion dictate the form of the monetary system.

The interwar gold exchange standard

The interwar gold exchange standard offers a radically different picture: on the one hand, there was no single dominant power like nineteenth century Britain or mid-twentieth century America; on the other, there were conscious efforts by rivals to shape the international monetary order to their national advantage.

Contemporary views of the design of the interwar monetary system were aired at a series of international meetings, the most important of which was the Genoa Economic and Financial Conference convened in April 1922.[20] Although the United States declined to send an official delegation to Genoa, proceedings there reflected the differing economic objectives of Britain and the United States. British officials were aware that the war had burdened domestic industry with adjustment problems, had disrupted trade, and had accentuated financial rivalry between London and New York. Their objectives were to prevent worldwide deflation (which was sure to exacerbate the problems of structural adjustment), to promote the expansion of international trade (to which the nation's prosperity was inextricably linked), and to recapture the financial business diverted to New York as a result of the war.[21] To prevent deflation, they advocated that countries economize on the use of gold by adopting the gold exchange standard along lines practiced by members of the British Empire. Presuming London to be a reserve center, British officials hoped that these measures would restore the City to its traditional prominence in international finance. Stable exchange rates would stimulate international trade, particularly if the United States forgave its war debt claims, which would permit reparations to be reduced and encourage creditor countries to extend loans to Central Europe.

The United States, in contrast, was less dependent for its prosperity on the rapid expansion of trade. It was less reliant on income from financial and insurance services and perceived as less urgent the need to encourage the deposit of foreign balances in New York. Influential American officials, notably Benjamin Strong of the Federal Reserve Bank of New York,

---

[19] Bloomfield, *Monetary Policy*, pp. 13–15.
[20] These are reviewed by Traynor, *International Monetary and Financial Conferences*.
[21] A more politically oriented assessment of policymakers' objectives is provided by Costigliola, *Awkward Dominion*.

opposed any extension of the gold exchange standard.[22] Above all, American officials were hesitant to participate in a conference whose success appeared to hinge on unilateral concessions regarding war debts.[23]

In the absence of an American delegation, Britain's proposals formed the basis for the resolutions of the Financial Committee of the Genoa Conference. These resolutions proposed the adoption of an international monetary convention formally empowering countries, "in addition to any gold reserve held at home, [to] maintain in any other participant country reserves of approved assets in the form of bank balances, bills, short-term securities, or other suitable liquid resources."[24] Participating countries would fix their exchange rates against one another, and any that failed to do so would lose the right to hold the reserve balances of the others. The principal creditor nations were encouraged to take immediate steps to restore convertibility in order to become "gold centers" where the bulk of foreign exchange reserves would be held. Following earlier recommendations by the Cunliffe Committee, governments were urged to economize on gold by eliminating gold coin from circulation and concentrating reserves at central banks. Countries with significantly depreciated currencies were urged to stabilize at current exchange rates rather than attempting to restore prewar parities through drastic deflation, which would only delay stabilization.

To implement this convention, the Bank of England was instructed to call an early meeting of central banks, including the Federal Reserve. But efforts to arrange this meeting, which bogged down in the dispute over war debts and reparations, proved unavailing. Still, even though the official convention advocated by the Financial Committee failed to materialize, the Genoa resolutions were not without influence.[25] Many of the innovations suggested there were adopted by individual countries on a unilateral basis and comprised the distinguishing features differentiating the prewar and interwar monetary standards.[26]

The first effect of Genoa was to encourage the adoption of statutes permitting central banks to back notes and sight deposits with foreign exchange as well as gold. New regulations broadening the definition of eligible as-

---

[22] For further discussion of Strong and the American position, see Clarke, *Central Bank Cooperation*.

[23] Frank Costigliola, "Anglo-American Rivalry"; and Traynor, *International Monetary and Financial Conferences*, p. 72.

[24] For the text of the resolution and related correspondence, see United Kingdom, *Papers Presented to Parliament*.

[25] Details are provided in Chapter 6.

[26] The significance of the Genoa resolutions is discussed at greater length in Chapter 10.

sets and specifying minimum proportions of total reserves to be held in gold were widely implemented in succeeding years. The second effect was to encourage the adoption of gold economy measures, including the withdrawal of gold coin from circulation and provision of bullion for export only by the authorities. The third effect was to provide subtle encouragement to countries experiencing ongoing inflation to stabilize at depreciated rates. Thus Genoa deserves partial credit for transforming the international monetary system from a gold to a gold exchange standard, from a gold coin to a gold bullion standard, and from a fixed-rate system to one in which central banks were vested with some discretion over the choice of parities.

Given its dominance of the proceedings at Genoa, Britain's imprint on the interwar gold exchange standard was as apparent as its influence over the structure of the prewar system. That British policymakers achieved this despite a pronounced decline in Britain's position in the world economy and the opposition of influential American officials suggests that planning and effort were substitutes, to some extent, for economic power.

The Bretton Woods system

Of the three cases considered here, U.S. dominance of the Bretton Woods negotiations is most clearly supportive of hegemonic stability theories of the genesis of the international monetary system. U.S. dominance of the postwar world economy is unmistakable.[27] Yet, despite the trappings of hegemony and American dominance of the proceedings at Bretton Woods, a less influential power – Great Britain – was able to secure surprisingly extensive concessions in the design of the international monetary system.

American and British officials offered different plans for postwar monetary reconstruction both because they had different views of the problem of international economic adjustment and because they represented economies with different strengths and weaknesses. British officials were preoccupied by two weaknesses of their economic position. First was the specter of widespread unemployment. Between 1920 and 1938, unemployment in

---

[27] In the immediate post–World War II period, the United States produced a majority of the global industrial output of the capital goods and equipment needed for economic reconstruction abroad. It was the largest holder of gold and the major creditor on long-term capital account. Observers anticipated that its creditor position would strengthen yet further as the United States continued to finance deficit spending for European reconstruction. Such observations lead Keohane to conclude that the extent of American predominance after World War II was unprecedented, unmatched even by Britain before World War I (*After Hegemony*, pp. 36–7).

Britain had scarcely dipped below double-digit levels, and British policy-makers feared its recurrence. Second was the problem of sterling balances. Britain had concentrated its wartime purchases within the sterling bloc and, because they were allies and sterling was a reserve currency, members of the bloc had accepted settlement in sterling, now held in London. Since these sterling balances were large relative to Britain's hard currency reserves, the mere possibility that they might be presented for conversion threatened plans for the restoration of convertibility.[28]

U.S. officials, in contrast, were confident that the competitive position of American industry was strong and were little concerned about the threat of unemployment. The concentration of gold reserves in the United States, combined with the economy's international creditor position, freed them from worry that speculative capital flows or foreign government policies might undermine the dollar's stability. U.S. concerns centered on the growth of preferential trading systems from which its exports were excluded, notably the sterling bloc.

The British view of international economic adjustment was dominated by concern about inadequate liquidity and asymmetrical adjustment. A central lesson drawn by British policymakers from the experience of the 1920s was the difficulty of operating an international monetary system in which liquidity or reserves were scarce. Given how slowly the global supply of monetary gold responded to fluctuations in its relative price and how sensitive its international distribution had proven to be to the economic policies of individual states, they considered it foolhardy to base the international monetary system on a reserve base composed exclusively of gold. Given the perceived inelasticity of global gold supplies, a gold-based system threatened to impart a deflationary bias to the world economy and to worsen unemployment. This preoccupation with unemployment due to external constraints was reinforced by another lesson drawn from the 1920s: the costs of asymmetries in the operation of the adjustment mechanism. If the experience of the 1920s were to be repeated, surplus countries, in response to external imbalances, would need only to sterilize reserve inflows, whereas deficit countries would be forced to initiate monetary contraction to prevent the depletion of reserves. Monetary contraction, according to Keynes, whose views heavily influenced those of the British delegation, facilitated adjustment by causing unemployment. To prevent unemployment, symmetry had to be restored to the adjustment mechanism through

---

[28] See R. S. Sayers, *Financial Policy, 1939–1945* (London, 1956), pp. 438–40; and Cairncross and Eichengreen, *Sterling in Decline*, chap. 4.

the incorporation of sanctions compelling surplus countries to revalue their currencies or stimulate demand.

From the American perspective, the principal lessons of interwar experience were not the costs of asymmetries and inadequate liquidity, but the instability of floating rates and the disruptive effects of exchange rate and trade protection. U.S. officials were concerned about ensuring order and stability in the foreign exchange market and preventing the development of preferential trading systems cultivated through expedients such as exchange control.

The Keynes and White Plans, which formed each side's basis for negotiations, are too well known to require more than a brief summary.[29] Exchange control and the centralized provision of liquidity ("bancor") were two central elements of Keynes's plan for an international clearing union. Provision of bancor was designed to permit "the substitution of an expansionist, in place of a contractionist, pressure on world trade."[30] Exchange control would insulate pegged exchange rates from the sudden liquidation of short-term balances. Symmetry would be ensured by a charge on creditor balances held with the clearing bank.

The White Plan acknowledged the validity of the British concern with liquidity, but was intended to prevent both inflation and deflation rather than to exert an expansionary influence. It limited the Stabilization Fund's total resources to $5 billion, compared with $26 billion under the Keynes Plan. It was patterned on the principles of American bank lending, under which decision-making power rested ultimately with the bank; the Keynes Plan resembled the British overdraft system, in which the overdraft was at the borrower's discretion.[31] The fundamental difference, however, was that the White Plan limited the total U.S. obligation to its $2 billion contribution, whereas the Keynes Plan limited the value of unrequited U.S. exports that might be financed by bancor to the total drawing rights of other countries ($23 billion).

It is typically argued that the Bretton Woods agreement reflected America's dominant position, presumably on the grounds that the International

---

[29] See, in particular, J. Keith Horsefield, ed., *The International Monetary Fund, 1945–1965: Twenty Years of International Monetary Cooperation,* 3 vols. (Washington, DC, 1969); and Richard N. Gardner, *Sterling-Dollar Diplomacy* (New York, 1956).

[30] Horsefield, *International Monetary Fund,* vol. 3, p. 26.

[31] See, for example, Benjamin J. Cohen, "Balance-of-Payments Financing: Evolution of a Regime," in Stephen D. Krasner, ed., *International Regimes* (Ithaca, NY, 1983), pp. 315–36.

Monetary Fund charter specified quotas of $8.8 billion (closer to the White Plan's $5 billion than to the Keynes Plan's $26 billion) and a maximum U.S. obligation of $2.75 billion (much closer to $2 billion under the White Plan than to $23 billion under the Keynes Plan). Yet, relative to the implications of simple versions of hegemonic stability theory, a surprising number of British priorities were incorporated. One was the priority Britain attached to exchange rate flexibility. The United States initially had wished to invest the IMF with veto power over a country's decision to change its exchange rate. Subsequently it proposed that 80 percent of IMF members be required to approve any change in parity. But the Articles of Agreement permitted devaluation without Fund objection when needed to eliminate fundamental disequilibrium. Lacking any definition of this term, there was scope for devaluation by countries other than the United States to reconcile internal and external balance. Only once did the Fund treat an exchange rate change as unauthorized.[32] If countries hesitated to devalue, they did so as much for domestic reasons as for reasons related to the structure of the international monetary system.

Another British priority incorporated into the agreement was tolerance of exchange control. Originally, the White Plan obliged members to abandon all exchange restrictions within six months of ceasing hostilities or joining the IMF, whichever came first. A subsequent U.S. proposal would have required a country to eliminate all exchange controls within a year of joining the Fund. But Britain succeeded in incorporating into the Articles of Agreement a distinction between controls for capital transactions, which were permitted, and controls on current transactions, which were not. In practice, even nondiscriminatory exchange controls on current transactions were sometimes authorized under IMF Article VIII.[33] As a result of this compromise, the United States protected itself from efforts to divert sterling bloc trade toward the British market, while Britain protected itself from destabilization by overseas sterling balances.[34]

[32] Kenneth W. Dam, *The Rules of the Game: Reform and Evolution in the International Monetary System* (Chicago, 1982), p. 92.

[33] Brian Tew, *The Evolution of the International Monetary System, 1945–88*, 4th ed. (London, 1988), p. 99.

[34] Fund procedures also represented a compromise between the British preference for free access to Fund resources and the American preference for conditionality. The Articles of Agreement flatly stated that a country "shall be entitled" to buy currency from the IMF providing only that currency is needed for purposes consistent with the fund agreement. Initially it was unclear whether the Fund had legal authority to make borrowing subject to conditions. But in 1948 the IMF's Board of Executive Directors asserted its right to limit

In comparison with these concessions, British efforts to restore symmetry to the international adjustment mechanism proved unavailing. With the abandonment of the overdraft principle, the British embraced White's "scarce currency" proposal, under which the Fund was empowered to ration its supply of a scarce currency and members were authorized to impose limitations on freedom of exchange operations in that currency. Thus, a country running payments surpluses sufficiently large to threaten the Fund's ability to supply its currency might face restrictions on foreign customers' ability to purchase its exports. But the scarce currency clause had been drafted by the United States not with the principle of symmetry in mind, but in order to deal with problems of immediate postwar adjustment – specifically, the prospective dollar shortage. With the development of the Marshall Plan, the dollar shortage never achieved the severity anticipated by the authors of the scarce currency clause, and the provision was never invoked.

If the "Joint Statement by Experts on the Establishment of an International Monetary Fund," made public in April 1944, bore the imprint of the U.S. delegation to Bretton Woods, to a surprising extent it also embodied important elements of the British negotiating position. It is curious from the perspective of hegemonic stability theory that a war-battered economy – Britain – heavily dependent on the dominant economic power – America – for capital goods, financial capital, and export markets was able to extract significant concessions in the design of the international monetary system.[35] Britain was ably represented in the negotiations. But even more important, the United States also required an international agreement and wished to secure it even as hostilities in Europe prevented enemy nations from taking part in negotiations and minimized the involvement of the allies on whose territory the war was fought. The United States therefore had little opportunity to play off countries against one another or to brand as renegades

---

access to fund reserves if the member was using its resources in a manner contrary to the purposes of the organization and to make that access subject to conditions. The conditionality that evolved treated access to successive credit tranches in different ways. Whereas attempts to borrow in the gold tranche would receive "the overwhelming benefit of any doubt," access to higher tranches would be subject to increasingly stringent conditions. Horsefield, *International Monetary Fund*, vol. 3, p. 230.

35 This portrayal of Bretton Woods as neither an American triumph nor a British defeat is at variance with characterizations of it as a construct of the American hegemon. But it is not inconsistent with the view that, as a compromise between the Keynes and White Plans, it "contained less of the Keynes and more of the White plans." Sidney E. Rolfe, *Gold and World Power: The Dollar, the Pound, and the Plans for Reform* (New York, 1966), p. 78.

any that disputed the advisability of its design. As the western world's second largest economy, Britain symbolized, if it did not actually represent, the other nations of the world and was able to advance their case more effectively than if they had attempted more actively to do so themselves.

What conclusions regarding the applicability of hegemonic stability theory to the genesis of international monetary systems follow from the evidence of these three cases? In the two clearest instances of hegemony – the United Kingdom in the second half of the nineteenth century and the United States following World War II – the leading economic power significantly influenced the form of the international monetary system, by example in the first instance and by negotiation in the second. But the evidence also underscores the fact that the hegemon has been incapable of dictating the form of the monetary system. In the first instance, British example did nothing to prevent significant modifications in the form of the gold standard adopted abroad. In the second, the exceptional dominance of the U.S. economy was unable to eliminate the need to compromise with other countries in the design of the monetary system.

The operation of monetary systems and the theory of hegemonic stability

It is necessary to consider not only the genesis of monetary systems, but also how the theory of hegemonic stability applies to the operation of such systems. I consider adjustment, liquidity, and the lender of last resort function in turn.

Adjustment

Adjustment under the classical gold standard has frequently been characterized in terms compatible with hegemonic stability theory. The gold standard is portrayed as a managed system whose preservation and smooth operation were ensured through its regulation by a hegemonic power, Great Britain, and its agent, the Bank of England. In the words of Cohen, "The classical gold standard *was* a sterling standard – a hegemonic regime – in the sense that Britain not only dominated the international monetary order, establishing and maintaining the prevailing rules of the game, but also gave monetary relations whatever degree of inherent stability they possessed." [36]

---

[36] Benjamin J. Cohen, *Organizing the World's Money: The Political Economy of International Monetary Relations* (New York, 1977), p. 81 (emphasis in original).

Before 1914, London was indisputably the world's leading financial center. A large proportion of world trade – 60 percent by one estimate – was settled through payment in sterling bills, with London functioning as a clearinghouse for importers and exporters of other nations.[37] British discount houses bought bills from abroad, either directly or through the London agencies of foreign banks. Foreigners maintained balances in London to meet commitments on bills outstanding and to service British portfolio investments overseas. Foreign governments and central banks held deposits in London as interest-earning alternatives to gold reserves. Although the pound was not the only reserve currency of the pre-1914 era, sterling reserves matched the combined value of reserves denominated in other currencies. At the same time, Britain possessed perhaps £350 million of short-term capital overseas. Though it is unclear whether Britain was a net short-term debtor or creditor before the war, it is certain that a large volume of short-term funds was responsive to changes in domestic interest rates.[38]

Such changes in interest rates might have been instigated by the Bank of England. By altering the rates at which it discounted for its customers and rediscounted for the discount houses, the Bank could affect rates prevailing in the discount market.[39] But the effect of Bank Rate was not limited to the bill market. Although, in part, this reflected the exceptional integration characteristic of British financial markets, it was reinforced by institutionalization. In London, banks automatically fixed their deposit rates half a percentage point above Bank Rate. Loan rates were similarly indexed to Bank Rate but at a higher level. Though there were exceptions to these rules, changes in Bank Rate were immediately reflected in a broad range of British interest rates.

An increase in Bank Rate, by raising the general level of British interest rates, induced foreign investors to accumulate additional funds in London and to delay the repatriation or transfer of existing balances to other centers. British balances abroad were repatriated to earn the higher rate of return. Drawings of finance bills, which represented half of total bills in 1913, were similarly sensitive to changes in interest rates. Higher interest rates spread to the security market and delayed the flotation of new issues for

---

[37] David Williams, "The Evolution of the Sterling System" in C. R. Whittlesey and J. S. G. Wilson, eds., *Essays in Money and Banking in Honour of R. S. Sayers* (Oxford, 1968), p. 268.

[38] Peter H. Lindert, "Key Currencies," pp. 56–7.

[39] Of course, the Bank might have to intervene with purchases or sales of bills and bonds to render its rate effective. Sayers, *Bank of England Operations*, chap. 2.

overseas borrowers. In this way the Bank of England was able to insulate its gold reserve from disturbances in the external accounts.[40]

Because of the size of the London market and the Bank of England's leverage over the interest rates prevailing there, Bank Rate seemed to have "a controlling influence on Britain's balance of payments, regardless of what other central banks were doing." When Bank Rate was raised, Britain's external position strengthened even when "other central banks raised or lowered their discount rates along with Bank rate, as they normally did."[41] Hence the hegemonic center was rarely threatened by convertibility crises under the classical gold standard.

But why did the Bank of England's exceptional leverage not threaten convertibility abroad? The answer commonly offered is that Britain's unrivaled market power led to a de facto harmonization of national policies. As the report of the Macmillan Committee characterized the prewar situation, Britain could "by the operation of her Bank Rate almost immediately adjust her reserve position. Other countries had, therefore, in the main to adjust their conditions to hers."[42] As Keynes wrote in the *Treatise on Money,* "During the latter half of the nineteenth century the influence of London on credit conditions throughout the world was so predominant that the Bank of England could almost have claimed to be the conductor of the international orchestra."[43]

Since fiscal harmonization requires no discussion in an era of balanced budgets, the stability of the classical gold standard can be explained by the desire and ability of central banks to harmonize their monetary policies in the interest of external balance. External balance, or maintaining gold reserves adequate to defend the established gold parity, was the foremost target of monetary policy in the period preceding World War I. In the absence of a coherent theory of unemployment, much less a consensus on its relation to monetary policy, there was little pressure for central banks to accommodate domestic needs. External balance was not the sole target

---

[40] This brief account draws on Moggridge, *British Monetary Policy*, pp. 8–9.

[41] Cleveland, "International Monetary System in the Interwar Period," in Rowland, ed., *Balance of Power or Hegemony*, p. 17.

[42] Committee on Finance and Industry, *Report*, p. 125.

[43] Keynes, *Treatise*, Vol. 2, pp. 306–7. Evidence to this effect is presented by Barry Eichengreen, "Conducting the International Orchestra: Bank of England Leadership under the Classical Gold Standard," *Journal of International Money and Finance* 6 (March 1987), 5–29. Regression results reported there reveal that, although the Bank of England's discount rate was responsive to changes in French and German rates, the influence of the Bank of England rate over foreign rates was stronger and more systematic.

of policy, but when internal and external balance came into conflict, the latter took precedence.[44] Viewed from an international perspective, British leadership played a role in this process of harmonization insofar as the market power and prominence of the Bank of England served as a focal point for policy coordination.

But if the Bank of England could be sure of defeating its European counterparts when they engaged in a tug of war over short-term capital, mere harmonization of central bank policies, in the face of external disturbances, would have been insufficient to prevent convertibility crises on the Continent. The explanation for the absence of such crises would appear to be the greater market power of European countries compared with their non-European counterparts. Some observers have distinguished the market power of capital-exporting countries from the inability of capital importers to influence the direction of financial flows.[45] Others have suggested the existence of a hierarchical structure of financial markets: below the London market were the less active markets of Berlin, Paris, Vienna, Amsterdam, Brussels, Zurich, and New York, followed by the still less active markets of the Scandinavian countries, and finally the nascent markets of Latin America and other parts of the non-European world.[46] When Bank Rate was raised in London, thus redistributing reserves to Britain from other regions, compensatory discount rate increases on the Continent drew funds from the non-European world or curtailed capital outflows. De-

---

[44] As Sayers, *Central Banking after Bagehot,* p. 61, described the British case, although the Bank of England was "a little sensitive to the state of trade," in deciding whether to change Bank Rate it "looked almost exclusively at the size of its reserve." An extensive literature analyzes the extent to which central banks of the classical gold standard era adhered to the rules of the game, which dictated that they should adjust their policies in order to bring about external balance. In a classic study, Bloomfield (*Monetary Policy under the International Gold Standard*) revealed that external considerations were by no means the sole determinant of monetary policies before 1913. But if central banks were in fact responsive to internal considerations, this raises the question of how they managed to defend their gold standard parities. A more recent study emphasizes the distinction between short-run and long-run policy responses and concludes that in the short run the Bank of England may have hesitated to take the steps needed to restore external balance and neutralize gold outflows, but in the long run the goal of maintaining the gold standard dominated, leading the Bank to reverse its initial sterlization of gold flows to ensure that external balance would be restored. See Pippenger, "Bank of England Operations."

[45] See A. G. Ford, *The Gold Standard, 1880–1914: Britain and Argentina* (Oxford, 1962); and Robert Triffin, "The Evolution of the International Monetary System: Historical Reappraisal and Future Perspectives," *Princeton Studies in International Finance,* no. 12 (June, 1964).

[46] See, for example, Cohen, *Future of Sterling as an International Currency.*

veloping countries, due to either the thinness of markets or the absence of relevant institutions, were unable to prevent these events. In times of crisis, therefore, convertibility was threatened primarily outside Europe and North America. If Britain and Europe managed the system, they did so "partly at the expense of its weakest members." [47]

Thus, insofar as hegemony played some role in the efficiency of the adjustment mechanism, it was not the British hegemony of which so much has been written but the collective hegemony of the European center relative to the non-European periphery. Not only does this case challenge the concept of the hegemon, therefore, but because the stability of the classical gold standard was enjoyed exclusively by the countries of the center, it supports only the weak form of hegemonic stability theory – that the benefits of stability accrued exclusively to the powerful. [48]

The relation between hegemonic power and the need for policy harmonization is equally relevant to the case of the interwar gold exchange standard. One interpretation of Nevin's argument that "the existence of more than one center . . . [led] to the existence of more than one policy" is that in the absence of a hegemon there was no focal point for policy, which interfered with efforts at coordination. [49] But more important than a declining ability to harmonize policies may have been a diminished desire to do so. Although the advent of explicit stabilization policy was not to occur until the 1930s and 1940s, during the 1920s central banks placed increasing weight on internal conditions when formulating monetary policy. [50] The rise of socialism and the example of the Bolshevik revolution in particular provided a counterweight to central bankers' instinctive wish to base policy

[47] Fred Hirsch, *Money International* (London, 1967), p. 28.

[48] As I indicated at the beginning of this chapter, I define the strong form of hegemonic stability theory as the benefits of stability accruing to both the hegemon and other countries and the weak form as benefits accruing only to the hegemon. It is tempting to suggest a parallel between this "collective hegemony of the center countries" and the argument by Joanne Gowa, which she attributes to Keohane and Snidal, that even in the absence of a hegemon the public good of collective stability might still be provided so long as the number of countries is sufficiently small for them to solve the free-rider problem. See Gowa, "Hegemons, IOs, and Markets." But the case considered here differs in that instability, rather than being eliminated, is shifted onto countries that are not members of the hegemonic cartel.

[49] Edward Nevin, *The Mechanism of Cheap Money: A Study of British Monetary Policy, 1931–1939* (Cardiff, 1955), p. 12.

[50] On the United States, see Wicker, *Federal Reserve Monetary Policy*. On the United Kingdom, see Chapter 4. A general discussion of the growing conflict between the needs of internal and external balance is provided by Beyen, *Money in a Maelstrom*, chap. 2.

solely on external conditions. External adjustment was rendered difficult by policymakers' increasing hesitancy to sacrifice other objectives on the altar of external balance. Britain's balance-of-payments problems, for example, cannot be attributed to "the existence of more than one policy" in the world economy without considering also a domestic unemployment problem that placed pressure on the Bank of England to resist restrictive measures that might have strengthened the external accounts at the expense of industry and trade.

Under Bretton Woods, the problem of adjustment was exacerbated by the difficulty of using exchange rate changes to restore external balance. Hesitancy to change their exchange rates posed few problems for countries in surplus. However, those in deficit had to choose between aggravating unemployment and tolerating external deficits; the latter was infeasible in the long run and promoted an increase in the volume of short-term capital that moved in response to anticipations of devaluation. Although the IMF charter did not encourage devaluation, the hesitancy of deficit countries to employ this option is easier to ascribe to the governments' tendency to attach their prestige to the stability of established exchange rates than to U.S. hegemony, however defined. Where the singular role of the United States was important was in precluding a dollar devaluation. A possible solution to the problem of U.S. deficits, one that would not have threatened other countries' ability to accumulate reserves, was an increase in the dollar price of gold, that is, a dollar devaluation.[51] It is sometimes argued that the United States was incapable of adjusting through exchange rate changes since other countries would have devalued in response to prevent any change in bilateral rates against the dollar. However, raising the dollar price of gold would have increased the dollar value of monetary gold, reducing the global excess demand for reserves and encouraging other countries to increase domestic demand and cut back on their balance-of-payments surpluses. But although a rise in the price of gold might have alleviated central banks' immediate dependence on dollars, it would have done nothing to prevent the problem from recurring. It would also have promoted skepticism about the U.S. government's commitment to the new

[51] This was advocated by, among others, Milton Gilbert, "The Gold-Dollar System: Conditions of Equilibrium and the Price of Gold," reprinted in Eichengreen, ed., *Gold Standard in Theory and History*, pp. 229–49; and Roy Harrod, "Triple the Dollar Price of Gold," reprinted in Gerald M. Meier, ed., *Problems of a World Monetary Order*, 2d ed. (New York, 1982), pp. 107–8.

gold price, thereby encouraging other countries to increase their demands for gold and advancing the date of future difficulties.

Does this evidence on adjustment support hegemonic theories of international monetary stability? The contrast between the apparently smooth adjustment under the classical gold standard and Bretton Woods and the adjustment difficulties of the interwar years suggests that a dominant power's policies served as a fixed target that was easier to hit than a moving one. As in Luce and Raiffa's "battle of the sexes" game, what mattered was not so much the particular stance of monetary policy but that the leading players settled on the same stance.[52] The argument, advanced by Snidal in a similar context, is that a dominant player is best placed to signal the other players the nature of the most probable stance.[53] The effectiveness of the adjustment mechanism under the two regimes reflected not just British and American market power but also the existence of an international consensus on the objectives and formulation of monetary policy that permitted central bank policies to be harmonized. The essential role of Britain before 1914 and the United States after 1944 was not so much to force other countries to alter their policies as to provide a focal point for policy harmonization.

Liquidity

Under the classical gold standard, the principal source of liquidity was newly mined gold. It is hard to see how British dominance of international markets could have much influenced the changes in the world price level and mining technology upon which these supplies depended. As argued previously, where Britain's prominence mattered was in facilitating the provision of supplementary liquidity in the form of sterling reserves, which grew at an accelerating rate starting in the 1890s. It is conceivable, therefore, that in the absence of British hegemony a reserve shortage would have developed and the classical gold standard would have exhibited a deflationary bias.

Liquidity was an issue of more concern under the interwar gold exchange standard. Between 1915 and 1925, prices rose worldwide due to the in-

---

[52] See R. Duncan Luce and Howard Raiffa, *Games and Decisions: Introduction and Critical Survey* (New York, 1957).

[53] This problem is referred to as a "coordination game," by Duncan Snidal, "Coordination versus Prisoners' Dilemma: Implications for International Cooperation and Regimes," *American Political Science Review* 79 (December 1985), 923–42.

flation associated with wartime finance and postwar reconstruction; these rising prices combined with economic growth to increase the transactions demand for money. Yet, under a system of convertible currencies, world money supply was constrained by the availability of reserves. Statutory restrictions required central banks to back their money supplies with eligible reserves, while recent experience with inflation deterred politicians from liberalizing the statutes. The output of newly mined gold had been depressed since the beginning of World War I, and experts offered pessimistic forecasts of future supplies. Increasing the real value of world gold reserves by forcing a reduction in the world price level would only add to the difficulties of an already troubled world economy. Countries were encouraged, therefore, to stabilize on a gold exchange basis to prevent the development of a gold shortage.

There are difficulties with this explanation of interwar liquidity problems, which emphasizes a shortage of gold.[54] For one, the danger of a gold shortage constraining the volume of transactions was alleviated by the all but complete withdrawal of gold coin from circulation during the war. As a result, the percentage of short-term liabilities of all central banks backed by gold was little different in 1928 than its level in 1913, whereas the volume of the liabilities backed by that gold stock was considerably increased. It is hard to see why a gold shortage, after having exhibited only weak effects in previous years, should have had such a dramatic impact starting in 1929. It is even less clear how the absence of a hegemon contributed to the purported gold shortage. The obvious linkages between hegemony and the provision of liquidity work in the wrong direction. The straightforward way of increasing the monetary value of reserves was to have a round of currency devaluation, which would revalue gold reserves and, by raising the real price of gold, increase the output of the mining industry. As demonstrated in 1931, when the pound's depreciation set off a round of competitive devaluations, sterling remained the linchpin of the international currency system; the only way a round of currency devaluation could have taken place, therefore, was if Britain had stabilized in 1925 at a lower level. But had its dominance of the international economy not eroded over the first quarter of the twentieth century, the political pressure on Britain to return to gold at the prewar parity would have been increased rather

---

[54] The leading exponent of the gold shortage explanation was Gustav Cassel. For a summary of his views, see Cassel, *Crisis in the World's Monetary System;* and for a critical perspective, Hardy, *Enough Gold?*

than reduced.[55] It seems unlikely, therefore, that a more successful maintenance of British hegemony, ceteris paribus, would have alleviated any gold
shortage.

An alternative and more appealing explanation for interwar liquidity
problems emphasizes mismanagement of gold reserves rather than their
overall insufficiency. It blames France and the United States for absorbing
disproportionate shares of global gold supplies and for imposing deflation
on the rest of the world.[56] Between 1928 and 1932, French gold reserves
rose from $1.25 billion to $3.26 billion of constant gold content, or from 13
to 28 percent of the world total. Meanwhile, the United States, which had
released gold between 1924 and 1928, facilitating the reestablishment of
convertibility in other countries, reversed its position and imported $1.49
billion of gold between 1928 and 1930. By the end of 1932 the United
States and France together possessed nearly 63 percent of the world's central monetary gold. The British Macmillan Committee attributed to this
maldistribution of gold "a large measure of responsibility for the heavy fall
in prices in recent years." [57]

The maldistribution of reserves can be understood by focusing on the
systematic interaction of central banks. This approach builds on the literature that characterizes the interwar gold standard as a competitive struggle
for gold between countries that viewed the size of their gold reserves as a
measure of national prestige and as insurance against financial instability.[58]
France and the United States, in particular, but gold standard countries in
general, repeatedly raised their discount rates relative to one another in
efforts to attract gold from abroad. By leading to the accumulation of excess

---

[55] The most compelling argument for returning to gold cited the importance of the prewar
parity for the maintenance of Britain's position in international transactions – specifically,
its importance for maintaining London's preeminent position in international finance. See
Moggridge, *Return to Gold.*

[56] Gold inflows into France can be attributed to stabilization of the franc at an undervalued
rate in 1926 in conjunction with statutory limitations that prevented the Banque de France
from expanding the domestic credit component of the money supply through open market
operations. Inflows into the United States can be attributed to the misguided policies of
the Federal Reserve: initially, its failure to moderate the Wall Street boom responsible for
curtailing U.S. foreign investment and for inducing capital inflows into the United States;
and subsequently, its failure to prevent the contraction of the money supply, which created
an excess demand for money that could be met only by gold inflows. On French policy,
see Chapter 5. On the controversy over U.S. policy, see Friedman and Schwartz, *Monetary
History;* and Wicker, *Federal Reserve Monetary Policy, 1917–1933.*

[57] Committee on Finance and Industry, *Report.*

[58] See Eichengreen, "Central Bank Cooperation"; and Chapter 6.

reserves, these restrictive policies exacerbated the problem of inadequate liquidity, but by offsetting one another they also failed to achieve their objective of attracting gold from abroad. As Keynes explained, "what helps each [central bank] is not a high Bank rate but a higher rate than the others. So that a raising of rates all round helps no one until, after an interregnum during which the economic activity of the whole world has been retarded, prices and wages have been forced to a lower level." [59]

The origins of this competitive struggle for gold are popularly attributed to the absence of a hegemon. The competing financial centers – London, Paris, and New York – worked at cross-purposes because, in contrast to the preceding period, no one central bank was sufficiently powerful to call the tune.[60] Before the war, the Bank of England had been sufficiently dominant to act as a leader, setting its discount rate with the reaction of other central banks in mind, while other central banks responded in the manner of a competitive fringe. By using this power to defend the gold parity of sterling despite the maintenance of slender reserves, the Bank prevented the development of a competitive scramble for gold. But after World War I, with the United States unwilling to accept responsibility for leadership, no one central bank formulated its monetary policy with foreign reactions and global conditions in mind, and the noncooperative struggle for gold was the result.[61] In this interpretation of the interwar liquidity problem, hegemony – or, more precisely, its absence – plays a critical role.

In discussing the provision of liquidity under Bretton Woods, it is critical to distinguish the decade ending in 1958 – when the convertibility of European currencies was restored and before which U.S. dominance of international trade, foreign lending, and industrial production was unrivaled – from the decade that followed. In the first period, the most important source of incremental liquidity was dollar reserves. Between 1949 and 1958, when global reserves rose by 29 percent, less than one-third of the increment took the form of gold and one-fifteenth was in quotas at the IMF. The role of sterling as a reserve currency was limited almost exclusively to Commonwealth members and former British colonies that had traditionally

[59] Keynes, "Is There Enough Gold?"
[60] Viner, "International Aspects of the Gold Standard," p. 28; and Gayer, *Monetary Policy and Economic Stabilisation*, p. 29.
[61] As one Bank of England official put it, "such leadership as we possessed has certainly been affected by the position which America has gained." Macmillan Committee evidence of Sir Ernest Harvey, reprinted in Sayers, *Bank of England, 1891–1944*, Vol. 3, p. 206.

held reserves in London and traded heavily with Britain. Consequently, the accumulation of dollar balances accounted for roughly half of incremental liquidity in the first decade of Bretton Woods.

In one sense, U.S. dominance of international markets facilitated the provision of liquidity. At the end of World War II, the United States had amassed 60 percent of the world's gold stock; at $35 an ounce, this was worth six times the value of the official dollar claims accumulated by foreign governments by 1949. There was little immediate question, given U.S. dominance of global gold reserves, of the stability of the gold price of the dollar and hence little hesitation to accumulate incremental liquidity in the form of dollar claims. But in another sense, U.S. international economic power in the immediate postwar years impeded the supply of liquidity to the world economy. Wartime destruction of industry in Europe and Japan left U.S. manufactured exports highly competitive in world markets and rendered Europe dependent on U.S. capital goods for industrial reconstruction. The persistent excess demand for U.S. goods tended to push the U.S. balance of payments into surplus, creating the famous "dollar shortage" of the immediate postwar years. Although U.S. hegemony left other countries willing to hold dollar claims, it rendered them extremely difficult to obtain.

Various policies were initiated in response to the dollar shortage, including discrimination against dollar area exports, special incentives for European and Japanese exports to the United States, and a round of European currency devaluations starting in September 1949. Ultimately the solution took the form of two sharply contrasting actions by the hegemon: Marshall Plan grants of $11.6 billion between mid-1948 and mid-1952, and Korean War expenditures. Largely as a result of these two factors, U.S. trade surpluses shrank from $10.1 billion in 1947 to $2.6 billion in 1952; more important, U.S. government grants and private capital outflows exceeded the surplus on current account. By 1950 the U.S. balance of payments was in deficit and, after moving back into surplus in 1951–52, deficits returned to stay. Insofar as its singular economic power encouraged the United States to undertake both the Marshall Plan and the Korean War, hegemony played a significant role in both the form and adequacy of the liquidity provided in the first decade of Bretton Woods.

Between 1958 and 1969, global reserves grew more rapidly, by 51 percent, than they had in the first decade of Bretton Woods. Again, gold was a minor share of the increment, about one-twentieth, and IMF quotas were one-eighth. While foreign exchange reserves again provided roughly half,

Eurodollars and other foreign currencies grew in importance; their contribution actually exceeded that of official claims on the United States.[62] In part these trends reflected rapid growth in Europe and Japan. More important, they reflected the fact that starting in 1965 the value of foreign government claims on the United States exceeded U.S. gold reserves. Prudence dictated that foreign governments diversify their reserve positions out of dollars.

The role of U.S. hegemony in the provision of liquidity during this second decade has been much debated. The growth of liquidity reflected both supply and demand pressure: both demands by other countries for additional reserves, which translated into balance-of-payments surpluses, and the capacity of the United States to consume more than it produced by running balance-of-payments deficits financed by the willingness of other countries to accumulate dollar reserves. The United States was criticized sharply, mainly by the French, for exporting inflation and for financing purchases of foreign companies and pursuit of the Vietnam War through the balance of payments.[63] Although these complaints cannot be dismissed, it is incorrect to conclude that the dollar's singular position in the Bretton Woods system permitted the United States to run whatever balance-of-payments deficit it wished.[64] Moreover, it is difficult to envisage an alternative scenario in which the U.S. balance of payments was zero but the world was not starved of liquidity. Owing to the sheer size of the American economy, new claims on the United States continued to exceed vastly new claims on any other nation. Moreover, U.S. economic, military, and diplomatic influence did much to encourage if not compel other countries to maintain their holdings of dollar claims. Thus U.S. dominance of inter-

---

62 Statistics are drawn from IMF publications, notably the *Annual Reports*.

63 The evidence typically invoked is that the Johnson administration financed the Vietnam War without a tax increase until 1968, and that except for 1969 monetary policy was expansionary over much of the period.

64 The size of the deficit, if not its existence, served as a significant constraint on policy. For example, when the dollar price of gold on the London market rose above the U.S. Treasury's selling price in 1960, inducing foreign monetary authorities to purchase substantial amounts of U.S. gold, the Eisenhower administration responded by reducing the number of military dependents abroad, cutting back foreign Defense Department procurement, and tying U.S. development assistance to American exports. Restrictions on capital outflows, including the interest equalization tax, the voluntary foreign credit restraint program, and the foreign direct investment program, were imposed starting in 1963. As Tew, *The Evolution of the International Monetary System, 1945–88*, put it, U.S. authorities "were not conspicuously less ready than those of other deficit countries to adopt measures to prevent [the deficit] getting worse" (p. 71).

national markets played a critical role in resolving the liquidity crisis of the 1960s.[65]

The distinguishing feature of Bretton Woods is not that other countries continued to hold dollar reserves in the face of exchange rate uncertainty and economic growth abroad, for neither development has deterred them from holding dollars under the flexible exchange rate regime of the 1970s and 1980s. Rather, it is that they continued to hold dollar reserves in the face of a one-way bet resulting from dollar convertibility at a fixed price when the dollar price of gold seemed poised to rise. In part, the importance of American foreign investments and the size of the U.S. market for European exports caused other countries to hesitate before cashing in their chips. Yet foreign governments also saw dollar convertibility as essential to the defense of the gold-dollar system and viewed the fixed exchange rates of that system as an international public good worthy of defense. Not until 1965 did the French government decide to convert into gold some $300 million of its dollar holdings and subsequently to step up its monthly gold purchases from the United States. But when pressure on U.S. gold reserves mounted following the 1967 devaluation of sterling, other countries, including France, sold gold instead of capitalizing on the one-way bet. They joined the United States in the formation of a gold pool whose purpose was to sell a sufficient quantity of gold to defend the official price. Between sterling's devaluation in 1967 and the closure of the gold market on March 15, 1968, the pool sold $3 billion of gold, of which U.S. sales were $2.2 billion. France purchased no gold in 1967 or 1968, presumably due in part to foreign pressure.[66] U.S. leverage undoubtedly contributed to their decisions. But a plausible interpretation of these events is that foreign governments, rather than simply being coerced into support of the dollar by U.S. economic power, were willing to take limited steps to defend the international public good of a fixed exchange rate system defined in terms of the dollar price of gold.

What does this discussion imply for the role of hegemony in the provi-

---

65 The most notable instance of the use of U.S. power – clearly an illustration of the stick variant of hegemonic stability theory – was in 1967 when Germany explicitly agreed to forgo any future conversions of dollars into U.S. gold in response to American threats to reduce troop levels in Europe. See Bergsten, *Toward a New International Economic Order*, chap. 4.

66 The world was reminded of the difficulties posed by the free-rider problem confronting efforts to supply a public good when Algeria purchased $150 million of gold from the United States in 1967, "presumably at French instigation." Robert Solomon, *The International Monetary System, 1945–1976: An Insider's View* (New York, 1977), p. 115.

sion of international liquidity? The strongest evidence for the importance of a hegemon is negative evidence from the interwar years, when the absence of a hegemon and the failure of competing financial centers to coordinate their policies effectively contributed greatly to the liquidity shortage. In other periods, when a dominant economic power was present, it is difficult to credit that power with sole responsibility for ensuring the adequate provision of liquidity. Under the gold standard, the principal source of incremental liquidity was newly mined gold; Britain contributed to the provision of liquidity only insofar as its financial stature encouraged other countries to augment their specie holdings with sterling reserves. After World War II, U.S. economic power similarly rendered dollars a desirable form in which to acquire liquid reserves, but the same factors that made dollars desirable also rendered them difficult to obtain.

The lender of last resort

If adjustment were always accomplished smoothly and liquidity were consistently adequate, there would be no need for an international lender of last resort to stabilize the international monetary system. Yet countries' capacity to adjust and the system's ability to provide liquidity may be inadequate to accommodate disturbances to confidence. Like domestic banking systems, an international financial system based on convertibility is vulnerable to problems of confidence that threaten to ignite speculative runs. Like depositors who rush to close their accounts upon receiving the news of a neighboring bank failure, exchange market participants, upon hearing of a convertibility crisis abroad, may rush to liquidate their foreign exchange balance because of incomplete information about the liabilities and intentions of particular governments. This analogy leads Charles Kindleberger, for example, to adopt from the domestic central banking literature the notion that a lender of last resort is needed to discount in times of crisis, provide countercyclical long-term lending, and maintain an open market for distress goods, and to suggest that, in the absence of a supranational institution, only a hegemonic power can carry out this international lender-of-last-resort function on the requisite scale.[67]

Of the episodes considered here, the early Bretton Woods era provides the clearest illustration of the benefits of an international lender of last re-

---

[67] See Kindleberger, *World in Depression;* and Kindleberger, *Manias, Panics, and Crashes: A History of Financial Crises* (New York, 1978).

sort. The large amount of credit provided Europe in the form of grants and long-term loans and the willingness of the United States to accept European and Japanese exports even when these had been promoted by the extension of special incentives illustrate two of the lender-of-last-resort functions identified by Kindleberger: countercyclical lending and provision of an open market for distress goods. Many histories of the Marshall Plan characterize it in terms consistent with the benevolent strand of hegemonic stability theory: the United States was mainly interested in European prosperity and stood to benefit only insofar as that prosperity promoted geopolitical stability. Revisionist histories have more in common with the coercive strand of hegemonic stability theory: they suggest that the United States used Marshall aid to exact concessions from Europe in the form of most-favored-nation status for Germany, IMF exchange rate oversight, and Swiss links with the Organization for European Economic Cooperation.[68] Although it is certain that the European countries could not have moved so quickly to relax capital controls and quantitative trade restrictions without these forms of U.S. assistance, it is not clear how far the argument can be generalized. The Marshall Plan coincided with a very special era in the history of the international monetary system, in which convertibility outside the United States had not yet been restored. Hence there was little role for the central function of the lender of last resort: discounting freely when a convertibility crisis threatens.[69] When convertibility was threatened in the 1960s, rescue operations were mounted not by the United States but cooperatively by the Group of Ten.

Kindleberger has argued that the 1929–31 financial crisis might have been avoided by the intervention of an international lender of last resort. The unwillingness of Britain and the United States to engage in countercyclical long-term lending and to provide an open market for distress goods surely exacerbated convertibility crises in the non-European world. Both the curtailment of overseas lending and the imposition of restrictive trade policies contributed greatly to the balance-of-payments difficulties that led to the suspension of convertibility by primary producers as early as 1929.[70]

[68] See the discussion in Alan S. Milward, *The Reconstruction of Western Europe, 1945–51* (London, 1984), pp. 113–25.

[69] The notable exception to this generalization is the abortive attempt to restore sterling convertibility in 1947, which was taken at the hegemon's insistence and failed in part because the United States was unwilling to supply the funds needed to defend sterling. See Cairncross and Eichengreen, *Sterling in Decline*, chap. 4; and Milward, *Reconstruction of Western Europe*, chap. 1.

[70] The links among foreign lending, foreign trade, and currency convertibility in this period

Gold movements from the periphery to London and New York in 1930 heightened the problem and hastened its spread to Central Europe.

But it is not obvious that additional U.S. loans to Britain and other European countries attempting to fend off threats to convertibility would have succeeded in altering significantly the course of the 1931 financial crisis. Heading off the crisis would have required a successful defense of the pound sterling, whose depreciation was followed almost immediately by purposeful devaluation in some two dozen other countries. Britain did succeed in obtaining a substantial amount of short-term credit abroad in support of the pound, raising $650 million in New York and Paris after only minimal delay. Total short-term lending to countries under pressure amounted to approximately $1 billion, or roughly 10 percent of total international short-term indebtedness and 5 percent of world imports (more than the ratio of total IMF quotas to world imports in the mid-1970s).[71] It is noteworthy that these credits were obtained not from a dominant power but from a coalition of creditor countries.

Could additional short-term credits from an international lender of last resort have prevented Britain's suspension of convertibility? If the run on sterling reflected merely a temporary loss of confidence in the stability of fixed parities, then additional loans from an international lender of last resort – like central bank loans to temporarily illiquid banks – might have permitted the crisis to be surmounted. But if the loss of confidence had a basis in economic fundamentals, no amount of short-term lending would have done more than delay the crisis in the absence of measures to eliminate the underlying imbalance. The existence of an international lender of last resort could have affected the timing but not the fact of collapse.

The fundamental disequilibrium that undermined confidence in sterling is typically sought in the government budget. The argument is that by stimulating absorption, Britain's budget deficit, in conjunction with the collapse of foreign demand for British exports, weakened the balance of trade. Although the second Labour government fell in 1931 precisely because of its failure to agree on measures to reduce the size of the budget deficit, historians disagree over whether the budget contributed significantly to the

are analyzed by Barry Eichengreen and Richard Portes, "The Anatomy of Financial Crises," in Richard Portes and Alexander K. Swoboda, eds., *Threats to International Financial Stability* (Cambridge, 1987), pp. 10–58.

71 These calculations are drawn from Donald E. Moggridge, "Financial Crises and Lenders of Last Resort: Policy in the Crisis of 1920 and 1929," *Journal of European Economic History* 10 (1981), p. 66.

balance-of-payments deficit.[72] The trade balance, after all, was only one component of the balance of payments. The effect on the balance of payments of shocks to the trade balance appears to have been small compared with the Bank of England's capacity to attract short-term capital. If this is correct and the 1931 financial crisis in Britain reflected mainly a temporary loss of confidence in sterling rather than a fundamental disequilibrium, then additional short-term loans from the United States or a group of creditor countries might have succeeded in tiding Britain over the crisis. But the loans required would have been extremely large by the standards of either the pre–1914 period of British hegemony or the post-1944 period of U.S. dominance.

The international lender-of-last-resort argument is more difficult to apply to the classical gold standard. Cohen asserts that the three lender-of-last-resort functions identified by Kindleberger – maintaining an open market, providing countercyclical foreign lending, and discounting freely in times of crisis – were practiced by Britain before 1913.[73] But, according to Moggridge, Kindleberger argues the opposite: that under the classical gold standard certain international crises, such as that of 1873, were rendered severe by the absence of an international lender of last resort.[74] On my reading, Kindleberger's views are more circumspect. He examines whether international loans were solicited and whether their extension might have moderated the 1873 crisis. But he notes that in 1873, as in 1890 and 1907, the hegemonic monetary authority, the Bank of England, would have been the "borrower of last resort" rather than the lender. These facts might be reconciled with the theory of hegemonic stability if the lender, Paris, is elevated to the status of a hegemonic financial center – a possibility to which Kindleberger is led by his analysis of late nineteenth century financial crises. But elevating Paris to parity with London would do much to undermine the view of the classical gold standard that attributes its durability to management by a single financial center.

What does this historical analysis of the lender-of-last-resort function imply for the validity of hegemonic theories of international monetary stability? It confirms that there have been instances, notably in the aftermath of World War II, when the economic power of the leading country so

---

72 Moggridge, "The 1931 Financial Crisis," argues yes, whereas Cairncross and Eichengreen, *Sterling in Decline*, argue no, largely on the basis of econometric simulations.

73 Cohen, *Organizing the World's Money*, pp. 81–2.

74 Moggridge, "Financial Crises and Lenders of Last Resort," p. 49, citing Kindleberger, *Manias, Panics, and Crashes*, p. 188.

greatly surpassed that of all rivals that it succeeded in ensuring the system's stability in times of crisis by discounting freely, providing countercyclical lending, and maintaining an open market. It suggests, at the same time, that such instances are rare. For a leading economic power to effectively act as lender of last resort, not only must its market power exceed that of all rivals, but it must do so by a very substantial margin. British economic power in the 1870s and U.S. economic power in the 1960s were inadequate in this regard, and other economic powers – France, in the first instance, the Group of Ten, in the second – were needed to cooperate in providing lender-of-last-resort facilities.

The dynamics of hegemonic decline

Might an international monetary system that depends for its smooth operation on the dominance of a hegemonic power be dynamically unstable? There are two channels through which dynamic instability might operate: the system itself might evolve in directions that attenuate the hegemon's stabilizing capacity; or the system might remain the same, but its operation might influence relative rates of economic growth in such a way as to progressively reduce the economic power and, by implication, the stabilizing capacity of the hegemon.[75]

The hypothesis that the Bretton Woods System was dynamically unstable was mooted by Robert Triffin as early as 1947.[76] Triffin focused on what he saw as inevitable changes in the composition of reserves, arguing that the system's viability hinged on the willingness of foreign governments to accumulate dollars, which depended in turn on confidence in the maintenance of dollar convertibility. Although gold dominated the dollar as a source of international liquidity (in 1958 the value of gold reserves was four times the value of dollar reserves when all countries were considered, two times when the United States was excluded), dollars were the main source of liquidity on the margin. Yet the willingness of foreign governments to accumulate dollars at the required pace and hence the stability of the gold-dollar

---

[75] After writing this section, I discovered its resemblance, both in general and in its particular emphasis on the role of foreign investment, to Gilpin, *U.S. Power and the Multinational Corporation*.

[76] See Robert Triffin, "National Central Banking and the International Economy," in *Postwar Economic Studies*, vol. 7 (Washington, DC: Board of Governors of the Federal Reserve System, 1947); Robert Triffin, *Gold and the Dollar Crisis: The Future of Convertibility* (New Haven, CT, 1960), pp. 46–81; and Peter B. Kenen, *British Monetary Policy and the Balance of Payments*.

system were predicated on America's commitment and capacity to maintain the convertibility of dollars into gold at $35 an ounce. The threat to its
ability to do so was that, under a system in which reserves could take the
form of either dollars or gold (a scarce natural resource whose supply was
insufficiently elastic to keep pace with the demand for liquidity), the share
of dollars in total reserves could only increase. An ever-growing volume
of foreign dollar liabilities was based on a fixed, or even shrinking, U.S.
gold reserve. Thus the very structure of Bretton Woods – specifically, the
monetary role for gold – progressively undermined the hegemon's capacity
to ensure the system's smooth operation through the provision of adequate
liquidity.[77]

Dynamic instability also could have operated through the effect of the
international monetary system on the relative rates of growth of the U.S.
and foreign economies. If the dollar was systematically overvalued for a
significant portion of the Bretton Woods era, this could have reduced the
competitiveness of U.S. exports and stimulated foreign penetration of U.S.
markets. If the dollar was overvalued due to some combination of European devaluations at the beginning of the 1950s, subsequent devaluations
by developing countries, and the inability of the United States to respond
to competitive difficulties by altering its exchange rate, how might this
have depressed the relative rate of growth of the U.S. economy, leading
to hegemonic decline? One can think of two arguments: one that proceeds
along Heckscher-Ohlin lines, another that draws on dynamic theories of
international trade.

The Heckscher-Ohlin hypothesis builds on the observation that the United
States was relatively abundant in human and physical capital. Since, under
Heckscher-Ohlin assumptions, U.S. exports were capital intensive, any
measure that depressed exports would have reduced the rate of return. Reducing the rate of return would have discouraged investment, depressing

---

[77] See Triffin, *Gold and the Dollar Crisis*. For a conventional view of the dollar shortage and
glut, see Donald MacDougall, "The Dollar Problem: A Reappraisal," *Essays in International Finance*, no. 35 (Princeton University, Department of Economics, November 1960).
Ironically, it was the hegemonic power – the United States – that had insisted on retaining a monetary role for gold at Bretton Woods. The British would have preferred to free
themselves from dependence on yellow metal, so long as the clearing union rather than
the United States regulated the creation of reserves. But the United States was suspicious
that the clearing union might be an engine of inflation and hesitated to demonetize gold
just when it had accumulated a majority of world stocks. Given U.S. opposition to British
plans for the large-scale creation of liquidity by the clearing union, the British had to settle
for restraints on U.S. ability to unilaterally determine global liquidity in the form of a
monetary role for gold.

the rate of economic growth and accelerating the U.S. economy's relative decline.

The dynamic trade theory hypothesis builds on the existence of learning curves in the production of traded goods. If production costs fall with cumulative output and the benefits of learning are external to the firm but internal to domestic industry, then exchange rate overvaluation, by depressing the competitiveness of exports, will inhibit their production and reduce the benefits of learning.[78] If overvaluation is sufficiently large and persistent, it will shift comparative advantage in production to foreign competitors. The weakness of this hypothesis is that it is predicated on the unsubstantiated assumption that learning effects are more important in the production of traded goods than nontraded goods. Its strength lies in the extent to which it conforms with informal characterizations of recent trends.

Precisely the same arguments have been applied to the downfall of the interwar gold exchange standard. The interwar system, which depended for liquidity on gold, dollars, and sterling, was if anything even more susceptible than its post–World War II analog to destabilization by the operation of Gresham's Law. As noted above, the legacy of the Genoa Conference encouraged central banks to accumulate foreign exchange. Promoting the use of exchange reserves while attempting to maintain gold convertibility threatened the system's stability for the same reasons as under Bretton Woods. But because foreign exchange reserves were not then concentrated in a single currency to the same extent as after World War II, it was even easier under the interwar system for central banks to liquidate foreign balances in response to any event that undermined confidence in sterling or the dollar. Instead of initiating the relatively costly and complex process of acquiring gold from foreign monetary authorities in the face of at least moral suasion to refrain, central banks needed only to swap one reserve currency for the other on the open market. Gresham's Law operated even more powerfully when gold coexisted with two reserve currencies than with one.[79]

This instability manifested itself when the 1931 financial crisis, by under-

---

[78] See Paul Krugman, "The Narrow Moving Band, the Dutch Disease, and the Competitive Consequences of Mrs. Thatcher: Notes on Trade in the Presence of Dynamic Scale Economics," *Journal of Development Economics* 27 (October 1987), 41–55; and Krugman, "Market Access and International Competition in High Technology: A Simulation Exercise," Massachusetts Institute of Technology, Department of Economics, 1985.

[79] The same argument is advanced by Bergsten, *Toward a New International Economic Order*, chap. 4, although he suggests that the existence of a well-defined institutional framework can minimize this source of instability.

mining faith in sterling convertibility, induced a large-scale shift out of London balances. Once Britain was forced to devalue, faith in the stability of the other major reserve currency was shaken, and speculative pressure shifted to the dollar. The National Bank of Belgium, which had lost 25 percent of the value of its sterling reserve as a result of Britain's devaluation, moved to liquidate its dollar balances. The Eastern European countries, including Poland, Czechoslovakia, and Bulgaria, then liquidated their deposits in New York. Between the end of 1930 and the end of 1931, the share of foreign exchange in the reserve portfolios of twenty-four European countries fell from 35 to 19 percent, signaling the demise of the exchange portion of the gold exchange standard.

The argument that structuring the international monetary system around a reserve asset provided by the leading economic power led eventually to that country's loss of preeminence has been applied even more frequently to Britain after World War I than to the United States after World War II. Because the gold exchange standard created a foreign demand for sterling balances, Britain was able to run larger trade balance deficits than would have been permitted otherwise. In a sense, Britain's reserve currency status was one of the factors that facilitated the restoration of sterling's prewar parity. Despite an enormous literature predicated on the view that the pound was overvalued at $4.86, there remains skepticism that the extent of overvaluation was great or that the effect on the macroeconomy was significant.[80] Though it is not possible to resolve this debate here, the point relevant to the theory of hegemonic stability is that evidence of reserve currency overvaluation is as substantial in the earlier period, when hegemony was threatened, as in the later period, when it was triumphant.

Of the three monetary systems considered here, the classical gold standard is the most difficult to analyze in terms of the dynamics of hegemonic decline. It might be argued that the pound was overvalued for at least a decade before 1913 and that Britain's failure to devalue resulted in sluggish growth, which accelerated the economy's hegemonic decline.[81] The com-

---

[80] See John Maynard Keynes, "Is Sterling Over-Valued?" in Moggridge, ed., *Collected Writings of John Maynard Keynes: Activities, 1922–1929: The Return to Gold and Industrial Policy,* pt. 1, pp. 349–54. See also John Maynard Keynes, *The Economic Consequences of Sterling Parity* (New York, 1923). A reassessment of Keynes's evidence is in Moggridge, *Return to Gold.*

[81] See R. C. O. Matthews, C. H. Feinstein, and J. C. Odling-Smee, *British Economic Growth, 1856–1973* (Stanford, 1982), pp. 455, 526. N. F. R. Crafts, following James Foreman-Peck, suggests that learning by doing and its associated externalities were particularly important in the new traded-goods industries of the turn of the century, such as

petitive difficulties of older British industries, notably iron and steel, and the decelerating rate of economic growth in the first decade of the twentieth century are consistent with this view.[82] The deceleration in the rate of British economic growth has been ascribed to both a decline in productivity growth and a fall in the rate of domestic capital formation.[83] This fall in the rate of domestic capital formation, especially after 1900, reflected not a decline in British savings rates but a surge of foreign investment. Thus, if Britain's hegemonic position in the international economy is to have caused its relative decline, this hegemony would have had to be responsible for the country's exceptionally high propensity to export capital. The volume of British capital exports in the decades preceding World War I has been attributed, alternatively, to the spread of industrialization to and associated investment opportunities in other countries and continents, and to imperfections in the structure of British capital markets that resulted in a bias toward investment overseas.[84] It is impossible to resolve this debate here. But the version of the market-imperfections argument that attributes the London capital market's lack of interest in domestic investment to Britain's relatively early and labor-intensive form of industrialization implies that the same factors responsible for Britain's mid-nineteenth century hegemony (the industrial revolution occurred there first) may also have been responsible for the capital market biases that accelerated its hegemonic decline.

Although the classical gold standard experienced a number of serious

motor cars, implying that the dynamic effects emphasized by new trade theory may have also come into play. See N. F. R. Crafts, *British Economic Growth during the Industrial Revolution* (Oxford, 1985); and James S. Foreman-Peck, "Tariff Protection and Economies of Scale: The British Motor Industry before 1939," *Oxford Economic Papers* 31 (July 1979), 237–57.

82 Donald N. McCloskey, "Did Victorian Britain Fail?" *Economic History Review*, sec. ser., 23 (December 1970), table 2, pinpoints the deceleration in the rate of British economic growth as taking place in the first decade of the twentieth century. The traditional view of the British climacteric is also criticized by D. J. Coppock, "The Climacteric of the 1890's: A Critical Note," *The Manchester School of Economic and Social Studies* 24 (January 1956), 1–31, but subsequently defended by W. P. Kennedy, "Foreign Investment, Trade and Growth in the United Kingdom, 1870–1913," *Explorations in Economic History* 11 (Summer 1974), 415–44.

83 See Matthews and others, *British Economic Growth*, table 8.1, p. 222.

84 For the traditional view that emphasizes capital market imperfections, see the Committee on Finance and Industry, *Report;* Charles P. Kindleberger, *Economic Growth in France and Britain, 1851–1950* (Cambridge, MA, 1964); or David S. Landes, *The Unbound Prometheus: Technological Change and Industrial Development in Western Europe from 1750 to the Present* (New York, 1969). The revisionist view is represented by McCloskey, "Did Victorian Britain Fail?"

disruptions, such as the 1907 panic when a financial crisis threatened to undermine its European core, the prewar system survived these disturbances intact. Eventually, however, the same forces that led to the downfall of the interwar gold exchange standard would have undermined the stability of the prewar system.[85] As the rate of economic growth continued to outstrip the rate of growth of gold (the supply of which was limited by the availability of ore), countries would have grown increasingly dependent on foreign exchange reserves as a source of incremental liquidity. As in the 1960s, growing reliance on exchange reserves in the face of relatively inelastic gold supplies would have eventually proven incompatible with the reserve center's ability to maintain gold convertibility.

De Cecco argues that the situation was already beginning to unravel in the first decade of the twentieth century – that the Boer War signaled the end of the long peace of the nineteenth century, thereby undermining the willingness of potential belligerents to hold their reserves as deposits in foreign countries. "In the years following the Boer War, the international monetary system once more showed a distinct tendency towards becoming a pure gold standard. . . ."[86] More important for our purposes, he suggests that the system was destabilized by the growth of U.S. economic power relative to that of Great Britain. Given the experimental nature of U.S. Treasury efforts to accommodate seasonal variations in money demand, the United States relied heavily on gold imports whenever economic conditions required an increase in money supply, notably during harvest and planting seasons.[87] When the demand for money increased, the United States imported gold, mainly from the Bank of England, which was charged with pegging the sterling price of gold on the London market with a gold reserve of only £30 million. As the American economy grew, both its average demand for gold from London and that demand's seasonal fluctuation in-

---

[85] In Charles Kindleberger's words, "The problem posed by Gresham's Law exists not only on the gold-exchange standard, but on the gold standard itself." Charles P. Kindleberger, *Power and Money: The Economics of International Politics and the Politics of International Economics* (New York, 1970), p. 213. See also James D. Hamilton, "Role of the International Gold Standard in Propagating the Great Depression," *Contemporary Policy Issues* 6 (April 1988), 67–89.

[86] De Cecco, *The International Gold Standard*, p. 125.

[87] At the beginning of the century, Treasury Secretary Leslie M. Shaw began managing public deposits in such a way as to provide some seasonal elasticity of money supply but these early efforts were modest and experimental. On the seasonality of U.S. money demand, see Barry Eichengreen, "Currency and Credit in the Gilded Age," in Gary Saxonhouse and Gavin Wright, eds., *Technique, Spirit and Form in the Making of the Modern Economies: Essays in Honor of William N. Parker* (Greenwich, CT, 1984), pp. 87–114.

creased relative to the Bank of England's primary reserve and its capacity to attract supplementary funds from other centers. To rephrase De Cecco's argument in terms of hegemonic stability theory, the growth of the United States relative to that of Britain undermined Britain's capacity to stabilize international financial markets: specifically, its ability to serve simultaneously as the world's only free gold market, providing however much gold was required by other countries, and to maintain the stability of sterling, the reference point for the global system of fixed exchange rates. In a sense, De Cecco sees indications of the interwar stalemate – a Britain incapable of stabilizing the international system and a United States unwilling to do so – emerging in the first decade of the twentieth century. From this perspective, the process of hegemonic decline that culminated in the international monetary difficulties of the interwar years was at most accelerated by World War I. Even before the war, the processes that led to the downfall of established monetary arrangements were already under way.

Conclusion

Much of the international relations literature concerned with prospects for international monetary reform can be read as a search for an alternative to hegemony as a basis for international monetary stability. Great play is given to the contrast between earlier periods of hegemonic dominance, notably 1890–1914 and 1945–71, and the nature of the task presently confronting aspiring architects of international monetary institutions in an increasingly multipolar world. In this chapter I have suggested that hegemonic stability theories are helpful for understanding the relatively smooth operation of the classical gold standard and the early Bretton Woods system, as well as some of the difficulties of the interwar years. At the same time, much of the evidence is difficult to reconcile with the hegemonic stability view. Even when individual countries occupied positions of exceptional prominence in the world economy and that prominence was reflected in the form and functioning of the international monetary system, that system was still fundamentally predicated on international collaboration. Keohane's notion of "hegemonic cooperation" – that cooperation is required for systemic stability even in periods of hegemonic dominance, although the presence of a hegemon may encourage cooperative behavior – seems directly applicable to international monetary relations. The importance of collaboration is equally apparent in the design of the international monetary system, its operation under normal circumstances, and the management of crises. Despite the usefulness of hegemonic stability theory when applied to short periods and well-defined aspects of international monetary relations, the international monetary system has always been "after hegemony" in the sense that more than a dominant economic power was required to ensure the provision and maintenance of international monetary stability. Moreover, it was precisely when an important economic power most forcefully conditioned the form of the international system that the potential for instability, in a dynamic sense, was greatest. Above all, historical experience demonstrates the speed and pervasiveness of changes in national economic power; since hegemony is transitory, so must be any international monetary system that takes hegemony as its basis. Given the costs of international monetary reform, it would seem unwise to predicate a new system on such a transient basis.

References

Abel, A. B. (1980), "Empirical Investment Equations: An Integrative Framework," *Carnegie Rochester Conference Series* 12 (Spring), 39–91.

Abel, D. (1945), *A History of British Tariffs 1923–1942*. London: Free Trade Union.

Aftalion, A. (1932), *L'Or et sa Distribution Mondiale*. Paris: Librairie Dalloz.

Aliber, R. Z. (1962), "Speculation in the Foreign Exchanges: The European Experience," *Yale Economic Essays* 2, 171–245.

Alt, J. E., R. Calvert, and B. Humes (1986), "Game Theory and Hegemonic Stability: The Role of 'Reputation and Uncertainty'," unpublished, Harvard University.

Ambrosi, C., M. Baleste, and M. Tagel (1984), *Economie Contemporaine*. Paris: Delgrave.

Arndt, H. W. (1944), *The Economic Lessons of the 1930's*. London: Oxford University Press.

Artus, J. R. (1973), "A Multilateral Exchange Rate Model," *Staff Papers* 20, 591–611.

Aukrust, D. (1977), "Inflation in the Open Economy: A Norwegian Model," in L. Krause and W. Salant (eds.), *Worldwide Inflation*. Washington, DC: Brookings Institution, pp. 107–66.

Avery, R. A., L. P. Hansen, and V. J. Kotz (1983), "Multiperiod Probit Model and Orthogonality Condition Estimation," *International Economic Review* 24, 21–35.

Baer, W. and I. Kerstenetzky (1964), *Inflation and Growth in Latin America*. Homewood, IL: Irwin.

Bagehot, W. (1873), *Lombard Street*. London: Murray.

Balogh, T. (1930), "The Import of Gold Into France: An Analysis of the Technical Position," *Economic Journal* 40, 442–60.

(1947), *Studies in Financial Organization*. Cambridge: National Institute of Economic and Social Research.

Bank for International Settlements (1934), *Annual Report*. Basle: BIS.

(1937), *The Tripartite Agreement of September 25, 1936 and Subsequent Monetary Arrangements*. Basle: BIS.

Bank of France (1928), *Compte Rendu au Nom du Conseil General de la Banque*. Paris: Paul Dupont.

(1930), *Compte Rendu au Nom du Conseil General de la Banque*. Paris: Paul Dupont.

Barro, R. (1979), "Money and the Price Level under the Gold Standard," *Economic Journal* 89, 13–33.

Bassett, R. (1958), *Nineteen Thirty-One: Political Crisis*. London: Macmillan Press.

Baudhuin, F. (1972), "Europe and the Great Crisis," in H. van der Wee (ed.), *The Great Depression Revisited*. The Hague: Martinus-Nijhoff, pp. 59–68.

312

Beenstock, M., B. Griffiths, and F. Capie (1984), "Economic Recovery in the United Kingdom in the 1930's," Bank of England Panel of Academic Consultants paper no. 23, London.

Beer, S. H. (1965), *Modern British Politics*. London: Faber and Faber.

Benham, F. and L. Robbins (1931), "Tariffs and the Trade Balance," *Manchester Guardian*, October 19, p. 9.

Benjamin, D. and L. Kochin (1979), "Searching for an Explanation for Unemployment in Interwar Britain," *Journal of Political Economy* 87, 449–78.

Bergmann, K. (1927), *History of Reparations*. London: E. Benn.

Bergsten, C. F. (1975), *Toward a New International Economic Order: Selected Papers of C. Fred Bergsten, 1972–1974*. Lexington, MA: Lexington Books.

Bernard, P. (1975), *La Fin d'un Monde, 1914–1929*. Paris: Sevil.

Berndt, E. R., B. H. Hall, R. E. Hall, and J. A. Hausman (1974), "Estimation and Interference in Nonlinear Structural Models," *Annals of Economic and Social Measurement* 3, 653–66.

Beveridge, W. H. (1909), *Unemployment: A Problem of Industry* (2nd ed., 1930). London: Longman Group.

 (1932), *Tariffs: The Case Examined*, 2nd ed. London: Longman.

Beyen, J. W. (1949), *Money in a Maelstrom*. London: Macmillan Press.

Bloomfield, A. E. (1959), *Monetary Policy Under the International Gold Standard: 1880–1914*. New York: Federal Reserve Bank of New York.

Blum, J. M. (1959), *From the Morganthau Diaries, vol. I: Years of Crisis, 1928–1938*. Boston: Houghton Mifflin.

Bonnell, S. (1981), "Real Wages and Unemployment in the Great Depression," *Economic Record* 57, 277–81.

Booth, A. (1983), "The 'Keynesian Revolution' in Economic Policy-Making," *Economic History Review*, sec. ser., 26, 103–23.

Bordo, M. (1981), "The Classical Gold Standard: Some Lessons for Today," *Federal Reserve Bank of St. Louis Review* 63, 2–17.

Bouvier, J. (1980), "Monnaie et Banque d'un Après-guerre à L'autre: 1919–1945," in F. Braudel and E. Labrousse (eds.), *Histoire économique et sociale de la France*. Paris: PUF, pp. 687–727.

 (1981), "A Propos de la Strategie D'Encaisse (or et devises) de la Banque de France de 1928 à 1932," unpublished, University of Paris.

 (1984), "The French Banks, Inflation and Economic Crisis, 1919–1939," *Journal of European Economic History* 13 (special issue), 29–80.

Branson, W. and W. Buiter (1983), "Monetary and Fiscal Policy with Flexible Exchange Rates," in J. Bhandari and B. Putnam (eds.), *The International Transmission of Economic Disturbances*. Cambridge, MA: MIT Press, pp. 251–85.

Broadberry, S. N. (1986), *The British Economy Between the Wars: A Macroeconomic Survey*. Oxford: Blackwell.

Brown, E. C. (1956), "Fiscal Policy in the Thirties: A Reappraisal," *American Economic Review* 46, 857–79.

Brown, W. A. (1940), *The International Gold Standard Reinterpreted, 1914–1934*. New York: National Bureau of Economic Research.

Bullock, A. (1960), *The Life and Times of Ernest Bevin*. London: Heinemann.

Butlin, N. G. (1984), "Select Comparative Economic Statistics, 1900–1941," Research School for Social Sciences, Australian National University, Source Paper No. 4.

Cahill, R. (1928), *Economic Conditions in France, 1928*. London: HMSO.

 (1934), *Economic Conditions in France, 1934*. London: HMSO.

Cairncross, A. and B. Eichengreen (1983), *Sterling in Decline: The Devaluations of 1931, 1949 and 1967*. Oxford: Blackwell.

Capie, F. (1978), "The British Tariff and Industrial Protection in the 1930s," *Economic History Review*, sec. ser., 31, 399–409.

(1981), "Shaping the British Tariff Structure in the 1930s," *Explorations in Economic History* 18, 155–73.

Capie, F. and A. Webber (1985), *Monetary History of the United Kingdom, 1870–1982, vol. I: Data, Sources, Methods*. London: Allen and Unwin.

Cargill, T. F. (1969), "An Empirical Investigation of the Wage-Lag Hypothesis," *American Economic Review* 59, 806–16.

Caron, F. and J. Bouvier (1980), "Les Années 1914–1930," in F. Braudel and E. Labrousse (eds.), *Histoire économique et sociale de la France*. Paris: PUF, pp. 633–54.

Carré, J. J., P. Dubois, and E. Malinvaud (1975), *French Economic Growth*. Stanford, CA: Stanford University Press.

Cassel, G. (1922), *Money and Foreign Exchange after 1914*. New York: Macmillan.

(1932), *The Crisis in the World's Monetary System*. Oxford: Clarendon Press.

(1936), *The Downfall of the Gold Standard*. Oxford: Oxford University Press.

Cassiers, I. (1980), "Une statistique des salaires horaires en Belgique, 1919–1939," *Recherches Economiques de Louvain* 46, 57–85.

Chéron, H. (1926), *Rapport au Sénat*, no. 84, February 22, 1926, Paris.

Choudri, E. and L. Kochin (1980), "The Exchange Rate and the International Transmission of Business Cycle Disturbances," *Journal of Money, Credit and Banking* 12, 565–74.

Clapham, J. A. (1941), *The Bank of England*. Cambridge: Cambridge University Press.

Clarke, S. V. O. (1967), *Central Bank Cooperation 1924–1931*. New York: Federal Reserve Bank of New York.

(1973), "The Reconstruction of the International Monetary System: The Attempts of 1922 and 1933," *Princeton Studies in International Finance*, no. 33 (November).

(1977), "Exchange-Rate Stabilization in the Mid-1930's: Negotiating the Tripartite Agreement," *Princeton Studies in International Finance*, no. 41 (September).

Clay, H. (1957), *Lord Norman*. London: Macmillan Press.

Cleveland, H. (1976), "The International Monetary System in the Interwar Period," in B. Rowland (ed.), *Balance of Power or Hegemony: The Interwar Monetary System*. New York: New York University Press, pp. 1–59.

Clough, S. B. (1964), *The Economic History of Modern Italy*. New York: Columbia University Press.

Cohen, B. J. (1971), *The Future of Sterling as an International Currency*. London: Macmillan Press.

(1977), *Organizing the World's Money: The Political Economy of International Monetary Relations*. New York: Basic.

(1982), "Balance of Payments Financing: Evolution of a Regime," in S. Krasner (ed.), *International Regimes*. Ithaca, NY: Cornell University Press, pp. 315–36.

Cohen, J. S. (1972), "The 1927 Revaluation of the Lira: A Study in Political Economy," *Economic History Review*, sec. ser., 25, 642–54.

Committee on Currency and Foreign Exchanges After the War (Cunliffe Committee) (1918), *First Interim Report*, Cmd. 9182. London: HMSO.

Committee on Finance and Industry (Macmillan Committee) (1931), *Report*, Cmd. 3897. London: HMSO.

Committee on National Expenditure (May Committee) (1931), *Report*, Cmd. 3920. London: HMSO.

Condliffe, J. B. (1940), *The Reconstruction of World Trade*. New York: Norton.

Conybeare, J. (1983), "Tariff Protection in Developed and Developing Countries: A Cross-Sectional and Longitudinal Analysis," *International Organization* 37, 441–68.

Cooper, R. (1972/3), "Trade Policy Is Foreign Policy," *Foreign Policy* 9, 18–36.

  (1982), "The Gold Standard: Historical Facts and Future Prospects," *Brookings Papers on Economic Activity* 1, 1–56.

  (1984), "Economic Interdependence and the Coordination of Economic Policies," in P. Kenen (ed.), *Handbook of International Economics*. Amsterdam: North Holland, pp. 1195–234.

Coppock, D. J. (1956), "The Climacteric of the 1890s: A Critical Note," *Manchester School of Economic and Social Studies*, 24, 1–32.

Costigliola, F. (1977), "Anglo-American Financial Rivalry in the 1920s," *Journal of Economic History* 37, 911–34.

  (1984), *Awkward Dominion: American Political, Economic, and Cultural Relations with Europe, 1919–1933*. Ithaca, NY: Cornell University Press.

Cowhey, P. and E. Long (1983), "Testing Theories of Regime Change: Hegemonic Decline or Surplus Capacity?" *International Organization* 37, 157–83.

Crafts, N. F. R. (1985), *British Economic Growth During the Industrial Revolution*. Oxford: Clarendon Press.

Cross, C. (1966), *Philip Snowden*. London: Barrie and Rockliff.

Cuddington, J. T. and J. M. Viñals (1986), "Budget Deficits and the Current Account: An Intertemporal Disequilibrium Approach," *Journal of International Economics* 21, 1–24.

Currie, R. (1979), *Industrial Politics*. Oxford: Clarendon Press.

Dam, K. (1982), *The Rules of the Game*. Chicago: University of Chicago Press.

Davis, J. S. (1975), *The World Between the Wars: An Economist's View*. Baltimore: Johns Hopkins University Press.

De Cecco, M. (1985), *The International Gold Standard: Money and Empire*. London: Francis Pinter.

DeLong, J. B. (1987), "Returning to the Gold Standard: A Macroeconomic History of Britain and France in the 1920s," Ph.D. dissertation, Harvard University.

Dessirier, J. (1935), "Secteurs 'abrités' et 'non abrités' dans le Déséquilibre Actuel de l'Economie Française," *Revue d'économie politique* 49, 1330–61.

Dornbusch, R. (1974), "Real and Monetary Aspects of the Effects of Exchange Rate Changes," in R. Z. Aliber (ed.), *National Monetary Policies and the International Financial System*. Chicago: University of Chicago Press, pp. 64–81.

  (1976), "Expectations and Exchange Rate Dynamics," *Journal of Political Economy* 84, 1161–76.

  (1980), *Open Economy Macroeconomics*. New York: Basic.

  (1987), "Lessons from the German Inflation Experience of the 1920's," in R. Dornbusch, S. Fischer, and J. Bossons (eds.), *Macroeconomics and Finance*. Cambridge, MA: MIT Press, pp. 337–66.

Dornbusch, R. and J. A. Frenkel (1984), "The Gold Standard and the Bank of England in the Crisis of 1847," in M. Bordo and A. Schwartz (eds.), *A Retrospective on the Classical Gold Standard*. Chicago: University of Chicago Press, pp. 233–64.

Dowie, J. A. (1975), "1919–1920 Is in Need of Attention," *Economic History Review*, sec. ser., 28, 429–50.

Drummond, I. M. (1972), *British Economic Policy and the Empire, 1919–1939*. London: Allen and Unwin.

(1974), *Imperial Economic Policy 1917–1939*. London: Allen and Unwin.

(1979), "London, Washington and the Management of the Franc, 1936–39," *Princeton Studies in International Finance*, no. 45 (November).

Dulles, E. L. (1929), *The French Franc, 1914–1928*. New York: Macmillan.

(1933), *The Dollar, the Franc and Inflation*. New York: Macmillan.

Dutton, J. (1984), "The Bank of England and the 'Rules of the Game' Under the International Gold Standard: New Evidence," in M. Bordo and A. Schwartz (eds.), *A Retrospective on the Classical Gold Standard*. Chicago: University of Chicago Press, pp. 173–202.

Edelstein, M. (1981), *Overseas Investment in the Age of High Imperialism*. New York: Columbia University Press.

Edgen, G., K. O. Faxen, and C. E. Odhner (1969), "Wages, Growth and the Distribution of Income," *Swedish Journal of Economics* 71, 133–60.

Edwards, S. (1983), "The Demand for International Reserves and Exchange Rate Adjustments: The Case of LDC's: 1964–72," *Economica* 50, 269–80.

Eichengreen, B. (1981), "A Dynamic Model of Tariffs, Output and Employment Under Flexible Exchange Rates," *Journal of International Economics* 11, 341–59.

(1982), "Did Speculation Destabilize the French Franc in the 1920s?" *Explorations in Economic History* 19, 71–100.

(1983), "Protection, Real Wage Resistance and Employment," *Weltwirtschaftliches Archiv* 119, 429–52.

(1984a), "Central Bank Cooperation Under the Interwar Gold Standard," *Explorations in Economic History* 21, 64–87.

(1984b), "Currency and Credit in the Gilded Age," in G. Saxonhouse and G. Wright (eds.), *Technique, Spirit and Form in the Making of the Modern Economies: Essays in Honor of William N. Parker*. New York: JAI Press, pp. 87–114.

(ed.) (1985), *The Gold Standard in Theory and History*. London: Methuen.

(1987), "Conducting the International Orchestra: The Bank of England and the Classical Gold Standard, 1880–1914," *Journal of International Money and Finance* 6, 5–29.

(1988a), "The Australian Economic Recovery in International Comparative Perspective," in N. G. Butlin and R. G. Gregory (eds.), *Recovery from the Depression*. Sydney: Cambridge University Press, pp. 33–60.

(1988b), "Did International Economic Forces Cause the Great Depression?" *Contemporary Policy Issues* 6, 90–114.

(1989), "The Political Economy of the Smoot-Hawley Tariff, *Research in Economic History* 11, 1–44.

Eichengreen, B. and F. Giavazzi (1984), "Inflation, Consolidation or Capital Levy? European Debt Management in the 1920's," unpublished, Harvard University and University of Venice.

Eichengreen, B. and R. Portes (1986), "Debt and Default in the 1930's: Causes and Consequences," *European Economic Review* 30, 599–640.

(1987), "The Anatomy of Financial Crises," in R. Portes and A. Swoboda (eds.), *Threats to International Financial Stability*. Cambridge: Cambridge University Press, pp. 10–58.

Eichengreen, B. and J. Sachs (1986), "Competitive Devaluation and the Great Depression: A Theoretical Reassessment," *Economics Letters* 22, 67–71.

Eichengreen, B., M. W. Watson, and R. S. Grossman (1983), "Bank Rate Policy Under the Interwar Gold Standard: A Dynamic Probit Model," Harvard Institute of Economic Research Discussion Paper no. 1008.

Eichengreen, B. and C. Wyplosz (1986), "The Economic Consequences of the Franc Poincaré." NBER working paper no. 2064, November.

Einzig, P. (1932), *Montagu Norman*. London: Macmillan Press.

(1937), *The Theory of Forward Exchange*. London: Macmillan Press.

Ellis, H. S. (1941), *Exchange Control in Central Europe*. Cambridge, MA: Harvard University Press.

Epstein, G. and T. Ferguson (1984), "Monetary Policy, Loan Liquidation, and Industrial Conflict: The Federal Reserve and the Open Market Operations of 1932," *Journal of Economic History* 44, 957–84.

Fayle, C. E. (1927), *The War and the Shipping Industry*. New Haven, CT: Yale University Press.

Feiling, K. (1946), *Life of Neville Chamberlain*. London: Macmillan Press.

Feinstein, C. H. (1972), *Statistical Tables of National Income, Expenditure and Output of the U.K. 1855–1965*. Cambridge: Cambridge University Press.

Feldman, G. (1926), *Le Franc Français Depuis 1914*. Paris: Eugène Figuière.

Feldman, G. D. (1977), "Socio-Economic Structures in the Industrial Sector and Revolutionary Potentialities, 1917–1922," in C. Bertrand (ed.), *Revolutionary Situations in Europe, 1917–1922*. Montreal: Interuniversity Centre for European Studies.

Findlay, R. (1934), *Britain Under Protection*. London: Allen and Unwin.

Fischer, S. (1983), "A Note on Investment and Lagged Q," unpublished manuscript, MIT.

Fleming, J. M. (1962), "Domestic Financial Policies under Fixed and under Flexible Exchange Rates," *Staff Papers* 9, 369–80.

Flood, R. P. and P. M. Garber (1980), "Market Fundamentals versus Price-Level Bubbles: The First Tests," *Journal of Political Economy* 88, 745–70.

Fohlen, C. (1966), *La France de l'Entre-Deux-Guerres, 1917–1939*. Paris: Casterman.

Ford, A. G. (1962), *The Gold Standard, 1880–1914: Britain and Argentina*. Oxford: Clarendon Press.

Foreman-Peck, J. (1979), "Tariff Protection and Economies of Scale: The British Motor Car Industry Before 1939," *Oxford Economic Papers* 31, 237–57.

Franco, G. H. B. (1987), "The Rentenmark 'Miracle'," *Rivista di Storia Economica*, sec. ser., 4, 96–117.

Frankel, J. A. (1986), "International Capital Mobility and Crowding Out of Investment in the U.S. Economy: Imperfect Integration of Financial Markets or of Goods Markets?" in R. W. Hafer (ed.), *How Open Is the U.S. Economy?* Lexington, MA: Lexington Books, pp. 33–67.

Frayssinet, P. (1928), *La Politique Monétaire de la France (1924–1928)*. Paris: Recueil Sirey.

Fregert, K. and L. Jonung (1986), "Monetary Regimes and the Length of Wage Contracts," unpublished, University of Lund.

Fremling, G. M. (1985), "Did the United States Transmit the Great Depression to the Rest of the World?" *American Economic Review* 75, 1181–5.

Frenkel, J. A. (1974), "The Demand for International Reserves by Developed and Less-Developed Countries," *Economica* 41, 14–24.

318   References

(1980), "Exchange Rates, Prices and Money: Lessons from the 1920's," *American Economic Review Papers and Proceedings* 70, 235–44.

Frenkel, J. A. and C. A. Rodriguez (1982), "Exchange Rate Dynamics and the Overshooting Hypothesis," *Staff Papers* 29, 1–30.

Friedman, M. (1953), "The Case for Flexible Exchange Rates," in *Essays in Positive Economics*. Chicago: University of Chicago Press, pp. 157–203.

Friedman, M. and A. Schwartz (1963), *A Monetary History of the United States, 1867–1960*, Princeton, NJ: Princeton University Press.

Galenson, W. and A. Zellner (1957), "International Comparisons of Unemployment Rates," in National Bureau of Economic Research, *The Measurement and Behavior of Unemployment*. Princeton, NJ: Princeton University Press, pp. 439–580.

Gardner, R. (1956), *Sterling-Dollar Diplomacy*. New York: Columbia University Press.

Garside, R. (1980), *The Measurement of Unemployment, 1850–1979*. Oxford: Blackwell.

Gayer, A. D. (1937), *Monetary Policy and Economic Stabilisation: A Study of the Gold Standard*. London: Black.

Geary, D. (1981), *European Labour Protest, 1848–1939*. London: Croom Helm.

Giffin, R. (1886), "Gold Supply, the Rate of Discount and Prices," in *Essays in Finance*. London: Putnam, pp. 37–88.

Gilbert, M. (1968), "The Gold-Dollar System: Conditions of Equilibrium and the Price of Gold," reprinted in B. Eichengreen (ed.), *The Gold Standard in Theory and History*. London: Methuen, 1985, pp. 229–49.

Gilpin, Robert (1975), *U.S. Power and the Multinational Corporation*. New York: Basic.

Goldstein, J. (1987), "Ideas, Institutions, and American Trade Policy," *International Organization* 42, 179–218.

Goodhart, C. A. E. (1972), *The Business of Banking*. London: Weidenfeld and Nicolson.

Goschen, G. J. (1863), *The Theory of Foreign Exchanges*. London: E. Wilson.

Gowa, J. (1984), "Hegemons, IOs and Markets: The Case of the Substitution Account," *International Organization* 38, 661–84.

Graham, T. N. (1948), *Willie Graham*. London: Hutchinson.

Grant, A. T. K. (1937), *A Study of the Capital Market in Postwar Britain*. London: Macmillan Press.

Grossman, R. S. (1982), "Bank Rate Policy by the Bank of England During the Gold Standard Years, 1925–1931," unpublished, Harvard College.

Haas, E. (1980), "Why Collaborate? Issue Linkage and International Regimes," *World Politics* 32, 357–405.

Haberler, G. (1937), *Prosperity and Depression*. Geneva: League of Nations.

Haig, B. D. (1974), "Manufacturing Output and Productivity, 1910 to 1948/49," *Australian Economic History Review* 14, 136–55.

Haig, R. M. (1929), *The Public Finances of Post-War France*. New York: Columbia University Press.

Hamada, K. (1976), "A Strategic Analysis of Monetary Interdependence," *Journal of Political Economy* 84, 677–700.

(1979), "Macroeconomic Coordination and Strategy Under Alternative Exchange Rates," in R. Dornbusch and J. Frenkel (eds.), *International Economic Policy: Theory and Evidence*. Baltimore: Johns Hopkins University Press, pp. 292–324.

Hamilton, J. (1987), "Monetary Forces in the Great Depression," *Journal of Monetary Economics* 19, 145–69.

(1988), "Role of the International Gold Standard in Propagating the Great Depression." *Contemporary Policy Issues* 6, 67–89.

Hancock, K. J. (1960), "Unemployment and the Economists in the 1920s," *Economica* 17, 305–21.

(1962), "The Reduction of Unemployment as a Problem of Public Policy, 1920–1929," *Economic History Review*, sec. ser., 15, 329–43.

Hardach, K. (1976), *The Political Economy of Germany in the Twentieth Century.* Berkeley, CA: University of California Press.

Hardy, C. (1932), *Credit Policies of the Federal Reserve System.* Washington, DC: Brookings Institution.

(1936), *Is There Enough Gold?* Washington, DC: Brookings Institution.

Harris, J. (1977), *William Beveridge: A Biography.* Oxford: Clarendon Press.

Harrod, R. (1951), *The Life of John Maynard Keynes.* London: Macmillan Press.

(1971), "Triple the Dollar Price of Gold," reprinted in G. H. Meier, *Problems of a World Monetary Order.* New York: Oxford University Press, 1982, pp. 107–8.

Hart, J. (1976), "Three Approaches to the Measurement of Power in International Relations," *International Organization* 30, 289–308.

Hawtrey, R. (1913), *Good and Bad Trade.* London: Constable.

(1923), *Monetary Reconstruction.* London: Longman Group.

(1925), "Public Expenditure and the Demand for Labour," *Economica* 13, 38–48.

(1932), *The Art of Central Banking.* London: Macmillan Press.

(1938), *A Century of Bank Rate.* London: Longman Group.

(1950), *Currency and Credit.* London: Longman Group.

(1954), *Toward the Rescue of Sterling.* London: Longman Group.

Hayashi, F. (1982), "Tobin's Marginal q and Average q: A Neoclassical Interpretation," *Econometrica* 50, 213–24.

Heckman, J. (1981), "Statistical Models for Discrete Panel Data," in C. Manski and D. McFadden (eds.), *Structural Analysis of Discrete Data with Econometric Application.* Cambridge, MA: MIT Press, pp. 114–78.

Heller, H. R. (1966), "Optimal International Reserves," *Economic Journal* 76, 296–311.

Hepburn, A. B. (1924), *A History of Currency in the United States,* revised edition. New York: Macmillan.

Hinton, J. (1973), *The First Shop Stewards' Movement and Workers' Control.* London: Allen & Unwin.

Hirsch, F. (1967), *Money International.* London: Penguin.

Horsefield, J. K. (1969), *The International Monetary Fund, 1945–65: Twenty Years of International Monetary Cooperation.* Washington, DC: IMF.

Howson, S. (1975), *Domestic Monetary Management in Britain, 1919–1938.* New York: Cambridge University Press.

(1980a), "Sterling's Managed Float: The Operations of the Exchange Equalisation Account, 1932–1939," *Princeton Studies in International Finance,* no. 46 (November).

(1980b), "The Management of Sterling, 1932–1939," *Journal of Economic History* 40, 53–60.

Howson, S. and D. Winch (1977), *The Economic Advisory Council, 1930–1939.* London: Cambridge University Press.

320   References

INSEE (1966), *Annuaire Statistique de la France: Résumé retrospectif.* Paris: INSEE.
Jack, D. T. (1927), *The Restoration of European Currencies.* London: P. S. King and Sons.
Jackson, J. (1985), *The Politics of Depression in France, 1932–1936.* Cambridge: Cambridge University Press.
James, H. (1986), *The German Slump.* Oxford: Clarendon Press.
Janeway, W. H. (1971), "The Economic Policy of the Second Labour Government, 1929–1931," unpublished Ph.D. dissertation, Cambridge University, Cambridge.
Jeffreys, J. B. (1945), *The Story of the Engineers.* London: Lawrence and Wishart.
Johnson, H. G. (1953/54), "Optimum Tariffs and Retaliation," *Review of Economic Studies* 21, 142–53.
   (1956), "The Revival of Monetary Policy in Britain," *Three Banks Review* 30 (June), 3–20.
Johnson, H. L. and S. Kotz (1970), *Distributions in Statistics: Continuous Multivariate Distributions.* New York: Wiley.
Jonung, L. (1981), "The Depression in Sweden and the United States: A Comparison of Causes and Policies," in K. Brunner (ed.), *The Great Depression Revisited.* Boston: Martinus-Nijhoff, pp. 286–315.
Kemp, T. (1971), "The French Economy under the Franc Poincaré," *Economic History Review* sec. ser., 24, 82–99.
   (1972), *The French Economy, 1913–1939.* London: Longman Group.
Kenen, P. (1960), *British Monetary Policy and the Balance of Payments, 1951–1957.* Cambridge, MA: Harvard University Press.
   (1986), *Financing, Adjustment and the International Monetary Fund.* Washington, DC: Brookings Institution.
Kenen, P. and E. Yudin (1965), "The Demand for International Reserves," *Review of Economics and Statistics* 47, 242–50.
Kennedy, W. (1974), "Foreign Investment, Trade and Growth in the United Kingdom, 1870–1913," *Explorations in Economic History* 11, 415–54.
Keohane, R. (1980), "The Theory of Hegemonic Stability and Changes in International Regimes, 1967–1977," in O. Holsti, R. Siverson, and A. George (eds.), *Change in the International System.* Boulder, CO: Westview, pp. 131–62.
   (1982), "Inflation and the Decline of American Power," in R. Lombra and W. Witte (eds.), *The Political Economy of International and Domestic Monetary Relations.* Ames, IA: Iowa State University Press, pp. 7–37.
   (1984), *After Hegemony: Cooperation and Discord in the World Political Economy.* Princeton, NJ: Princeton University Press.
Kessel, R. A. and A. A. Alchian (1960), "The Inflation-Induced Lag of Wages," *American Economic Review* 50, 43–66.
Keynes, J. M. (1923), *A Tract on Monetary Reform.* London: Macmillan Press.
   (1925a), *The Economic Consequences of the Sterling Parity.* New York: Harcourt-Brace.
   (1925b), "Is Sterling Overvalued?" *The Nation and Athenaeum* April 4 and 18, 1925, reprinted in *The Collected Writings of John Maynard Keynes: Activities, 1922–1929: The Return to Gold and Industrial Policy,* D. Moggridge (ed.) Cambridge: Cambridge University Press, Part I, pp. 349–54.
   (1929), "Is There Enough Gold? The League of Nations Inquiry," *The Nation and Athenaeum* January 19, reprinted in D. Moggridge (ed.), *The Collected*

Writings of John Maynard Keynes, Activities 1922–1929: The Return to Gold and Industrial Policy. Cambridge: Cambridge University Press, 1981, Part II, pp. 775–80.

(1930), *A Treatise on Money.* London: Macmillan Press.

(1931), *Essays in Persuasion.* London: Macmillan Press.

(1933), "National Self-Sufficiency," *Yale Review,* new series, 22, 755–69.

(1936), *The General Theory of Employment, Interest and Money.* London: Macmillan Press.

(1981), *Activities 1929–31: Rethinking Employment and Unemployment Policies,* vol. 20 of *The Collected Writings of John Maynard Keynes.* London: Macmillan and St. Martin's Press.

Keynes, J. M. and H. Henderson (1972), " 'Can Lloyd George Do It?' – The Pledge Examined," in *The Collected Writings of John Maynard Keynes, Vol. 9, Essays in Persuasion.* London: Macmillan Press, pp. 86–125.

Kindleberger, C. (1964), *Economic Growth in France and Britain, 1851–1950.* Cambridge, MA: Harvard University Press.

(1970), *Power and Money: The Economics of International Politics and the Politics of International Economics.* New York: Basic.

(1973), *The World in Depression, 1929–39.* Berkeley, CA: University of California Press.

(1978), *Manias, Panics and Crashes: A History of Financial Crises.* New York: Basic.

(1986), "International Capital Movements and Foreign Exchange Markets in Crisis: The 1930s and the 1980s," in I. Berend and K. Borchardt (eds.), *The Impact of the Depression of the 1930s and Its Relevance for the Contemporary World.* Budapest: Karl Marx University Press.

Kirkaldy, A. W. (1916), *Labour, Finance and the War.* London: Pitman Books.

Kooker, J. (1976), "French Financial Diplomacy: The Interwar Years," in B. M. Rowland (ed.), *Balance of Power or Hegemony: The Interwar Monetary System.* New York: New York University Press, pp. 83–146.

Krasner, S. D. (1976), "State Power and the Structure of International Trade," *World Politics* 28, 317–47.

Krugman, P. (1984), "The Narrow Moving Band, the Dutch Disease, and the Competitive Consequences of Mrs. Thatcher: Notes on Trade in the Presence of Dynamic Scale Economies," *Journal of Development Economics* 27, 41–55.

(1985), "Market Access and International Competition in High Technology: A Simulation Exercise," unpublished, MIT.

Kunz, D. (1987), *Britain's Battle for the Gold Standard in 1931.* London: Croom-Helm.

Kydland, F. E. and E. C. Prescott (1982), "Time to Build and Aggregate Fluctuations," *Econometrica* 50, 1345–70.

Lake, D. A. (1988), *Power, Protection and Free Trade: International Sources of U.S. Commercial Strategy, 1887–1939.* Ithaca: Cornell University Press.

Landes, D. S. (1969), *The Unbound Prometheus.* Cambridge: Cambridge University Press.

Lawson, F. (1983), "Hegemony and the Structure of International Trade Reassessed: A View from Arabia," *International Organization* 37, 317–38.

Leaf, W. (1926), *Banking.* London: Williams and Norgate.

League of Nations (various years), *Monthly Bulletin of Statistics.* Geneva: League of Nations.

(various years), *International Statistical Yearbook*. Geneva: League of Nations.

(1930a), *Legislation on Gold*. Geneva: League of Nations.

(1930b), *Interim Report of the Gold Delegation of the Financial Committee*. Geneva: League of Nations.

(1931a), *Selected Documents on the Distribution of Gold*. Geneva: League of Nations.

(1931b), *Course and Phases of the World Economic Depression*. Geneva: League of Nations.

(1932a), *Report of the Gold Delegation*. Geneva: League of Nations.

(1932b), *World Economic Survey, 1931/32*. Geneva: League of Nations.

(1935), *World Economic Survey, 1934/35*. Geneva: League of Nations.

(1936), *Review of World Trade*. Geneva: League of Nations.

(1937a), *Monetary Review*. Geneva: League of Nations.

(1937b), *Review of World Trade*. Geneva: League of Nations.

(1938), *Monetary Review*. Geneva: League of Nations.

(1939), *Statistical Yearbook*. Geneva: League of Nations.

(1942), *Commercial Policy in the Interwar Period: International Proposals and National Policies*. Geneva: League of Nations.

(1943), *Europe's Overseas Needs, 1919–1920*. Geneva: League of Nations.

Lewis, W. A. (1949), *Economic Survey, 1919–1939*. London: Allen and Unwin.

Liepman, H. (1938), *Tariff Levels and the Economic Unity of Europe*. London: Allen and Unwin.

Lindert, P. (1969), "Key Currencies and Gold, 1900–1913," *Princeton Studies in International Finance*, no. 24 (August).

Lippincott, I. (1919), *Problems of Reconstruction*. New York: Macmillan.

Lipson, C. (1982), "The Transformation of Trade: The Sources and Effects of Regime Changes," *International Organization* 36, 417–56.

London and Cambridge Economic Service (1970), *The British Economy: Key Statistics, 1900–1970*. London: Times Newspapers Ltd.

Loriot, J. (1930), "Les Banques," *Revue d'économie politique* 44, 538–56.

Loveday, A. (1931), *Britain and World Trade*. London: Longman Group.

Lowe, M. E. (1942), *The British Tariff Movement*. Washington, DC: American Council on Public Affairs.

Luce, R. D. and H. Raiffa (1957), *Games and Decisions: Introduction and Critical Survey*. New York: Wiley.

McCloskey, D. N. (1970), "Did Victorian Britain Fail?" *Economic History Review*, sec. ser., 23, 446–59.

McCloskey, D. N. and J. Richard Zecher (1976), "How the Gold Standard Worked, 1880–1913," in Jacob A. Frenkel and Harry G. Johnson (eds.), *The Monetary Approach to the Balance of Payments*, London: Allen and Unwin, pp. 184–208.

McDougall, D. (1960), "The Dollar Problem: A Reappraisal," *Princeton Essays in International Finance*, no. 35 (November).

McKeown, T. (1983), "Hegemonic Stability Theory and 19th Century Tariff Levels in Europe," *International Organization* 37, 73–92.

MacLeod, H. D. (1856), *The Theory and Practice of Banking*. London: Longman Group.

Maddison, A. (1964), *Economic Growth in the West*. New York: Twentieth Century Fund.

Maier, C. (1976), *Recasting Bourgeois Europe*. Princeton, NJ: Princeton University Press.

March, J. (1966), "The Power of Power," in D. Easton (ed.), *Varieties of Political Theory*. Englewood Cliffs, NJ: Prentice-Hall, pp. 39–70.

Marjolin, R. (1939), "Structure Monétaire," *Revue d'économie politique* 53, 271–90.

Marquand, D. (1977), *Ramsay MacDonald*. London: Cape.

Marshall, A. (1887), *Evidence Before the Gold and Silver Commission*, Official Papers, no. 9677–81, London.

Matthews, Kent (1987), "Was Sterling Overvalued in 1925?" *Economic History Review*, sec. ser., 39, 572–98.

Matthews, R. C. O., C. H. Feinstein, and J. Odling-Smee (1982), *British Economic Growth, 1856–1973*. Stanford, CA: Stanford University Press.

Meltzer, A. (1976), "Monetary and Other Explanations for the Start of the Great Depression," *Journal of Monetary Economics* 2, 455–72.

Methorst, H. W. (1938), *Recueil international de statistiques économiques 1931–1936*. La Haye: Office Permanent de L'Institut International de Statistique.

Meynial, P. (1930), "La Balance des Comptes," *Revue d'économie politique* 44, 470–83.

Middlemas, K. and J. Barnes (1969), *Baldwin: A Biography*. London: Weidenfeld and Nicolson.

Middleton, R. (1981), "The Constant Employment Budget Balance and British Budgetary Policy, 1929–1939," *Economic History Review*, sec. ser., 34, 266–86.

Mills, J. S. (1922), *The Genoa Conference*. New York: Dutton.

Milward, A. (1984), *The Reconstruction of Western Europe, 1945–51*. London: Methuen.

Mitchell, B. R. (1975), *European Historical Statistics 1750–1970*. London: Macmillan Press.

Mlynarski, F. (1929), *Gold and Central Banks*. London: Macmillan Press.

Moggridge, D. E. (1969), *The Return to Gold, 1925: The Formulation of Economic Policy and Its Critics*. Cambridge: Cambridge University Press.

(1970), "The 1931 Financial Crisis – A New View," *The Banker* 120 (August), 832–9.

(1972), *British Monetary Policy 1924–1931: The Norman Conquest of $4.86*. New York: Cambridge University Press.

(1975), *Keynes*. London: Macmillan Press.

(1981), "Financial Crises and Lenders of Last Resort: Policy in the Crises of 1920 and 1929," *Journal of European Economic History* 10, 47–69.

Morgenstern, O. (1959), *International Financial Transactions and Business Cycles*. Princeton, NJ: Princeton University Press.

Moulton, H. G. and L. Pasvolsky (1932), *War Debts and World Prosperity*. Washington, DC: Brookings Institution.

Mundell, R. (1963), "Capital Mobility and Stabilization Policy under Fixed and Flexible Exchange Rates," *Canadian Journal of Economics* 29, 475–85.

(1972), "The Future of the International Monetary System," in A. L. K. Acheson et al., eds., *Bretton Woods Revisited*. Toronto: University of Toronto Press, pp. 91–106.

Mussa, M. (1986), "Nominal Exchange Rate Regimes and the Behavior of Real Exchange Rates: Evidence and Implications," *Carnegie Rochester Conference Series on Public Policy* 25, 117–214.

Nathan, O. (1944), *The Nazi Economic System*. Durham, NC: Duke University Press.

National Monetary Commission (1910), *Interviews on the Banking and Currency Systems of England, Scotland, France, Germany, Switzerland, and Italy*, Senate Document no. 405, Washington, DC.

Neary, P. and J. Stiglitz (1983), "Toward a Reconstruction of Keynesian Economics: Expectations and Constrained Equilibria," *Quarterly Journal of Economics* 98, 199–228.

Neurrisse, A. (1967), *Histoire du Franc*. Paris: PUF.

Nevin, E. (1955), *The Mechanism of Cheap Money: A Study of British Monetary Policy, 1931–1939*. Cardiff: University of Wales Press.

Niehans, J. (1968), "Monetary and Fiscal Policies in Open Economies Under Fixed Exchange Rates: An Optimizing Approach," *Journal of Political Economy* 76, 893–920.

Nurkse, R. (1944), *International Currency Experience*. Geneva: League of Nations.

Odell, J. (1982), "Bretton Woods and International Political Disintegration: Implications for Monetary Diplomacy," in R. Lombra and W. Witte (eds.), *The Political Economy of International and Domestic Monetary Relations*. Ames, IA: Iowa State University Press, pp. 39–72.

Ogburn, W. F. and W. Jaffe (1929), *The Economic Development of Postwar France*. New York: Columbia University Press.

Ohkawa, K. and H. Rosovsky (1973), *Japanese Economic Growth*. Stanford, CA: Stanford University Press.

Ohlin, B. (1929), "The Reparation Problem: A Discussion," *Economic Journal* 39, 172–8.

Olson, M. and R. Zeckhauser (1966), "An Economic Theory of Alliances," *Review of Economics and Statistics* 48, 266–79.

Oye, K. (1986), "The Sterling-Dollar-Franc Triangle: Monetary Diplomacy 1929–1937," in K. Oye (ed.), *Cooperation Under Anarchy*. Princeton, NJ: Princeton University Press, pp. 173–99.

Palyi, M. (1972), *The Twilight of Gold*. Chicago: Henry Regnery.

Parrini, C. (1969), *Heir to Empire: United States Economic Diplomacy, 1916–1923*. Pittsburgh: University of Pittsburgh Press.

Pasvolsky, L. (1933), *The Necessity for a Stable International Monetary Standard*. Paris: International Chamber of Commerce.

Patinkin, D. (1976), *Keynes' Monetary Thought*. Durham, NC: Duke University Press.

Peden, G. C. (1980), "Keynes, the Treasury and Unemployment in the Later Nineteen-thirties," *Oxford Economic Papers* 32, 1–18.

Perrot, M. (1955), *La Monnaie et l'opinion publique en France et en Angleterre, 1924–1936*. Paris: Presses de la fondation nationale des sciences politiques.

Pigou, A. C. (1947), *Aspects of British Economic History, 1918–1925*. London: Macmillan Press.

Pippenger, J. (1984), "Bank of England Operations, 1893–1913," in M. Bordo and A. Schwartz (eds.), *A Retrospective on the Classical Gold Standard*. Chicago: University of Chicago Press, pp. 203–32.

Pollard, S. (1969), *The Development of the British Economy, 1914–1967*, 2nd ed. London: Arnold.

(ed.) (1970), *The Gold Standard and Employment Policies Between the Wars*. London: Methuen.

Redmond, J. (1980), "An Indicator of the Effective Exchange Rate of the Pound in the 1930's," *Economic History Review*, sec. ser., 33, 83–91.

(1988), "Effective Exchange Rates in the 1930s: North America and the Gold Bloc," *Journal of European Economic History* 17, 379–410.

République Française, Direction générale des douanes et droits indirects (various issues), *Tableau général du commerce extérieur*. Paris: Républic Française.

Ricard, V. (1929), "Le Marché Monétaire et les Changes," *Revue d'économie politique* 43, 438–70.

Rist, L. and P. Schwob (1939), "Balance des Paiements," *Revue d'économie politique* 53, 528–50.

Robbins, L. (1971), *Autobiography of an Economist*. London: Macmillan Press.

Robinson, J. (1975), "What Became of the Keynesian Revolution?" in M. Keynes (ed.), *Essays on John Maynard Keynes*. London: Cambridge University Press, pp. 123–31.

Rogers, J. H. (1929), *The Process of Inflation in France, 1914–1927*. New York: Columbia University Press.

Rogoff, K. (1985), "Can International Policy Coordination Be Counterproductive?" *Journal of International Economics* 18, 199–218.

Rolfe, S. (1966), *Gold and World Power: The Dollar, the Pound, and the Plans for Reform*. New York: Harper and Row.

Royal Institute of International Affairs (1931), *The International Gold Problem*. Oxford: Oxford University Press.

(1932), *British Tariff Policy*. London: Royal Institute of Economics and London School of Economics and Political Science.

Ruggie, J. G. (1975), "International Responses to Technology: Concepts and Trends," *International Organization* 29, 557–84.

Russell, H. (1898), *International Monetary Conferences*. New York: Harper Brothers.

Ruud, P. (1981), "Conditional Minimum Distance Estimation and Autocorrelation in Limited Dependent Variable Models," Ph.D. dissertation, MIT.

Sachs, J. (1980), "Wages, Flexible Exchange Rates and Macroeconomic Policy," *Quarterly Journal of Economics* 94, 737–47.

(1986), "The Uneasy Case for Greater Exchange Rate Coordination," *American Economic Review Papers and Proceedings* 76, 336–41.

Sachs, J. and C. Wyplosz (1984), "Real Exchange Rate Effects of Fiscal Policy," Harvard Institute of Economic Research Discussion Paper 1050 (April).

Saint-Etienne, C. (1983), "L'offre et la demande de monnaie dans la France de l'Entre-Deux-Guerres (1920–1939)," *Revue Economique* 34 (March), 344–67.

(1984), *The Great Depression, 1929–1938: Lessons for the 1980's*. Stanford, CA: Hoover Institution Press.

Salter, W. (1959), "Internal and External Balance: The Role of Price and Expenditure Effects," *Economic Record* 35, 226–38.

Saposs, D. J. (1931), *The Labor Movement in Postwar France*. New York: Columbia University Press.

Sargent, T. (1983), "Stopping Moderate Inflations: The Methods of Poincaré and Thatcher," in R. Dornbusch and M. H. Simonsen (eds.), *Inflation, Debt, and Indexation*. Cambridge, MA: MIT Press, pp. 54–96.

Sauvy, A. (1984), *Histoire Économique de la France Entre les Deux Guerres*. Paris: PUF.

Sayers, R. S. (1936), *Bank of England Operations 1890–1914*. London: P. S. King.

(1956), *Financial Policy, 1939–1945*. London: HMSO and Longman Group.

(1957), *Central Banking After Bagehot*. Oxford: Clarendon Press.

(1970), "The Return to Gold, 1925," in S. Pollard (ed.), *The Gold Standard and Employment Policies Between the Wars*. London: Methuen, pp. 85–98.

(1976), *The Bank of England, 1891–1944*. Cambridge: Cambridge University Press.

(1979), "Bank Rate in Keynes' Century," *Proceedings of the British Academy* 65 (May), 191–206.

Schmid, G. C. (1974), "The Politics of Currency Stabilization; The French Franc, 1926," *Journal of European Economic History* 31, 359–77.

Silverman, D. (1982), *Reconstructing Europe After the Great War*. Cambridge, MA: Harvard University Press.

Skidelsky, R. (1967), *Politicians and the Slump*. London: Macmillan Press.

(1975), *Oswald Mosley*. New York: Holt, Rinehart, and Winston.

Snidal, D. (1985a), "The Limits of Hegemonic Stability Theory," *International Organization* 39, 579–614.

(1985b), "Coordination versus Prisoners' Dilemma: Implications for International Cooperation and Regimes," *American Political Science Review* 79, 923–42.

Snowden, P. (1930a), *The Menace of Protection*. London: The Labour Party.

(1930b), *The Truth About Protection – The Worker Pays*. London: The Labour Party.

(1934), *An Autobiography*. London: Nicholson and Watson.

Solomon, R. (1977), *The International Monetary System, 1945–1976*. New York: Harper and Row.

Stamp, J. (1931), *Papers on Gold and the Price Level*. London: P. S. King.

Statistique Générale (1951), *Indices général du mouvement économique en France de 1901 à 1931 et de 1929 à 1939*. Paris: Statistique Générale.

Stein, A. (1984), "The Hegemon's Dilemma: Great Britain, the United States, and the International Economic Order," *International Organization* 38, 355–86.

Strange, S. (1982a), "Cave! hic dragones: A Critique of Regime Analysis," in S. Krasner (ed.), *International Regimes*. Ithaca, NY: Cornell University Press, pp. 337–54.

(1982b), "Still an Extraordinary Power: America's Role in a Global Monetary System," in R. Lombra and W. Witte (eds.), *Political Economy of International and Domestic Monetary Relations*. Ames, IA: Iowa State University Press, pp. 73–93.

Svennilson, I. (1954), *Growth and Stagnation in the European Economy*. Geneva: United Nations.

Swan, T. (1960), "Economic Control in a Dependent Economy," *Economic Record* 73, 51–66.

Temin, P. (1971), "The Beginning of the Great Depression in Germany," *Economic History Review*, sec. ser., 24, 240–8.

(1976), *Did Monetary Forces Cause the Great Depression?* New York: Norton.

Tew, B. (1988), *The Evolution of the International Monetary System, 1945–88*. London: Hutchinson.

Tinbergen, J. (ed.) (1934), *International Abstract of Economic Statistics 1919–1930*. London: International Conference of Economic Services.

Tiwari, R. D. (1942), *Modern Commercial Policy*. Bombay: New Book Company.

Tobin, J. (1969), "A General Equilibrium Approach to Monetary Theory," *Journal of Money, Credit and Banking* 1, 15–29.

Toi-Phang, H. (1962), "L'étalon or en France de 1820 à 1960: Contribution statistique à l'étude de 'Règles du jeu'," *Revue d'économie politique* 72, 877–90.

Traynor, D. (1949), *International Monetary and Financial Conferences in the Interwar Period*. Washington, DC: Catholic University of America Press.

Triffin, R. (1947), "National Central Banking and the International Economy," in Federal Reserve System, *Postwar Economic Studies*, vol. 7. Washington, DC: Federal Reserve.

(1960), *Gold and the Dollar Crisis: The Future of Convertibility*. New Haven, CT: Yale University Press.

(1964), "The Evolution of the International Monetary System: Historical Reappraisal and Future Perspectives," *Princeton Studies in International Finance*, no. 12 (June), excerpted in B. Eichengreen (ed.), *The Gold Standard in Theory and History* (1985). London: Methuen, pp. 121–40.

Tsiang, S. C. (1959), "Fluctuating Exchange Rates in Countries with Relatively Stable Economies," *Staff Papers* 7, 244–73.

Ueda, K. and H. Yoshikawa (1986), "Financial Volatility and the q Theory of Investment," *Economica* 53, 11–28.

United Kingdom (1922), *Correspondence between His Majesty's Government and the French Government Respecting the Genoa Conference*, Cmd. 1742. London: HMSO.

(1924), *International Economic Conference, Genoa, April–May 1922, Papers Presented to Parliament by Command of His Majesty*, Cmd. 1667. London: HMSO.

United Nations (1949), *International Capital Movements During the Interwar Period*. New York: United Nations.

United States Department of Commerce (1976), *Historical Statistics of the United States*. Washington, DC: GPO.

United States Senate (1879), *International Monetary Conferences held in Paris under the Auspices of the Republic of Washington in August, 1878*, Senate Executive Document No. 58, 45th Congress, Third Session, Washington, DC: GPO.

Urquhart, M. C. and K. A. H. Buckley (1965), *Historical Statistics of Canada*. Cambridge: Cambridge University Press.

van der Wee, H. and K. Tavernier (1975), *La Banque Nationale de Belgique et l'histoire monétaire entre les deux guerres mondiales*. Brussels: Banque Nationale de Belgique.

Viner, J. (1932), "International Aspects of the Gold Standard," in Q. Wright (ed.), *Gold and Monetary Stabilization*. Chicago: University of Chicago Press, pp. 3–39.

Walker-Smith, D. (1939), *Neville Chamberlain*. London: Hale.

Warren, G. F. and F. A. Pearson (1933), *Prices*. New York: Wiley.

Webb, S. B. (1985), "Four Ends to the Big Inflation in Germany, 1920–1924," unpublished, University of Michigan.

West, K. (1987), "A Standard Monetary Model and the Variability of the Deutchemark-Dollar Exchange Rate," *Journal of International Economics* 23, 57–76.

White, H. D. (1933), *The French International Accounts 1880–1913*. Cambridge, MA: Harvard University Press.

Wicker, E. (1966), *Federal Reserve Monetary Policy, 1917–1933*. New York: Random House.

Williams, D. (1959), "Montagu Norman and Banking Policy in the 1920's," *Yorkshire Bulletin of Economic and Social Research*, 11, 38–55.

328   References

(1963a), "The 1931 Financial Crisis," *Yorkshire Bulletin of Economic and Social Research* 15, 92–110.

(1963b), "London and the 1931 Financial Crisis," *Economic History Review*, sec. ser., 15, 513–28.

(1968), "The Evolution of the Sterling System," in C. R. Whittlesey and J. S. G. Wilson (eds.), *Essays in Money and Banking in Honour of R. S. Sayers.* Oxford: Clarendon Press, pp. 266–297.

Williams, F. (1952), *Ernest Bevin.* London: Hutchinson.

Willis, H. P. (1901), *A History of the Latin Monetary Union: A Study of International Monetary Action.* Chicago: University of Chicago Press.

Winch, D. (1969), *Economics and Policy.* New York: Walker.

Wolfe, M. (1951), *The French Franc Between the Wars, 1919–1939.* New York: Columbia University Press.

Woo, W. T. (1985), "The Monetary Approach to Exchange Rate Determination Under Rational Expectations," *Journal of International Economics* 18, 1–16.

Yamamura, K. (1972), "Then Came the Great Depression: Japan's Interwar Years," in H. van der Wee (ed.), *The Great Depression Revisited.* The Hague: Martinus-Nijhoff, pp. 182–211.

Yarborough, B. V. and R. M. Yarborough (1985), "Free Trade, Hegemony and the Theory of Agency," *Kylos* 38, 348–64.

Young, O. (1980), "International Regimes: Problems of Concept Formation," *World Politics* 32, 331–56.

(1983), "Regime Dynamics: The Rise and Fall of International Regimes," in S. Krasner (ed.), *International Regimes.* Ithaca, NY: Cornell University Press, pp. 93–113.

Zaalberg, C. J. P. (1928), *The Netherlands and the World War, vol. 2: The Manufacturing Industry.* New Haven, CT: Yale University Press.

Index